D1607608

EVANGELICAL PROTESTANTISM
IN ULSTER SOCIETY
1740–1890

EVANGELICAL PROTESTANTISM IN ULSTER SOCIETY 1740–1890

David Hempton and Myrtle Hill

LONDON AND NEW YORK

First published 1992
by Routledge
11 New Fetter Lane, London EC4P 4EE

Simultaneously published in the USA and Canada
by Routledge
a division of Routledge, Chapman and Hall, Inc.
29 West 35th Street, New York, NY 10001

Typeset in 10 on 12 point Bembo by Fotographics (Bedford) Ltd
and printed in Great Britain by The University Press, Cambridge

British Library Cataloguing in Publication Data

A catalogue record for this book is available
from the British Library

Library of Congress Cataloging in Publication Data

A catalog record for this book is available on request

ISBN 0 415 07823 7

Contents

List of tables

List of figures

List of maps

Preface

'The flavour of Protestantism in Modern Ulster', wrote David Miller over a
decade ago, 'is distinctly "evangelical".' All would agree that evangelical
Protestantism has exercised a profound influence on the religion, politics,
social mores and attitudes of mind in Ireland's northernmost ancient province.
It is all the more surprising, therefore, that despite a handful of books on Irish
evangelicalism and a great many more histories of Irish Protestant denominations, evangelicalism in Ulster has still not received serious historical
treatment. Whereas national studies of Irish religion have tended to diminish
the distinctiveness of Ulster religion, denominational studies of Protestantism
limit the perception of how important evangelicalism actually was as it
proceeded from splinter groups and voluntary societies to infiltrate every
aspect of institutionalized religion. A realistic appraisal of the impact of
evangelicalism on Ulster life can be achieved only by a regional, not a
denominational, study and by looking at the way in which evangelical religion
affected not only the churches but society as a whole. Our aim has been to
make good some of these deficiencies by conducting a regional study of
evangelicalism in Ulster from its complex origins in the 1740s to the political
and cultural shock of the Home Rule crisis in the late 1880s.

As with all regional studies of religion there is a danger of imagining that it
is a peculiar study of a peculiar people in a peculiar place. This danger is
magnified in Ulster because of the perceived eccentricity of its people in
refusing to come to terms with the modern world by holding onto its divisive
religious heritage. Ulster is no doubt a distinctive sort of place, but in the
period of this study not only did its religious life intersect with many of the
age's most characteristic developments in Britain, Europe and North
America, but evangelical Protestantism in Ulster encountered very similar
problems to its sister movements in other countries in adjusting itself to much
wider social and economic changes. The challenges to traditional religion
occasioned by the spread of industry and the growth of cities, the relationship
of religion, culture and ethnicity to the concept of nationhood, the application
of an historically patriarchal faith to changing gender relations, the alignment
of religion with 'respectable' values in a period of cultural differentiation and
class formation, the processes by which old religious rituals acquire new social
meanings and the role of religion as a legitimizing force in social conflict were
the great religious issues of the eighteenth and nineteenth centuries. All

Christian churches in the industrializing west had to face them, or ignore them, in one way or another. Ulster Protestants may have taken some tortuous paths through these dark forests, but their journey was not as unique as some of their stoutest defenders and severest critics may suppose. One of the themes of this book is therefore to highlight both the distinctiveness and the universality of Ulster Protestantism in a period of extraordinarily rapid social and political change.

At a time when many books on Ireland seem to be judged in terms of their contribution or otherwise to the understanding and solution of the 'Irish Question', the authors wish to make clear that they did not set out with any such intentions or expectations. In so far as this book makes some contribution to the understanding of a small province over a short period of time then our limited ambitions have been realized. We also wish to make clear that our main objective has been to bring to life a vigorous *religious* tradition, not to offer a causal explanation of the distinctive development of Ulster politics in the nineteenth century. Evangelical religion intersected with all other frameworks within which Ulster people expressed their cultural aspirations, including politics and national identity, but we are much too aware of the complex mechanisms by which such exchanges took place to offer crude or monocausal solutions to well-known problems. Evangelicalism contributed to the creation of an Ulster Protestant identity and ultimately to the rise of unionism, but it has not been our intention to push forward a specifically religious interpretation of such developments to the neglect of other factors. This book rests, therefore, on the belief that the role of evangelical religion in Ulster society is worth studying for the insights it offers into the province's distinctive religious and political configurations.

The main themes of this study are evident from its structural division into four parts. Part One deals with the rise of evangelicalism in Ulster as part of a wider 'awakening' from the Urals in the east to the Appalachians in the west. Inevitably, the troubled decade of the 1790s made a profound impact on evangelical religion as it did on most other aspects of Irish life. Part Two focuses on the rise of the evangelical voluntary agencies and their contribution to cooperation and schism in the churches and to religious competition in the society as a whole. Part Three is an attempt to penetrate beneath the surface of religious and political conflict to investigate the way in which evangelical religion encountered the problems of urban living, and also how it affected the lives of women, who were always a clear majority within its ranks. Part Four deals with two kinds of climax. The first is a quite remarkable outbreak of religious revivalism which evangelicals had prayed and worked for since the mid-eighteenth century. The second is the emergence of a Protestant provincial identity which was determined to maintain its way of life against what it regarded as an alien creed and an inferior culture. Both earthquakes have had their aftershocks over the past century. Ulster evangelicals still hope for 'a mighty revival' and still say no to a predominantly Catholic nationalism.

As those who have studied it already know, evangelicalism is a difficult phenomenon to define. In the main we have relied on Dr Bebbington's fourfold emphasis on biblicism, activism, conversionism and the centrality of the cross both in its theology and in the personal experiences of its adherents. Its social constituency is more easily determined in specifically evangelical movements such as Methodism than in the older Protestant denominations in which the boundaries between evangelical and orthodox churchmanship are never clear-cut. A similar problem emerges over anti-Catholicism. Evangelicalism as much inherited older forms of 'No Popery' as it added emotional and theological urgency to renewed conflict in the nineteenth century. Not all evangelicals were anti-Catholic any more than all liberal churchmen were supporters of Catholic claims, but generally speaking the hotter the Protestantism the more fervent was the accompanying anti-Catholicism. As these qualifications indicate, no definition can either be scientifically precise or encapsulate the sheer diversity of religious traditions which have been grouped collectively under one term. Moreover, we are conscious that a study such as this inevitably focuses on the public and the controversial aspects of a religious tradition which has many more dimensions to it. The quiet spirituality and daily charities of generations of Ulster evangelicals are as much part of the tradition as are its great protest or revival meetings. No uncommitted reader of the sources we have used could possibly doubt the existence of genuine religious motivation in its subjects, however mixed up with other interests it inevitably became. Human beings, like evangelicalism itself, are complicated creatures not easily reduced to historical categories.

Much of the research for this book has been carried out in the archives and libraries of the Northern Ireland Public Record Office, the Linenhall Library, the National Library of Ireland, the Royal Irish Academy, Trinity College, Dublin, Queen's University, Belfast, Union Theological College, the Representative Church Body Library in Dublin, the Irish Wesley Historical Society, the Methodist Archives and Research Centre in the John Rylands Library in Manchester, the School of Oriental and African Studies in London, the British Library, Cambridge University Library, the Bodleian Library in Oxford and the Church Missionary Society Archives in Birmingham. The level of cooperation was universally high, especially from those who maintain church and missionary society records with small budgets and immense enthusiasm. Nothing is more indicative of the value of living religious traditions than their meticulous care for their past.

Over the many years of preparation for this volume we have incurred debts to a great many individuals and institutions. We wish to record our thanks to the staff of the Department of Modern History and the Institute of Irish Studies in Queen's University, Belfast, for the time that was made available for research in a climate of painful restructuring. In addition, our research would never have been completed without financial assistance from Queen's University and a substantial grant from the Economic and Social Research Council. Our thanks go also to the little army of researchers into Irish religious history who still sustain a cooperative ideal in these individualistic times. These include Professor Holmes, Dr Liechty, Ms Irene Whelan, Dr Jacqueline Hill, Dr Connolly, Professor Corish, Professor Kerr and Dr Brooke. Professor Holmes and Dr Connolly generously read the book in typescript and saved us from many inaccuracies and some inappropriate interpretations. We are also grateful to Frank Wright for allowing us to consult his doctoral thesis and for sympathetically dealing with our queries. The flaws that remain are entirely our own responsibility.

Our chief debt is to our respective spouses, Reg and Louanne, for their patience and tolerance of the outrageous demands historical research makes on family life. Catherine, Joanne, Stephen and Jonathan have been similarly inconvenienced. Now that the exit button on the word processor has been pressed for the last time Jonathan will have to find another machine to play with.

Myrtle Hill
David Hempton

PART ONE

From international origins to an Irish crisis 1740–1800

Map 1   Places mentioned in the text

[1]

The rise of
evangelical religion 1740–80

And I will multiply upon you man and beast; and they shall increase and bring
fruit: and I will settle you after your old estates, and will do better unto you than
at your beginnings: and ye shall know that I am the Lord. (Ezekiel 36:11)

And I will gather the remnant of my flock out of all countries whither I have
driven them, and will bring them again to their folds; and they shall be fruitful
and increase. (Jeremiah 23:3)

Writing in the middle of the nineteenth century the prolific clerical essayist
Abraham Hume suggested – ironically, in the light of modern views – that
when 'a Prime Minister states, that of all the parts of the United Kingdom,
Ireland is his "greatest difficulty", the Province of Ulster is an understood
exception'. Most of his contemporaries would have endorsed both his opinion
and his explanation.

> It is there that the people of Anglo-Saxon ancestry are found in greatest numbers,
> and that the modes of thoughts and habits of action bear the closest resemblance
> to those which are found in Great Britain. There is the stronghold of the United
> Church of England and Ireland; and there also are found the numerous
> Presbyterian communities which claim proximate or remote relationship to the
> Established Church of Scotland. In Ulster, too, partly as a consequence, and
> partly as a collateral fact, law and order are respected, life and property are secure.
> The wheels of commerce and social life move smoothly on; allowing for slight
> exceptional cases, property and population maintain a steady increase; and the
> vigour of enlarged views finds that, as in Scotland, a soil which was naturally
> unproductive has nourished a population of high promise. In short, except
> geographically, Ulster is not Irish at all.[1]

The links between Protestantism, the British connection, economic
prosperity, social stability and enlightened thought were frequently asserted
throughout the modern period and, although a vast oversimplification, such

assumptions underpinned the cultural and religious attitudes of most Ulster Protestants. Revealingly, perhaps, the above quotation is to be found in Hume's introduction to a study of the settlement patterns of English and Scottish immigrants, for it is on the canvas of the original *settlement* patterns that the various shapes and shades of Ulster religion are primarily to be located. The transfer of land from the native Irish population to successive waves of English and Scottish immigrants began on a relatively small scale with the Tudor monarchy, but at the end of the sixteenth century some 90 per cent of Irish land was still in the possession of Roman Catholics.[2] The first decade of the seventeenth century brought an acceleration of land confiscation, with the counties of Antrim and Down, and to a lesser extent Monaghan, falling into the hands of private adventurers from Britain. In addition, the Flight of the Earls in 1607 facilitated the more systematic plantation of Armagh, Cavan, Coleraine (later Londonderry), Donegal, Fermanagh and Tyrone. It was the violent upheavals of the Cromwellian and Williamite periods, however, which most decisively altered the balance of political power in the hands of Protestant landlords.[3] Their position was further consolidated in subsequent years by the limited but effective imposition of penal laws against Roman Catholics so that by the mid-eighteenth century only a small fraction of Irish land was owned by them. It would be difficult to exaggerate the long-term impact of confiscation and immigration on the social and religious geography of Ulster in the eighteenth and nineteenth centuries.

The settlers in Ulster came chiefly from the lowlands of Scotland where the displacement of small Presbyterian farmers and a long tradition of social and economic links with Ulster both encouraged migration and eased its stresses. Those Scottish farmers seeking a better way of life in Ulster were mainly concentrated in the rural areas of the northeast, especially in the counties of Antrim and Down, but they spread also into Donegal and Tyrone. The areas favoured by the English settlers – parts of Counties Armagh, Fermanagh, Cavan and Monaghan, and the eastern shores of Lough Neagh – were easily distinguishable by travellers from Britain long after the first settlements took place. The large farms, neat hedgerows and orchards, and general 'air of comfort and tidiness' offered a welcome sign of civilization and effective land utilization to English civil and ecclesiastical dignitaries who found themselves posted to Ireland.[4] The native Irish, in contrast, managed to survive in the south and west of Ulster, but in the northeast they were pushed out to the more infertile and inhospitable regions – the mountains, boglands and glens – and were for the most part reduced to the status of under-tenants and labourers.[5] It was no accident, therefore, that in eighteenth-century Ireland contemporaries distinguished men chiefly by their ethnicity, wealth and religion, which were held to be, and generally were, closely related to one another. By the mid-eighteenth century, then, Ulster's religious geography was primarily established by settlement patterns and by three ethnically distinctive denominations – Roman Catholic, Church of Ireland and Presbyterian – which, generally speaking, ministered to pre-assigned communities and only occasionally attempted any kind of proselytism. The fact that the Roman Catholic Church enjoyed the adherence of the vast majority of the Irish population (even in so-called Protestant Ulster Catholics outnumbered Protestants in five of the nine counties), that the Church of Ireland was the established church of a small minority, and that Ulster Presbyterianism was virtually a state within a state, ensured that the province's religious life would have more than its fair share of ecclesiastical and political turbulence.

It is important at the outset, therefore, to make quite clear that the evangelical Protestantism which affected Ulster religion from the mid-eighteenth century did not create the characteristic divisions of the province, it merely made them more vibrant and more complicated. Secondly, although the 'Great Awakening' brought important new features to Ulster's religious landscape, hotter forms of Protestantism predated this international movement of the mid-eighteenth century. Not only were there small cells of gathered churches including Baptists, Quakers and Congregationalists stemming from the Cromwellian period,[6] but there was an indigenous tradition of piety and revivalism within the Scots-Irish Presbyterianism of the seventeenth century. Firmly at the centre of this piety was a ritualized experience of community purification and conversion reaching back to the Sixmilewater revival in Ulster in 1625. Often initiated by populist itinerant preachers and sustained by a zealous laity, revivals in Ulster and the west of Scotland established a tradition which then served as a source of legitimization for fresh outbreaks of religious enthusiasm. Prolonged communion services lasting several days served the same function in Scots-Irish Presbyterian revivalism as love-feasts did in later Methodist revivals. The revivalist tradition in Scots-Irish Presbyterian piety survived into the eighteenth century despite, and partly because of, the growth of a more progressive and rationalist theology and the accompanying disputes over subscription to the Westminster Confession. Conflicts between ministers respectively devoted to moral philosophy and saving faith and between educated ministers and a more simple laity temporarily sapped the revivalistic energies of Scots-Irish Presbyterians, but the tradition was never buried. Indeed the same elements of itinerancy, conversionist preaching and community zeal for holiness and purity emerged again among the Scots-Irish emigrants to the American middle colonies in the 1730s. George Whitefield's role in the American Great Awakening was therefore not to initiate, but to reinforce, a pre-existing revivalistic strain in Scots-Irish culture. He was thus a catalyst of religious revival, not its instigator.[7]

The various migrations of the lowland Scots, first to Ulster and then to North America, is but one example of the international dimensions of the mid-eighteenth-century evangelical revival which until quite recently had been studied within absurdly narrow national boundaries.[8] Professor Ward has convincingly shown that the roots of eighteenth-century pan-revivalism can be traced to the displaced and persecuted minorities of Habsburg-dominated

Central Europe, in Silesia, Moravia and Bohemia.[9] This revival was partly a reaction against the confessional absolutism of much of early eighteenth-century Europe, and was also an attempt to express religious enthusiasm outside the stranglehold of politically manipulated established churches. The social background of these displaced minorities was low and their idea of religion fitted well into the dominant motif of the German Enlightenment, that is, religion 'as the means and way to a better life'. Revivalistic religion and pietism – the former was simply more urgent than the latter – survived on a diet of bible study, Reformation classics and a cell structure pastored by itinerant preachers. In terms of the international diffusion of evangelical pietism, the most influential group was the Moravians, who not only exercised a decisive influence over the religious development of John Wesley, but made an important and almost unrecorded contribution to the growth of evangelical religion in Ireland. The origins of the Renewed Unity of the Brethren – Moravianism – are extraordinarily complicated. Both at the time and ever since it has been variously interpreted as a rebirth of the old pre-Reformation Unity of the Brethren, as a new and potentially destabilizing sect with no right of toleration in the Holy Roman Empire and as an interconfessional religious movement seeking salvation outside the straitjacket of confessional orthodoxy.[10] It was in fact a unique product of religious revival with an emphasis on religious empiricism, international mission, the community of believers and an eclectic openness to the spirituality of other religious traditions. The most 'characteristic expression of their belief', according to Ward, 'was not the confession of faith, in the Reformation tradition, but the accumulation of archives, the evidence of the way God operated in history. Their leaders, though they were usually theologically aware, were not professional theologians defending a line, but pastors and evangelists writing letters and journals, preaching daily.'[11] One such was John Cennick, a Wiltshire itinerant preacher of Bohemian descent and early Methodist associations, who arrived in Ireland in 1746 and quickly built up a large religious society in an old Baptist meeting house in Dublin's Skinner's Alley.[12] Cennick had come to Ireland with the good wishes of Count Zinzendorf, the Moravian patron of Herrnhut, whom Cennick had met on a visit to the Moravian synod in Zeist in the Netherlands. Cennick's journal for the next few years is a mine of information about the state of popular Protestantism in Ireland before Wesley's first visit.[13] By the mid-1740s Dublin already had an informal network of religious societies, some established church, some Presbyterian, some Bradilonian and some Baptist. They formed a colourful, argumentative, eclectic and messy religious subculture, full of disputes about the nature of grace, the efficacy of the sacraments and the ownership of buildings. Allowing for the risk of reproducing Cennick's own evangelical hyperbole it seems that he quickly achieved a pre-eminent position among Dublin's popular Protestants owing to his preaching ability and his connections with the English and continental Moravian communities. Cennick's journal conveys a sense of the excitement of those early days.

In this time all things went on with blessed effects in Skinners-Alley where I preach'd twice daily, and the Crowds were so great that those who would hear must be 2 or 3 hours before the time else they could not get in, and tho' all the windows were taken down that people might hear in the Burrying-Ground Yards etc, yet multitudinous were oblig'd to be disappointed. On Sundays all the Tops of Houses near us, all walls and windows were cover'd with people, and I must get in at a window and creep over their heads to the pulpit if I would preach. Often 7 or 8 Priests have been together to hear me, as well as many of the Church-Clergy and Teachers of all religions and constantly many of them Collegians. Some curious people have several times counted the Congregation and found it generally more than a thousand and once 1323.[14]

Apart from itinerant preaching and the formation of religious societies, two other early characteristics of popular Protestantism in Ireland soon became evident. First, since voluntary religious societies had no standing before the law,[15] they were repeatedly the victims of mobs which Cennick firmly believed were composed of Roman Catholics. A second feature was that early society and band lists showed an unmistakable preponderance of women. A trawl of Cennick's Moravian society in 1747 showed that out of 526 members, 350 were female, half of whom were either unmarried or widowed. A denominational survey of band leaders showed that 13 were of the established church, 8 were Presbyterian, 6 were Baptist and 5 more comprised a Muggletonian, a Quaker, a Bradilonian, a separatist and a Roman Catholic.[16] Early evangelicalism had a knack of gathering up the flotsam and the jetsam of Ireland's Protestant past.

Perhaps it was inevitable, therefore, that Cennick as a popular evangelical preacher should come to the heartland of Irish Protestantism in Ulster. He was invited by a Ballymena grocer who had been impressed by Cennick's firm stand against Roman Catholicism, but Cennick's Arminianism was not well received by Ulster Presbyterians. His second visit in 1748 was more successful both in terms of the crowds he drew and in the pioneer planting of religious societies. By the early 1750s some 30 to 40 Moravian preachers were itinerating in Ulster, servicing 10 chapels and over 200 societies.[17] R. H. Hutton's comment that 'around Lough Neagh the Brethren lay like locusts' was no doubt exaggerated, but it was nevertheless surprising that Cennick's labours were so productive in such a short time.[18] His success shows that in areas largely settled by puritans, the traditions of a strict and self-denying religious culture had by no means died out. The voluminous surviving records of early Moravian societies reveal the importance of the Reformation emphasis on the priesthood of all believers and a distrust of Irish Catholicism based on a curious mixture of enlightenment hostility to superstition and priestcraft and more conventional bigotry. Unfortunately for the long-term future of Moravianism in Ulster, 'Swaddler Jack', as Cennick had become known was not as successful in organizing Moravian societies as he had been in encouraging their formation, and by the time of his death in 1755 the apex of Moravian expansion in Ulster had already passed. The one substantial survival of early Moravian enthusiasm in Ulster was the Gracehill community which was built after the Herrnhut model with Dutch and German help. The aim was to establish a self-regulating Christian village with a chapel, a school, an inn for travellers, and accommodation and workshops for single men and women. Thus, the Moravian approach to evangelism envisaged the creation of numerous quasi-monastic settlements which would be not only inward-looking in the sense that the inhabitants would seek to live a disciplined and charitable Christian life, but also outward-looking to work for the conversion of the whole world. In fact Gracehill never fulfilled its most optimistic aspirations. Its population never exceeded 400, reached its peak between 1790 and 1845 and thereafter became a more mixed religious community.[19] Cennick's importance should not be overlooked, however, as a link between seventeenth-century pietist societies, continental revivalism and eighteenth-century evangelicalism in Dublin and in Ulster.[20] The biographer of Peter Roe, whose own generation led an evangelical movement within the Church of Ireland, stated that 'at the time Mr Roe commenced his clerical career, the Moravian Church was the body which seemed most alive to the Christian duty . . . of sending "portions to them for whom nothing was prepared" '.[21]

The year after Cennick's first visit to Ireland in 1746 there arrived another English evangelical whose faith had also been influenced by the Moravians. John Wesley's visit in 1747 was the first instalment of a 40-year commitment to the cause of Methodism in Ireland in which 21 visits were made, including his first to the province of Ulster in 1756.[22] The small minority of historians who have followed the course of the Methodist revival in both England and Ireland in the eighteenth century have been struck by a remarkable difference of strategy and tactics employed by Wesley in the two countries. Whereas in England Wesley saw himself as having a special – but not exclusive – ministry to the poor, and frequently made barbed criticisms of the worldliness of the English Church and its gentry patrons, 'in Ireland his mission worked downward from the gentry class and outward from the garrison in a way that would have been unthinkable in England'.[23] The editors of the recently published and definitive edition of Wesley's *Journal* state that the total number of Wesley's contacts among the Irish gentry was 'so great as to make it clear that Wesley's self-consciously asserted English mission to the poor was in Ireland refracted through the Protestant gentry class'.[24] Similarly, Wesley devoted a considerable amount of his preaching time to military garrisons, court-houses and other places resonant of Ascendancy control, thereby guaranteeing that 'he could reap no great Catholic harvest'.[25] In like vein Warner has suggested that Wesley was better received by the bishops and clergy of the Church of Ireland than by their counterparts in the Church of England, and was consequently a good deal less critical of the Irish Church.[26]

The evidence suggests that Wesley's approach to Ireland was based not so much on a planned and considered strategy as on a set of religious and social assumptions which travelled with him from his Epworth and Oxford days. The first is that, contrary to a powerful but erroneous tradition of ecumenical scholarship since the Second World War, Wesley was not well disposed to Roman Catholicism in England or in Ireland.[27] It was, however, in Ireland that Wesley thought he detected the baleful influence of Roman Catholicism in its most developed form. On his early visits to Ireland he devoured the standard Protestant accounts of Catholic atrocities in the seventeenth century,[28] encountered what he deemed to be bloodthirsty papist mobs,[29] had his congregations removed by Catholic priests,[30] and wrote nervously about the potential disloyalty of Irish Catholics should a suitable opportunity present itself.[31] There was, therefore, 'a gulf which it would be a mistake to regard as racial, but which went very deep, separating Wesley from the Catholic Irish, ... Wesley found the Irish "indolent" (which implied "squalid") and "fickle" '.[32] It is scarcely surprising, therefore, that Wesley found himself most at home among the unassimilated foreign Protestants – Huguenots and Palatines – who had been forced to leave their homelands by the Catholic intolerance he so much despised.[33] He equally enjoyed his encounters with those aspects of English culture – buildings, landscape, dress and mannerisms – which had been satisfactorily transplanted in Ireland. On his first visit to Ulster in 1756 Wesley immediately noted the general superiority of the countryside: 'no sooner did we enter Ulster, than we observed the difference, the ground was cultivated just as in England, and the cottages not only neat, but with doors, chimneys and windows'.[34] Wesley endorsed the Protestant ethic he thought he had discovered by exhorting the society in Derry 'to avoid sloth, prodigality, and sluttishness, and on the contrary to be patterns of diligence, frugality, and cleanliness'.[35] Wesley's admiration of Ulster Protestant thrift did not extend, however, to its predominantly Presbyterian spirituality. Of Belfast he remarked that 'between Seceders, old self-centred Presbyterians, New-Light men, Moravians, Cameronians, and formal "Churchmen", it is a miracle if any here bring forth fruit to perfection'.[36]

Methodism's early recruitment in Ireland was largely determined by the geography of Wesley's missionary journeys and the characteristics which have already been described. Most early growth took place in southern ports and market towns, in military garrisons, and among European Protestant minorities.[37] By 1760 it was estimated that of the 2,000 in Methodist societies, approximately half were located in the province of Leinster and only a tenth lived in Ulster. The following decade saw the beginning of a dramatic and irreversible trend toward the concentration of Methodism in the north of Ireland. By 1770, 47 per cent of Irish Methodists lived north of a line drawn from Sligo to Dundalk, and by 1815 that had gone up to 68 per cent.[38] Even in a religious movement that made its first impression in the south of Ireland, the steadily increasing proportion of its members living in Ulster from the late eighteenth century is a striking manifestation of a wider demographic trend of incalculable importance to the future history of the island. Thus, the evangelical revival helped reinforce the peculiar concentration of Protestantism in the north of the country and, if anything, sharpened its anti-Catholic characteristics.

Explaining the growth of Irish Methodism from a tiny minority of 2,000 in 1760 to a society membership of 15 times that number (and the number of adherents was at least twice as many again) half a century later is not as straightforward as one might think, for it raises much wider questions about the growth of evangelicalism throughout the western world in the second half of the eighteenth century. In looking at the history of Methodism, for example, one is immediately presented with a paradox. No religious movement has left more accurate statistical information on its growth and development yet, predictably, no subject has occasioned as much debate, often intensely ideological, among its historians. Thus, Methodist expansion in England has been interpreted in many different, if not mutually exclusive, ways. It has been seen both as a component of the psychic process of counter-revolution and as a religious expression of popular radicalism.[39] Its success has been attributed to weaknesses in Anglican parochial machinery and to its creative interaction with English popular culture.[40] Its growth has been related to specific kinds of community, to certain occupational categories and to the booms and slumps of the economy.[41] More recently the origins and growth of evangelicalism have been placed in a proper international setting, and have been related to important changes in the history of ideas as Enlightenment empiricism was translated into a dynamic evangelical doctrine of assurance.[42] More traditional Methodist historians still like to emphasize Methodism's theology and pragmatic organization, its standards of pastoral care and innovations in worship, its evangelistic zeal and concern for education, and its emphasis on conversion as a compelling catalyst in religious motivation.[43] Since no religious movement is either a mere product of social forces or a spiritual island entire unto itself, numerical growth must be the result of both endogenous and exogenous factors. In explaining Irish Methodist growth, however, the relative weight given to each of these categories, region by region, would be difficult to determine even if all the necessary data had survived. As it is, the problems are compounded by lack of information about the age, sex and occupation of early Methodists and, compared with England, the lack of detailed research on Irish social and economic history before the famine. Against these difficulties must be offset the rare advantages of having a full set of Methodist membership figures for every circuit in Ireland after 1770, a good collection of Conference minutes from 1752, with details of preachers, chapel building and financial organization, and a large number of preachers' biographies, reminiscences and private letters.

Not surprisingly, the overwhelming impression from such material is that Methodism grew rapidly through a combination of its own resources and divine favour. This explanation deserves serious treatment from the historian, not only to do justice to what contemporaries thought was happening, but because the early Methodist organization is now the subject of admiration from modern church renewal movements.[44] The most striking features of eighteenth-century Methodism were its itinerant ministry, cell groups, outdoor preaching, love-feasts, hymn-singing and spiritual discipline. The itinerancy in particular was well suited to a pioneering religious movement with few financial resources. Even allowing for inevitable exaggeration and nostalgia, the autobiographical fragments of Wesley's early Irish itinerants tell a remarkable story of miles travelled, sermons preached, persecutions suffered and illnesses endured.[45] When Henry Moore, Wesley's literary executor, was appointed to the relatively poor Charlemont circuit in 1779 he left his new bride at a neighbouring parsonage and spent six weeks riding once round the circuit.[46] As money was scarce among such humble people the travelling preacher depended on simple hospitality, and this further cemented the links between preacher and people. Thus the itinerants serviced the small societies, which in turn collected a penny a week from each member to finance the itinerancy. This was remarkably cost-efficient and pastorally successful until the increase in married preachers and expensive new chapels put the whole system under stress in the early nineteenth century when Irish Methodism became a financial burden to its equally hard-pressed English counterpart. By then the rate of membership growth per preacher had gone into an irreversible decline (Table 1.1). But in their pioneering phase, Methodist missionaries and itinerant preachers, disparagingly called 'black caps', 'swaddlers' and 'cavalry preachers', spoke wherever they could attract a crowd – at markets, fairs, wakes, pilgrimages, court-houses, public executions, Volunteer meetings and Orange gatherings.[47] As a result a high percentage of Irish Methodists in the eighteenth century had their first contact with Methodism through the public preaching of Wesley and his itinerant preachers.

Table 1.1   Rate of membership growth per minister in
Irish Methodism 1770–1830

	Total ministers[1]	Members[2]	Quinquennial increase of members per minister
1770	20	3,124	
1775	24	4,237	46.4
1780	34	6,109	55.1
1785	40	7,817	42.7
1790	67	14,106	93.9
1795	76	15,266	15.3
1800	88	19,292	45.8
1805	104	23,321	38.7
1810	120	27,801	37.3
1815	132	29,357	11.8
1820	169	36,529	42.4
1825	190	34,217	−12.2
1830	205	36,903	13.1

The average growth of members per minister for the period 1770–1800 is 49.9.
The average growth of members per minister for the period 1800–30 is 21.9.
[1] 'Ministers' includes full ministers, probationers, supernumeraries and missionaries, all of whom were supported by the connexion.
[2] The figures for the years 1820–30 include Wesleyan Methodists and Primitive Wesleyan Methodists.

Many of the early itinerants in Ireland were brought from England, but as classes were established they acted as channels through which new preaching talent could flow. Described by one Methodist theologian as a 'sort of spiritual hospital', the class system was at the heart of Methodism.[48] In the classes mutual confession of sins brought psychological release, prayer meetings heightened revivalistic expectancy, and the sharing of burdens encouraged companionship and commitment. The class was also the basic unit of pastoral care and the hub of Methodist finances. Of course its intense discipline must have scared away as many as it attracted, but for the Methodist faithful, especially women, it was at the very centre of their allegiance.[49] Moreover, as classes were home-, rather than chapel-, based they were easily subdivided in times of expansion. Holders of Methodist class membership tickets also gained automatic entry to the love-feasts, which were simple fellowship meals held at least four times a year.[50] These times of hymn-singing, prayer and exhortation attracted large crowds and were often important catalysts of religious revival. In the midst of the Cavan revival of 1801, for example, James Rennick told Dr Coke, the father of Wesleyan missions, that 'shortly after the love-feast was opened, the cry of mourners arose; and it was thought no less than thirty were converted; and great were the rejoicings of the truly pious'.[51] Such accounts were common, not only from Ireland, but from contemporaneous Methodist revivals in Yorkshire and Cornwall.[52] The love-feast, in a special way, combined community solidarity with intense religious emotions.

All contemporary accounts of Methodist expansion in the eighteenth century mention the centrality of itinerant preaching, class and band meetings, love-feasts and hymn-singing, but behind these distinctive features of Methodism there are other, more complex, reasons for growth. One is the strategic contribution made by women in early Methodism (see chapter 7) through their preaching and class leadership, their hospitality and family influence, and their spiritual endurance, and as models of piety. In many Methodist families the wife or daughter was the first to be converted, resulting either in family hostility and division or in the swift conversion of other members. So marked was this pattern that enemies of Methodism alleged that creeping into homes and making captives of 'silly women' was a speciality of the itinerant preachers. Another important factor in early Methodist growth was the psychological impact of frequent 'special providences'. As one would expect many of the most extravagant examples were passed down by oral tradition or were associated with particularly flamboyant preachers such as the American frontier preacher Lorenzo Dow who arrived in Ireland in the immediate aftermath of the '98 rebellion and penned an exotic account of his *Works: Providential Experience*.[53] More substantially, the biographies of the Irish itinerants show how special providences sustained their missionary zeal in what was otherwise a hostile environment. The *Life of Henry Moore*, despite being a biography of a man of considerable learning, is full of providential interventions, including the story of his first open-air service in Dublin when he was mocked by a drunken sailor who subsequently drowned in the Liffey.[54] One of the most embellished of early Methodist providences was the sudden death in 1795 of J. D. Bourke, the Anglican Archbishop of Tuam, after he had threatened to take legal proceedings against the Methodists under the Conventicles Act. The main facts of the case are easily authenticated but not the prophetical dreams of the Methodist faithful.[55] The wide circulation of countless providences gave an immediate spiritual authenticity to the Methodist message in a predominantly superstitious rural culture. Predictably, many of the most remarkable providences were directed against the rich, the powerful and the scoffers. If God was indeed for the Methodists who could stand against them?

With such evidence in mind some have sought to explain the appeal of Methodism in terms of its interaction with a wider folk culture. In England, for example, labour historians have drawn attention to Methodist success in mining and fishing villages allegedly because 'Wesleyan superstition matched the indigenous superstitions of tinners and fishermen who, for occupational reasons . . . were dependent upon chance and luck in their daily lives'.[56] In addition to matching popular superstitions, Methodism had the capacity to translate them into religious idioms. Thus, Cornish Methodists declared holy war on drink, hurling, wrestling, bull-baiting, cock-fighting and folk superstitions, but replaced them with revivals, love-feasts, providential interventions and colourful local versions of the cosmic conflict between God and the devil.[57] Irish Methodists enjoyed a similarly complex relationship with their surrounding culture. The itinerant preachers, for example, were expert at explaining difficult theological ideas in simple rustic parables such as the scutching of flax (stripping the husk from the fibre), and the cutting of peat in the summer for use in the winter.[58] The predominantly agricultural nature of biblical imagery thereby worked in their favour. Moreover, some Methodists were keen to gain a greater understanding of the culture in which they ministered. Adam Clarke, a native of County Londonderry and Irish Methodism's most eminent scholar asked the itinerant preachers for detailed information on the Irish Catholic poor, especially 'their *peculiar* civil and religious customs – their superstitions, legends, tales, belief in a spiritual world, and the agents employed in it, etc., etc., as from such things as these, the character and genius of a people may be more readily collected than from any philosophical reasonings'.[59] Clarke later used his considerable influence on the British and Foreign Bible Society (BFBS) to get the scriptures printed in the Irish language. Indeed the concern of some Methodists and Evangelicals for the preservation of the Irish language, not only on grounds of missionary expediency, is a forgotten aspect of Irish cultural history.[60]

The idea that Methodism, through its providences, folk preaching and concern for the Irish language, chimed in with certain aspects of Irish popular culture should not be pressed too far. The Methodists after all condemned a range of rural sports from cock-fighting to horse-racing and tried hard, not always successfully, to suppress smuggling, illicit alcohol production and sexual irregularities within their own societies.[61] In fact the private minutes of Conference show that the preachers were themselves occasionally guilty of such misdemeanours. Despite their own special providences, Methodists were opposed to most rural superstitions, bawdy rituals, feasts and festivals – whether Catholicized or not – and to the purveyors of local magic. In short, the Methodists opposed the world of divinations and portents by offering what some might regard as the alternative magic of theology and the new birth. Ultimately, however, Methodism appealed as much to the mind as to the heart, and it both depended upon and encouraged a more literate approach to religion than was common in the Irish countryside. Indeed all the churches found it hard to penetrate the superstitious shield of Irish peasants, who were willing to use Catholic rites of passage without coming under the control of the Catholic Church.[62] Methodism experienced similar problems. It attracted thousands of curious Irishmen to outdoor meetings, but only a small proportion was willing to exchange rural entertainment for the discipline of class meetings. As this became evident, Methodism's mission to the disreputable increasingly gave way to recruitment from the respectable.

Perhaps Methodism's most important contribution to Irish society was the stimulus it gave to a much wider evangelicalism, initially in the Dublin area and then later in the province of Ulster. Many Methodist characteristics, particularly itinerant preaching and the establishment of voluntary religious societies, were taken up by individuals, missionary organizations and eventually the churches themselves. When William Gregory toured Ulster in the summer of 1800 under the auspices of the Evangelical Society he found evangelical enthusiasm in all denominations, even in the most obscure corners of rural Ulster.[63] As in England the Irish Methodists did not create this religious enthusiasm single-handed, nor were they necessarily the dominant force within it, but by pioneering more flexible religious forms and structures they opened up new possibilities which others were able to exploit.

With the history of the Church of Ireland in the eighteenth century still to be written, it is as yet too early to be precise about the relationship between Methodism and the established church or about the origins and strength of evangelicalism within the church before the late eighteenth century when its growth is well charted by Alan Acheson and Joseph Liechty.[64] Indeed any study of church evangelicalism before the emergence of a coherent and self-conscious ecclesiastical party, within which members of the Church of Ireland were either welcomed or excluded, is beset with problems of definition. Sensitive to the problems of defining evangelicalism in the eighteenth century, David Bebbington's recent book describes it as a religious movement based on the centrality of the cross, the importance of religious conversion, the authority of the Bible and the energetic campaigns for the reformation of manners and the propagation of mission.[65] Inevitably, the boundary lines between avowed evangelicals and those traditional members of the Church of Ireland who were devoted to its holy mission are by no means exact. Wesley's journal offers some help, however, because in his encounters with the clergy of the Irish Church he distinguishes between those who were 'blind leaders of the blind' and those who at least had some grasp of the religion of the heart and of the importance of a righteous and pious life. Among such were Dr Hort of Longford, Arthur Grueber of Athlone and Philip Skelton of Fintona; Wesley also seems to have had good relations with a section of the learned and congenial clergy of Ulster.[66] There was, of course, a handful of more overtly evangelical clergy in the Irish Church from the mid-eighteenth century, foremost among whom were Edward Smyth, who later became a Methodist, Charles Caulfield, Thomas Tighe and Walter Shirley. Shirley had built up quite a reputation as a worldly priest before he was converted on a visit to his niece, Selina, Countess of Huntingdon from which he emerged with a more pious life-style and a new dedication to evangelism. Such clerical conversions were nevertheless rare in the Church of Ireland until the late eighteenth century when the pace of evangelical growth within the church significantly increased. In 1797 a Dublin bookseller estimated that there were 29 evangelical clergymen in the Church of Ireland, the vast majority of whom were educated at Trinity College, Dublin. Despite the fact that there appear to have been only three evangelical fellows of Trinity before 1800 – John Walker, Henry Maturin and Joseph Stopford – Trinity was undoubtedly the educational powerhouse of early episcopalian evangelicalism in Ireland.[67] The spread of evangelicalism from Trinity's cloisters was first evident in the growth of proprietary chapels – 'a kind of voluntary system within the Establishment' – the most important of which was Bethesda Chapel founded in 1786. In the following decade two evangelical clerical associations were formed in Ossory and Dromore. By the beginning of the nineteenth century, therefore, evangelicalism was a force to be reckoned with in the Church of Ireland, and as with Ireland's other Protestant denominations there were already signs that Ulster was likely to be its most productive territory.

One of the most important themes in the early history of evangelicalism in Ireland is its lack of denominational and doctrinal homogeneity. Not only was Wesley's Arminian Methodism disliked by some evangelical churchmen for its ecclesiastical novelties, it was also challenged by a Calvinistic version associated with George Whitefield and the preachers sponsored by Selina, Countess of Huntingdon. Whitefield came to Belfast, Lambeg and Lisburn in 1751, 1752 and 1757 and seems to have had a bigger influence than Wesley among the Calvinistic Presbyterians of Ulster. By 1773 Lady Huntingdon, the foremost aristocratic sponsor of Calvinistic Methodism, had determined to provide 'poor wicked Ireland' with a 'Gospel day'.[68] Throughout the next two decades she not only enlisted popular evangelical preachers from Britain in the Irish cause, but sent her own preachers – and even probationers – as demand continued to outrun the supply. Dubbed 'the genteel Methodists' Lady Huntingdon's preachers played an important role in the formation and running of the General Evangelical Society in Dublin (1787) the purpose of which was to furnish 'a succession of zealous and popular ministers of every denomination who shall be employed to preach . . . wherever an opportunity should offer'.[69] The growing acceptance of itinerant preaching as a legitimate ministry and the much publicized problems of Ireland led to the involvement of several prominent English and Welsh evangelical preachers, some of whom had a reputation for anti-Catholic rhetoric, in the Dublin society.[70] This was followed a decade later by the formation, on similar principles, of the Evangelical Society of Ulster which gave a boost to Calvinistic evangelicalism in Ulster in the wake of the '98 rebellion.

Calvinistic evangelicalism may have needed a boost, but Calvinism itself did not, for Ulster was the home of the only Protestant church in Ireland whose members were overwhelmingly concentrated in the province and whose structure and government was provincial not national.[71] The high concentration of Presbyterian congregations in a relatively small geographical area gave them a firm power base, while the education of their ministers at liberal Scottish universities often led to political as well as theological radicalism. At the head of this community was the Synod of Ulster, the first Protestant dissenting synod in the British Isles, which, despite pressures, harassments and 'influences' from outside, attracted the loyalty of the vast majority of Ulster Presbyterians throughout the eighteenth century.[72] The Presbyterian Church in Ulster was in effect a state within a state, a self-regulating community organized according to its own principles and virtually independent of the wider structures of church and state. It selected its own ministers, built its own churches, administered its own discipline and developed a reflective and vibrant intellectual tradition based on its complicated position within the wider polity. In Ireland it was technically a dissenting church yet it received, through the *regium donum*, a state contribution to the cost of its ministry.[73] It suffered from substantial religious and political disabilities in relation to one of Britain's established churches, yet it was virtually a sister church of another British established church, the Church of Scotland. As with the American colonists in the 1770s it was effectively shut out from exercising political control of the civilization it had largely built and therefore nurtured deep-seated grievances against episcopalianism. Equally, its Calvinist eschatology and *Weltanschauung* bequeathed to it a powerful anti-Catholic theology which was, if anything, strengthened by its settler experience of religious conflict in the seventeenth century. The eighteenth century brought little relief. A combination of legal disabilities and economic distress resulted in mass emigration to North America, while some of the lower orders who stayed at home were attracted to Protestant secret societies. A church with such a history was correctly regarded by late eighteenth-century British administrations as by no means unconditional in its loyalty to the state.

Meanwhile within the church, classical divisions emerged during the eighteenth century between conservatives and radicals, Old and New Light, subscribers and non-subscribers, and those who emphasized ecclesiastical orthodoxy and confessions of faith against free thought and independent judgement.[74] The cohesiveness of Ulster Presbyterianism was further eroded by its propensity to reflect disputes within Scottish Presbyterianism even when the point of division in Scotland had no equivalent cause in Ireland. One such was the formation of the Associate Synod, or the Seceders, who left the Church of Scotland over a patronage dispute which was largely irrelevant to Ulster Presbyterianism.[75] With their conversionist zeal and strong emphasis on fighting sin, expressed in days of fast and humiliation, the Seceders had all the emotional intensity of a new religious movement, but they strenuously avoided novelty. Rigid orthodoxy and strict discipline were their hallmarks. After first inviting Whitefield to minister to them and then repudiating him 'as a wild enthusiast engaged in the work of Satan', they distanced themselves – at considerable cost to their long-term prospects – from the remarkable revivals at Kilsyth and Cambuslang which, revealingly, had no Ulster counterpart.[76] Whether this was because Whitefield did not visit Ulster in the 1740s, or, more likely, because of the weakness of an individualist and conversionist evangelical tradition within Ulster Presbyterianism, the result was the same. Ulster had no popular revival in the 1740s, but it did see the beginning of a substantial Seceder community, despite a further division into Burgher and Anti-Burgher synods. By 1760 there were over twenty Secession congregations in Ulster and this figure was more than doubled within the next twenty years. Seceders benefited from the Ulster synod's unwillingness to create new congregations because of scarce resources, from disputes within local congregations, and from a reputation for intense religiosity at a time when some sections of the Ulster Presbyterian laity were disenchanted with its more urbane ministerial leadership.[77] The geographical distribution of Secession congregations in Ulster is also compatible with the last stages of the Scottish settlements. Their main concentration was in west Down and mid and south Armagh with only a scattering elsewhere, proving yet again that the historian of Ulster religion is unwise to drift too far from the settlement patterns of the early modern period.[78]

Another Presbyterian minority which made some progress in eighteenth-century Ulster was the Reformed or Covenanting Presbyterian Church which originated in the second Scottish Reformation of 1638–49 and put down somewhat delicate roots in Ulster during the troubled years of the mid-seventeenth century.[79] Although a couple of 'mountain ministers' had been active in the mid-eighteenth century, this body had no settled minister in Ulster until 1761. The Covenanters' rejection of any civil authority in the church and their refusal to take oaths hampered their progress, but their commitment to ardent preaching in the later eighteenth century produced a modest growth. While both the Covenanters and the Secessionists strongly attacked New Light tendencies and the complacency of the Synod of Ulster, there was little harmony between them. The Covenanters insisted on the full liberty and independence of the church, while the Seceders took the view that 'rendering unto Caesar the things that were Caesar's and unto God the things that were God's meant that a full testimony against the evils of the religious establishment was compatible with a full profession of loyalty to the civil establishment'.[80] These minority Presbyterian groups nevertheless offered an outlet for a more intense religiosity in areas traditionally hostile to the conversionist imperative of evangelical Arminianism. By creating a viable and theologically attractive alternative to New Light tendencies, they also ensured that those who objected to what they saw as excessive moderation and tolerance in the Synod of Ulster could leave the synod without abandoning a committed Presbyterianism. The fact that such options were open contributed to the maintenance of a tradition of 'serious religion' among the Presbyterian laity, while ensuring that the creeping invasion of a more conversionist evangelicalism was slower in Ireland than in Scotland.

Despite internal divisions, Ulster Presbyterians, with their strong Scottish links and sense of religious and political identity, formed a close-knit community. Most Presbyterian ministers were local men, serving the farming communities from which they came. Professor Barkley's survey of the 619 Irish ministers (there were also 30 Scots and 1 American) of the Synod of Ulster in the eighteenth century shows that 71 per cent were sons of farmers, 20 per cent sons of the manse, 4 per cent sons of merchants (and these towards the end of the century), 1 per cent of other backgrounds and 4 per cent untraceable.[81] The social background of the Presbyterian ministry thus clearly reflected the interests of a predominantly middle-class rural community. The session minutes of eighteenth-century congregations paint a similar picture of closely integrated communities. The minutes, taken at monthly meetings, generally dealt with the financial arrangements of the church itself, with social duties such as alms-giving and with the exercise of discipline.[82] Elders, each of whom was allocated a quarter or a district to visit, were required to report on the moral and spiritual welfare of the congregation and to offer themselves for twice-yearly examination.[83] Fornication seems to have been the most frequent misdemeanour coming before the session courts, and this was absolved by public confession before the congregation.[84] All aspects of Presbyterian church life, therefore, seem to reaffirm the separate and self-sufficient identity of the Ulster-Scots community. As David Miller suggests, their main 'task was to keep the reformed church true to her standards within their own closed community'.[85] It is difficult to see how a more individualist and conversionist evangelicalism – as opposed to the serious practice of the reformed religion – could make much headway in such communities without being accompanied by more profound religious, social and political changes in the wider environment. Such conditions occurred in the following century.

Although nothing very dramatic happened, 1746 is an important date in Irish religious history. It was the year of the first Secession minister to settle in Ulster and it coincided exactly with the arrival in Ireland of the first itinerant preacher, John Cennick, with experience of continental pietism and English Methodism. Within the next five years the two most influential revivalist preachers of the eighteenth century, Wesley and Whitefield, had both visited Ireland, and for the former it was the beginning of a lifetime's commitment to 'vital religion' in Ireland. In the following 40 years the province of Ulster did not experience the kind of revivalism that changed the religious temperature in the west of Scotland and the middle colonies of America, but evangelicalism had nevertheless made considerable progress. In particular, a new kind of associational, voluntaristic and non-credal religion, serviced by itinerant preachers and committed to evangelism, had been established in Ireland. It was a country in which the major eighteenth-century denominations – Anglican, Presbyterian and Roman Catholic – had generally kept within their own ecclesiastical boundaries: 'each was a church ministering to a pre-assigned community – none was a sect seeking converts'.[86] But by the end of the century this was a pattern already showing signs of change. Ulster Presbyterianism was a more fragmented community at the end of the century than it was at the beginning, and the influence of Methodism and church evangelicalism had persuaded a dynamic minority within the Church of Ireland that the unfinished work of the Reformation might yet be completed. Within the Roman Catholic Church the relative social and political stability of the eighteenth century had enabled it to improve its diocesan and parish system. Its achievements were regionally uneven and mostly confined to better-off urban dwellers, but it was in a better position to defend its corner in 1790 than it had been in 1740. Moreover, as Professor Corish has remarked, 'in the eighteenth century Irish patriotism had been very much a Protestant preserve. After the crucial decade of the 1790s it was well on the way to becoming a Catholic one.'[87] This has to be placed in the context of the anti-Catholicism of much early evangelicalism. In the case of the Moravians, Palatines, Huguenots and Methodists, anti-Catholicism was more than a crude expression of bigotry; it was rooted in a folk memory of persecution within continental Protestantism and a settled conviction that Roman Catholicism was an enemy of enlightened values and economic progress. In short, Irish religion, beneath the surface of apparent denominational stability, was, by the late eighteenth century, beginning to exhibit signs of profound change, the direction of which boded ill for the future of religious tranquillity on the island. Moreover, Irish Protestantism had already shown its capacity to reflect religious innovations in central Europe, England and Scotland, and to re-export some of them to the new world. Ireland, as Europe's last offshore island, and as an unrivalled exporter of humanity, has played an important role in the evolving religious traditions, both Catholic and Protestant, of a surprisingly large part of the globe.

[2]

Rebellion and revolution:
c. 1780–1800

This know also, that in the last days perilous times shall come. (2 Timothy 3:1)

Even now are there many antichrists: whereby we know that it is the last time. (1 John 2:18)

The interaction of political, religious and economic developments in Ulster was an almost inevitable consequence of the settlement patterns already traced. As well as distinctive religious and ethnic traits, the immigrants of the seventeenth century brought with them new skills upon which came to depend the economic life of the province, and which combined with other factors further to distinguish its socioeconomic development from that of the rest of Ireland. The most important ingredient in the opening up of the interior of Ulster to economic prosperity, for example, was the development of the linen industry.[1] Although the Huguenots have been traditionally credited with this important economic contribution, it is now clear that these late seventeenth-century entrepreneurs were able to build upon the hand-loom weaving and basic bleaching skills brought from the north of England by earlier seventeenth-century immigrants, who had themselves acquired the indigenous spinning skills for which the Irish had long been noted.[2] It was this combination of influences and enterprises which made Ulster the 'cradle of the linen trade in Ireland' by the last quarter of the eighteenth century. However, the prosperity of the domestic linen industry in south Ulster had significant repercussions on the localities in which it took strongest root. It put severe pressure on traditional social and administrative structures and resulted in periodic outbursts of violence.[3]

Agrarian outrage was not a new feature in Irish society, but it is possible to distinguish between rural disturbances in Ulster and the resurgent outbursts of agrarian protest in the rest of Ireland. The latter were primarily concerned with the regulation of rent and tithe payments and were undertaken by an expanding population of small farmers and cottiers under pressure from enclosure and other effects of the growing trend away from tillage and towards pasture farming. In south Ulster on the other hand economic and demographic factors combined to give a particularly bitter sectarian dimension to a conflict where the threat seemed to come from within peasant society itself.[4] By the end of the eighteenth century, Armagh not only was one of the most populous counties in Ireland, but its population was made up of almost equal numbers of Protestants and Catholics. While this demographic equilibrium created the potential for sectarian conflict, industrial expansion helped produce 'favourable conditions for institutionalizing the sectarian consciousness of the Protestant lower orders'.[5] In the first place, the rise of independent smallholders, directly employed by drapers or bleachers, caused a breakdown in traditional forms of social control, temporarily weakening the bond between Protestant gentry and Protestant weavers. Secondly, and more ominously, although Roman Catholics were latecomers to the weaving trade in the eighteenth century, the relaxation of the penal laws and the prosperity generated by the linen industry put them in a position to compete in the land market and thus challenge traditional Protestant notions of ascendancy. The acquisition of arms by Catholics through the Volunteer movement, and continuing radical demands for political concessions, further eroded social stability in Armagh.[6] This dangerous fusion of social, economic and political competition between the religious communities produced the conflicts fought out by the Protestant Peep O'Day Boys and the Catholic Defenders. While the gentry of north Armagh were at first concerned to protect the Catholic victims of Peep O'Day activities, their initial sympathy could not be maintained during the heightened tensions of the 1790s. When the Defender movement spread outside the area of its initial impact and its actions became more organized and more overtly political, Protestant landlords withdrew their support and united with their Protestant tenantry against a threat which was thought to be linked with the contemporary bloody upheavals in France.[7] The Orange Order then became the channel through which their common Protestant – and inevitably anti-Catholic – identity was expressed.[8]

These local outbreaks of sectarian violence must also be placed in the context of increasing interdenominational tension at the national level. Although the eighteenth century had seen the gradual relaxation of the penal laws, events in the 1780s and 1790s revealed the limits of religious toleration. For example, while the grievances of secret societies such as the Whiteboys were economic in origin, their activities were often interpreted by the ruling class as popish conspiracies directed against the Protestant state, and were used as an argument against granting Catholic relief.[9] Similarly, although the Rightboy anti-tithe campaign of the mid 1780s focused the attention of Dublin Castle on the need for reform, conservative Protestants claimed that the Church of Ireland itself was under attack. Protestant pamphleteers whipped up public feeling in defence of the religious establishment, warned that the granting of Roman Catholic rights was irreconcileable with the maintenance of Protestant privilege and, by drawing attention away from the issue of tithes to that of the security of Protestantism itself, ensured that in 1787 the political initiative passed from those advocating conciliation to those favouring coercion. As James Kelly demonstrates, the involvement of Church of Ireland clergy in this polemical warfare, and their anti-Catholic propaganda, underlined the importance of religion in shaping political attitudes.[10]

Religious differences were thus deep-rooted, particularly in south Ulster, and involved more than a particular interpretation of Christianity:

> If a person was a Catholic, it invariably meant that he was of old Gaelic stock, that his ancestors were a defeated race, that he was never to be fully trusted by the planter stock, that his intention was some day, perhaps some distant day, to become master in his own house again. And if he were a Protestant it also meant that he was a foreigner, a persecutor, a privileged person, an enemy.[11]

In the volatile 1790s, when the campaign for Roman Catholic liberties was again gathering momentum and the possibility of widespread rebellion was given credibility by events in France, those on each side of the religious divide drew deeply on religious traditions to justify their social and political stance. The language of the Defenders' catechisms is rich in biblical imagery, reflecting the mysticism and symbolism of the freemasonry on which it was modelled.

> Who is your father? God. Who is your mother? The true Catholic Church. Who is your brother? The second person of the Holy Trinity. What order are you from? From the order of St Patrick. Where do you stand? I stand upon the rock that St Peter built the church on.[12]

Statements like these, particularly when combined with rumours of French support for the Irish Catholic cause, heightened Protestant awareness of the potentially revolutionary nature of the Defender movement.

The Orange Order also had strong religious foundations. Meetings of the society were opened with prayers and members were forbidden to curse, swear or drink in the Lodge room. It was required of an Orangeman that

> He should have a severe love and veneration for his Almighty Maker, productive of those happy fruits, righteousness and obedience to his commands, a firm and steadfast faith in the Saviour of the World, convinced that he is the only Mediator between a Sinful Creature and an Offended Creator. . . . Lastly, he should pay the strictest attention to a religious observance of the Sabbath, and also to temperance and sobriety.[13]

This did not of course prevent members from taking direct action against their political and religious enemies, and the strength of the Orange Order throughout the nineteenth century waxed and waned in direct proportion to the perceived urgency of the Catholic threat. In this period, however, the Orange Order was probably more significant for what it was than for what it did. 'While the social structure of Ulster was being drastically altered,' writes

Miller, 'Orangeism sustained for Protestant workers in town and country the sense that the most important feature of the old structure – a special relationship between them and their betters – still existed'.[14]

The importance of this build-up of sectarian conflict (in religious terms at least) lies in the need for a more distinctive and assertive religious identification which its tensions produced. Religion itself had not been immune from the general competition between the two communities, but in the heightened atmosphere of the 1790s it became a more critical element. The upsurge of evangelical activity in the south Armagh area in the late eighteenth and early nineteenth centuries reveals a strong link between social disruption and religious excitement, suggesting that this new and vibrant faith met many of the needs of an anxious and vulnerable society. The events of the last decades of the century particularly focused attention upon the potential of its moral creed and its anti-Catholicism as antidotes to civil and political unrest.

W. R. Ward has written that the generation overshadowed by the French Revolution was the most important in the modern history of western European religion, 'for the Revolution altered for ever the terms on which religious establishments, the chief device on which the nations of the West had relied for christianising the people, must work'.[15] So much is true, but the revolution also cast its shadow over dissenting churches in Britain and Ireland, especially in the last decade of the eighteenth century, when the relationship between political and theological radicalism came under close scrutiny. While the major churches in Ulster were thus considerably disrupted by ideologies and events emanating from France, underlying social tensions, culminating in the rebellion of 1798, further highlighted the inadequacies of civil and religious institutions and deepened the division between the Catholic and Protestant communities they served.

The preface to *Ireland's Mirror* in 1804 stated 'we live in an age when not only the pillars of Government, but the adamantine foundations of religion itself, shaken as it were by an earthquake, tremble to their base.'[16] While there was nothing new in revelations of the inadequacies and degraded state of existing institutions, the rapidity and urgency of secular events shook many out of their former complacency. The implications of revolution for upholders of the old order were particularly felt by the established church in Ireland, which was partly upheld by English patronage and the operation of discriminatory laws against Roman Catholics and dissenters. The Bishop of Cloyne's widely-circulated pamphlet response to the Rightboys in 1787 had focused attention on the link between the Irish religious establishment and the Protestant constitution, pointing to the vulnerability of both, and stating that Protestantism itself was in danger from deep-laid popish plots.[17] Such fears were intensified by news of the abolition of tithes and the overthrow of civil and ecclesiastical institutions in France. When revolutionary fervour spread to Ireland in 1798, the ineffectiveness of the established church in terms of social and religious leadership was further highlighted. The Reverend Charles

Warburton complained bitterly about the bishops and clergy who had gone to England, 'leaving their flocks to the certain seduction of revolutionary agents who sleep not'. 'The absence of our clergy from their respective charges', he concluded, 'creates disaffection, and is, at this moment, the strongest engine in the hands of our revolutionists to pull down the whole fabric of the Church and State.'[18] As R. A. Soloway points out, secular events 'placed the question of clerical effectiveness and responsibility in a different and critical perspective'.[19]

For Presbyterians too the events of the 1780s and 1790s produced new strains in their relations with the state. Many dissenting liberals saw in the revolutionary ardour of the times the opportunity for political and religious equality with both their episcopalian and Catholic neighbours. Although much has been written about this period of Presbyterian radicalism some points need re-emphasizing.[20] In the first place the radicalism (or liberalism) which gained ground within Irish Presbyterianism in this decade was not a creation *ex nihilo*, nor was it politically monochrome. In fact the picture is altogether more complicated because there was not one radical ideology but many. One strand had its origins in the Commonwealth tradition and was carried on by Dublin enlightenment coteries, such as the one dominated by Frances Hucheson in the period 1719–29, and by the Scottish universities. This antique republicanism stressed the right of resistance, electoral reform and equality before the law. Another strand could be described as a kind of high-minded dissenting cantankerousness in its hostility to war, slavery and blood sports. Yet another strand drew its ideas and encouragement from the American and French revolutions, Paine's *Rights of Man* and the democratic corresponding societies. As well as emphasizing the diversity of radical ideology, one must be careful not to overestimate its appeal. To say that Presbyterians were to the forefront of Belfast radicalism is not the same thing as saying that Belfast radicalism was the dominant feature of Ulster Presbyterianism.

What was remarkable about the Presbyterian radicalism of the 1790s was its clubbable character, its close family and economic networks and its mercantile, professional and clerical membership. This educated elite, partly upset by the fact that it could not control the electoral politics and patronage of the town it had built, disseminated its opinions through radical newspapers, a sprinkling of Presbyterian pulpits and Belfast town meetings.[21] This was precisely the kind of radicalism that could not sink deep roots into the Ulster countryside where Protestant and Catholic peasants were fighting a life-and-death struggle against small holdings, increasing rents and, ultimately, each other. The crude sectarianism of rural Ulster had its urban liberal counterpart in the fragmentation of radical Presbyterian opinion over Catholic relief. For if the Irish problem in the twentieth century is about what Irish Catholics plan to do with Ulster Presbyterians, the reverse was the case in the 1790s. Although there were perfectly respectable liberal reasons for not trusting Catholics with political power, while at the same time refraining from actual persecution, many Belfast Presbyterian radicals wanted to do something for the Catholics – the real issue was how much, how quickly and with what securities.[22] Long before the rebellion of the United Irishmen, therefore, Catholic Emancipation was the rock upon which the fragile unity of Presbyterian radicalism perished.

Disillusionment with revolutionary ardour was clearly in evidence from about 1793, when many Ulster liberals began to feel that the French revolutionary government was deviating from the principle of liberty in both politics and religion. The French were accused of exercising a despotic power over the small nations within their control, and of setting up an irreligious regime.[23] As the Reign of Terror unfolded it became necessary to distinguish between reforming and revolutionary actions and between the concept and the reality of political freedom for Irish Roman Catholics, particularly in the light of the sectarian outrages which were disrupting the southern border counties of Ulster. The choice was by no means clear-cut and Presbyterian involvement in both United Irish and government forces in '98 reveals the lack of solidarity within the community.[24]

The political activism of several of its clergy and a considerable number of the laity was a major embarrassment for the governing body of the Presbyterian Church. At its autumn meeting in 1798, anxious to clear itself from the suspicion under which it was placed, the church's religious leaders condemned the conduct of 'those few unworthy members of our Body whose conduct we can only view with grief and indignation' and reaffirmed its 'Fidelity to the Crown' and 'Attachment to the Constitution'.[25] Such protestations of loyalty from the Synod of Ulster were to some extent provoked by the fear that their much-vaunted 'special relationship' with the state was endangered. In the event, however, Ulster Presbyterians were to be offered an increased and differential *regium donum* from a government concerned to encourage a more respectable, more conservative and more loyal dissenting leadership.[26] Thus a combination of disillusionment with French and Irish revolutionary violence, fear of a more strident Irish Catholicism, and government policy ensured that a more conservative ethos would dominate nineteenth-century Ulster Presbyterianism. Throughout the eighteenth century both theological and political radicalism had coexisted with more conservative and orthodox elements in the Synod of Ulster. In the aftermath of rebellion, however, this essentially religious, middle-class community with a vested interest in social order and stability, began to reassess both its doctrinal and political position. The interrelation between the two is most plainly seen in the popular misconception, fostered by nineteenth-century Presbyterian conservatives and historians, that it was 'New-Light' ministers – that is those who opposed subscription to the Westminster Confession of Faith – who were most closely implicated in the rebellion. Unorthodox views in both religion and politics thus came to be seen as mutually reinforcing when in reality, as recent surveys have shown, no such convenient relationship can be demonstrated.[27]

The circumstances which presented the established and semi-established churches with new challenges to their authority simultaneously generated a popular religious enthusiasm which was readily accommodated by a variety of evangelical sects and individuals whose flexibility proved conducive to the excitement and uncertainty of the times. In purely religious terms, the pastoral and missionary zeal of the Presbyterian Church, like that of the Church of Ireland, was limited by internal tensions and by financial and legal restraints. In the second half of the eighteenth century both churches were thus subject to strident criticism from pious sects and individuals operating both within and outside their boundaries. In Presbyterian circles, the problem of spiritual complacency was energetically tackled by the Seceders and Covenanters. By 1800 the Covenanters had formed congregations in seven of the nine Ulster counties and the Seceding Presbyterians likewise increased the number of their congregations from 41 in 1770 to 91 in 1809.[28] The zealous activities of these Presbyterian sects offered an important outlet for popular piety, which in less rigidly Calvinist circles was enthusiastically expressed by Moravians, Methodists and other evangelicals.

Impatient of the slow, grinding machinery of bureaucracy and galvanized by a sense of urgency which transcended the legal, the geographical and often the theological limitations of ecclesiastical orthodoxy, evangelicalism's radical approach and popular appeal presented a clear challenge to existing religious institutions. Motivated by a religious ardour which was all too often interpreted as spiritual arrogance, evangelicals demanded a more urgent and intense religious commitment from both clergy and laity. To be God's chosen instrument was a responsibility not to be taken lightly, nor was the task an easy one. Matthew Lanktree, for example, who for over forty years actively promoted the Methodist cause in the north of Ireland, like most of his colleagues endured many hardships, suffered verbal and physical abuse and made great personal and family sacrifices. The deep sincerity of his rejection of worldly values is evident in his justification of itinerancy in reply to a pamphlet attack from a Presbyterian minister. Upholding 'divine' over human appointments, he explained the guiding principles of his life.

> Why did I first think of being a Preacher? Was it because I thought myself in every respect qualified? Far from it, but I believed I should perish if I did not preach the Lord Jesus. When I pleaded my unfitness for the work, and said, 'I will speak no more in his name', I strove to settle in the world, and roll the burden from my mind, the ground withered over my head, and his word became like fire in my bones. I felt, woe is me if I preach not the Gospel . . . I am acquainted with hundreds who are influenced by the same motives.[29]

The dissemination of the gospel message came to be seen as the first duty of all who considered themselves Christians. Rowland Hill wrote to the Scottish evangelical James Haldane, that

> I am now an old stager in the itinerants' work, and I bless God for the line in which I have been called, being assured that I have followed the will of God

therein; and I am satisfied the salvation of many souls has been promoted thereby. In preaching through England, Scotland, Ireland and Wales, I always conceived I stuck close to my Parish. We are to 'preach the Gospel to every creature, even to the end of the world'.[30]

As these examples suggest, any attempt to come to terms with evangelical expansion at the turn of the century must address itself to the psychology of religious motivation in the lives of the individuals who made it happen, as well as to the social and economic circumstances which facilitated its progress.

Rowland Hill was one of several independent preachers who toured Ireland in the latter half of the eighteenth century on behalf of the General Evangelical Society, sponsored by Lady Huntingdon.[31] The society strengthened the links between Ireland and the wider British evangelical movement by attracting many prominent revivalists. Such popular and influential men, who were often notorious in orthodox ecclesiastical circles,[32] caused a considerable stir in the local religious community. The earnest pietism of these itinerants was to become, in the nineteenth century, a crucial factor in the revitalization of the churches, but in the revolutionary era their enthusiasm was viewed as at best irresponsible, and at worst dangerous. Both the Presbyterians and episcopalians regarded the recruiting ardour of evangelical sects and individuals as disruptive and schismatic rather than as a stimulus to genuine religious experience.[33] Itinerancy in particular was condemned as a threat to ecclesiastical authority. Although disruptive in terms of ecclesiastical discipline, however, there is little evidence of evangelical support for political radicalism or revolution. But some individuals did express enthusiasm either for the American colonists or the early stages of the revolution in France. Rowland Hill's constant references to the plight of the American colonists prompted Wesley to accuse him of political and seditious preaching, while Adam Clarke apparently 'remained convinced that if the French had been left alone, they would have constructed a Government "which would have been the glory of the whole earth" '.[34] However, these tendencies were more likely to reflect a love of religious freedom than political radicalism and were widely exaggerated by orthodox churchmen who regarded all interdenominational activities with alarm. Church of Ireland evangelicals, already critical of spiritual apathy, saw 'the ominous implications of the French Revolution as God's judgment on all Christians, but especially ministers', but, in a climate which linked schism with sedition, most reiterated their loyalty to the establishment and remained to strengthen the church from within.[35] So long as political radicalism involved concessions to Catholics, evangelical ardour in Ireland was constrained by the wider implications of disruptive behaviour.

The French Revolution not only altered for ever the terms on which established churches throughout the western world must work, but also seemed to be the key to unlock the treasure chest of biblical prophecy.[36] Within Ulster Presbyterianism, in particular, a millenarian subculture fastened eagerly on the events of the French Revolution for signs and portents. Calvinists and Covenanters with an extravagant cosmology believed that God was hastening the downfall of Popery and Prelacy. Even the *Northern Star*, supposedly the journal of rational radicalism, was not above dabbling in the strange world of Antichrist, the Beast, the millennium and Armageddon.[37] The reason for all this millennial excitement was, of course, the revolutionary ditching of the French Catholic Church by erstwhile French Catholics. If that church had indeed reached its nemesis in the very nerve centre of the European *ancien régime* was not a new day about to dawn? In the general atmosphere of tension and unrest in Ulster in the 1790s, both national and international events were infused with religious significance. By interpreting secular events as part of a divine plan, prophetical speculations offered both an explanation for contemporary turmoil and religious legitimacy for those seeking to transform the world. Local events thus acquired new significance by being placed not only in an international, but a universal setting. The full extent and impact of millennial ideology and millenarian excitement in late eighteenth-century Ulster are difficult to estimate, since they were expressed in a wide variety of academic and popular forms. Indeed the intricate complexities of millenarian ideologies are often much misunderstood. For those with a vested interest in the world changing quickly it was perfectly possible to construct an optimistic eschatology in which temporal events were interpreted as the ushering in of a new and a better age. For those with most to lose from rapid social change, however, the reverse was the case, though for them divine providence was still regarded as incomparably superior to temporal misfortunes. In addition, for those whose view of the last times incorporated a post-millennial emphasis on a new 'gospel age' before the final curtain descended on the world, eschatological excitement could inspire a new enthusiasm for evangelism. All three strands were evident in the millenarian enthusiasms of late eighteenth-century Ulster.

Specialized theological studies on the approach of the millennium pre-occupied sections of the Presbyterian community in the 1790s, with the printing and distribution of several publications lending weight to United Irish pressure for radical political reform. While expositions of the books of Daniel and Revelation often differed in precise details of interpretation, they generally agreed on the overriding significance of events in France. For Presbyterian radicals the struggle between Christ and Antichrist was identified with the struggle between liberty and despotism in a characteristic mingling of theological and political ideologies which was a recurring feature of Ulster Protestantism.[38] The biblical interpretation of political events, whether construed as an academic theological exercise, or, more commonly, expressed in the general linking of contemporary social upheaval with the unfolding of a divine plan for mankind, invested all aspects of life with a compelling urgency. 'Be ye ready also, for the Son of Man cometh at an hour when ye think not' was a text taken up by all Presbyterian synods in the last decades of the century.[39] During years when murder and looting were commonplace, secret societies proliferated, a repressive military presence was established, and the daily newspapers were full of the dramatic occurrences in France and the progress of the war in Europe, references to the imminence of the Latter Day abounded.[40] Lord Charlemont, after receiving an alarming report from Ballymena in 1797, wrote that

> We are like Christians in the first century, who every day expected the world would be at an end, and in contemplation of that great event, every idea was absorbed. So here, nothing can persuade us but that some great event is at hand (invasion, massacre). God grant it may be otherwise, but we are generally (however it happens) pretty well informed.[41]

In the aftermath of the rebellion, when it did indeed seem that things would never be the same again, the Union debates perpetuated popular excitement and unrest. Few, however, could link political and religious principles with such ingenious simplicity as Francis Dobbs, MP for Charlemont, whose interpretations of both biblical and daily events enlivened the House of Commons in the first summer of the nineteenth century. Dobbs saw the immediate Second Coming as inevitable, given the attempt to unite Ireland with Britain, since Ireland's independence was 'written in the immutable records of Heaven'. He identified Armagh with Armageddon, and viewed the proposed union as an attempt to annihilate God's chosen nation.[42]

Events in both Britain and the wider world also inspired those with a more optimistic eschatology. Many evangelicals saw in contemporary events the fulfilment of God's promise that 'the Gospel would be preached to all inhabitants of every nation prior to the establishment of His Kingdom'.[43] 'The people of Europe, and particularly Ireland', wrote T. L. Birch in 1799, 'are inspired (as they think) with a well-grounded belief, and hope that the time is arrived when the prophecies concerning the universal dominion of Christ's kingdom, and the peaceful happy state upon earth, that is thereupon to ensue . . . are to be fulfilled.'[44] The breakdown of the old order was thus seen as the prelude to spiritual regeneration on a worldwide basis, a perception boosted by the steady progress of evangelicalism and the apparent success of the proliferation of newly formed foreign missionary societies.[45] The spirit of self-confidence and optimism which characterized this period of evangelicalism also encouraged local revivalist initiatives. Thomas Coke, president of the British Methodist movement, wrote to an American preacher of his hopes that Ireland would partake of the revivalistic fervour that had swept America in the Second Great Awakening: 'Surely you cannot be mistaken in the signs of the times. The Lord is hastening apace the great Millennium, when Christ shall reign with his ancients gloriously a thousand years . . .! One of the most sure signs of the approach of the Millennium will be the having a multitude of real possessors of that mighty blessing on our society.'[46]

The intensity and urgency of Methodist preaching were particularly appropriate to the current climate of social convulsion and apocalyptic expectancy. The intervention of divine providence in the daily affairs of men became a familiar theme in sermons and anecdotes. This providentialism was closely connected to elements of popular culture, allowing what would formerly have been classed as 'superstition' or even magic, to be interpreted as religious phenomena.[47] In 1798 the threat of French invasion and popish rebellion gave rise to many 'remarkable deliverances' and 'miraculous preservations'. 'Our little company', wrote Adam Averell, 'is like the Israelites in the wilderness, surrounded by warlike and inimical nations, yet we are perfectly safe, and rest in peace.'[48] The Irish Methodists' address to the English Conference in 1798 told of the dreadful sense of 'carnage and desolation' witnessed by all, but went on

> However, in the midst of this national confusion, we and our people in general, blessed be God! have been wonderfully preserved. Though some of us were imprisoned for weeks by the rebels, exposed also to fire and sword in the heat of battle, carried into the enemy's camp, and plundered of almost every valuable, yet we have not suffered the least injury in our persons![49]

The Christian system of rewards and punishments thus acquired immediacy and a new significance. Widely disseminated through the work of itinerant preachers, in tracts, sermons and addresses, this kind of popular interpretation of events had an effect which was ultimately more pervasive than political or religious liberalism. The evidence of God's near presence gave a new impetus to those of evangelical faith and, particularly after the disillusionment of the 1790s, came to have a directly spiritual as opposed to political significance. The incentive to conversionist zeal was reflected in a variety of missionary initiatives undertaken in the period 1798–1810 by both Presbyterians and Methodists, and by British as well as local evangelicals.

Even before the dramatic events of the late 1790s prompted its leaders to develop a more comprehensive and urgent home missionary programme, Methodism was undergoing significant expansion in the north of Ireland, especially in two quite distinct areas – the 'Linen Triangle of Ulster' and a rectangular area with Lough Erne at its centre (Figure 2.1).[50] By 1830, 47 per cent of Irish Methodists lived within those boundaries. The most notable feature of Methodist growth in the Lough Erne area between 1770 and 1830 is that it is more volatile than in any other part of Ireland (Figure 2.2). Methodist growth in the nation as a whole exceeded 20 per cent a year on only three occasions, but this area had ten such years, including remarkable periods of growth in 1772–3, 1783, 1785–7, 1799–1802 and 1819–20 (Table 2.1). Predictably perhaps these years of rapid growth were often followed by periods of stagnation or decline. The membership figure for 1802, for example, is not exceeded until 1820, and the figure for 1830 is only marginally larger than that for 1820. This erratic pattern was the product of a well-established rural revivalist tradition in the predominantly English settlements of Fermanagh, where profitable dairy farming and small-scale linen weaving

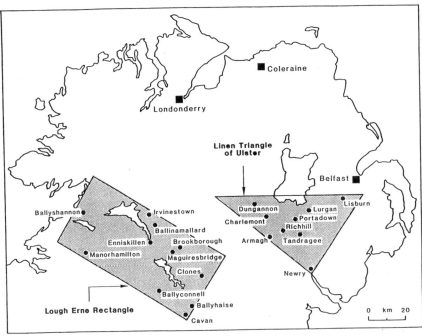

Figure 2.1 The 'Linen Triangle of Ulster' and the 'Lough Erne Rectangle'

led to a rapid expansion of markets and communications. Moreover, as with Armagh, this area had an evenly balanced ratio of Protestants and Catholics.[51]

The most dramatic of all the revivals in this area occurred in the immediate aftermath of the rebellion of the United Irishmen in 1798 when Methodism more than doubled its membership within three years and attracted huge crowds to outdoor meetings. This local success was at least partly attributable to a wider initiative. In 1799, as a direct response to the rebellion of the previous year, and reflecting the evangelical belief that Ireland's problems required religious solutions, the Irish Conference appointed three itinerant missionaries, James McQuigg, Charles Graham and Gideon Ouseley, to travel throughout the country without being confined to any one circuit, to preach, exhort, advise and pray.[52] In the Lough Erne area, at least, their early efforts were crowned with remarkable success. After visiting Enniskillen on Christmas Day 1800, Charles Graham told his son that 'superstition and formal religion are flying like the chaff of the summer threshing floor'. Dr Coke, chief organizer of the mission, received a string of letters on the progress of the revival.[53]

> O! Sir, to see the fields covered with the spiritually slain, what a blessed sight it was! Husbands and wives, parents and children, all in a kind of regular confusion, weeping, exhorting, praying, and rejoicing alternately with and for each other. So graciously has God engaged the hearts of the people in quest of salvation, that at times I have had much to do to prevail on them to disperse and go home.[54]

We have preached to thousands in the open streets and in the fields, in the fairs and markets, and in the principal towns of the North . . . the preachers and people thought it impossible that we could hold out, having not only the labours of the streets and fields, but a revival almost in every part, that keeps us preaching, exhorting and praying for hours.[55]

The Methodists attributed the success of the revival to the work of the newly appointed Irish-speaking evangelists, together with the spiritual power generated by the cottage prayer meetings of the Methodist faithful. It would be unwise to ignore this explanation altogether, because the journals of the missionaries themselves and the reports on their activities from other sources testify to the unique role they played.[56] In his most productive period Gideon Ouseley travelled over 4,000 miles a year, preached about 20 times a week and

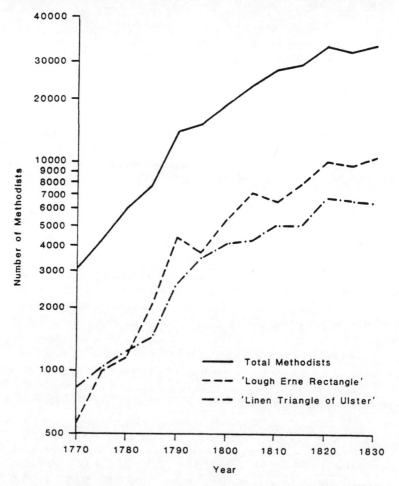

Figure 2.2   Members of Methodist societies in Ireland in the 'Lough Erne Rectangle' and in the 'Linen Triangle of Ulster', at five-yearly intervals (hundreds: semi-log)

Table 2.1   Methodist membership and growth rates
in the 'Lough Erne Rectangle' 1770–1830[1]

1770	569		1800	5,413	37.0
1771	669	17.6	1801	8,412	55.4
1772	937	40.1	1802	9,079	7.9
1773	1,160	23.8	1803	8,426	− 7.2
1774	937	−19.2	1804	7,293	−13.5
1775	990	5.7	1805	7,248	− 0.6
1776	872	−11.9	1806	7,153	− 1.3
1777	996	14.2	1807	7,103	− 0.7
1778	972	− 2.4	1808	6,661	− 6.2
1779	1,175	20.9	1809	6,690	0.4
1780	1,184	0.8	1810	6,664	− 0.4
1781	1,196	1.0	1811	6,750	1.3
1782	1,284	7.4	1812	7,190	6.5
1783	1,819	41.7	1813	6,829	− 5.0
1784	1,861	2.3	1814	6,869	0.6
1785	2,059	10.6	1815	8,000	16.5
1786	2,968	44.2	1816	7,995	− 0.1
1787	3,837	29.3	1817	7,503[2]	− 6.2
1788	3,821	− 0.4	1818	7,010	6.6
1789	3,995	4.6	1819	8,500[3]	21.3
1790	4,423	10.7	1820	10,201	20.0
1791	4,345	− 1.8	1821	10,888	6.7
1792	4,541	4.5	1822	10,313	− 5.3
1793	4,043	−11.0	1823	10,314	0.0
1794	3,891	− 3.8	1824	9,915	− 3.9
1795	3,771	− 3.1	1825	9,834	− 0.8
1796	4,291	13.8	1826	10,133	3.0
1797	4,116	− 4.1	1827	10,958	8.2
1798	4,139	0.6	1828	11,227	2.5
1799	3,950	−4.6	1829	10,807	− 3.7
			1830	10,883	0.7

[1]   See Figure 2.1 for the approximate area of the sample. Since Methodist circuits changed their boundaries through expansion in this period the actual geographical area is not absolutely precise. The circuits included in the sample are Enniskillen, Clones, Ballyconnell, Brookborough, Cavan, Ballinamallard, Manorhamilton and Killeshandra. From 1817 onwards the figures include Wesleyan and Primitive Wesleyan Methodists, though their circuits were not identical.
[2]   Because of the chaos in circuit geography after the split of 1816, this figure is an average of those for 1816 and 1818.
[3]   The recorded figure is arrived at by adding the Wesleyan numbers to an estimate of Primitive Wesleyan numbers, calculated by averaging the figures for 1818 and 1820.

generally found himself at the centre of intense spiritual excitement wherever he went. He understood this to be a sign of approval from the Holy Spirit, while his opponents made allegations of credulity and fanaticism.[57] Neverthe-less, the novelty of preaching in both English and Irish to large crowds at markets, fairs and county assizes, along with an extensive distribution of literature, brought notoriety to the Methodist missionaries, and in the economy of rural revivalism all publicity is good publicity.

The Methodist explanation for their remarkable success in Fermanagh and Cavan between 1799 and 1802 is, however, too simple. The Irish-speaking preachers made little impact on other parts of Ireland, and their record in the Lough Erne area after 1802 was much less impressive. Rather it could be argued that a well-established revivalistic tradition in southwest Ulster was given added urgency in the period 1799–1802 by the psychological impact of the '98 rebellion in an area of sectarian equilibrium. It was also a period of high food prices and serious scarcities. The missionaries were, therefore, both the conscious and unconscious catalysts of more tangible emotions.

> We have preached two market-days and one Sabbath in the streets of Ballyshannon to vast congregations, who heard with the greatest attention. We met with no opposition; the rich and learned seemed astonished, standing at a distance, and hearing us denounce the judgements of Heaven against the crimes of a guilty nation.[58]

In such circumstances the old Methodist command to flee from the wrath to come had obvious temporal applications in the rural environs of post-rebellion Ireland.

Despite the remarkable Methodist growth in this period two cautionary notes should be struck. First, only a fraction of those who attended outdoor meetings actually committed themselves to the discipline of Methodist societies. Second, there was considerable leakage from those societies throughout the following decade.[59] Facts like these from all over the British Isles persuaded influential Methodists of Jabez Bunting's generation that Methodist revivalism obeyed a law of diminishing returns. Instead, they put their faith in denominational consolidation. The resultant tensions between denominationalists and revivalists led to division in England and to heated quarrels in Ireland between the wealthy Dublin Methodists and folk preachers like Ouseley, whose sermons were described as all 'nonsense and noise'.[60] The almost rhythmic pattern of generational revivalism did not die out in south-west Ulster at the start of the nineteenth century, but thereafter it was on a smaller scale and there was much less at stake. In this area Methodism emerged as a force to be reckoned with by the older denominations, but it never again threatened to supplant them altogether.

Methodist growth in the linen triangle of Ulster shows some similarity to that of the Lough Erne area (Table 2.2). Both grew rapidly in the 1780s, 1800–2, and 1819–21, and in both areas expansion slowed down considerably in the

1820s. Although early Methodist growth in this area may be accounted for in the traditional way by emphasizing the importance of itinerant preachers encountering an expanding and more independent population,[61] the period 1784–1802 can be understood only against the background of economic, political and religious competition between Protestants and Catholics. Methodism was therefore, a beneficiary of, and partly a contributor to, the increased sectarian tensions of the last two decades of the eighteenth century.

Table 2.2 Methodist membership and growth rates
in the 'Linen Triangle of Ulster' 1780–1830[1]

1780	1,257	− 2.3	1805	4,294	− 0.1
1781	1,138	− 9.5	1806	4,600	7.1
1782	1,126	− 1.1	1807	4,574	− 0.6
1783	1,108	− 1.6	1808	4,299	− 6.0
1784	1,125	1.5	1809	4,494	4.5
1785	1,463	30.1	1810	5,105	13.6
1786	1,750	19.6	1811	5,231	2.5
1787	2,104	20.2	1812	5,108	− 2.4
1788	2,395	13.8	1813	5,119	0.2
1789	3,100	29.4	1814	5,096	− 0.5
1790	2,614	−15.7	1815	5,066	0.6
1791	2,928	12.0	1816	4,913	3.0
1792	3,181	8.6	1817	4,896[2]	− 0.4
1793	3,004	− 5.6	1818	4,875	− 0.4
1794	3,071	2.2	1819	6,383[3]	30.9
1795	3,515	14.5	1820	6,906	8.2
1796	4,007	14.0	1821	7,267	5.2
1697	4,071	1.6	1822	7,335	0.9
1798	3,720	− 8.6	1823	7,079	− 3.5
1799	3,687	− 0.9	1824	6,702	− 5.3
1800	4,161	12.9	1825	6,639	− 0.9
1801	4,145	− 0.4	1826	6,282	− 5.4
1802	4,488	8.3	1827	6,257	− 0.4
1803	4,367	− 2.7	1828	6,365	1.7
1804	4,300	− 1.5	1829	6,498	2.1
			1830	6,512	0.2

[1]   See Figure 2.1 for the approximate area of the sample. Since Methodist circuits changed their boundaries through expansion in this period the actual geographical area is not absolutely precise. The circuits included in the sample are Armagh, Tandragee, Newry, Lisburn, Charlemont, Lurgan and Dungannon. From 1817 onwards the figures include Wesleyan and Primitive Wesleyan Methodists, though their circuits were not identical. Figures exist for the 1770s, but are unreliable for present purposes because of circuit expansion.
[2]   Because of the chaos in circuit geography after the split of 1816, this figure is an average of those for 1816 and 1818.
[3]   The recorded figure is arrived at by adding the Wesleyan numbers to an estimate of Primitive Wesleyan numbers, calculated by averaging the figures for 1818 and 1820.

The relationship between this new religious movement and established religious institutions remained uneasy. Methodist leaders aimed to complement rather than replace the established church, and continually stressed their desire to cooperate with the regular clergy in spreading 'scriptural Holiness over the land'. The antipathy of the Church of Ireland towards Methodist itinerants, however, and the latter's complaints of the spiritual deadness of many of the ordained clergy, led to demands for the sacraments to be administered by Methodist preachers, within their own society.[62] The question of separation from the church was first raised in 1773 and recurred regularly thereafter, adding credence to establishment accusations of dangerous 'fanaticism'. Their 'schismatic' tendencies were particularly condemned in the revolutionary era when the government of both church and state were seen to be under threat.[63]

Despite Methodism's popular base, widespread influence and ambiguous relationship with the established church, however, accusations of radicalism were unfounded. Methodist individualism was firmly based on scriptural principles which stressed the interrelationship between personal morality and social order. Moreover, its smallness (only 14,000 by 1789), its close links with the established church, from which it did not separate until 1817,[64] and its military connections, made it an unlikely vehicle for radical opinions in Ireland. In the context of the rebellion, however, loyalty could no longer be merely assumed, but needed to be demonstrated, and Methodist leaders were anxious to dissociate themselves from the disruptive elements operating in Irish society. Individual members who 'swerved from their allegiance to lawful authority' were at once expelled and Methodists swelled the ranks of the yeomanry which helped put down the rebellion.[65] Growing confidence in Methodist loyalty was reflected in the government decision to permit the 1798 Conference of the society to go ahead despite the disturbed state of the country, and the prohibition of all meetings of more than five men. At the conclusion of the Conference, letters were received from the government granting permission and protection to preachers setting out to their respective destinations. None the less, in an age of political innovation, debates on the nature of government, whether civil or ecclesiastical, were regarded as dangerous, and never more so than in 1798. Thus, a challenge to the Methodist constitution from 32 stewards and leaders in the Lisburn circuit prompted Conference leaders into firm and decisive action. The Lisburn protesters' demand 'that the people shall have a voice in the formation of their own laws, in the choice of their own ministers, and in the distribution of their own property', left them open to charges of jacobinism from both Dublin and London.[66] While it seems clear that these men were in fact sincere Christians, wishing only for greater lay involvement in the leadership of the Methodist connexion, the prevailing political situation determined the outcome of their requests. A Conference anxious to exhibit its loyalty to both civil and religious establishments presented their 'delinquent' views as 'the result of the spirit of insubordination and lawlessness so prevalent'. The protesters were expelled and their subsequent appeal rejected. Over 200 members joined the dissidents in the formation of the Methodist New Connexion.[67] That the leaders of the Dublin Conference went so far as to send a list of the protesters' names to the military authorities again shows the way in which political and religious ideas were thought to be interrelated, and established Methodism's credibility as a champion of the established order.[68] Within the Methodist organization the ousting of dissidents was followed by a greater emphasis on clericalism and centralization – a development which was paralleled in Presbyterianism in the 1820s when the introduction of new tests for ordinands resulted in an organizational split between theological radicals and conservatives. The revolutionary atmosphere thus ensured that in ecclesiastical as in civil government, reaction was ultimately victorious over reform.

The formation of the Methodist mission in 1799 was an important stimulant to the activities of local societies, and Irish membership figures more than doubled from 16,227 in 1799 to 36,527 in 1820 (Table 2.3 and Figure 2.3). It also had a wider social impact. The stipulation that the itinerant missionaries should be Irish speakers was significant. While individual evangelists had already recognized the importance of using the native tongue in gaining easier access to the illiterate Roman Catholic peasantry, official sanctioning of this policy was a new step. The decision was directly related to social and political disorder, and reflected the evangelical conviction that the problems of Ireland were directly attributable to the pernicious doctrines of a heretical church and the manipulation of its people by a corrupt priesthood.[69] Thus, when Gideon Ouseley called for the emancipation of the Catholic populace he was eager to free them from the trammels of their religion, not from civil laws. In purely religious terms, this aspect of Methodism was by no means so significant as its revitalizing effect on all varieties of Protestantism. It did, however, arouse the wrath of the Roman Catholic Church and contributed to the sectarian bitterness already prevalent in south Ulster. It also offered an example for evangelicals throughout Britain whose attention was focused upon Ireland by the rebellion and the subsequent Act of Union, and who realized they did not have to travel thousands of miles to satisfy their missionary enthusiasm.

The Evangelical Society of Ulster, like the Methodist missionary initiative, was a direct response to the crisis of 1798, and in its make-up and development can be seen the coming together of several strands of Ulster evangelicalism. The society was founded by five Presbyterian Seceding ministers acting independently of their synod, and inspired by the example of evangelicals in America and Britain. The new secretary's explanation of the impulse behind the society reveals the sense of individual responsibility and constant vigilance by which evangelicals were motivated.

> To be found at any time, slumbering upon Zion's walls, is very inconsistent with the character of a faithful watch-man; but in times like the present, it must be peculiarly so. Never surely was there a more eventful period than this, in which

Table 2.3   Methodist membership and growth rates
in Ireland 1767–1830[1]

1767	2,801		1801	24,233	25.6
1768	2,700	− 3.6	1802	26,700	10.2
1769	3,180	17.8	1803	24,605	− 7.9
1770	3,124	− 1.8	1804	22,954	− 6.7
			1805	23,321	1.6
1771	3,632	16.3			
1772	3,792	4.4	1806	23,773	1.9
1773	4,013	5.8	1807	24,560	3.3
1774	4,341	8.2	1808	24,550	0.0
1775	4,237	− 2.4	1809	25,835	5.2
			1810	27,801	7.6
1776	4,798	13.2			
1777	5,211	8.6	1811	28,194	1.4
1778	5,336	2.4	1812	27,823	− 1.3
1779	5,940	11.3	1813	28,770	3.4
1780	6,109	2.9	1814	29,388	2.2
			1815	29,357	0.1
1781	6,175	1.1			
1782	6,512	5.5	1816	28,542	− 2.8
1783	6,053	− 7.1	1817	27,167	− 4.8
1784	6,427	6.2	1818	27,147	− 0.1
1785	7,817	21.6	1819	32,987[3]	21.5
			1820	36,527	10.7
1786	10,345	32.3			
1787	11,313	9.4	1821	37,100	1.6
1788	12,213	8.0	1822	35,643	− 3.9
1789	14,010	14.7	1823	34,654	− 2.8
1790	14,106	0.7	1824	33,969	− 2.0
			1825	34,217	0.7
1791	14,158	0.4			
1792	15,018	6.1	1826	35,289	3.1
1793	13,974	− 7.0	1827	35,833	1.6
1794	14,551[2]	4.1	1828	36,156	0.9
1795	15,266	4.9	1829	36,457	0.8
			1830	36,903	1.2
1796	16,762	9.8			
1797	17,004	1.3			
1798	16,630	− 2.2			
1799	16,227	− 2.4			
1800	19,292	18.9			

[1]   Figures are taken from the annual minutes of Conference and refer to the numbers of Methodists enrolled in societies. From 1817 onwards the figure given is the added number of Wesleyan Methodists and Primitive Wesleyan Methodists. Growth rates are calculated by expressing the annual net turnover of membership as a percentage of the total membership in the previous year.

[2]   Figure is based on an estimate for the Newry circuit which sent no return.

[3]   Since the Primitive Wesleyan numbers for 1819 are not available, the recorded figure is arrived at by adding the Wesleyan numbers to an estimate of Primitive Wesleyan numbers, calculated by averaging the figures for 1818 and 1820.

our lot has been cast. What lover of the gospel, who that ever prays in sincerity, 'thy kingdom come;' we ask, what soldier of the cross can stand neuter at present, or remain at ease in Zion?[70]

Its organizers clearly saw this local society as part of an international pan-evangelical movement. Among those attending its first meeting in October 1798 were 13 ministers from four different Presbyterian denominations, and the society is thus of particular interest as a Calvinist parallel to Arminian Methodist evangelicalism. The society applied to British missionary bodies such as the London Missionary Society for a supply of itinerant preachers in a (vain) attempt to deflect synodical criticism. As a result, popular and controversial preachers such as Rowland Hill and William Cooper, renowned for their zeal and anti-Catholicism, toured the north in the summer of 1799, preaching wherever a crowd gathered, in fields, barns, schoolhouses and mills.[71] Reports indicate that the excitement and drama of the post-rebellion period, with talk of curfews, the army presence and a pervading atmosphere of tension, contributed to their popular success. Presbyterian involvement in this particular society was short-lived, but its records give an insight into the state of Ulster Presbyterianism in the immediate post-rebellion period.

William Gregory, who had been one of the London Missionary Society's first ambassadors to the South Seas in 1798, toured Ulster in 1800 and his observations on the religious community of Ulster are particularly

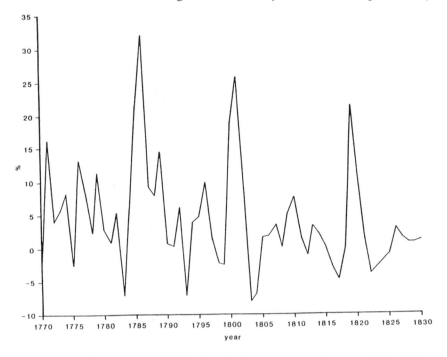

Figure 2.3   Growth rates of Methodism in Ireland at annual intervals 1770–1830

revealing.[72] While he was received in parish churches and Methodist meeting houses by ministers already committed to interdenominational cooperation, his visit caused disruption in Presbyterian circles. The response from the Seceding synods was particularly hostile. They spoke out against the Evangelical Society's latitudinarian principles, claiming that interdenominationalism was schismatic and general itinerancy unconstitutional.[73] The General Synod was less vehement in its opposition, and despite its reputation for lacking evangelical fervour in this period, several of its ministers appear to have opened their pulpits to the agents of the society.[74] Indeed, there seems to have been a considerable gap between official and popular perceptions resulting in frequent clashes within the Presbyterian community. When confronted by Gregory's request for premises in which to preach, elders clashed with ministers and congregations with elders. Ministers could find themselves locked out, or a congregation find the meeting-house doors closed against it. The missionary records therefore suggest a degree of complexity at local level which is disguised by the official response. Evangelicalism within Presbyterianism was still a matter of individual commitment, but the reception which many within the community gave to the itinerants of this society suggests that the transition to the more evangelical Presbyterian church of the mid-nineteenth century was perhaps not as dramatic as it is sometimes portrayed.

Although it faded in the early years of the new century, the Evangelical Society of Ulster stirred up a good deal of religious enthusiasm and controversy in the area around Armagh. It not only was a pioneering step in the direction of interdenominational cooperation within Ulster evangelicalism, but also drew attention to the importance of popular revivalists within that tradition. William Gregory's tales of his colourful life as a South Seas missionary, for example, were guaranteed to hold the attention of his listeners. Similarly, the flamboyant style of the American revivalist Lorenzo Dow, fresh from his heady successes in the frontier revivalism of Kentucky, attracted large crowds when he toured Ireland in 1800 and again in 1806.[75] Many observers claimed they 'had never seen any person who so much reminded them of the Lord Jesus'. Both the General Evangelical Society and the Evangelical Society of Ulster attracted prominent revivalist preachers from the mainland. In the pervading atmosphere of social disruption and millenarian excitement, the voices of emotional orators and enthusiasts were particularly acceptable. Anti-Catholic polemicists such as Ouseley, Cooper and Hill were able to capitalize on the general aura of turbulence and unrest, and both to contribute to, and draw from, the popular anti-Catholic sentiments of the period. Their zeal in proclaiming religious certainties to a generation made anxious by revolution in Europe and Catholic resurgence in Ireland was quite remarkable.

The life of Gideon Ouseley in particular testifies to the intense religious energy which the most passionate evangelists devoted to reclaiming Irish Catholics, lukewarm Protestants and the irreligious in a period of social tumult and political upheaval. Ouseley was born in the year of John Wesley's second visit to County Galway, was 'converted' in the year of Wesley's death, and died on the one hundredth anniversary of Wesley's first introduction to field preaching. A Methodist rural revivalist could have no better pedigree.[76] Of English ancestry, the Ouseley family was one of a declining group of substantial Protestant farmers who were surrounded by an overwhelmingly Catholic peasantry.[77] Despite his father's anticlericalism, Ouseley was bound for a career in the Church of Ireland and was tutored by the local Catholic priest. After failing to win a place at Trinity College, he married into a respectable Protestant family and acquired a farm which was subsequently surrendered after a lawsuit.[78] Ouseley then entered a phase of dissolute living which was dramatically brought to an end by a drunken shooting accident in which he lost an eye and very nearly his life. With Young's gloomy *Night Thoughts* as his unlikely convalescent reading, Ouseley's close encounter with death resulted in a lasting preoccupation with death and eternity.

His first experience of evangelical religion was in the meetings conducted in a local inn by a Methodist quartermaster attached to the Royal Irish Dragoons and stationed in Dunmore barrack.[79] His 'conversion' was one of those agonizing evangelical experiences, and so intense was Ouseley's mental turmoil at this time that it became the emotional and conceptual foundation of much of his later preaching.[80] Indeed so frequently did Ouseley recall in tears 'that Sunday morning' when 'I got such a sight of hell' that the more sophisticated Dublin Methodist congregations came to dread the very sight of him.[81] His conversion opened up the way for half a century of itinerant preaching characterized by unremitting zeal and energy. One-eyed, barrel-chested, and with a liberal dose of native humour, Ouseley cut an extraordinary figure in the troubled landscape of post-rebellion Ireland.

> On Monday we came to Baillieborough. The market-people were assembled when we came into the street. We did not alight, but prepared to attack the devil's kingdom which still remained strong in this town. The Methodists wished us out of the street, when they saw the manner of our proceedings, riding on our horses, with our umbrellas over our heads, the day being wet, but a young girl was so alarmed that she feared the day of judgement was at hand.[82]

His preaching was unashamedly emotional and often produced disturbing signs of physical and psychological excesses. He rang bells to announce his presence, stood in front of apothecaries' windows to deter missiles and used simple agrarian illustrations to engage his hearers – the bulk of whom were made up of the Irish peasantry. Ouseley's view of Irish peasants was that they adhered to a deeply pagan and superstitious form of religion upon which was grafted a veneer of Roman Catholicism that was itself superstitious and irrational. The Roman Catholic priests were therefore, in his opinion, the beneficiaries of ignorance which they had a vested interest in maintaining. Likewise, poor Protestants, because of the failings of the episcopal clergy, availed themselves of Catholicized quasi-magical practices to ward off death, demons, fairies and banshees.[83]

It is perhaps in its anti-Catholic fervour that Ouseley's career is most closely bound up with the wider development of Irish evangelicalism in this period. The different phases in the development of his anti-Catholic opinions is thus of wider significance. Ouseley's anti-Catholicism predated his evangelical conversion and was part of a wider anticlericalism, but his experiences as an itinerant evangelist confirmed his prejudices. Between 1799 and 1807 Ouseley and his missionary colleagues experienced a number of unpleasant incidents at the hands of Irish priests, but these were generally shrugged off as one of the hazards, even blessings, of missionary endeavour. Three circumstances combined to produce a more hostile climate. The first was Dr Coke's request for accurate numbers of Roman Catholic converts, presumably to stimulate fund-raising for the Irish mission in England.[84] The published figures were sufficiently large to engage Catholic attention. Secondly, the reports of the Irish missionaries were reproduced in the connexional magazine and even taken direct to the secretive Committee of Privileges by Joseph Butterworth, the Methodist MP, with the result that both English and Irish Methodists began to ascribe a significance to the Irish mission quite disproportionate to its actual size and impact.[85] Thirdly, after a period of acute opposition from priests, Ouseley wrote a series of letters to Dr Bellew, the Roman Catholic Bishop of Killala, detailing names, dates and places of anti-Methodist persecutions.[86] Bellew's response was that since the Methodist missionaries were neither ordained nor specifically legitimized by the civil authorities then they could scarcely expect protection from a Roman Catholic bishop. As a bishop of a church emerging from a century of penal laws, albeit loosely enforced, Bellew had no desire to clear the paths for itinerant zealots. After 1807, therefore, Ouseley was much more willing to engage in public controversies against Catholics.

While Ouseley's style was highly individualistic, his attitude to Irish Catholicism was reflected in wider evangelical circles. The view was frequently expressed that 'the hope that the Irish will ever be a tranquil and loyal people, and, still more, that piety and virtue will flourish among them, must be built on the anticipated reduction of Popery'.[87] Evangelical religion both fostered this hope and provided the opportunities for its realization. Emotive reports of Catholic attacks on Protestants by Ouseley and other evangelical itinerants made a deep impression on the wider British evangelical community. While assurances sent to the Methodist Missionary Committee in London or the London Missionary Society that 'Popery is falling off before us' were more optimistic than realistic, they were nevertheless enthusiastically received, and played an important part in promoting the belief that mass conversion was possible.[88] This was the impulse behind the formation of the variety of voluntary religious agencies which in the early years of the nineteenth century concentrated their efforts on the religious welfare of the Irish peasantry. In the immediate post-rebellion atmosphere, religious revival seemed a viable alternative to political reform which was now firmly linked with social and religous anarchy. Combining educational and religious principles, and with the scriptures as their major tool, the agents of the voluntary societies stressed the links between morality, political loyalty and social stability. Preaching, teaching and bible distribution were the major, and interdependent, strands of the campaign. The societies' exclusive use of the Bible, without note or comment, and the extensive use of the Irish language by teachers and itinerants brought them, and the faith they wished to disseminate, into direct conflict with those engaged in the political and social rejuvenation of Irish Catholicism.[89] The troubled area of south Ulster proved particularly attractive and responsive to the evangelical societies. Their preachers and agents capitalized on the political excitement and social unrest which deepened the significance of religious loyalties. In this cultural conflict, the religious societies quickly became identified with the social and political conservatism of the alarmed Protestant nation, and evangelicalism in Ireland became embroiled in controversial political issues. Accusations of proselytism and cultural imperialism thus became a recurring feature of nineteenth-century religious life.

In the long term, however, the strident nature of Irish evangelicalism was more significant in shaping Protestant identity than in changing religious allegiances. Its influence was felt both within the churches and in the wider society. Both the Presbyterian and Anglican churches, anxious to reassert their social and religious authority, came to recognize the relevance and effectiveness of at least some aspects of evangelicalism in the campaign against Catholicism and secularism. By the mid-nineteenth century many of its methods were adapted to denominational forms.[90] Not only did the use of Irish-speaking preachers, missions, bible distribution and auxiliary societies revitalize Ulster's major churches in terms of pastoral and missionary work, but increased anti-Catholic zeal left them better placed to reassume the role of leadership in the Protestant community. At the same time, the perception that Protestantism itself was in danger ensured a degree of evangelical support for the religious institutions of the state.

Within the wider society, only a minority ever adopted evangelicalism's strict religious code. Nevertheless, its influence on nineteenth-century Ulster was pervasive,[91] endowing the most vulnerable elements of society with a creed which justified and upheld the status quo. With radical politics, secularism and industrialization threatening the stability of long-held privileges, and with memories of the Reign of Terror a stark indicator of the transience of worldly things, evangelicalism offered the upper classes a creed which reaffirmed the old values and supplied a vigorous defence of social and political conservatism. In an age when class divisions were assuming greater significance, evangelicalism stressed the mutual interdependence of the rich and poor in a divinely ordained society, and defined the common enemy as immorality and ignorance, which were thought to be the products of Roman Catholicism. Sunday schools, temperance movements, town missions, tract and bible societies were the main agencies employed in the campaign to promote Protestant respectability. It success can still be measured in rural Ulster.

While the French Revolution was not a cause of religious revivalism, fear of the passions and forces which it unleashed gave a new urgency to religious commitment and encouraged a more emotional type of religious activity. Although the failure of the United Irishmen was complete, the sectarian nature of the rebellion in southeast Ireland left the Protestant community with an anxious understanding of its vulnerability in a predominantly Catholic nation. Far from the 'one and indivisible republic' envisaged by the would-be revolutionaries, religious identity assumed a heightened significance in any discussion of social and political tensions. The withdrawal of many Presbyterians from radical politics reinforced the view that Catholicism and disloyalty were synonymous. With the religious divide deepening as the new century progressed, the relevance of evangelical principles to local political and social circumstances was even more vigorously asserted. In these years it gained widespread acceptance, a new prominence and the support of the most important elements of ecclesiastical and secular society. From a long-term perspective, it could, of course, be argued that far from being a stabilizing force in Irish society, evangelical religion proved to be the most disruptive of influences. It imbued the Ulster Protestant community with a sense of divine approval in its continued resistance to assimilation into the wider Irish culture, in which the Roman Catholic religion was regarded as the most central and most pernicious element.

PART TWO

Voluntarism, denominationalism and sectarianism 1800–50

[3]
Evangelical expansion: cooperation and conflict

For the preaching of the cross is to them that perish foolishness; but unto us which are saved it is the power of God. (1 Corinthians 1:18)

They that were scattered abroad went every where preaching the word. (Acts 8:4)

The late eighteenth-century revival had a profound effect on religious life, not only in Britain and Ireland, but throughout the rest of the world. It has been suggested that 'no outburst of missionary zeal, unless it be the Jesuit mission of the late 16th century, has ever paralleled the missionary developments resulting from the Evangelical Awakening between 1790 and 1820'.[1] The 'passion for evangelism' which it promoted was also channelled into a crusade for moral and social reform involving Christians of all denominations and nurtured by a variety of voluntary religious agencies.[2] In bible, preaching and missionary societies, evangelical clergy and laity were given a new sense of cohesion and direction, as well as the organizational facilities required for their campaign against irreligion and immorality. In the first two decades of the nineteenth century manifold societies were set up to encourage recruitment, manage funds and stimulate public interest in foreign and domestic missions.

During this period the great British evangelical societies, such as the Church Missionary Society (CMS) and the British and Foreign Bible Society (BFBS), not only established Hibernian auxiliaries, but made Ireland one of the chief targets for their conversionist zeal. Ireland thus helped to fund its own deliverance or, more accurately, an evangelical minority contributed modest sums to organizations based in London whose more considerable assets were then used to convert the Irish and civilize their country. Such arrangements not only released far more resources for the evangelization of Ireland than were available from within its own boundaries, but resulted in a much closer identification of interests between British and Irish evangelicals than would otherwise have been the case. Thus the great evangelical societies, with their

Hibernian auxiliaries, gave fresh impetus to a centuries-old civilizing mission which Irish evangelicals made their own.

The formation of evangelical missionary societies at the end of the eighteenth century sprang from a genuine sense of Christian duty and responsibility. Nowhere is this more clearly expressed than in William Carey's *Enquiry into the Obligations of Christians to use means for the Conversion of the Heathen*, which resulted in the formation of the Baptist Missionary Society in 1792.[3] Carey's pamphlet, calling for a new approach to the heathen by those who claimed to be Christians, excited a good deal of interest in evangelical circles. Published accounts of his subsequent mission to Bengal were an inspiration to adventurous Christian spirits and set an example for other denominations to follow. One consequence of the renewed missionary spirit was a degree of unity and cooperation between Christians of all denominations and theological traditions which threatened to upset some of the more established religious institutions. The London Missionary Society (LMS), for example, formed in 1795, set out to 'combine churchmen and nonconformists in the cause of missions'. One of its founders optimistically claimed that its formation represented the 'funeral of bigotry'.[4] In the turbulent final years of the eighteenth century the LMS was an important focal point for the pan-evangelical fervour stimulated by millennial expectancy. Interdenominational cooperation was particularly evident in the foreign mission field where Methodists, Anglicans, Presbyterians and even Roman Catholics, brought into frequent contact with one another, recognized their interdependence and unity of purpose. Harmony on home ground was less easily maintained, however, as the practicalities of administration, recruitment and finance inevitably reinforced denominational divisions.[5] The formation in 1799 of the Church Missionary Society for Africa and the East was a sign of things to come.[6] From about 1813 interdenominational rivalry intensified as the various missionary societies sought to extend their influence by the formation of local auxiliaries. In Ireland, evangelicals of all denominations, keen to contribute to the great cause of bringing the light of the gospel truth to the darkened continents of the globe, were assiduously courted by all parties.

In the first twenty years of its operations, the LMS played a particularly important role in awakening interest in missionary work among Ulster Presbyterians. Local interest had already been aroused by the Calvinist evangelicals who itinerated through Ireland in the late eighteenth and early nineteenth centuries.[7] Visiting deputations also helped. One of the founders of the LMS, Alexander Waugh, a Secession minister from London, won the support of the General and Associate (Burgher) Synods on a trip to the north of Ireland in 1812.[8] The importance of synodical support for missionary enterprises should not be underestimated. The opportunity to address the assembled ministers and elders from all over the country, and of gaining permission from ministers to open their pulpits to visiting speakers, facilitated the formation of auxiliary societies and the recruitment of enthusiastic young clergy. As a result of visits from missionary deputations, LMS auxiliaries were

Map 2 The ecclesiastical province of Armagh, 1800

formed in Tyrone, Armagh, Antrim and Down in 1813.[9] Members of the Scottish Missionary Society (SMS) were likewise introduced to the Synod of Ulster in Moneymore in 1824, and these two Calvinist organizations thereafter visited the synod in alternate years. Support from members of the established church was also forthcoming and the society formed numerous auxiliaries throughout Ulster until the increased denominational exclusiveness of the 1830s embittered relations with the major churches.[10]

The early encouragement given to the London and Scottish missionary societies, by the Presbyterians in particular, can be seen as evidence of a growing emphasis on evangelism which came to the fore within the next three decades. This was a significant change of direction. As late as 1796, when the Assembly of the Church of Scotland debated a motion to send the gospel to the heathen, it was defeated on the grounds that philanthropy and learning must take precedence. The Church of Scotland had no foreign mission until 1826, and although the Presbyterians of Ulster did not form their own foreign missionary society until 1833 (1838 in the case of the Seceders), missionary sermons and visiting deputations had their effect much earlier.[11]

It was inevitable, however, that the energy invested in funding and recruitment campaigns would introduce a spirit of denominational competition into the missionary societies, and the example set by evangelical dissenters acted as a spur to local episcopalians anxious to secure support for the established church's own foreign missionary society. The prominent Irish evangelicals Henry Maturin from County Donegal and John Walker from Dublin were county members of the CMS London Committee as early as 1801.[12] The lack of an Irish auxiliary, however, meant that many churchmen supported the LMS and the SMS, ignorant of the existence of a Church of Ireland alternative. Despite a distinctly lukewarm response from the bishops an Hibernian auxiliary to the CMS was formed in 1814, and by 1825 there were 88 local associations, primarily located in Ulster.[13] The formation of the Methodist Missionary Society in 1813 and its Hibernian auxiliary in 1817 was also a product of denominational competition as Methodists tried to stem the flow of funds from their chapels into the coffers of the predominantly Calvinist London Missionary Society.[14] Despite continued pleas for Christian unity, these denominational initiatives inexorably weakened cooperative ventures. Thus by the 1830s the LMS had in effect become the missionary arm of the Congregationalists.

With opportunities for world mission apparently unlimited, only the shortage of funds seemed to stand in the way of a rich harvest. The chronic problems of financing the missionary crusade made the enlistment of the wealthy an important aspect of the work on the home front. The success or failure of local auxiliaries was largely dependent on the commitment of individual ministers and the support of well-connected laymen. In Ireland, as in England, the evangelical aristocracy, or at least those who saw social benefits from being attached to worthy causes, dominated the annual published lists of subscribers.[15] The evangelical societies therefore, gave full scope to the leadership qualities of those unconstrained by ecclesiastical authority or fine doctrinal distinctions, and in return the evangelical elite was able to add religious respectability to the social deference it already enjoyed.[16]

Although large donations from the rich were especially welcome, foreign mission fund-raisers were also able to capitalize on the popular appeal of a quest which combined the crusading ardour of the religious zealot with the adventurous, romantic spirit of the times. Lengthy, detailed reports of the progress of the mission in exotic-sounding, and often dangerous, locations drew in ordinary men, women and children through their penny societies. The appeal of personal involvement, in the life of an African child, for example, was especially attractive to ladies and juveniles, for whom separate auxiliaries were formed.[17] Monthly prayer meetings, local church sermons, missionary registers and reports, as well as visits by leading British evangelicals, helped sustain interest or revive flagging spirits.[18] The idea that foreign missionary work was an integral responsibility of the church gradually gained acceptance as the nineteenth century progressed. The formation and spread of local societies reflected a general awakening of interest in religious matters, both within and outside the traditional religious institutions. The work of conversion in foreign lands retained its romantic and adventurous flavour as conversionist zeal and benevolence were dispensed without any practical consequences for the everyday life of the sponsors. The situation on the home front, on the other hand, was much more controversial as the repercussions of the missionary campaign in Ireland both enlivened politics and embarrassed the churches.

Both the rebellion of the United Irishmen and the Union had focused the attention of the rest of Britain on Ireland as a vulnerable and unstable corner of the empire, while numerous surveys stressed the impoverished and ignorant state of its population. Whereas the civil authorities concentrated on the political dangers inherent in Irish instability, evangelicals quickly realized that there was a mission field on their own doorstep. Reports of the primitive superstitions of a peasantry ignorant of the word of God were rife. An agent of the London Hibernian Society (LHS) dubbed Ireland 'a land of beads, not bibles'.[19] William Gregory's comments in 1800 were also typical.

> The long neglected state of religion in Ireland surely demands some attention from those who profess to have, as the object in view, the conversion of sinners. . . . When it is reflected that an island so near to England, under the same Government, where the gospel is tolerated, but where so many thousands are under the gross darkness of superstition, and have never an opportunity of once hearing the glorious gospel of the Grace of God; means hath been employed and have proved successful to answer a political purpose. The civil sword has made rebels subjects of King George, and a new century is ushered in with a new Union. But, alas! Little hath been done in England to extend in Ireland the territory of Christ's kingdom, or bring spiritual rebels by the sword of the spirit to the feet of Jesus, or to bring about a Union with the Son of God.[20]

The desire to make good this deficiency became a major evangelical priority in the first quarter of the nineteenth century. Since ignorance was regarded as the midwife of both Catholicism and irreligion, the methods most commonly employed to reach Ireland's poor were preaching, teaching and bible distribution. All three encouraged the notion that evangelical Protestantism was a civilizing, improving and literate faith, which had little time for ancient superstitions or popular rituals. The evangelical crusade was, therefore, primarily a war against ignorance, but it carried with it wider religious, cultural and economic consequences. However, the Irish evangelical societies which proliferated in the decades after the Act of Union scarcely considered these implications. The paucity of educational provision in early nineteenth-century Ireland simply offered an opportunity to combine instruction with vital religion which zealous evangelicals were determined to grasp. The Hibernian Bible Society (HBS) and the Hibernian Sunday School Society were the largest and most influential of Ireland's Protestant religious agencies, but there were many others, including the London Hibernian Society (1806), the Baptist Society for Ireland (1814), the Irish Evangelical Society (1814), the Irish Society for Promoting the Education of the Native Irish through the Medium of their Own Language (the Irish Society) (1818), the Irish branch of the Religious Tract and Book Society (1816) and the Scripture Readers Society, formed in 1822.[21]

One of the most important tasks confronting missionaries, whether in India and Africa or in Ireland, was surmounting language barriers. But whereas in most parts of the world this represented logistical and technical problems which simply had to be overcome, in Ireland the language issue was resonant of much wider concerns relating to England's civilizing mission in the country over many centuries. Not surprisingly, therefore, there was much acrimonious debate among all those concerned with the enlightenment of the Irish masses about whether, or to what extent, they should conduct their mission in the native language. Although the Methodists, despite Wesley's own indifference to the Irish language, were to the forefront in promoting Irish preaching at the end of the eighteenth century, individual members of both the Presbyterian and established churches had advocated the use of the Irish language as a means of conversion from a much earlier period, and the task of translating the gospels into the native tongue had been undertaken as far back as 1602.[22] This and subsequent attempts, however, met with opposition even from within the Protestant community, and many of the old arguments were resurrected in the early nineteenth century.

The British and Foreign Bible Society, which supplied the evangelical societies, conducted several inquiries into the feasibility of publishing the Bible in Irish. Early responses from Irish religious quarters were negative. It was felt that those Irish peasants who could read at all, and these were few enough, read in English,[23] and in 1806 a decision was taken against the publication of an Irish edition of the Bible.[24] There were, however, some dissident voices including Whitley Stokes, who was a fellow of Trinity College and a passionate defender of the Irish poor.[25] Stokes refuted the notion that the native language was rapidly dying out, pointing out that even in Ulster 'there is a greater proportion of Irish speakers than is generally supposed. Cavan and Monaghan contain many; Tyrone about half of its inhabitants, Donegal more than half; Derry a few in the mountains to the south-west; Fermanagh scarcely any.'[26] His recommendation that Bibles be printed with the two languages in parallel columns met with immediate opposition, particularly from the Dublin Association for the Purpose of Discountenancing Vice (ADV). Apart from stating that the native language was declining as the Irish strove to better themselves, the society's officials pointed also to wider political implications in their suggestion that its promotion could be exploited by those advocating separation and independence.[27]

Another point of view which was beginning to win favour, however, was expressed by the distinguished Methodist scholar, Adam Clarke, himself an Ulsterman. 'The Irish language is with the natives a *sacred* language. . . . They allow themselves to *feel* from that tongue, what they do not consider themselves obliged to feel from another'.[28] Rural itinerants endorsed this view, and after further inquiries the BFBS resolved towards the end of 1809 that it was expedient to print the New Testament in Irish. The arguments were given an important boost in 1815 by the publication of an influential pamphlet by Christopher Anderson, who had conducted a survey on the topic for the Baptist Missionary Society.[29] This work echoed the sentiments of Adam Clarke by stressing the importance of using what was after all 'the language of the heart', in implanting a thirst for knowledge, from which instruction in English could follow. In the same year an even closer identification with the Gaelic tradition was established when the use of the Irish character as well as language was adopted.[30] From this date, and particularly after the formation of the Irish Society, the more extensive distribution of the scriptures in the Irish language was demanded. By 1823, the BFBS committee was calling for 5,000 copies of the whole scriptures to be printed in the Irish character and language.[31] From the mid-1820s copies of Irish Bibles, New Testaments and numerous tracts poured from the printing presses in response to the demands of the various preaching and teaching agencies. Despite their contrary intentions, therefore, early nineteenth-century evangelicals must take credit for at least slowing down the decline of the native tongue. They thus played a part, however unwittingly, in the preservation of the cultural heritage of Gaelic Ireland. Their inquiries into the state of the Irish language, and their intensive studies of its grammar and dialects, stimulated a new interest in its fate. In the long term, however, the fears of the ADV proved well founded, as this early tradition was built upon by later nationalists who were not particularly concerned to acknowledge the breadth of the tradition they appropriated. The language problem in Ireland was, of course, symbolic of much wider historical, cultural and political barriers, which evangelical missionary enthusiasm both confronted and inexorably deepened.

Evangelical intentions were, however, strictly religious. The Baptist Missionary Society, acting on Anderson's recommendations, set up a system of circulating schools in which the Bible could be taught by Irish-speaking masters.[32] The London Hibernian Society contented itself with providing Irish classes where it was thought necessary, but reported that Irish scripture readers were particularly well received.[33] The Irish Society for Promoting the Education of the Native Irish through the Medium of their Own Language, as its title suggests, was more specifically concerned with the Irish language, but not for its own sake. Rather the aim was

> to instruct the native Irish who still use the vernacular, how to employ it as a means for obtaining an accurate knowledge of English; and for this end, as also for their moral amelioration, to distribute among them the Irish version of the Scriptures by AB Russell and Bishop Bedell, the Irish prayer-book, where acceptable, and such other works as may be necessary for school-books, disclaiming at the same time any intention of making the Irish language a vehicle for the communication of general knowledge.[34]

To facilitate the eventual mastery of the English language by students, English translations were given on parallel pages or columns, and it was insisted that schoolmasters must be proficient in both languages. Bedell's Bible was the version favoured by most agencies involved with bible distribution, since it was felt to be acceptable to both the Roman and Protestant churches.

The main agency for the bible distribution was the Hibernian Bible Society, which from its inception was supported by the BFBS.[35] Reports from all over Ireland showed that the need was great. According to Archbishop Singer in 1805, there were not twelve provincial towns in Ireland in which Bible might be had.[36] Even in the Protestant northeast there was cause for concern. The society recorded a letter in 1808 from 'a clergyman in a very populous district of the north of Ireland' where 'the Bible could not be procured for *any* money'.[37] To meet such deficiencies the HBS was founded in Dublin in 1808 by W. B. Mathias and William Shaw and quickly won the support of Ireland's most influential social and ecclesiastical leaders, who clearly felt that bible distribution was part of the acceptable face of evangelicalism and carried with it no ecclesiological or political ramifications.[38]

The HBS was open to, and worked on behalf of, all denominations. The higher administrative levels were largely confined to Church of Ireland clergy and laity, while at committee level, and throughout the provinces, Presbyterians and Methodists played their part. Presbyterian concern for bible distribution, like that of the Anglican ADV, preceded the formation of the new society, and in 1807 an attempt was made to supply the gospel to the poor.[39] Although the response from local clergy was disappointing, aid was granted to the synod by both the ADV and the BFBS, and special arrangements were made for the inclusion of the metrical psalms in all copies of the scriptures.[40] The formation of auxiliaries of the HBS in the north, however, duplicated and superseded the work of the synod's bible committee which was dissolved in 1811. All ministers were then urged to support the formation of new branches, and to become active members of the national Bible Society.[41]

In the first year of the society's operations, when 3,500 Bibles and 2,000 testaments were distributed, every county in Ulster except Fermanagh and Donegal formed auxiliaries. In Belfast, where the Seceding Presbyterians were particularly active, a branch was formed with its own depository, and this became an important centre for evangelical work in the north.[42] The Hibernian Bible Society and its close relation the Religious Tract and Bible Society distributed countless thousands of Bibles and religious tracts despite the lack of booksellers.[43] Serviced by an army of volunteers, print and Protestantism were on the march throughout the country. Mathias's optimism in 1820 spoke for many.

> There is a Home Mission on a very extensive scale already formed at 22 Sackville Street, which sent out, throughout the last year, no less than 365,000 Missionaries through the country. They are the cheapest Missionaries on earth – they require no food or clothing – they will cost you little or nothing for carriage – as you are leaving town you may procure whatever number of them you wish – and if you should even throw any of them out of your carriage window on the road, they will be nothing the worse for it, nor in the least diverted from their labours.[44]

Despite the apparent success of the society, however, underlying denominational tensions came to the fore in the 1820s as churches realized that voluntary societies were eroding ecclesiastical control and church discipline.

In the meantime, evangelicals were firmly convinced that access to the scriptures was all that was necessary for the moral transformation of Ireland. This belief was based on the popular Protestant perception of Catholicism as a mixture of ignorance and superstition, promulgated by a cunning priesthood, and explained the widely held assumption that a system of education based on Protestant principles would convince the peasantry of the error of their ways.[45] Between 1810 and 1825 a formidable array of evangelical societies set out to educate the Irish peasantry in scriptural principles. As Bishop Doyle remarked, 'There were not as many verse-makers in Rome in the days of Horace, as there are writers and speakers on education now-a-days in a single assembly of ladies and gentlemen in Ireland.'[46] Although some Roman Catholics had at first been keen to cooperate in the expansion of education for the obvious temporal benefits it offered, it was not long before allegations of proselytism began to muddy the waters.

The most important of the evangelical educational societies, the London Hibernian Society was formed in 1809 as a result of an English deputation sent to Ireland at the request of Irish evangelicals.[47] The society complemented the work of rural itinerants and had three related aims during its first six years – the ministry of the gospel, the formation of schools and the distribution of tracts and Bibles. Theological problems over preaching practices, however, as well as the increasing degree of specialization resulting from the proliferation of religious societies in these years, necessitated a change of policy.[48] In 1814, therefore, the Irish Evangelical Society was formed to continue with the promotion of gospel preaching and the LHS was left to concentrate on education.[49] By 1830 the LHS had 1,373 schools with 80,513 scholars receiving a combination of religious and secular instruction.

> Persons of every religious description are freely received into the schools of this institution – they are instructed in the Irish and English language, or both – they are taught reading, writing and arithmetic – all the scholars who have been a certain time in the schools are required to commit at least four chapters of the New Testament to memory every quarter – the teachers are only paid in proportion to the proficiency of the scholars, as determined at quarterly inspections, and deserving scholars are rewarded with gifts of Bibles or Testaments, as their respective cases may require.[50]

About one quarter of the scholars of the LHS were distinguished as Roman Catholic, which in itself shows how far early evangelical attempts to reclaim the Irish poor, both Catholic and Protestant, inexorably gave way to recruitment among those from within the Protestant community.

The Irish Society had a greater emphasis on the Irish language, and was therefore more involved in Roman Catholic areas of Ireland. By 1830 it had a total of 491 schools.[51] The main distinction between these two organizations was in their approach to the language question. Teachers of the Irish Society sought out Irish-speakers as the main objects of their care, using English only as a means of translation where necessary, while the teachers of the LHS taught in English, and used Irish only with those who, having acquired English, wished to master the native tongue. Irish-speaking classes were a particular bone of contention for Roman Catholic clergy, who saw this as a way for Protestant evangelicals to insinuate themselves into the rural community. The policy of giving premiums and of paying teachers in proportion to the proficiency of their scholars was also condemned as taking advantage of the most vulnerable section of society. The annual reports of both societies frequently record the hostility of the Catholic clergy on the one hand and the appreciation of the peasantry on the other. Not surprisingly, the 'covert' methods of the Irish Society, of which its supporters were so proud, enraged local priests:

> In truth, an Irish master teaches his scholars where and when he can find opportunity; and, to avoid exciting the opposition of the Priest, the inspection is frequently obliged to be confined to one, two or three scholars at a time, according as they can be induced to come, or are enabled to avoid suspicion – and seldom can they be inspected in a body at one fixed place, – while the establishment has nothing of a school but the teacher and the name – no school room, no tables, no benches, no apparatus, no registration, but a collection of scholars. In order to avoid discovery, the little batch will be sometimes found behind the hay-stack, or the turf-clamp, generally in some neighbour's cabin in

the evening. It is quite needless to say that all this must pass unobserved to anyone who does not follow the proper mode of inquiry through the persons
concerned.[52]

Both the necessity for, and the exercise of, such subterfuge increased the
mutual hostility between evangelical Protestants and the Catholic church.
Although the society's publicists stressed, as did the LHS, that it was their
'bounden duty to respect the religious prejudices of those whom they wish to
improve and benefit', it was more difficult to ensure that these instructions
were actually carried out in practice.[53] The evangelical belief that 'tolerance'
in religious matters was merely the child of 'indifference' is an indication of
how fine the line was between education and proselytism.[54] The LHS's
response to charges of proselytism speaks for itself:

> the Committee would draw the distinction between instances of reported
> conversion, and cases of practical interference with the tenets of children in
> school. Cases of the description which are usually stated in the report [of the
> Education Committee] are, *facts of conversion wrought by the simple efficacy of divine
> truth, not by interference upon the part of the society with the religious peculiarities of the
> scholars*; and however the policy of such statements may be questioned by some,
> the statements themselves supply no proof of improper deviation from a strictly
> neutral practice in the schools.[55]

What is offered here is a convoluted and disingenuous distinction between
conversion and proselytism in which evangelical educationalists drew a
narrow line between 'the simple efficacy of divine truth' in opening the eyes
of Roman Catholics to vital religion, and specific interference with the
'peculiarities' of Catholic belief and practice. The inadequacy of this
distinction was based not so much on hypocrisy and moral chicanery as on the
fervent evangelical belief in the supremacy of scripture and the benefits that
would accrue to the recipients of their version of 'godliness and good learning'.
As with all fine distinctions its actual operation in a specific place at a specific
time must have depended a great deal on the balance between zeal and
sensitivity in the minds of its operators. But in practice the viability of such a
distinction also depended on the goodwill and passive acceptance of those on
the receiving end of evangelical instruction. Even in a climate of perfect
religious harmony such ambiguities would have been difficult to cope with,
but with the increase in religious controversy and Catholic self-consciousness
in the 1820s the fine distinctions of evangelical missionary strategy became
more difficult to apply. The evangelical educational societies were thus both
instigators and victims of a renewed spirit of controversy in Irish religion.

While the Roman Catholic clergy were convinced of the LHS's proselytizing intentions, the attempts of evangelicals to emphasize the common ground
on which Protestants and Catholics rested also caused problems with fellow
Protestants. The degree of cooperation from the Protestant churches varied
considerably. The LHS claimed to be a fully interdenominational society, and

this is borne out by the annual reports which record the denominational allegiances of its school supervisors. In 1831 it was reported that, of 675 day schools, 331 were supervised by Church of Ireland ministers, 44 by other ministers, 263 by noblemen, ladies, etc., while in 37 schools the local situation meant that no supervision was available.[56] The Irish Society, on the other hand, claimed to be 'a society managed by a committee of members of the Church of England, doing a work which is in its nature truly Catholic, and which receives the co-operation of Christians of every denomination'.[57] Although the Archbishop of Tuam was the society's first president, the church hierarchy was slow to become involved.[58] The hesitation of church leaders reflected their concern about who controlled the operations of the voluntary societies. They were anxious to ensure both that their own doctrinal practices were adhered to in public meetings and that the enthusiasm and efforts of their clergy and laity would be channelled into denominational expansion. They also wished to avoid damaging religious and political controversy. Thus the interests of the Protestant establishment and the 'needs' of the Irish peasantry were balanced on a tightrope. The organizers of the evangelical societies found from experience, therefore, that it was better to rely on individual clergymen and wealthy laymen than on the goodwill of the denominations themselves.[59]

The circumspection of church leaders was partly justified, because some of the evangelical societies, convinced of the link between Catholicism, poverty and ignorance, initially chose Roman Catholic areas for their special attention. The London Hibernian Society, for example, proclaimed that 'the most legitimate field of labour . . . is . . . in the confessed region of Popery, where there are few or no Protestants to show the deluded multitude a more excellent way'.[60] But in reality, as the records of the LHS make clear, it was the provincial border counties of Ulster that were the most important areas of expansion for the more controversial evangelical societies.

Table 3.1   London Hibernian Society:
number of schools and scholars by county in 1818

County	Schools	Scholars	County	Schools	Scholars
Sligo	47	4,140	Fermanagh	53	3,671
Leitrim	58	4,712	Donegal	47	4,202
Roscommon	9	799	Cavan	35	2,817
Mayo	52	4,188	Tyrone	21	2,087
Galway	23	1,699	Monaghan	38	3,596
Longford	6	459			
Cork	1	46	Total	194	16,373
Waterford	2	100			
Total	198	16,143			

Thus, the number of schools in the five border counties of Ulster almost equalled the total number in the eight counties of southern Ireland, and the number of scholars was more or less the same.[61] By 1837, 68 per cent of the total number of LHS schools were based in Ulster.[62] The figures for the Irish Society in 1839 show a similar trend, with more than half its schools concentrated in the provincial border counties of Ulster which were experiencing rapid demographic growth in the early decades of the nineteenth century.[63]

The chief explanation for the success of the voluntary agencies in Ulster was the need for a strong network of Protestant supporters and a cultural bedrock of religious seriousness upon which to build. Aristocratic patrons, resident gentry and the existence of a prosperous middle class of shopkeepers, farmers and craftsmen, ensured a supply of teachers, inspectors and sponsors. The importance of such advantages can be seen most clearly in the popularity of Ireland's most successful voluntary religious agency, the Hibernian Sunday School Society (also known as the Sunday School for Ireland), formed in Dublin in 1809. In the 1820s, for example, there were more Sunday school teachers in Ulster than there were scholars in Munster, and the provincial statistics reflect the particular appeal of the movement to the Protestant middle classes of Antrim and Down (Table 3.2).[64] The Sunday School Society was primarily a coordinating body that offered Bibles, grants and support where requested.[65] It had an interdenominational constitution, though the preponderance of upper-class supporters weighted it heavily on the Anglican side.

Unlike the other religious societies, the Sunday School Society did not pay its teachers, and no doubt this policy served its intended purpose of promoting a bond of sympathy between the instructors and the instructed. Certainly, their involvement as patrons or Sunday school teachers imbued at least some members of the upper and middle classes with a new understanding of the harsh and unrelenting poverty in which many of the lower orders lived out their daily lives. Early accusations of parental indifference, for example, were withdrawn when it was recognized that many could not send their children to schools of any sort because they lacked sufficient clothes or shoes. Sunday schools also offered tangible advantages to the poor:

(1)   Bibles, Testaments or other improving or instructive books.
(2)   Plain, useful clothing.
(3)   The privilege of procuring books from the Library.
(4)   Admission to an evening school, where writing, arithmetic and plain work are taught.
(5)   Marks of kindness and attention to deserving children or their families, recommendations for service, etc.
(6)   A testimonial on leaving the school.[66]

There is little doubt that Sunday schools made an important contribution to the inculcation of religious respectability which was so predominant a feature of nineteenth-century Ulster life.[67]

Table 3.2 (a)   Hibernian Sunday School Society: number of Sunday schools in each province at five-yearly intervals

Year	Ulster	Leinster	Munster	Connaught	Total
1816	256	57	11	11	335
1821	1,193	281	77	89	1,640
1826	1,300	297	103	104	1,804
1831	1,841	387	131	222	2,581
1836	2,007	432	259	165	2,863
1841	2,010	455	394	169	3,028

Table 3.2 (b)   Hibernian Sunday School Society: proportion of scholars to population, 1831

Ulster	1:14
Leinster	1:68
Munster	1:148
Connaught	1:173

Table 3.2 (c)   Hibernian Sunday School Society: proportion of scholars to population in the province of Ulster, 1831

County Antrim	1:9
County Armagh	1:11
County Cavan	1:44
County Donegal	1:25
County Down	1:11
County Fermanagh	1:19
County Londonderry	1:10
County Monaghan	1:27
County Tyrone	1:14

Statistics are extracted from the printed annual reports of the Sunday School Society for Ireland, held by the RCB, Dublin.

The first third of the nineteenth century saw an unprecedented attempt to convert Irish Catholics, not by the power of established churches or coercion by the state, but by the voluntary religious zeal of a host of evangelical societies. It would be a serious misunderstanding of the evangelical mind to deny that the chief motivation for such activity was what evangelical Protestants claimed it to be, that is, an earnest desire to see 'vital religion' expand at the expense of Romish superstition and popular indifference. But the fact that many of the societies were either founded in England or had the support of English evangelicals, and that they were patronized by Anglo-Irish landowners, ensured that there was more at stake than conversion alone. The potential for controversy was there from the start because the most common evangelical methods – preaching, teaching and the distribution of literature – carried with them overtones of religious proselytism and cultural imperialism. The acrimonious disputes over the use of the Irish language, for example, both within Protestantism and between Protestants and Catholics, show that what was at stake was no less than a contest between incompatible religious and national cultures for the heart and soul of the nation. But even by 1830 it was clear that the evangelical campaign to convert the Irish peasantry could not succeed in the face of the Catholic Church's stout resistance. Ironically, therefore, the evangelical crusade to convert Catholic Ireland contributed further to the concentration of Protestantism in Ulster. The extent to which the provincial frontier with the rest of Ireland was the chief theatre of evangelical proselytism is itself indicative of the changes that were taking place.

To state, however, that the evangelical societies failed to achieve their main objective is only part of the story. The voluntary agencies, with their preachers, teachers, distributors, collectors and visitors, bureaucratized evangelicalism and brought into being an army of subalterns beyond the immediate control of churches and their clergy. Committed to evangelical zeal and mutual improvement, this army at once destabilized the old conventional boundaries between the Catholic and Protestant churches, and promoted class harmony within Ulster Protestantism. What was happening was both new and exciting for those wrapped up in it. The evangelical societies, with their fund-raising activities and annual round of meetings and speeches, constituted a religious sub-culture which in the long term was more significant for the participants than for those to whom they reached out. James Digges La Touche, for example, found the annual April meetings in Dublin 'soul stirring', inspirational and exciting as they broke away from the complacency of 'old-fashioned habits' and reached out to include in their audiences those who could not normally be induced to attend monotonous church services.[68] The voluntary agencies thus contributed to the spread of a revived Protestantism both within and outside churches and offered a new outlet for those whose degree of commitment overreached the confines of existing religious institutions. Much was achieved, but much also had to be faced up to by churchmen and politicians who now had to manage a society made more unpredictable by religious zeal.

[4]
The churches:
schism and consolidation

I hear that there be divisions among you; and I partly believe it. For there must be also heresies among you. (1 Corinthians 11:18–19)

He that hath an ear, let him hear what the Spirit saith unto the churches. (Revelation 2:7)

There is little doubt that such voluntary organizations as the London Hibernian Society, the Irish Society and the Bible Society made a lasting contribution to the Protestant churches. Bible distribution, better levels of literacy, and the growing popularity of religious seriousness helped to increase attendances at church and communion. The societies also drew together otherwise isolated rural clergy whose involvement in the supervision of schools and distribution of Bibles kept them in close touch with their parishioners and with other evangelicals throughout Britain. But if evangelical voluntarism brought fresh enthusiasm to the churches, it also threw up a new range of problems. On the formation of a Hibernian auxiliary to the CMS, for example, Daniel Wilson stated that 'It will now form a center of friendly acquaintance and union between them and that suspected class of churchmen who cherish the vital interests of Religion. By making both approximate to each other, it may be the means of improving both.'[1] Wilson's statement not only reflects the aspirations of ardent evangelicals, but hints at the degree of dissension which separated them from their more orthodox colleagues. For, although evangelicalism had already taken root among certain sections of the major churches by the end of the eighteenth century, its advocates were, at that stage, a powerless minority. Lacking authority either at Presbyterian synodical level or among the Anglican hierarchy, their influence was largely confined to the localities in which they operated. The evangelical societies not only organized such 'godly' individuals into more cohesive units, but also increased their capacity for disruption. The practice of itinerancy, for example, both undermined the professionalism of the clergy and encouraged an individualism which was difficult to control. Moreover, the voluntary societies appropriated functions, such as teaching and bible distribution, which the churches considered to be in their own domain. The resultant tension between voluntarism and denominational loyalty was one of the most important features of early nineteenth-century religion.

For both the Anglican and Presbyterian churches, therefore, this period was one of introspection and reconstruction. The growing weight of criticism – from political reformers, social observers and religious zealots – pushed church leaders out of their complacency and onto the defensive. Only by overcoming internal dissensions and divisions, and by enforcing a greater degree of discipline and uniformity within their own denominations, could the distinctive tenets of their respective faiths be upheld, and authority imposed, at both ministerial and popular levels. This process, however, necessitated the clarification of points of doctrine and practice, which inevitably flushed disputed issues into the open and sometimes resulted in damaging divisions. The hierarchy of the Church of Ireland, by undertaking an energetic programme of internal reform, managed to contain its disruptive elements, but both the Methodists and the Presbyterians experienced serious splits. For the Presbyterians the 'purge' of 1829 was a necessary preliminary to evangelical consolidation and expansion. Methodism, by contrast, was damaged by the financial hardship, legal wranglings and protracted bitterness which followed the schism of 1816.

THE CHURCH OF IRELAND

D. H. Akenson labels the period 1800 to 1830 as 'The Era of Graceful Reform' for the Irish established church. A series of administrative improvements rendered it 'a much more efficient organization by the end of the period than it had been at the time of the Union'.[2] By the late 1820s even the Presbyterians and Methodists commented on the increased spiritual zeal of the established clergy.[3] The success of the established church in redeploying its assets and reasserting its authority was attributable to several different causes operating simultaneously. These included pressure from clergy and laity involved in the various evangelical societies, the contribution of evangelicals striving to revitalize the church from within, and the committed churchmanship of an increasing number in both the upper and lower ranks of the church hierarchy. Important areas nevertheless remained outside the control of even the church's most well-intentioned and influential champions. The limitations imposed by the state detracted from the Church of Ireland's credibility and hampered the efforts of reformers. Archbishop William Stuart (1800–22), outraged by the arbitrary and indiscriminate exercise of political patronage to fill the Irish bench in the years immediately following the Union, could only threaten to embarrass the government by taking the unprecedented step of resigning the primacy. Stuart's persistent and unqualified opposition to government wishes on this occasion, and his equally unequivocal failure to impose his authority – he was eventually persuaded to withdraw his threats – served only to accentuate the problems facing the church at the highest level.[4] However, once the obligations incurred at the Union had been discharged, political considerations became less important in the appointment of Irish bishops because there was no longer a House of Lords to be managed. The Irish establishment's desire to put its own house in order was invested with a new sense of urgency in the early nineteenth century by commissions of inquiry and the related possibility of legislative intervention. Questions on the state of the Irish Church were frequently raised in Parliament and English politicians displayed a growing lack of patience with Irish prelates.[5] Nonetheless, in those areas where action could be taken, there is some statistical evidence of an improvement which was seriously underestimated by hostile contemporaries and which has, until recently, been neglected by historians.[6]

The Church of Ireland's most intractable deficiencies – pluralism, non-residence and the related problems of an inadequate supply of churches and glebe houses – were tackled by a series of practical measures in the early nineteenth century. By 1830 the province of Armagh could boast of 79 new benefices since 1782, while the number of glebe houses had increased to 93 per cent of all parishes. The corollary of such improvements was an increase in the number of resident clergy, church services and communicants.[7] It was clear by the early 1830s, however, that internal reform was not enough even to placate some of the Church of Ireland's ambivalent supporters let alone its severest critics.[8] With the Whigs determined to make the Irish established church more defensible on utilitarian grounds, a pragmatic reorganization of its resources seemed inevitable. The Church Temporalities Act, dramatic both in its implications and in its immediate impact, was the first instalment in the erosion of the old order. The number of Irish bishoprics was reduced from 22 to 12, church cess and the Board of First Fruits were abolished, and a new body, the Ecclesiastical Commissioners for Ireland, was set up to deal with church administration and finance.[9] Funds to augment poor livings and for church building were made available from the revenue of the suppressed bishoprics, the reduction of the substantial revenues of the dioceses of Armagh and Derry and a graduated tax on ecclesiastical livings. The ancient and inefficient structure of the Irish Church was thus thoroughly overhauled, with more respect paid to efficiency than tradition.

The response of most Irish churchmen to Whig pragmatism was predictably hostile. Archbishop Beresford reluctantly accepted the need for wide-ranging reforms in order to ward off even worse dangers. But the general feeling was that this kind of rationalization, based on 'expediency', was yet another sop to the enemies of the Protestant religion.[10] The Bishop of Killala was of the opinion that Parliament was exceeding its rightful powers in intruding in ecclesiastical affairs and feared that 'the plan introduced would tend to establish the Church of Rome here on the ruin of the Protestant church'.[11] The bishops were particularly concerned about the future financial welfare of the parochial clergy which was brought into even sharper focus by the anti-tithe agitation of the 1830s.[12] Early attempts to solve the problem proved unsuccessful and merely contributed further to party disagreements over the financing of the Irish Church.[13] A compromise Act in 1838 converted tithes into a concealed payment set at a lower rate, and this temporarily put a stop to further agitation against religious endowments. As a result of such legislation Anglican churchmen and laity felt themselves to be increasingly thrown back on their own resources. They also recognized that more fundamental issues were at stake. Landlords identified the church reforms as preludes to an attack 'on every species of property'.[14] Even a moderate, anti-Orange landlord such as Lord Downshire now found himself cooperating with 'ultra' Lord Roden in defence of the clergy and their rights.[15] Similarly, Hereward Senior explains the increased number of Church of Ireland clergy on the Grand Committee of the new Irish Grand Lodge in 1830 as a result of the anticipated attacks on church and establishment.[16] This fusion of political, social and religious interest, while having little short-term impact, gave further impetus to evangelical zeal, and simultaneously stressed the importance of the established church to the survival of Protestantism in Ireland.

The activities of evangelicals posed different kinds of problems for the Church of Ireland. The tendency of 'bible' Christians to disregard the finer distinctions of their church in the wider interests of a gospel mission undermined both the hierarchical structure and the wider authority of the established church. In such circumstances the schismatic tendencies of evangelical enthusiasts were particularly threatening. The secession from the church led by John Walker, 'the most important figure in Irish evangelicalism',[17] established an unhappy precedent. As chaplain of Bethesda Chapel from 1794 to 1805, Walker was an unambiguous, passionate and outspoken evangelical. He contemptuously dismissed the 'baptized infidels' of the established church, with whom he severed all connections in 1804 to form the Church of God. Walker was not the first seceder, but he was the most prominent, and while his subsequent career is indicative only of his highly individualistic approach, his actions in 1804 caused ripples of anxiety throughout the Irish Church. Up to that point evangelicals, in their attempts to rejuvenate the established church, had generally relied more on self-restraint and pragmatism than on principled or doctrinaire arguments.[18] Walker's secession was not only a body-blow to that tradition, but made interdenominational cooperation among evangelicals far more difficult to defend. A deputation of English churchmen visiting Ireland in 1814 felt that the effects of Walker's actions were still in evidence. They reported: that 'Pure and active religion . . . is young in Ireland, cherished by few in number, and not without some of the errors and luxuriance of youth.' They clearly thought that, in Dublin at least, Irish evangelicalism was more contentious than helpful and exhibited 'too much of nicety and fastidiousness about religious opinions and human distinctions . . . too little of a sound, practical, bible-spirit'.[19]

Despite the damage caused by Walker's secession, the development of evangelical churchmanship within the Church of Ireland proved that a synthesis between orthodox churchmanship and evangelicalism was possible. The process was nevertheless gradual and beset with difficulties. The attempt to establish a Hibernian auxiliary to the CMS in Armagh, for example, offers a well-documented insight into the tensions of the early period. Viscount and Lady Lifford, while confident of the full support of the aristocracy of the Armagh area and of its local clergy, were adamant that the approval of Archbishop Stuart was an essential prerequisite to the setting up of a local auxiliary.[20] Orthodox church leaders naturally pointed to the existence of the two older Anglican missionary societies, the Society for Promoting Christian Knowledge (SPCK) and the Society for the Propagation of the Gospel (SPG). But the real point at issue, and one which was to recur all too often in the subsequent history of religious societies, was that of the mutual antipathy between 'sound, pious and rational Christians' and the whole body of evangelical 'enthusiasts'. Evangelical disdain for the original church-based missionary societies was probably based on their inability to exercise any real influence over them. On the other hand, church authorities remained resentful of the criticism of evangelicals, and their tendency to make invidious distinctions between worldly clergymen and genuine 'converts and believers'.[21] The cool and unhelpful response of the Archbishop of Armagh to the CMS proposals and the general hostility manifested by other leading churchmen led to hesitancy and caution on the part of many clergy.[22] When the Hibernian auxiliary was eventually formed in June 1814 it relied heavily on lay initiative and lay support. For the first six years of its existence the Deans of Armagh and Cloyne were the only leading churchmen officially associated with it. Not until mid-century were all dioceses fully represented by their ecclesiastical leaders, though by then the evangelical clergy had already made a substantial contribution to the CMS in Ulster.[23] This dichotomy between the church hierarchy and the parochial clergy, especially in Armagh, had the effect of cementing a popular evangelicalism outside the direct control of a more urbane leadership.

The interdenominational nature of the Hibernian Bible Society (HBS) posed even more serious problems for the church hierarchy and occasioned a revival of old 'Church in Danger' sentiments.[24] It was felt that, merely by associating with Methodists and dissenters, church leaders could be accused of conferring legitimacy upon them instead of defending the establishment from their attacks.[25] By 1821, the diversity of views existing within the society, and the increasingly controversial nature of its relationship with the Roman Catholic population,[26] led the Archbishop of Armagh to withdraw his support in the interests of prudence and religious harmony. His lead was followed by all the prelates except the Archbishop of Tuam, and he too ceased to attend HBS meetings in 1830.[27] Since one of the most frequent criticisms made against the Bible Society by church leaders was its rivalry with existing church organizations such as the Society for Promoting Christian Knowledge, the split with the HBS stimulated more enthusiasm for the older societies. The threat of evangelical enthusiasm thus rekindled interest in the Anglican denominational societies.[28] The withdrawal of church leaders from the Bible Society was part of a wider campaign to reassert hierarchical control, internal discipline and distinctive church forms against the perceived dilution of Anglican authority by pan-evangelical societies. Even well-established local arrangements for the sharing of buildings and facilities fell victim to the new mood of denominational consolidation.[29] When Bishop Mant was translated to Down and Connor in 1823, for example, he found that the degree of cooperation in the northeast between Anglican clergy and their Presbyterian neighbours was unacceptable.[30] He was determined to put a stop to such mutual accommodation, whether it was on the question of the timing of services, the announcement of 'rival' activities, or the content of sermons. He expressed a fear that his clergy were 'compromising their principles' in order to conciliate their Presbyterian counterparts. His intervention in long-established local traditions of interdenominational cooperation was often unwelcome, but by instilling a sense of authority and distinctiveness the hierarchy was going some way towards counteracting the interdenominational tendencies of the voluntary agencies in which many Anglican clergy and laity were involved.

The delicate task of church leaders in these years was to encourage religious zeal without stirring up religious controversy, and to harness evangelical enthusiasm to the broader interests of the church. Disciplinary problems were thus a recurring feature of the period. The chief causes of tension between orthodox and evangelical churchmen were untempered 'enthusiasm' and the conduct of public worship. The growing popularity of extempore prayer and popular hymn-singing, for example, was a worrying development for a church rooted in liturgical tradition.[31] The laws of the church were regarded as a safeguard, not only against Romanism, but against the equally pernicious threat of Puritanism, which was thought to be the unwelcome result of uncontrolled religious enthusiasm. The response of Bishop Mant to the issues raised by the evangelical revival thus represented the new standards of Anglican churchmanship which Archbishop Beresford sought to impose on the Irish Church, and reflects both the new seriousness and the strict adherence to the distinctive principles of the establishment that was to play an important role in its spiritual rejuvenation. By upholding sound churchmanship and rational Christianity over Methodistic enthusiasm, Mant dismissed the narrow rigidity of some aspects of evangelicalism. He claimed he was no friend of extempore prayer and warned that, while it was the duty of every Protestant to 'search the Scriptures', not all were qualified to explain them. He reinforced the value of 'slow, secure and permanent' conversions and published sermons on the necessity of scriptural education.[32] But despite the proclamations of bishops and archbishops, evangelical clerics continued to interpret the laws of the church with considerable flexibility. According to the *Christian Examiner*, the chief organ of the evangelicals, they were all too aware of the willingness of churchmen to dub them 'enemies of everything vital in the doctrine and discipline of the established church'.[33] Writers were therefore anxious to stress their devotion to the episcopal government, liturgy and doctrine of their church, but their simultaneous promotion of a wider evangelicalism often left them balancing precariously on an ecclesiastical tightrope. While there were many articles on Prophecy and on Reformation meetings, for example, words of caution were necessary to ward off unwelcome accusations of 'fanaticism'. Reformation supporters, and these included many Church of Ireland clergy, were advised to keep themselves away 'from the violence and ebullition of popular meetings' and to exhibit 'sobriety of view and restraint of imagination in their enquiries into unfulfilled prophecy'.[34]

But there were occasions when evangelical missionary enthusiasm could not be reconciled with official restraints. On the question of Home Missions, for example, it was felt that the national church was standing by while its role was usurped by others.

> We are aware that there are some quietists in the establishment who would shudder to think that our National Church could assume a character so active, who would circumscribe her exertions within the pale of her own communion, and while they allow her to be a city placed upon a hill, would so fence her round with protective ordinances, that her light would be of little effectual use or advantage to others – who would limit the labours of the established church to the work of educating her people, and satisfied with this partial performance of positive duty, would devolve upon others the task of conversion.[35]

The formation of the Established Church Home Missionary Society in October 1828 was an attempt by leading Dublin evangelicals to overcome official obstacles to their missionary enthusiasm. Although they were keen to secure episcopal approval for the use of itinerant clergy in neglected areas, this was not forthcoming. Bishop Mant, in a call for 'discipline, order and decency', attacked the mission's agents for neglecting to seek diocesan permission, for using extempore prayers and for mutilating liturgical forms. He further claimed that 'the outward decencies and solemnities of public worship were disregarded; that without any preference of consecrated over unholy ground, any place where it is possible to collect a congregation was employed for these ministerial tours'.[36] No matter how much supporters of the mission claimed to be working in the church's interest,[37] indisciplinary behaviour on the part of the established clergy undermined the very hierarchical authority which distinguished it from dissenting churches. But although the work of this particular society was effectively ended by legal action which deemed it 'illegal and irregular' and 'an anomalous appendage to an established church',[38] it became clear by the 1830s and 1840s that evangelicals and churchmen were working towards roughly the same ends, if from different starting points. Although style and methods were still contested territory, the spread of 'vital religion' in Church of Ireland parishes was increasingly a shared objective.

The political attacks on the church in the 1830s not only highlighted the need for internal unity and a more public display of spiritual zeal, but also shifted the focus to those areas on which evangelicals and other churchmen could agree. By the second half of the decade population growth and migration, especially to Belfast, made the problem of church extension a major priority, and the formation of diocesan societies to deal with it showed how evangelicalism and orthodox churchmanship could harmoniously coexist. The formation of the Down and Connor Clergy Aid Society,[39] for example, despite superficial similarities with the controversial Church Home Mission,[40] was endorsed by Bishop Mant, as was the formation of the Additional Curates' Society in 1838.[41] In his Charge of 1839 Mant pointed out that these new societies involved 'no compromise, sacrifice, nor suspension of principle': 'They are Church societies, calculated to advance Christ's Holy Religion by means of the doctrine and discipline, the religious training, the liturgy, the ministers, and the solemn ordinances of the Church.'[42] By such means evangelical zeal was harnessed to the cause of church reform and was consequently regarded as an asset rather than a nuisance. Administrative reforms and evangelical enthusiasm, when properly controlled, were thus complementary components of the revitalization of the established church.

Any survey of the Church of Ireland's history, however, makes it clear that its claim to be a national church, within a predominantly Roman Catholic country, was the overriding factor in determining its fate in the decades surrounding Catholic Emancipation. Whereas evangelicals, with varying degrees of sensitivity, were determined to convert Roman Catholics, the hierarchy was understandably more cautious. Most church leaders retained an acute awareness of their social and political responsibilities in not stirring up unnecessary religious conflict, but in the 1820s the growing confidence and aggression of Roman Catholicism, as both a religious and political force, ensured that the established church – which after all had the most to lose – was inevitably drawn into acrimonious debates. The 1830s and 1840s brought no relief as disputes over education, tithes and endowments fuelled the flames of ecclesiastical controversy. Ironically, the Church of Ireland was being undermined by political events beyond its control at the same time as administrative reform and evangelical zeal made its holy mission more efficient.

THE PRESBYTERIAN CHURCH

The rise of nineteenth-century Presbyterian evangelicalism is traditionally associated with the name of Henry Cooke and, more particularly, with the Arian controversy of the late 1820s. Cooke, an able and impressive orator, popularized evangelical principles within the Synod of Ulster and rallied its 'Old-Light' or orthodox members. But it should already be clear that the view of a sudden transformation from theological and political liberalism to conservative evangelicalism is, like the popular tradition of an all-pervasive Presbyterian radicalism in 1798, a dangerous oversimplification. The 'purge' of the Synod of Ulster in the late 1820s has to be placed in the context of increasing evangelical influence within Presbyterianism during the first quarter of the nineteenth century.

The rapid extension of the Seceding and Reformed churches in this period was itself an indication of the growing demand for doctrinal orthodoxy and a stricter religious life-style within the Presbyterian community. The union in 1818 of 97 Burgher and Anti-Burgher congregations, first discussed in 1800 but delayed by the contentious *regium donum* issue, was a logical first step towards Presbyterian consolidation.[43] The newly enlarged Secession synod reflected its commitment to evangelism by increased support for the London Missionary, the Hibernian Bible and the London Hibernian societies.[44] In 1820 it also established its own Home Mission which appointed itinerant preachers to work in the south and west of Ireland. An emphasis on synodical control and strictly Presbyterian principles permitted the synod, which twenty years earlier had denounced the Evangelical Society of Ulster, to present its new policy without appearing to compromise its orthodox heritage.[45] By 1829 the Secession Synod had increased its strength to 114 ministers, and four years later approached negotiations on unity with the Synod of Ulster from a strong and respected position. The Seceding and Covenanting varieties of Presbyterianism in this period have been correctly viewed as 'a stabilizing factor, reducing the chances that dissatisfaction may have taken an enthusiastic and/or non-Presbyterian form'.[46] That such an outlet was necessary is evident from the increasing Presbyterian participation in Methodist and inter-denominational evangelical societies in the early nineteenth century.[47]

In the Synod of Ulster, as in the Church of Ireland, the response to the inconveniences of evangelical enthusiasm took the form of increased central control and a greater emphasis on clerical discipline.[48] The tightening of synodical discipline was not, however, an entirely straightforward process. The right of individual ministers to follow their private judgement was a long-established tradition in the Presbyterian community, resulting in a variety of opinions on issues such as subscription to the Westminster Confession of Faith, as well as on details of doctrine. The most long-running and tenacious doctrinal dispute in the Synod of Ulster was over Arianism, which, although it could take various forms, was based on a rejection of the traditional Christian doctrines of the divinity of Christ and the Trinity. The hold which this brand of theological liberalism had on the synod was probably greatly exaggerated. The prestige and influence of this dissident minority was based on their control of the wealthy, urban congregations and on their high public profile.[49] The government's legalization of Unitarianism in 1813 (extended to Ireland in 1817) also gave a degree of respectability to their cause and made it easier to define. It has been suggested that at least part of the explanation for the anti-Arian controversy in the 1820s was that it was only in these years that a distinct Arian position was clarified. Previously, it had been known 'by defect rather than by declaration'.[50] The whole question of doctrinal orthodoxy, which was closely related to that of subscription, had been bubbling under the surface for some time, and had caused frequent congregational clashes over competing orthodox and Arian candidates. But in the early nineteenth century external pressures symbiotically interacted with the growth of evangelicalism to give fresh urgency to old disputes.[51] As with many deep-seated religious quarrels, the subscription controversy centred on a particularly powerful personality.

Born in Maghera in 1788, Henry Cooke became a religious and political hero for successive generations of Ulster Protestants. Cooke's most recent biographer stresses the formative influence of the violence of 1798 in the development of his opinions. Cooke himself stated that 'impressions were left on my mind that I have never forgotten'. This experience was felt to have determined his later career in the same way as his arch-rival, Henry Montgomery, drew inspiration for his religious and political liberalism from the association of his 'kith and kin' with the principles of the United Irishmen.[52] To see the lives of the two men as determined by political events which took place in their youth would, however, be an oversimplification. It is nevertheless on the difficulty of disentangling his political and theological views that much of the historical interest in Cooke's campaign against Arianism is centred. Since this duality is an important feature of Ulster evangelicalism in a much wider sense, the development of Cooke's particular form of Presbyterianism merits closer examination.

While it is indicative of future developments that Cooke resigned from his first post at Duneane, County Antrim, after only two years because 'his orthodoxy and enthusiasm offended his latitudinarian senior minister', his theological views were not as rigidly conservative as they later became. Throughout his early years in the ministry he associated, both personally and professionally, with those holding Arian views.[53] It was while minister of Killyleagh from 1818 onwards that Cooke first became popularly known as the 'Champion of Orthodoxy'.[54] His first public controversy was occasioned by the arrival of the Unitarian missionary, the Reverend J. Smethurst, from Exeter in the spring of 1821. The prospect of a popular tour by a minister who publicly denounced the doctrine of the Trinity provoked a reaction on behalf of the fundamental doctrines of the gospel by a man reared on strict Calvinist principles. Cooke attacked Smethurst's theology, first in Killyleagh, and then relentlessly pursued the disconcerted Englishman around the towns and villages of Ulster.[55] Smethurst's view that theological conservatism was also hampering the cause of liberal politics in the north of Ireland suggests a wider dimension to his debates with Cooke, but it is notoriously difficult to separate the religious, political and cultural aspects of opinions which are best left in the undifferentiated form in which they were originally expressed.[56]

It was, however, the theological liberalism of some of those involved in Belfast's Academical Institution which gave Cooke the opportunity to carry his anti-Arian campaign into the synod. Founded in 1810 to provide for the academic preparation of Presbyterian ministers, the well-known political liberalism of the staff of this institution was of particular concern to a government which had reason to be anxious about Presbyterian loyalty.[57] In 1816 the synod had rejected government attempts to impose a degree of control over its relations with the college, but in 1822 Cooke raised the question of the doctrinal orthodoxy of its teaching staff. He objected in particular to the appointment of an Arian, William Bruce, as Professor of Latin, Hebrew and Greek rather than the theologically conservative Reverend R. J. Bryce. Cooke warned the synod of the dangers to the Presbyterian faith which could arise from the unorthodox views of those entrusted with the teaching of its probationers.[58] The synod was not, however, prepared to be constrained by the polemics of Cooke, any more than by those of the government, and a dislike of airing theological controversies in public easily overrode Cooke's arguments, both in 1822 and again in the following year.

Cooke had to move outside the well-regulated formality of the synod to gain support for his campaign on behalf of orthodoxy. His 'plain and powerful' speaking as he travelled on foot and horseback throughout Ulster won him considerable support from those with deep roots of antagonism against educated and enlightened ministers. He was later able to claim, in defence of his views on Protestant attitudes to Catholic Emancipation, that 'those who know my habits will believe me – there is not a man in Ulster, who had better means of knowing the state of mind of the common people among orthodox Presbyterians than I have'.[59] This closeness to the rank and file of Ulster Protestantism, and his ability to both express and identify with the fears of those for whom the theoretical debates had an ominous and everyday relevance, was Cooke's main strength. His reputation was also enhanced in evangelical circles by a promotional tour of Scotland in 1824 on behalf of the Synod of Ulster's Home Mission, and he was appointed moderator in the same year. His new position eased the passage of his resolution for greater, though still limited, synodical control over the Belfast Institution's appointment of professors, which he continued to claim militated against the orthodoxy of the synod itself.[60]

It was during his period in office as moderator that Cooke, in giving evidence to the government Commission of Enquiry into Irish Education, came under the spotlight as a figure of public controversy. As the foremost representative of the Presbyterian community, his evidence carried a greater degree of authority than that of a private individual. Although other members of the synod questioned the representative nature of Cooke's opinions, leaks from the Commissioner's Report revealed two important points. First, Cooke stated that although the Synod of Ulster had supported the principle of Catholic Emancipation in 1813, the 'less informed' of the Presbyterians of Ulster 'almost entirely disapproved of it'. Second, on being questioned about the Belfast Academical Institution, he 'entertained very great fears that the Institution as at present constituted, would finally become, as it had already in some degree, a great seminary of Arianism'.[61] The reaction to Cooke's claims from Arians, Roman Catholics and those of a generally liberal disposition was predictably vehement. The Presbytery of Antrim, a stronghold of Arianism, insisted on its political loyalty and pointed out that the theological difference between Arians and the orthodox had nothing to do with scriptural authority, which all accepted, but revolved around the question of the 'liberty to exercise free enquiry and to differ among themselves on controverted doctrines'.[62] Although suspected Arians were neither theologically nor politically monochrome, the political liberalism of supporters of Catholic Emancipation and the theological liberalism of those accused of Arian tendencies were linked in the public mind. Cooke himself stated that 'the man who weakens the authority of the Scriptures, shakes to their foundations, the pillars of civil society',[63] and his vigorous defence of orthodoxy was thus seen as a defence of Protestantism itself. Although the press became the forum of much heated debate, caution prevailed within the synod. While a majority of its members might have been persuaded to agree with his theological points, the vigour with which Cooke promoted and publicized his cause alienated more moderate men. With the Committee of Enquiry concluding that Arianism was declining rather than spreading, and well-respected Presbyterian figures paying favourable tribute to the Belfast Institution's 'political and theological neutrality', Cooke was dismissed in 1826 as an alarmist.[64]

A summer spent in the company of leading evangelicals, however, injected Cooke's campaign against the unorthodox elements of Presbyterianism with a degree of urgency. At the same time, religious conflicts in the wider political arena seemed to confirm his view that the Synod of Ulster was out of touch with popular opinion, particularly on the issue of Catholic Emancipation. Although Cooke himself had favoured 'limited concessions' for Irish Catholics, his personal involvement with ardent defenders of the Protestant Constitution and supporters of the Reformation movement brought him into closer contact with the anti-Catholic and controversial elements of both the local and the wider evangelical world in the late 1820s.[65] Such connections helped to forge a link in the public mind between evangelical religion, doctrinal orthodoxy and anti-Catholicism. Cooke's main role in the development of evangelical Presbyterianism was to introduce these ideas to, and to insist on their predominance in, the Synod of Ulster.

In 1827 Cooke launched a strident and uncompromising attack on the 'indifference' of the synod to those who denied – or at least refused to profess publicly – the full trinitarian doctrine. In his newly confident and unequivocal mood he rejected the compromise on subscription which had been reached in the Presbyterian Code of 1825 and which had seemed to satisfy both Arians and orthodox.[66] Although he had been personally involved in drafting that code, which allowed a degree of flexibility while maintaining control at Presbytery level, he now spoke of the impossibility of 'maintaining the unnatural and uncoalescing admixture of our doctrines'.[67] In the synod's meeting at Strabane, noted for its anti-Emancipation, anti-Arian and pro-Orange sentiments, he called for subscription to an explicit formula: 'That there are three persons in the Godhead, the Father, the Son and the Holy Ghost, and these three are one in God, the same in substance, equal in power and glory.'[68] Leaders of the New Light element in the synod, most notably Henry

Montgomery, were not so much against the wording of the creed as in favour of the traditional Presbyterian position, 'that great Protestant principle, the sufficiency of Scripture, and the right of judgement in matters of faith and duty'.[69] Cooke summarily dismissed such views.

> Have we not been told, a thousand times, that the Protestant religion is built upon the right of private judgement: God forbid it were built upon any such flimsy foundation. The Protestant religion is built upon the command, the word of God – upon Prophets and Apostles, Jesus Christ himself being the chief cornerstone. There it rests unshakeable upon the rock of ages, and the gates of hell shall not prevail against it.[70]

These two positions are clearly illustrative of the separate strands in Presbyterianism which had for so long coexisted within the Synod of Ulster. Cooke, however, saw no point in 'operating the horrible apparatus of suspensions and degradations against a man's opinion: my plan was merely the unshackled exercise of our respective judgements, and a peaceable separation between men who could not agree'.[71] With the defence of Protestantism itself becoming a matter of public concern, it now seemed both politically and theologically expedient to accept separation as the price to be paid for synodical orthodoxy. The interests of a publicly proclaimed, unified evangelical cause demanded the sacrifice of the broad intellectual basis of traditional Presbyterianism. From this position the doctrine of personal salvation, dependent upon the divinity of Christ, could be disseminated without ambiguity or restraint.

Cooke clearly felt that only such a dramatic step as the separation of its liberal and orthodox elements could achieve the internal discipline and doctrinal purity necessary for such a spiritual revitalization of the synod. Despite liberal and even orthodox protests (over methods and principles rather than doctrine), he achieved his goal in 1829 after a bitter polemical debate, played out in synod, press and pamphlet.[72] In 1830, in recognition of the growing support for Cooke both within and outside the synod, and of the increasing isolation of their own minority position, the Arian party pre-empted expulsion by withdrawing to set up their own Remonstrant Synod. Despite fears to the contrary, the numerical loss to the Synod of Ulster was minimal and was soon made up, though locally, in areas where congregations were doctrinally divided, disputes over meeting houses continued for some time.[73] The 'purification' of the synod continued in 1835 with a resolution requiring full subscription to the Westminster Confession of Faith, and its increasingly narrow and rigid doctrinal requirements also led to a final breach with the Belfast Academical Institution in 1841.

Cooke's role in this Presbyterian 'purge' indicates how a strong personality can simultaneously influence and represent current trends. His powerful oratorical ability was employed as a manipulative and highly successful tool which played on popular fears and prejudices.[74] Although his ability to sway the synod was often limited, his popular acclaim was undoubted: 'A grateful Presbyterian people honoured him for the courage and constancy with which he had witnessed against Arianism, and, at the termination of the struggle, were prepared joyfully to exclaim, "Thou wast he that leddest out and broughtest in Israel",'[75] It is clear that while its growing evangelical ethos made the synod more receptive to Cooke's religious views during the 1820s, it was the wider political dimension to his campaign that gave it a sense of urgency, and determined his future direction. It was as a popular religiopolitical leader that he was primarily engaged in the following decades when issues such as education revealed that Emancipation had not seen the end of an old era, but had ushered in a new age of danger for Irish Protestantism. Cooke and his allies within the synod benefited therefore from the increase in religiopolitical controversies from the late 1820s, but, as Presbyterian voting behaviour clearly shows, the old liberal tradition within Presbyterianism was neither eradicated nor moribund in the early Victorian era.

It is a commonplace in Presbyterian history that the split of 1829 was both a recognition of the growth of evangelicalism within the church and a powerful stimulant to the evangelical cause. Cooke's personality no doubt forced a quicker pace, but many of the most important religious initiatives had already been taken as part of a growing trend towards 'vital religion' in the first quarter of the nineteenth century. This sprang both from the synod itself and, more importantly, from the demands of the laity. Undoubtedly, however, the 'purge' eliminated time-consuming preoccupations with doctrine and marked an important transition from the old self-regulating dissenting community to a renewed emphasis on the conversion of those outside its jurisdiction. The minutes of 1833, for example, record that 'the first duty of a church is the care of her own members – the next, the evangelization of the country in which she may be placed'.[76] The Synod of Ulster, with the long debate on trinitarian orthodoxy at last settled, was now well placed to engage in the pursuit of both these ends. The minutes of the next few years reveal a new impetus in the formation of congregations, supplemented by building programmes and increases in the number of services, as well as a stronger emphasis on the importance of domestic mission.[77]

It became increasingly clear that by the 1830s little divided the Synod of Ulster from the Seceders. Ministers from both synods were concerned with the same essential issues – doctrinal orthodoxy, missionary zeal, church extension, pastoral care, Sabbatarianism, scriptural education and temperance. In July 1840, in recognition of their common principles and purposes, the two synods united to form the General Assembly of the Presbyterian Church in Ireland.[78] Its first resolutions heralded a new age of missionary enterprise, with the setting up of a Foreign Mission, a Mission to the Jews, the first missionary ordained for the Home Mission, and attention given to the need for a Presbyterian church for Ulstermen in London. The creation of the new Presbyterian assembly was a consolidation of the work of the previous decades, but it was a beginning as much as an end. It was an important step towards the religious vigour and political strength of Ulster Presbyterianism which was evident in the 1859 revival and in the later battle against Home Rule.

METHODISM

The Methodists, who had begun the nineteenth century with such zest, experienced serious internal difficulties in this period. These were primarily caused by the lack of the solid and long-established traditions which enabled the Presbyterian and Anglican communities to emerge from the turmoils of the period 1800–40 with their institutional structures relatively intact. Paradoxically, it was the absence of a rigid framework that had been Methodism's greatest strength in the eighteenth century. Rapid membership growth and the mushrooming of local societies, however, inevitably required greater organizational control. The growing emphasis on uniformity and discipline which affected all denominations brought the long-running problems of being a 'society' rather than a church to the surface. The question of how best to organize itself as a religious movement came to dominate this period of Methodist history and, perhaps inevitably, the issue crystallized over the administration of the sacraments.

Although this question had been firmly dealt with in 1798, resulting in the ousting of dissatisfied ministers and the formation of the Methodist New Connexion, the problem did not go away. Its re-emergence can be attributed to Irish Methodism's ambiguous relationship with the already independent English connection and to the success of Methodism in the north of Ireland where it recruited from both the established and dissenting churches. In many cases too, both Anglican and Presbyterian churches were unwilling to offer the sacraments to those of their flock who frequented Methodist meeting-houses. Those who had been led into the movement by the failure of their original churches to perform their spiritual duty thus faced a new dilemma. Their problem was essentially a religious one. All those requesting a change in the Methodist rules to enable them to administer their own sacraments were at pains to insist that their loyalty to the British and Protestant constitution would remain unaffected by a religious separation from the established church.

A printed circular from the Methodists of Belfast to the stewards and leaders of other societies in 1812 marked the beginning of a more intensive agitation of the sacramental dispute.[79] This stated that the purely practical aspects of the issue, while unresolved, left many Methodists with no access to the sacraments at all, and an uncoordinated but vociferous campaign for the introduction of sacraments got under way. Although the Conference of 1814 seemed to favour the petitioners, deliberation and caution led to delay and gave both opponents and supporters of change an opportunity to engage in pamphlet controversy.[80] Opponents denounced the self-interest and opportunism of preachers and warned of dangers to the Establishment. Popular preachers such as Gideon Ouseley and Matthew Lanktree, well known for putting wider 'gospel' interests over the stipulations of Conference, supported the pro-sacrament view.[81] The increased acrimony generated by the debate led the Conference to acknowledge both the necessity for some action, and the possibly hazardous consequences of separation from the established church. An attempted compromise – that Adam Averell, a former Church of Ireland clergyman should administer the sacraments where requested – was recognized as an inadequate and contradictory stop-gap.[82]

Clear committed leadership, one way or the other, might perhaps have rallied the discontented elements in 1814. It might, at the very least, have encouraged an agreement to differ, but the irresolute and inconsistent attitude of Conference ensured that the opportunity of a peaceful settlement was lost. In 1816, when Conference finally announced a decision in favour of Methodist administration of the sacraments, it was hedged around with qualifications, designed not only to modify any changes in members' relations with other churches, but to prevent any further discussions or divisions.[83] But, with excitement at fever pitch, and with as many divisions within as between societies, any hopes that this belated decision would settle the issue were rapidly dispelled. On a question of such fundamental importance it is difficult to see how the two sides could have accommodated each other. Many society members felt that those preachers favouring change were planning to betray original Methodist principles by forming an independent church. Stewards and leaders on the other hand formed the core of the opposition to the administration of the sacraments outside the confines of the established church.

In the event, the leaders and stewards of the Charlemont, Tandragee, Aughnacloy and Newtownstewart societies refused to accept the Conference resolution. When no preacher came forward to 'join the people who adhered to first principles', they took steps to form an alternative to the authority of the Dublin Conference.[84] Sufficient numbers of dissatisfied Methodists came forward to make the formation of the Primitive Wesleyan Methodist Society a viable proposition. Meeting at Clones on 2 October 1816, the new society reported 21 circuits applying for preachers, and appointed 19 brethren as local preachers or 'special messengers'. None of these men was a regular Methodist preacher, and this emphasizes once again the extent to which the split reflected different concepts of ministry. Primitive Wesleyans proclaimed themselves 'Church Methodists' and expected preachers and society members to share responsiblity, whereas in the alternative Methodist organization preachers came to occupy a more prestigious position.[85]

Whereas in England after 1797 all Methodist secessions were outside the jurisdiction of the established church, the peculiarities of Irish religion meant that some Methodists feared the Protestant interest would be weakened by their withdrawal from the Church of Ireland. As a result the split of 1816 produced two different types of Methodism in Ireland. On the one hand was a church offering full ecclesiastical rites to its people, and on the other there was a religious society within the Church of Ireland. The setting up of an alternative in itself irrevocably hardened divisions and the ramifications of the dispute overshadowed the next decade of Irish Methodism. The vigorous pamphlet war continued, and at local level legal proceedings were frequently initiated to determine the right of ownership of meeting-houses.[86] The resulting shortage of suitable buildings exacerbated an already serious financial crisis and the loss of leaders hampered the initial development of the newly constituted Wesleyan society.[87] Although the years immediately after the split were marked by difficulties and hardships, once the dust had settled there were some advantages. Members were able to choose where their allegiance lay, and the difficulties of starting afresh were often viewed as a challenge.[88] As in the Presbyterian Church, the eradication of internal problems allowed missionary work to proceed with renewed energy. Before the schism 6 to 8 missionaries were annually sent out from the Irish Methodist Conference; by 1828 the Wesleyans employed 23 missionaries, and the Primitive Methodists 16.[89] In both societies, the geographical concentration of mission stations in the northeast reflected a familiar trend in Irish Protestantism.[90]

The progress of the Second Reformation was also a stimulus to Methodist missionary work. To landlords like Roden, Farnham and Mountcashel, 'the Wesleyan Methodists were a most useful body of persons . . . there could be no better soldiers to fight against the Pope and his party'.[91] The prospect of legislative concessions to the religious majority further served to intensify Methodist zeal to 'educate' the Catholic masses into a realization of their state of spiritual enslavement.[92] The importance of the Irish mission to Roman Catholics had also been recognized at an early stage within British Methodism.[93] As the nineteenth century got under way, and with it the campaign for Catholic Emancipation, the English became increasingly concerned by the alarmist reports of the Irish missionaries. Joseph Butterworth, the English Methodist MP, was an assiduous gatherer of information on the state of Irish Catholicism and the fears of Irish Protestants.[94] In 1820 he sent a circular letter to the Irish Methodist preachers asking their opinion about the probable consequences of Catholic Emancipation. The replies were unanimous: Henry Deery told him that 'Protestants would be driven to defend their liberties at the expense of blood';[95] Andrew Hamilton wrote that 'political power in the hands of R.C.s would greatly convulse this part of the country';[96] and John Stuart stated that 'I can see no change for the better in the Roman Catholics of Ireland. I firmly believe they are as bigoted as ever they were, and therefore, that it would not be safe to trust them now with political power as at any former period.'[97] Methodist fears grew worse throughout the 1820s, so that by 1828 Matthew Tobias, the only Irish Methodist preacher in favour of Catholic Emancipation, was having a hard job upholding the traditional Methodist 'no politics' rule. After hearing that several Methodist preachers had spoken at Brunswick Constitutional Clubs he told Jabez Bunting that 'we have great difficulty at present in our attempts to do good to the Roman Catholics – making speeches at Brunswick Clubs will increase that difficulty a thousand fold.'[98] One year later Tobias sadly acknowledged that 'our people are kept in perpetual political fever' and was forced to recognize that the preaching of the gospel in Ireland carried political consequences quite beyond his control.[99]

Once the Catholic Emancipation Act was on the statute book, the Methodists, in common with the Presbyterians and episcopalians, directed their attention to Irish national education. With some 150 Sunday schools and a sprinkling of day schools, the Methodists had experienced the same problems as all the other evangelical societies in the 1820s. They had to make an unwelcome choice between accommodating the curriculum to the satisfaction of the Catholic clergy or having no Catholic children in their schools. The annual reports of the Irish Methodist schools, like those of the London Hibernian and Irish Societies, reflect the increasingly contentious nature of the whole educational question, and the way in which it was fast becoming the central focus for the conflict between evangelical Protantism and Catholicism.[100] The right to sit in Parliament was as nothing compared with the right to educate the nation's children in principles of godliness and good learning.

Methodism's revivalist and popular nature and the dedication of its itinerants enabled it to continue to recruit successfully among the lower classes in the most neglected areas of Ireland and, increasingly, of Ulster. But a powerful combination of clerical professionalism, more elaborate buildings and crippling emigration limited the capacity of future Methodist growth. As in England, Irish Methodist growth rates evened off in the 1840s despite a temporary surge in the wake of the 1859 revival. Its main contribution had been to establish evangelical voluntarism as a major new feature on the Irish religious landscape and to play a catalytic role in the growth of evangelicalism within the other Protestant churches. By 1840 Irish Methodism was far from a spent force, but it no longer threatened to create a new configuration of religious loyalty in Ulster society.

In the first third of the nineteenth century the questions facing Irish Protestantism were on one level no different from those facing churches in other European societies. How established churches should operate in the post French-revolutionary world and how popular religious movements should be controlled were issues that transcended national boundaries. The problem of control was nevertheless particularly acute within Ulster Protestantism because evangelical religion turned out to be both ecclesiastically disruptive and socially divisive. The Irish churches struggled, with varying degrees of success, to harness evangelical zeal to denominational interests without abandoning the core of their religious traditions. Despite inevitable and painful divisions, this task was largely accomplished, but the price to be paid was a more competitive relationship with Irish Catholicism. The fact that much evangelical zeal was sponsored from Britain and took strongest root among the settlers of the north, ensured that religious competition had important political and cultural dimensions. But so long as ethnic and cultural identities were bound up with religious affiliations, the outlook for the churches was not altogether unpromising.

In the years between 1800 and 1840 evangelical religion made steady progress in all the Protestant churches, but its gains were regionally uneven and difficult to assess. Notwithstanding enthusiastic efforts to convert Catholics in the south of Ireland, the heartland of evangelical strength became even more concentrated in the province of Ulster. Moreover, despite earnest attempts at interdenominational cooperation, evangelicalism, if anything, hardened denominational divisions, except at times of crisis when anti-Catholicism acted as a powerful solvent. In one respect evangelicalism had made the churches stronger by giving them an injection of conversionist zeal, but the defensive side of evangelicalism was also not without foundation. The Protestant constitution had been breached, the established church could no longer rely upon unqualified state support, the old self-regulating Presbyterian community had been shaken up, and evangelical realists were beginning to accept that there were formidable obstacles in the way of mass conversions. It remained to be seen whether the individualism implicit in evangelical theology offered as substantial a bulwark against 'popery' and secularism as these older methods had done. The alternative, which was scarcely imagined in 1840, was the development of a new kind of Protestant nationalism centred on only one of the ancient provinces of Ireland.

[5]

Religion and society: conversions and controversy

Let him know, that he which converteth the sinner from the error of his way shall save a soul from death, and shall hide a multitude of sins. (James 5:20)

Think not that I am come to send peace on earth: I come not to send peace, but a sword. (Matthew 10:34)

The nineteenth-century confrontation between a more assertive Protestant evangelicalism and the emerging nationalism of the Catholic Irish has been recognized as a significant contributor to the deep divisions in contemporary Irish society.[1] What is less clear, however, is the precise relationship between cause and effect. Was political conservatism, for example, a stimulant or a consequence of anti-Catholicism? What precisely was the mixture of religious and political convictions in the minds of those Protestant enthusiasts who committed themselves to the conversion of the masses? Any attempt to unravel the complexities of the Irish Protestant psychology must take as its starting-point the overriding sense of moral responsibility with which evangelicals were imbued, and which blurred the distinctions between religious and political activities. For evangelical contempt for the Roman Catholic Church emanated not only from its doctrinal 'heresies' but from their social and political consequences. Evangelicals throughout Britain saw the Catholic Church in Ireland as another branch of the same international institution that was so busily engaged in perpetuating its own wealth and despotic power in Spain and Rome. The Protestant Union, formed in London in 1813, pointed out that Catholic Emancipation would give Roman Catholics, 'not only the exercise of unlimited and uncontrolled religious liberty, but . . . the grant of the most extensive political power'.[2] It was felt that Irish peasants, already burdened by poverty and ignorance, were exploited in every manner by a devious priesthood under vows of obedience to the 'man of sin'. Their submission to superstitious ritual and their inability to rise above their poor standards of living were seen as a direct result of their lack of access to religious truths which alone could inspire them to better themselves. Gideon Ouseley's diagnosis of the nation's ills was not untypical: 'the Priests and their fatal doctrines are the chief, if not the sole, cause of the peculiar sorrows of Ireland.'[3] The belief that the fault lay not with the people, but with their priests, inspired evangelicals with confidence in their ability to convert Ireland to Protestantism.

Since Irish priests were regarded as fundamentally opposed to Britain's Protestant constitution and were thought to be engaged in inciting their ignorant charges to rebellion, it was felt that political loyalty, social stability and moral improvement could be secured only by a reduction in the power and influence of Roman Catholicism.[4] An anecdote reported by a London Hibernian Society agent, and whose frequent repetition reflects the importance with which it was held, shows the extent to which political loyalty and social improvement were seen as natural corollaries of religious education.

> A gentleman mentioned to a Roman Catholic the importance of reading the Scriptures, and that the knowledge of them was conducive to present and eternal happiness. He referred to, and explained, some of the doctrines of Christianity. The Roman Catholic, after a considerable pause, and with a degree of surprise and energy said – 'If I believe these things, I cannot be a rebel'.[5]

The separation of the people from the influence of their priests was thus a favourite topic at evangelical meetings and in the reports of proselytizing societies. This interpretation of Ireland's difficulties enabled evangelical Protestants to sympathize with the Catholic peasantry by suggesting a mutual enemy lying between them and the spiritual and temporal blessings to which they were properly entitled.

The increased vigour with which this campaign against the Roman Catholic Church was waged in the 1820s can only be understood in the context of the general resurgence of Irish Catholicism which was viewed with mounting alarm by Protestants of all denominations. The reorganization of the Irish Catholic Church, under way from the late eighteenth century, was by this stage beginning to have a visible effect. The number of chapels under construction was increasing rapidly. In 1814 it was reported that in the diocese of Clogher 'upwards of thirty good chapels have been built and covered in within these twenty-eight years'.[6] A revitalized administration was evident in the annual general meetings of the bishops to discuss ecclesiastical affairs, which were under way by 1820.[7] The increased diligence of the hierarchy resulted in greater clerical discipline which in turn led to improvements in pastoral care. The education of students for the priesthood received renewed attention, and the number of priests in Ulster dioceses increased by 52 per cent between 1800 and 1835.[8] These institutional reforms laid a firm foundation for future growth and generated confidence in the strength and viability of the Catholic religion, while initiatives such as the Catholic Bible Society (1813) and the Irish Catholic Society for the Diffusion of Religious Knowledge, formed in Dublin in 1823, helped counteract the work of the Protestant educational societies.[9]

However, the growing confidence of the Roman Catholic Church in these years was not only due to internal developments but was a reflection of changes in the wider social and political setting in which it operated. An important aspect of the revitalization of Irish Catholicism was the contribution of a growing Catholic middle class which used its recently acquired mercantile wealth to invest in land. By buying leases for the next generation they built up a respectable and substantial class whose interconnections were repeatedly cemented by marriage with others of the same background.[10] In this process they were aided and abetted by the British government's piecemeal but progressive legislation. Evangelical Protestants also had a role to play, albeit a negative one, in raising Catholic consciousness. Their persistent and vehement denunciations occasioned a vigorous defence of the Roman Catholic Church and clergy, and a clearer exposition of its particular doctrines.

But it was Daniel O'Connell's campaign for Catholic Emancipation which most effectively instilled a sense of solidarity and unity of purpose among all classes of Catholics. The Catholic Association, formed in 1823, followed the example of the evangelical agencies in encouraging the participation of ordinary men and women by the giving of small, regular subscriptions, and brought what were after all essentially middle-class issues to the peasantry of every parish and village in Ireland.[11] The issues raised by the Catholic Association, including education, tithes, church rates and the administration of justice as well as political emancipation, inevitably increased religious divisions.[12] Thus, while instilling the peasantry with a sense of national pride and purpose, O'Connell also contributed to an increase in religious conflict which was such a potent factor in the second half of the 1820s, especially in the southern counties of Ulster.[13] Moreover, the close involvement of the priests in the Catholic Association was regarded by Protestants as further evidence of their manipulative role and subversive influence. This gave additional ammunition to the already virulent anti-Catholic polemics of evangelical agencies and individuals and established yet again the link between politics and religion.

The gradual removal of legislative barriers to Catholic progress which was part of a much wider liberalization of the British state in the nineteenth century, was perceived in Ireland as a process of conciliation to tyranny, and evidence of governmental weakness comparable with that of the seventeenth century:

No reasonable person can shut his eyes to the fact, that there are many features in the political aspects of the present times bearing a very strong resemblance to the days of James the Second: The same laxity of principle, the same lukewarmness in religious feeling, the same drivelling incapacity in some parts of the Government, the same corruptness in others, the same judicial blindness and infatuation as to the genuine interests of the Empire, and the same untiring efforts and deadly hatred in Popery; labouring for the destruction of everything Protestant, everything really free and loyal throughout Ireland.[14]

As early as 1812, pamphleteers, writing of the ingratitude and intolerance of Catholics, expressed the opinion that since all major disabilities had already been removed, no more could safely be conceded.[15] *The Benevolent and Religious Orange Reporter* stated in 1825 that 'popery is no longer hoping, it has become confident, even arrogant, and if not speedily checked, will usurp that tyranny with which it governed the nations for many generations'.[16] Landlords were particularly aware that the granting of further political concessions to their largely Catholic tenantry carried serious social implications. In 1826 their confidence was badly shaken by revolts of Catholic freeholders against landlord control in Counties Monaghan and Cavan.[17] Further down the social scale, fear of the territorial aspirations of Catholic tenants was heightened by the shortage of land and jobs endemic in the economy of south Ulster.[18] In the tense political atmosphere preceding emancipation which was aggravated by continuing agitation against tithes, Protestant churchmen, landlords, labourers and peasants all had a common interest in warding off Catholic encroachments on their respective positions. Religious, social and political threads were inextricably interwoven, with each side in the conflict developing a religious justification for its political position.

As in the 1790s millennial speculation played a part in increasing tension at the popular level, and in further uniting the political and religious elements of current debates. The Catholic cause was given added impetus by the reprinting and widespread circulation of the Prophecies of Pastorini – an interpretation of the Apocalypse of St John, published originally in 1771 by the English Catholic bishop, Charles Walmsley.[19] These writings, which predicted the overthrow of Protestantism on Christmas Day 1824, unexpectedly justified Protestant fears of a superstitious and essentially vengeful Catholic nation. Gideon Ouseley, busily engaged in missionary work throughout rural Ireland, reported the Prophecies to be extensively circulated, and that they were 'exercising a powerful influence over the minds of those to whom they were read'. He claimed they encouraged readers to 'cut off heresy, i.e., exterminate all Protestants and overturn the present government'.[20] The Roman Catholic hierarchy, concerned to differentiate between scriptural prophecy and folk superstition, played down this popular interpretation. They pointed out that the writings were 'perverted to very different ends from those which the pious author intended', and advised their flock to 'lay aside Pastorini and listen to your own pastors'.[21] Protestant polemicists, however, related the heightened sectarian tensions to which the beliefs contributed to the need for Roman Catholics to cast off their false doctrines and turn instead to the scriptures for guidance. 'Had you and your children, then, but read and learned from this Book, or indeed from Christ . . . would ye not be an affectionate, pious, loyal people as kind to Protestants as each other.'[22] Millenarian excitement was certainly an element in the recurring battles between Catholics and Protestants which were particularly bitter in south Ulster.[23] The peasantry, for example, excitedly interpreted the popular success of O'Connell's movement as evidence of much more than a mere political victory.[24] Such views infused the activities of Orangemen and Ribbonmen alike with a sense of righteousness and purpose.

Sectarian outrages and a bad 'party spirit' instilled a fear of revolution in the minds of political observers, and severely tested the administrative capabilities of the civil authorities.[25] It seemed to many observers that the whole area of law and order, particularly at the local level, reflected the sectarian biases of the market-place rioters. And while Protestant evangelists had little to fear from officials,[26] Catholics had less grounds for optimism.

> Lord Redesdale has said, and it has been repeated with surprise and indignation, that in Ireland there is one law for the rich and another for the poor: our proverb, 'there is no law for a Catholic' expresses the truth more concisely and more justly, for a poor Protestant does obtain justice in Ireland, and is protected not only by the law, but by the passions.[27]

Such statements were supported by reports of Orangemen evading justice through making their allegiance known to partisan magistrates. They could use secret signs, whistle party tunes, or simply rely on their connections in the local lodge.[28] Such prejudicial behaviour was not only deeply resented by Catholics, but was the source of much concern for those in London and Dublin committed to the impartiality of the judicial system.[29]

The problem was that the Orange Order, whose strength waxed and waned in response to the Protestant perception of Catholic aggression, infiltrated many important institutions. The success of O'Connell's movement, combined with anti-tithe demonstrations, general economic hardships and sectarian fervour roused by priestly opposition to voluntary religious agencies, swelled the ranks of the Order. This not only resulted in provocative displays of power and violent clashes with those of the opposing tradition,[30] but also prompted the greater involvement of the upper and middle classes in defence of Protestantism. It was generally felt that in areas where the gentry joined the Order they could exercise a considerable degree of control, whereas in counties such as Cavan, with low gentry recruitment, trouble was much more likely to occur.[31] It was reported that 'a great number' of the magistrates of Monaghan, Armagh and Tyrone were Orangemen.[32] As one witness called before the Select Commitee on Orange Lodges put it, 'It is useless to prosecute an Orangeman when one is on the Bench.'[33] The tension caused in the minds of the Irish evangelical elite by the progress of Catholicism is clearly evidenced in this consolidation of strength between the middle and lower classes. Outside the court-house, the yeomanry of the north were also believed to be 'almost entirely Orange', which again eroded Catholic trust in the instruments of local authority. Protestants on the other hand, who regarded themselves as naturally superior, viewed such partiality as their privilege rather than an abuse requiring reform.[34]

Throughout the 1820s and 1830s successive administrations in Dublin Castle made determined efforts to tackle the problem. In 1822 the Magistracy list was revised and the Lord Lieutenant was given power to appoint special stipendiary magistrates to disturbed areas. These government-paid employees, independent of local patronage, came increasingly to be used as substitutes for, rather than additions to, the local men.[35] The Constabulary Act of the same year set out to provide an efficient police force in every county in Ireland, and thus cut out much of the need for the 'troublesome and costly' Orange-dominated yeomanry. But while recruitment in the new force outside Ulster indicated a marked degree of Roman Catholic involvement, within the nine counties police officers and men were predominantly Protestant, even in those counties with large Roman Catholic populations.[36] Continued suspicion and mistrust were thus inevitable. Palmer concludes that in Ireland as a whole, 'despite the growing proportion of Catholics in its rank and file, the constabulary continued to be seen as representing English rule in Ireland, ascendancy politics and Orangeism'.[37] An act of 1836 continued the process of centralization and increased the level of Catholic recruitment in the police force,[38] but, in Ulster particularly, the image of a nation divided into the privileged and the persecuted, identifiable by religious allegiance, remained as potent as ever.

It was against this background of mutual hostility and distrust that the Second Reformation was introduced into the southern counties of Ulster. This new phase of the evangelical campaign was an intensification of the work of the voluntary religious agencies, and testified to the strength of evangelical belief in religious solutions to political problems. Conversion of the majority to Protestantism rather than concession to their political demands was viewed as the only way of solving Ireland's difficulties. While such attempts were by no means new, the Second Reformation movement, as an open and direct challenge to the Catholic Association, bore all the hallmarks of a well-coordinated campaign. It was widely publicized in the local, national and evangelical press, had outreach provision in the shape of local societies and was supplemented by a series of public meetings. County Cavan became the major arena for evangelical proselytism and religious controversy for two reasons. First, the plight of the tenantry in the area was particularly acute after the virtual collapse of the linen industry. Second, the evangelical aristocrats, Lord and Lady Farnham, exercised extensive local influence.[39] As events unfolded, these features were by no means unconnected. Farnham's social power in the locality and his position as either a prospective or present employer was obviously of some significance to the peasantry with whom he and his agents came into contact in the course of their evangelical campaign. The principles behind the scheme of estate management on which the Cavan 'Reformation' was based need to be considered in detail. Used as a model by other estate owners, they show how Cavan's politics, religion and economics were inextricably bound together.

Farnham took over his 29,000-acre estate in 1823. In *A Statement of the Management of the Farnham Estates*, drawn up in 1830 in response to the request of local proprietors, he explained the foundation of his system as the religion of the Bible, and his chief motivation as 'the moral and religious character and improvement of the tenantry'.[40] To facilitate its 'moral management' the estate was divided into five districts. Each was overseen by a land agent and a moral agent under the 'friendly supervision' of an inspectorate. The relation between landlord and tenant was understood to be one of mutual benefit, as each was dependent on the goodwill and cooperation of the other. The landlord would supply churches, day schools, Sunday schools, a lending library, and material aid for those who earned it. In return the tenant was expected to be responsive to such liberality. Punctual payment of rent, for example, was beneficial to both parties and rendered the employment of the much-hated 'drivers' unnecessary.[41] The 'moral agent', a new term in the tenurial system,[42] was the mainspring of the plan, and the appointment of a worthy individual to the position was a particular concern of evangelical landlords preoccupied with the spiritual welfare of their tenantry.[43] Lord Farnham's moral agent between 1826 and 1838 was William Krause whose evangelical credentials were impeccable.[44] Born in the West Indies in 1796 but resident in England from an early age, Krause had experienced a religious conversion after a dangerous illness ended his army career. His thoughts turned to the ordained ministry, and the position of moral agent on Farnham's estate was felt by both employer and employee to be an admirable preparation for spiritual and pastoral duties. Eventually ordained as a curate in Cavan church in 1838, Krause availed himself of every opportunity to expound to large congregations on the estate. He fully endorsed the system he administered and interpreted his task as one of 'trying to free Roman Catholics from bondage'. He regretted that many other gentry were too afraid of persecution to follow a similar course. It was with the moral agent that tenants had the most frequent contact. Besides his practical duties of removing paupers and supervising schools and buildings, it was through him that all requests of the tenantry were passed. He in turn reported their conditions to the inspectors and land agent. On principle, he was kept apart from the business of rent collection, and was expected to be 'continually urging and exhorting the tenantry'.

The system professed to heighten the individual responsibility of the tenants by cutting out middlemen and coercion. But the emphasis – indeed insistence – on high standards of personal and social morality meant that their lives were closely monitored and tightly controlled and their choices were strictly limited. Children on the estate were expected to attend the schools sponsored by Farnham which operated on the familiar but highly controversial evangelical pattern. The schools were remorselessly scriptural and opened and closed with the singing of a psalm or hymn, the reading of a Bible chapter and a prayer. Some provision was made for more practical instruction in arithmetic and needlework. But, while only Church of Ireland members were expected to learn their church catechism, the reading and memorizing of biblical passages was expected of all children, Protestant and Catholic. The giving of premiums, to which the Catholic Church was particularly opposed, was forbidden, but the children's progress was recorded in a Judgement Book. As Farnham was kept personally informed of the behaviour of all his tenants – in and out of school – tenurial arrangements were clearly dependent on conformity to a moral and social code. The whole system seemed designed to erode traditional rural folk culture and replace it with an alternative set of values. The singing of bawdy ballads, for example, was discouraged, with psalmody taught in the schools in a direct attempt to replace them. Evangelical Protestantism and social and economic progress were therefore inextricably linked in the minds of its promoters in the same way as Irish Catholic culture was associated with backwardness and inefficiency.[45]

By offering an all-embracing framework for the salvation of one's fellow man, this system, whether through specially appointed agents, or more directly, as practised by Lord Roden in County Down, came into operation in several of Ulster's largest estates, and in numerous smaller ones.[46] There was, however, a more practical side to this exercise in paternalism. It should be seen as part of a more general overhaul of methods of estate management which was one aspect of the process of improvement already under way on Irish farms by the late 1820s.[47] The consolidation of holdings, the closer relationships between landlord and tenants, and the implementation of a more streamlined and efficient system of management were entirely reconcilable with the new 'moral order'.[48] This reform of estate administration was, of course, in many cases carried out with regard to purely materialistic considerations. But, as in other areas of Irish life, evangelicalism supplied a religious justification for other more prosaic concerns. At the same time, the Report of the Devon Commission and the controversy surrounding the Cavan 'Reformation' indicate all too clearly how contemporaries were prepared to interpret all events in the light of sectarian animosities.[49] The importance of the work of landowners such as Roden, Farnham and Mandeville in Armagh in giving both political and religious leadership belies their small numbers. Their marital connections and social contacts with evangelical and political leaders in England, along with the sheer size of their holdings gave them a disproportionately strong influence in county and provincial society. The personalizing of estate management, and the obvious temporal advantages to be gained by conforming to the landlord's expectations, forged a bond between landlord and Protestant tenant. This was further strengthened by the landed leadership of local Orange movements. Where the tenantry was mostly Catholic, however, the system of 'moral management' had major political and religious ramifications.

The growing importance of evangelical Protestantism in relations between landlords and tenants came under close scrutiny in 1826–7 when it was seen as a decisive factor in the wave of conversions associated with the 'Second Reformation'. Farnham was closely implicated in this movement whose progress he outlined in a series of pamphlets. He stated that, following a public recantation in Cavan by three Roman Catholic schoolmasters, 17 persons had assembled at the local parish church on 8 October to renounce their native faith.[50] Two weeks later they were followed by 20 more converts, and these had subsequently continued at the rate of about 30 a week. By 6 January 1827 a total of 450 conversions was recorded in the county. An extensive and highly effective publicity machine swung into action to keep the public informed of the 'Progress of the Reformation'. Regular statistics and reports appeared in pamphlets and in local, national and denominational papers.[51] By October 1827, according to evangelical sources, 1,903 conversions had been publicly proclaimed throughout Ireland. It was added:

> We have been confidently assured from various parts of the Kingdom, that full as many more as above recorded, have privately abjured the errors of popery and joined various religious societies. Now that light is breaking upon our hitherto benighted country, and the everlasting Gospel must and will be read, we anticipate, every succeeding year, a harvest more and more abundant.[52]

This conversionist movement was highly concentrated in County Cavan, with 783 converts reported there by October 1827. The 'Reformation' had little direct impact on the rest of Ulster,[53] however, except as a stimulus to other, less controversial, aspects of evangelical enthusiasm.[54]

Given the extensive publicity surrounding the 'Second Reformation, the Roman Catholic Church found it necessary to investigate the claims of conversion. A deputation consisting of the primate and four bishops was sent to investigate events in Cavan. They finally announced themselves unimpressed either by the nature of the conversions or the character of the converts, stating that if 'names and places be specified . . . it will be found that many of the new converts are old Protestants, and that others are such as to make every decent Protestant blush for his new allies'.[55] Apparently satisfied that the Cavan conversions represented not so much a Protestant victory as an exercise in polemics, they refused to become embroiled in public debate with evangelical preachers. This decision, however, was interpreted as a sign of weakness and their accusations were dismissed as 'a tissue of the grossest falsehoods'. Despite Farnham's insistence that none of the reported converts were his immediate tenants, and that no rewards were given for recantation,[56] the most common criticism levelled at evangelical estate management was that it was characterized by manipulation on the one side and pragmatism on the other. It was claimed that the evangelicals carried out 'systematic deception', using a combination of 'fraud and force' to encourage the poor of the area to convert in exchange for clothing, food or employment. 'Misery acquaints us with strange bedfellows', wrote G. K. Ensor in a scathing attack on those attempting to 'convert six million Roman Catholics to Protestant Parliamentary faith.'[57] 'The converts were like birds, which visit milder climates at intervals – but their coming is proof of a great severity in their native country, and they return when the iron days are passed and the sun cheers them from home.'[58] With bible and missionary society agents, landlords and clergy joining forces in their campaign to dissuade the peasantry of their native faith, both Desmond Bowen and Irene Hehir depict the Catholic peasantry of Cavan as caught between Protestant enthusiasts on the one hand, and the Catholic clergy on the other, each battling for control of their souls.[59] George Ensor detected a hint of desperation in the 'unholy alliance' of Protestants. 'The Protestants had hitherto despised the Methodists and other interlopers on the episcopal domain – yet in this gossiping time of theology, this sacerdotal saturnalia, the lowest of tradesmen were employed to read the Bible to the unreading Catholics.'[60] Farnham himself was subjected to the derision and scorn of pamphleteers.

> A pious yell doth smite the air,
> With note like bugle call;
> Inviting converts to repair
> With speed to Farnham Hall.
> The Moral Agents sally forth
> And cry throughout the land,
> 'Come all ye vagrants of the north,
> Salvation is at hand!'[61]

If it was difficult for critics to see Farnham's system of estate management as one of paternalistic benevolence in an area of great poverty, hardship and Catholicism, his insistence on the spontaneity of the movement was also questionable. The 'Second Reformation' was a concerted campaign in which the concentrated efforts of the Irish and London Hibernian societies in this area were an important component. The involvement of both societies was reflected in the verbal and physical attacks to which their agents were subjected in the heightened sectarian tensions of these years.[62] The emotion generated on both sides of the debate complicated any attempt to evaluate the Cavan conversions. Clearly, the combination of economic hardship, the material ease which could result from conversion, and Lord Farnham's extensive and powerful influence, were potentially persuasive factors. These have to be balanced, of course, against the family and social difficulties which would undoubtedly follow the decision to reject one's native religion and culture, a problem to which evangelical leaders had to apply themselves.

Indeed, it became clear in the 1830s that in areas where Catholicism was strong, Protestantism needed not only to be promoted, but to be protected. The setting up of small communities, Protestant missions or settlements, particularly in the west of Ireland, thus became an important feature of the evangelical campaign. The Protestant Colonization Society (1830) was one such experiment, the chief aim of which was to stem the the increasing flow of Protestant migrations. While many landlords supported and indeed sponsored emigration to alleviate overcrowding and poverty on their estates, this evangelical enterprise was yet another attempt to redress the religious balance. Its founders planned to use the new society to settle selected families on waste or reclaimed land, and secure their future prosperity by providing them with scriptural education and 'a sound and pious ministry'.[63] Twelve families were initially settled in Donegal, but it quickly became clear that they would be a source of contention rather than a religious influence in the area.[64] Refuges for Roman Catholic converts, such as those established at Lough Corrib in Connemara, Dingle, Achill and Doon, in the 1830s and 1840s were of course much more controversial, and accusations of 'souperism' – perhaps inevitable in famine-stricken areas – soured relations between the two religious communities.[65] Mostly associated with the Irish Church Mission, these endeavours reflected the established church's growing concern to highlight its missionary role in response to allegations of negligence and complacency.[66] Despite the enthusiasm of their own 'soul-stirring' reports,[67] however, it is unlikely that these missions made an enduring impact on religious statistics or local conditions. Although they were important in offering employment for pioneer work in famine-stricken areas, visitors reported that the inhabitants of such settlements were very often imported from outside the local area.[68]

Much interest in the Reformation movement was expressed on the other side of the channel, particularly among those who were opposed to Catholic Emancipation, and who saw events in Ireland as crucial to their cause. The Irish Church Missions to the west of the country, for example, were largely funded and promoted by English evangelicals.[69] Both sides of the religious divide in Ireland likewise recognized the importance of influencing English opinion. Irish Catholic leaders were alarmed by the publicity given by English newspapers to Farnham's claims that popery was in the course of being abolished.[70] They accused evangelicals of sending different reports to England from those which were circulated in Ireland. Irish evangelicals, in response, energetically cultivated their English counterparts. 'We must rouse them by exploding Rome's own artillery under their nose, and if they sleep on, it will be the sleep of death.'[71] This was achieved primarily through the structural links of the voluntary religious agencies, and by the frequent communications and correspondence between Methodists and Anglican evangelicals on both sides of the channel. Tours were also undertaken by evangelical lay leaders such as Roden, Farnham and Manchester on behalf of the Reformation Society. These were designed specifically to drum up anti-popery feeling in support of the Union and the Irish established church. The Reverend M. G. Beresford, returning from a tour of Staffordshire in 1834, reported to Farnham, 'From what I saw I am convinced there is a splendid and unfathomed mine of good Protestant feeling in England which only requires to be well-worked. When I spoke of the persecutions suffered by Protestant clergy and people I excited a feeling that must be seen to be understood.'[72] Gideon Ouseley also toured the north of England in 1828 under the auspices of the Wesleyan Methodist Missionary Society and, as with his previous visit in 1818, he attracted large crowds and seemed to be particularly successful in reviving the faith and the anti-Catholicism of Ulster Protestant migrants. More generally, he was disappointed with the level of awareness about Ireland and the Catholic question in English cities only a year before the passage of the Catholic Emancipation Act. He wrote that 'the Protestants this side of the water are filled with apathy about popery, as if the case were *hopeless*, or that it is not worthy of notice. The latter is it'.[73]

Although critics preferred to dwell on the material consequences of conversion, the Reformation movement was also concerned to highlight the distinctions between Protestant and Catholic doctrine. The nature of the campaign ensured that theological niceties were translated into slogans which popularized and oversimplified the issues. Catholics were bombarded by addresses and appeals from Protestants[74] who advised them to ask themselves:

1.   Why do our clergy pray, and cause us to pray, in a language we do not understand?
2.   Why do they forbid us to read the Holy Scriptures, which are the words of Eternal Life?
3.   Why did not the clergy of the Roman Catholic persuasion meet the clergy of the established church, to discuss the differences of doctrine between them, when challenged thereto?[75]

The final question refers to one of a series of great public meetings associated with the setting up of auxiliaries to the Reformation Society. While the majority of these were held in the south of Ireland during the late 1820s, the north too had its share. Downpatrick, Newry, Maghera, Derry, Cookstown, Ahoghill, Ballymena, Randalstown, Doagh and Belfast all hosted such events. Their aim was 'to promote a spirit of religious enquiry' among Roman Catholics by engaging clergy from both traditions in debates over disputed doctrines. The six points tabled for discussion at the Downpatrick meeting, from 22 to 23 April 1829, were typical.

(a)   Right of Luther to dissent from the General Church.
(b)   To justify the use of any authority except the written word of God in support of any faith or morals.
(c)   The right of private interpretation of the Scriptures.
(d)   Invocation of Saints and Angels.
(e)   Perpetual visibility of the Church of Christ.
(f)   Transubstantiation.[76]

Ministers of the established, Presbyterian and Methodist churches participated in the meetings and leading evangelical figures from London and the provinces, keen to stir up interest in this stronghold of Irish Protestantism, were also welcome participants.[77] The long campaign to distribute and teach 'gospel truth' was here reaching its climax. Its promoters felt its claims to be irresistible, with little now standing in the way of the 'peaceable triumph of truth'.[78] With Protestants insisting that their only intention was to enlighten the masses about the 'erroneous' views held by their leaders, the role of the Catholic Church was largely defensive.[79] Catholic bishops were reluctant to become involved because of the threat to public order of debates which often lasted several days.[80] By absenting themselves from meetings, however, they merely supplied the Protestant spokesmen with additional ammunition to let loose on their excited assembly. Many local priests professed a willingness to explain the finer points of their doctrine. This, however, demanded considerable theological sophistication on the part of the audience, and expositions were also hampered by the stipulation that the verification of all points must rest on 'undisputed and undeniable authority', that is, the word of God as interpreted by evangelicals.[81] A description of the protagonists of the Ballymena debate illustrates the propaganda value of such occasions.

> The Protestant advocate, a tall and strong made man, constitutionally fearless and firm; the confident, but half ironic smile that played on his countenance bespoke endurance and good temper, but keen satire and reading wit, forcing us to say, this is surely a man fitted to strip a Jesuit of his cloak, and foil a priest with his own weapons. He brought to our mind a lively youth who had just been emancipated from the drudgery of a collegiate course, and with gun, and net, and hawk, and hound, determines to amuse himself and recreate his friends with the fruits of his pleasing exertion. The priest, on the contrary, was rather a knight of rueful countenance, occasionally appearing animated, but the prevailing expression of which was melancholy; there was a plaintiveness and suavity of manner that led us to think he would aim his shaft at the feelings rather than the understanding – about middle-sized, well-formed head and forehead, his hue pale; he looked like an unwilling captive, but rendered bold by his situation, and from his determined look, you would conclude, that neither threatening, nor railing, nor argument, should drive him from his position.[82]

Reports of attendance at these meetings vary according to the source, but they usually continued for several days and stirred up considerable local interest. They can be seen as a popular extension of the conflict between the two religious traditions exemplified at a more official level by the Archbishop of Dublin, William Magee, and the Roman Catholic Bishop of Kildare and Leighlin, James Doyle. Desmond Bowen claims that the militancy exhibited in their defences of their respective churches heralded a new age of theological conflict.[83] It is perhaps more accurate to say that this highly publicized phase of theological controversy showed a new willingness on the part of the churches to extend the debate beyond conventional channels. The 'Second Reformation' did have an important long-term effect, though not in the number of conversions, which were probably always insignificant. The contemptuous dismissal of basic Catholic doctrines, and the vilification of the Catholic religion in which Protestant polemicists indulged, united all classes in defence of the ancient faith. As Irene Hehir points out, the impetus given to speeches and writings upholding Catholic doctrine 'as the supreme moral authority in the country, provides yet another example of how the evangelical movement served to entrench Catholicism in the minds of the ordinary people'.[84] In the short term, however, such public confrontations, played out in a spirit of hostility and tension, both fed upon and contributed to the sectarian disturbances of the period. Ensor's comment on this stage of Protestant triumphalism was that 'the Bible, without note or comment, is not less a means of Protestant dominion than the Orange Yeoman's military array'.[85]

Even the most sanguine Irish Protestants were nevertheless forced to recognize that the passage of Catholic Emancipation was a major turning-point in the religious history of their country.[86] That crisis proved, as predicted, to be merely a prelude to the threat of further erosions of Protestant privileges. Agitation for further legislation on education, tithes and the church establishment followed in its wake. All were met with the determined, scriptural-based opposition of a diverse Ulster Protestantism, which found in anti-Catholicism a tentative and temporary unity. One indication of the evangelical reaction to the shifting political context was the growth of pre-millennialism as an alternative to earlier, more optimistic eschatological interpretations of events. The distinctive feature of pre-millennialism was that Christ's coming, which was still regarded as imminent, would precede rather than follow the downfall of Catholic and heathen nations.[87] Ian Rennie dates its origin among third generation evangelicals between 1825 and 1860.[88] It can be explained with reference to current political developments, the growth of romanticism, and as a reflection of the loss of earlier confidence in the ability of evangelical missions and religious initiatives to transform a largely secular world. New and convincing evidence of the prosperity of Catholicism both in Ireland and on the continent raised doubts as to its decline.[89] Pre-millennialism combined greater temporal realism with a comforting belief that the current generation was witnessing the unfolding of a divine plan. This enabled contemporary evangelicals to transform even the possibility of political defeat into a religious conviction which promised eventual victory. Day-to-day events – local, national and international – could thus be interpreted as part of the process of prophetic fulfilment. From the midst of strife and unrest in County Cavan in 1831, Krause wrote:

> I firmly believe that the day of the Lord's Coming is not far off. I believe that the restless, dissatisfied spirit which is abroad is rapidly maturing that distress of nations and perplexity which we are taught to consider as a forerunner of that day. I believe that the infidel, Popish, and every other abomination will gather daily strength to the day of battle.[90]

The speeches and writings of Edward Irving,[91] along with the prophetical conferences at Albury Park, Surrey and Powerscourt, Wicklow, were an important factor in the spread of pre-millennial ideas.[92] The importance of these conferences in the history of Irish evangelicalism lies primarily in the emergence of the Brethren movement which owed much to the ex-Church of Ireland clergyman, J. N. Darby.[93] The inaptly named Plymouth Brethren drew together discontented Dublin Anglican evangelicals and a few dissenters to pursue a comprehensive vision of a pure church set free from worldliness and hypocrisy.[94] Darby's dispensationalist theology supplied much of the intellectual cohesion of early Brethrenism and the evangelistic urgency which characterized its later development in Ulster.[95]

The epidemic of prophetical speculation in the 1820s and 1830s, far from being the preoccupation of an esoteric minority, attracted men of surprisingly cultivated tastes and high social standing. They met in the drawing-rooms of great country houses, not in the alleys of urban slums. They were, suggests Rennie, men with much to lose from the religious and political challenges of their generation.[96] In Ulster, for example, both the Earl of Roden and the Duke of Manchester kept a wary eye both on the Book of Revelation and on the 'Signs of the Times'.[97] Lower down the social scale, and operating at a more prosaic level, outbreaks of cholera, fever, or famine could equally serve as reminders of the close proximity of the next world, and as an incentive to prepare for divine judgement.[98]

Evangelical anxiety about the shape of events in Ireland in the late 1820s and early 1830s was given a specific temporal focus by the apparently irresistible liberalism of much government policy. Once Catholic Emancipation was out of the way it was the government's educational policies of the 1830s that seemed most threatening to evangelical principles. Until the beginning of the nineteenth century the major educational provision in Ireland came in the form of state-endowed schools whether of the parish, diocesan, royal or chartered variety. This tradition of state interference supported by penal laws against Catholic education was designed primarily to bolster up the Protestant ascendancy. Roman Catholics were consequently forced to set up a network of 'hedge schools' to which they clung with the same kind of tenacity as the English working classes did to their dame schools. In the wake of the evangelical revival, however, Irish education was transformed by the establishment of Protestant education societies with a vested interest in proselytism.[99] Although the educational achievements of the evangelicals were far from negligible, the most important gains were made between 1805 and 1825 before the Catholic Church fought back with the only effective instruments at its disposal, boycott and protest.[100] The one society which enjoyed a measure of Catholic support was the originally undenominational Kildare Place Society, but it too fell victim to Ireland's growing religious tensions when its managers allocated grants to the Protestant societies. O'Connell's resignation from the society, and condemnation of it from Catholic church leaders as far apart as the liberal Doyle and the conservative McHale, meant that the Kildare Place Society, as an undenominational institution, was living on borrowed time. Thus, a powerful combination of evangelical proselytism and Catholic self-consciousness rendered obsolete the old educational pattern of pre-Catholic Emancipation Ireland.

A royal commission was set up in 1824 to investigate alternatives, and through the maze of prolific reports it became clear that any future national system of education must be based on two principles neatly summed up by Peel in the House of Commons: 'first to unite as far as possible . . . the children of Protestants and Catholics under one common system of education; and secondly, in so doing, studiously and honestly to discard all idea of making proselytes'.[101] The obvious way of achieving these objectives was to have a system of combined literary and separate religious instruction for Protestant and Catholic children,[102] an idea which seemed logical enough in theory but which upset nineteenth-century churchmen who did not see such a sharp distinction between the secular and the sacred. This principle nevertheless formed the basis of the new Irish education system proposed by Stanley in his famous instructions to the Duke of Leinster in 1831.[103] The single most important fact about the new system is that it failed to achieve its chief objective, namely the creation of denominationally mixed schools with no proselytism. Although there were demographic and administrative reasons for this failure, the main problem was that the so-called religious consensus, upon which the scheme was based, was only skin-deep from the beginning and depended for its survival on an older tradition of liberal churchmen who composed the Board of Education. Interdenominational and moderate in outlook, such men were unrepresentative of the more highly charged religious atmosphere of the 1830s. Henry Cooke's response to the new board was more in tune with Ulster evangelical opinion. He described it as 'a supreme despotic Board. Three parts establishment, two parts Roman Catholic, one part Unitarian, and one part Church of Scotland.'[104] Ironically, the attempt to forge an undenominational system not only heightened denominational rivalries, but also increased tensions within denominations as pro- and anti-national education factions fought it out in Presbyterian synods, Methodist conferences, Anglican periodicals and even within the Catholic episcopate. No measure could have rebounded more completely on its own intentions. In short, the very thing that made the old system unacceptable – increased religious competition – also made the new proposals unworkable.

As an established church already aware of the ground shifting beneath its privileged foundations, the Church of Ireland felt it had strong grounds for defending its right to be the chief supplier of education in the country. Thus on this issue evangelicals were in line with the vast majority of their bishops, with the notable exception of Archbishop Whateley of Dublin.[105] The established church predictably set up its own educational society on a diocesan pattern,[106] but as with all such ventures in the British Isles in the nineteenth century, financial burdens imposed strict limits on what could be achieved.[107] Methodist and Presbyterian responses to the national education scheme were remarkably similar. Within Methodism the new scheme was given a cautious welcome until Jabez Bunting, with the Irish preachers solidly behind him, described the Whig proposals as 'inconceivably mischievous'.[108] For Bunting it was one thing to allow Catholics a seat in parliament, but quite another to employ government money for the benefit of the Roman Catholic religion itself. Bunting as usual was able to swing Methodist opinion his way by appealing to a trinity of evangelical nonconformist values in education: the centrality of the whole Protestant Bible in the curriculum, the absolute minimum of bureaucratic control over schools, and the conviction that public money should never be used for the support of religious heresy.[109] Ironically Bunting's position, along with that of the Irish preachers, was strengthened by the conservative wing of the Catholic Church led by McHale, Archbishop of Tuam who objected to the national scheme because it was not sufficiently Catholic.[110] Within Presbyterianism the main conflict was between James Carlile, an evangelical of liberal views, who was therefore a skilful political appointment to the Board of Education, and Henry Cooke. When under attack in the synod Carlile defended his commitment to Irish national education because 'it had a more direct tendency than any public measure which had yet been tried, to unite the mass of the people in affection, to diffuse civilization and knowledge of the sacred oracles of God'.[111] The problem lay in determining the centrality of 'the sacred oracles of God', because Carlile's Presbyterian critics claimed that the national board's decision to exclude the Bible from the hours of combined education was a sinister attempt to overthrow the Protestant religion. The use of scriptural extracts on the principle of the lowest common denominator was, according to Cooke and his evangelical supporters, a sorry attempt to create a sort of doctrinally insipid humanism.[112] In the short term Presbyterians formed their own system of voluntary schools, although practical considerations ensured that mixed schooling did continue in some areas. In the long term they joined with the other denominations in subverting the national system from within.

The various theological objections to national education were super-imposed on the controversies surrounding the 'Second Reformation' to generate yet more heat in the conflict between evangelical Protestantism and Roman Catholicism. Speaking at a 'great meeting of the friends of scriptural education and the whole bible', McGhee stated that 'every clergyman in Ireland is being forced by authority into direct and practical collision with the principles of the hierarchy of the Church of Rome'.[113] At similar events up and down the country, attended by members of all denominations, the same points were reiterated. The government was not only defending or protecting Catholicism, but, particularly by denying the free use of the Bible in schoolrooms, was actively 'confirming and propagating Romish errors'. What was worse, they expected local clergy to do the same by accommodating the priesthood in their dissemination of 'the peculiar dogmas, the superstitious rites, the dangerous deceits, and in a word, all the errors of Popery'.[114] By contrast, the scriptures were once again held forth as mankind's surest guide in all walks of life.[115] With such attitudes in the ascendancy it is scarcely surprising that by mid-century the three-way vested interests of Catholics, Anglicans and Presbyterians had made the Irish educational system thoroughly denominational in practice if still not in theory.[116] Perhaps the most remarkable feature of this whole episode in retrospect is not that undenominational schooling failed, but that anyone acquainted with the religious polemics of the 1820s could have imagined that it would succeed.

Throughout the 1830s, the combination of Whig concessions to Catholicism and the evangelical presentation of popery as dangerous to the fundamental liberties of the empire, forged a link between evangelical religion and political conservatism. This was most ardently articulated by the 'Protestant Champion' Henry Cooke, and formed the basis of his campaign for a Protestant alliance.[117] Cooke, and at least some of his colleagues in the Synod of Ulster, saw the political attacks on the church as an indication of greater and more fundamental dangers. The established church, historic and enduring, was regarded as the last guarantor of Protestant supremacy. 'In the forefront of the battle against the enemies of our Lord', it was seen 'like a vast break-water, resisting the impulses of the waves and tempests of the tumultuous ocean of fluctuating opinions, and behind which men may remain safely anchored'.[118] Cooke, in a letter to his wife in 1831, expressed his fears of its downfall.

> I should regret this event – partly because I do not wish to disturb things that are established – partly because, that when the Church is robbed, it is a question whether the spoils will go to better men – partly because I believe the hatred of the Church is just covetousness and envy on the part of a vast majority of those who would fleece her; but mainly because the principle of Establishments is Scriptural, and the Church now established, with many serious blemishes, is sound at the bottom.[119]

The ecclesiastical question which dominated political debates in the 1830s was, on what basis should established churches exist within the state after they had lost either the numerical support or the passive acceptance of the majority of the population? The Irish Church never had the former and was close to losing the latter, while the Church of England, though in a much stronger position, was also facing unparalleled challenges. In such a climate Whig attempts to promote religious peace by reforming, but essentially conservative, legislation, rebounded in an extraordinary way. Tractarianism, Orangeism, Nonconformist voluntaryism and Catholic nationalism all gathered pace in the 1830s, the first two because the Whigs had gone too far and the others because they had not gone far enough. In Ireland, fears for the future of the established church were reinforced by a combination of Repeal and anti-tithe agitation and proposals for a thorough administrative reform of the church's structure. Anxiety was expressed in a series of 'Great Protestant Meetings' in both England and Ireland in opposition to the prevailing 'horrid spirit of concession'.[120] Speaking at Hillsborough, County Down, alongside Lord Roden, Cooke called for a 'platform of common Protestantism' to oppose 'the threefold cord of the priesthood and laity of Rome, the Socinian and the Infidel'. 'Between the divided churches I publish the banns of a sacred marriage of Christian forebearance where they differ, or Christian care where they agree, and of Christian cooperation in all matters where their common safety is concerned.' Two points need to be made about Cooke's position in 1834. The first is that Cooke, as with Bunting and the Methodists, was supporting prelacy not so much for its own sake but rather for what it prevented: it was as a bulwark against Romanism that the Church of Ireland was most valued by its dissenting supporters in the 1830s. Secondly, Cooke was not speaking as an official representative of the Synod of Ulster; indeed Presbyterianism was actually moving in a more strictly denominational direction, and many of his colleagues bitterly opposed his public support for both Tory politics and church ascendancy.[121] The meeting at Hillsborough was nevertheless an important display of popular Protestant unity, which recurred thereafter at times of political danger to the Protestant cause in Ireland. With Cooke vigorously stating that 'a minister *may* and *must* interfere with politics, *whenever politics interferes with religion*',[122] evangelicals in Ireland were preparing themselves for a more active political campaign against further concessions to Irish Catholics. Cooke appeared at a number of ultra-Protestant meetings in London's Exeter Hall alongside the evangelical nobility and notorious polemicists such as R. J. McGhee and Mortimer O'Sullivan. Such meetings had the desired effect of drawing the attention of the British religious public to the intensity of 'No Popery' feeling in Ireland. Not only Protestantism, but the future of the empire itself was thought to be in danger from the renewed militancy of Irish Catholics.[123]

The Methodists, who saw themselves as being in the front line of the Protestant advance in Ireland, and whose missionary reports had an important impact on their English co-religionists, were regarded as a particularly strategic group because of their apparently disinterested support for the established church.[124] Despite the opposition of many of their numbers, however, Jabez Bunting, himself convinced of the political necessity of Catholic Emancipation, managed to uphold the 'no politics' rule in 1829 to prevent coordinated canvassing.[125] But although Methodists were thus denied opposing political measures as a body, individuals, particularly in Ireland, continued to exert popular pressure against political changes which they saw as antithetical to the religious welfare of the nation. Gideon Ouseley's plans for 'securing Ireland's peace' were, to him at least, 'simple, rational and practical'.[126] His remedies were more responsible landlordism, a more equitable and rational assessment of tithes, the state payment of Roman Catholic priests without asking for a veto or any other security,[127] and an electoral register based on minimum educational standards to ensure that landlords would have a vested interest in building schools for their freeholders. Ouseley expected these proposals to loosen the bonds between Catholic priests and their flocks and to strengthen those between good landlords and their tenants. Agrarian grievances would thus disappear and the population would be delivered from Romish ignorance into truth, knowledge, equity, industry and prosperity, all of which were linked in Ouseley's mind. Indeed there is much populist enlightenment rhetoric underpinning his more detailed proposals.

Ouseley's views were unpopular even among his friends, for few evangelicals could accept that bad means – the state payment of Catholic clergy – could ever produce a good end. But if some of Ouseley's political views were unpopular, his reputation as a second Saint Patrick in his zeal to convert pagan Ireland never stood higher. For the first quarter of a century of his itinerant labours he had been disliked by the vast majority of the Catholic clergy, by most episcopalian and Presbyterian clergy, and even by a powerful group of preachers within his own connection. He had been an embarrassment to most Protestant landlords and had posed problems for the civil magistrates. But by the late 1820s he was defended by the Protestant press in Ireland, patronized by the evangelical aristocracy, on agreeable terms with the most influential Protestant clergy,[128] and the recipient of more invitations from Britain and North America than he could ever hope to fulfil. It was not only that the religious world had a soft spot for ageing evangelists; Ouseley's career also shows how activities which were regarded as fanatical and dangerous at the beginning of the century had by the 1830s become an essential component in the defence of Protestantism. Not surprisingly his portrait was published and his praises were sung in the august pages of the *Methodist Magazine*.

> There is a heartiness in Mr. Ouseley's Protestantism which is quite refreshing in these days of spiritual liberality. He is thoroughly acquainted with all levels of popery, and has a deep conviction of their anti-Christian character and destructive tendency, and therefore treats them with uncompromising opposition. Few men have been so successful in exposing those pernicious dogmas in Ireland as this indefatigable missionary, and his tracts strongly remind one of the straightforward honesty and logic of the Latimers of a former age. Those who read merely to find the elegance and graces of style will derive little gratification from his homely pamphlets; but such as desire to know the truth will find them replete with sound sense, and scriptural argument.[129]

The significance of the evangelical crusade against popery in the 1820s and 1830s lies not so much in the number of converts it won or in the number of schools it controlled, but rather in the religious legitimacy it conferred upon a wider political cause. This is reflected in the sheer variety of clubs and associations formed in defence of Protestantism. The Brunswick Constitutional Clubs, for example, were formed in 1828 when Protestant uneasiness at O'Connell's election victory in County Clare was compounded by the sensational about-turn of the formerly staunch anti-Catholic MP George Dawson. At an Orange meeting in Derry Dawson announced his conversion to the necessity of Catholic Emancipation. Further anxiety was created by the appearance, brief but alarming, of O'Connell's agent John Lawless in a County Monaghan village.[130] Entrance to the new organization depended only on a commitment to 'simply and solely preserve the integrity of our Protestant constitution, and the preservation of our Protestant Establishment'. No oaths, signs, or passwords were necessary. Over a hundred Brunswick clubs were formed in two weeks and they were particularly successful in the Orange areas of Ulster.[131] Dominated by peers prominent in Orange and evangelical circles, such as Lords Roden, Farnham and Manchester, the clubs were another way of mobilizing the masses against their common enemy.

The aims of the Protestant Conservative Society similarly expressed the need of the aristocracy to identify their Protestant tenantry with their own interests and against the combined threat of liberalism and Catholicism. It planned the 'protection of Landed Proprietors, Magistrates, and the lower orders, against the Combinations with which they are assailed, and to secure the interests of Property and Religion at the ensuing General election'. A National Protestant fund was set up to maintain both the 'poor man's rights and the rich man's property'.[132] The Protestant Associations formed throughout Britain and Ireland in this period reflected similar interests, with 'Great Meetings' in Armagh, Down, Fermanagh, Tyrone, Antrim, Cavan, Monaghan and Londonderry offering platforms for emotional defences of the constitution. Lord Roden, for example, coloured his warnings against further Roman Catholic concessions with emotive tales of Protestant loyalty in the face of armed Catholic agitators, led by an aggressive priesthood intent on ascendancy. 'The Protestants scarcely dared to venture from their homes after sunset; they feared to transact their business in the fair or market; they were waylaid, insulted, beaten and robbed, or assassinated on their return.'[133] British evangelicals visiting Ireland eulogistically reported on the zeal, diligence and industry of these Protestant peers who were valiantly opposing the 'destruction of the Protestant church, and the dismemberment of the empire'.[134] The Protestant Association in London, with its headquarters in Exeter Hall became a particularly important forum for English, Scottish and Irish anti-Catholic polemics. Its supporters aimed to apply 'the standard of the Word of God to every measure of public policy . . . Thus, on the neglect of religion in public affairs, on the false system of education endowed by the State, it is the duty of a Protestant Association to protest again and again.'[135] Its extensive campaign of public meetings throughout the country not only widely diffused a vigorous attack on Irish Catholicism, but also nudged the opposition Conservative Party in a more Protestant direction. Ironically one of the Protestant Association's most deeply felt grievances was the payment of public money to Maynooth College which Peel substantially increased in 1845.[136] Not for the last time, Irish evangelicals found the Conservative Party a more ardent supporter of the Protestant cause in opposition than in power. The proliferation of tracts and pamphlets issued by the Protestant Association is nevertheless an indication of its effectiveness as a propaganda machine.[137] In Britain and in Ireland its support transcended social class and denominational distinctions, but as with many ultra-Protestant societies it found it hard to pursue a consistent political strategy and maintain its support beyond periods of immediate crisis.

The banning of the Orange Order in 1836 and the Maynooth crisis of 1845 led to the formation of yet another society. The Protestant Alliance, formed in Armagh in 1845, was an initiative designed to meet the 'extreme and increasing peril' in which the interests of Protestantism were placed. Prominent in the Alliance were the Earls of Manchester, Roden, Enniskillen and Downshire, who expressed concern about the apparently inexhaustible list of concessions to Irish Catholics since the passage of the Catholic Emancipation Act in 1829.[138] Urging Protestants to take immediate steps to secure their future, the Alliance was particularly keen to suppport an MP to speak for the Protestant interest in the House of Commons.[139] The maintenance of the united established churches in England and Ireland, the promotion of a scriptural system of education, and the protection of the rights and liberties of *all* subjects were among their declared objectives. As with so many of these organizations, however, the first object of the Protestant Alliance was to 'support the principles of the Reformation in Religion, and of the Revolution of 1688 in Politics'.[140] This dual goal, theologically clear-cut and politically unyielding, was at the heart of nineteenth-century evangelical anti-Catholicism.

The response of men like Cooke, Ouseley, Roden and Farnham to the events of the second quarter of the nineteenth century was informed by a powerful mixture of religious, social and political convictions. With religious faith as the chief motivating force, responsibility for personal, local and national affairs logically followed one another. It was regarded as the duty of all in positions of responsibility to use their providentially ordered status to resist Rome and all its devious works. Opposition to what was regarded as an intolerant social regime and a threat to the British Empire, as well as a heretical faith, was strengthened by the conviction that Catholicism was on the march again and needed to be stopped. Both the passage of Catholic Emancipation and the urgency of acute social problems stemming from rapid population growth made Ireland an increasingly important focus for Protestant opposition to the 'Man of Sin'. British evangelicals also made a contribution to the evangelical campaign to bring 'Vital Religion' to every corner of Ireland. Despite early optimism, however, the conversion of the native population was eventually recognized as an unrealistic goal; but in Ulster, in particular, Protestantism became both more vigorous and more defensive as it became clear that neither British governments nor British public opinion could be relied upon to resist Irish Catholicism with sufficient fortitude.

PART THREE

Culture and society
in evangelical
Ulster

[6]

Religion in the city: evangelicalism in Belfast 1800–60

For I have seen violence and strife in the city. (Psalm 55:9)

For I have much people in this city. (Acts 18:10)

The greatest challenge to evangelical ardour throughout the British Isles was posed by the new industrial centres which rendered existing religious structures inadequate and irrelevant. The real test for churches and voluntary religious organizations in the nineteenth century, therefore, was how well they could adapt to the realities of urban living and, more particularly, how much support they could attract from a predominantly youthful and mobile working class. A plethora of local studies has indicated that church extension programmes in the 1830s and 1840s were too late and too limited to enable religious institutions to make any real impact on the lives of working people in terms of formal observance. It has also been recognized, however, that to conclude – as did many Victorians – that the urban working classes were steeped in irreligion, atheism or scepticism, is too simplistic. For a minority of working-class men and women regular church attendance reflected a desire for an orderly, 'respectable' life-style. Many others accepted the churches' services at important stages of the life-cycle – for baptisms, marriages and funeral services – as a matter of culture and tradition and used the churches' social facilities without feeling any need to attend more overtly 'religious' activities. Recent studies also suggest that while the doctrinal, dogmatic, church-based conventions of orthodox Christianity were largely rejected by the urban masses, religious ideas, symbols and values permeated popular culture at a less official level. The relationship between religion and the culture of a community is thus richer and more complex than statistical analysis alone can reveal. While sectarian competition is particularly characteristic of Ulster's major town, a study of its religious development in the first half of the nineteenth century shows that working-class attitudes to evangelical attempts to transform their lives are much the same in Belfast as in London, Manchester or Glasgow.[1]

THE URBAN MISSION

The effects of urbanization and industrialization in the town of Belfast posed special problems. Social, political, economic and religious developments had combined to transform the liberal market town of the late eighteenth century into a crowded, bustling centre of activity which, by the middle of the next century, was poisoned by sectarianism, strife and distress. The most striking aspect of the emergence of Belfast as Ulster's capital city was the rapidity of its growth in the first half of the nineteenth century.[2] This process was closely related to basic changes in the local economic structure and consequent rural depopulation. The decline of the domestic linen industry, particularly in the densely populated counties of Monaghan, Cavan and south Armagh, forced many rural dwellers to choose between reliance on a vulnerable potato crop or migration to new manufacturing centres.[3] In 1800 Belfast, Londonderry and Newry were the only towns in Ulster with more than 1,000 houses,[4] but a trade boom in the 1820s ensured growth and a degree of prosperity for all three ports. Belfast, however, took the lead in urban development in these years with the percentage increase of the town's population almost three times that of the province as a whole between 1821 and 1841 (Table 6.1).

The rapid industrialization of what had been primarily a centre for trade and commerce was advanced by the introduction of cotton-spinning machines in

Table 6.1 (a)   Population of Belfast 1821–91

1821	37,277	1861	119,393
1831	53,287	1871	174,412
1841	75,308	1881	208,122
1851	97,784	1891	255,950

Table 6.1 (b)   Number and percentage of Roman Catholics in the Belfast population 1808–91

	No. of Roman Catholics	Percentage of population
1808	4,000	16
1834	19,712	32
1861	41,406	33.9
1871	55,575	31.9
1881	59,975	28.8
1891	67,378	26.3

the late eighteenth century and was further encouraged by the application of steam power. The Belfast cotton industry reached its peak in 1825, after which the introduction of the wet flax process facilitated the switch of capital and labour from cotton back into linen.[5] This successful adaptation to the mechanization of the textile industry stimulated further investment, most visible in the enlargement of the port itself and in the extension of its facilities.[6] Similarly, a proliferation of smaller, consumer-related industries sprang up to meet the needs and demands of the growing workforce.[7] The increased prosperity generated by economic growth was reflected in the façade of the city itself, especially after 1822 when a new Donegall family settlement resulted in the granting of leases on terms which encouraged tenants to build and improve.[8] With the establishment of shops and banks in the town centre, wealthy citizens gradually began to abandon their town residences for the fine Georgian and Victorian terraces which came to predominate in the southern suburbs.[9]

Industrialization had, of course, another face. While the great factories and mills provided employment for the labourers who flocked in from the surrounding countryside, the rapid shift in settlement patterns also generated new social problems. Work in the textile factories carried its own health hazards, but it was the living conditions of the poor in Belfast's industrial areas which most adversely affected the quality of their lives. Overcrowding and bad sanitation in back-to-back houses in narrow streets led to recurrent outbreaks of fever and a mortality rate significantly higher than elsewhere in Ireland.[10] Periodic depressions in trade and industry also contributed to the cycle of poverty, crime and violence which was the most familiar aspect of early Victorian urbanization.

The religious affiliations of the influx of rural families also contributed to the changing character of the town. In 1785 there were only 1,000 Catholics living in Belfast, which represented around 8 per cent of the total population. This percentage doubled every 25 years until the mid-1830s when the proportion of Catholics stood at 32 per cent and continued to climb, possibly to around 40 per cent, in the 1840s when the ethnic tide started to turn as a result of the famine, the growth of shipbuilding, engineering and skilled trades in the 1850s and the increased rate of Catholic emigration to other parts of Ireland and the rest of the world.[11] The absolute numbers of Roman Catholics in Belfast nevertheless continued to grow very rapidly. There were, for example, more Roman Catholics in Belfast in 1871 than the total number of inhabitants in 1831. As with other Victorian cities in the British Isles, population increase was due to migration from outside. This is particularly true of Belfast where infant mortality and fever death rates were among the highest in the British Isles. Where exactly the migrants came from is nevertheless insufficiently clear for statistical precision, but reliable figures of household heads within street categories from the late nineteenth century show different patterns of Protestant and Catholic migration. Whereas 50 per cent of Protestant migrants came from the counties of Down and Antrim,

Roman Catholics were more likely than Protestants to have been born in Belfast or to have migrated from other counties of Ulster and from the rest of Ireland. What can be said with certainty is that whereas Catholics had migrated to Belfast in larger numbers than Protestants before and during the famine, the position was reversed from the 1860s.[12]

Historians of ethnic conflict among migrants to American cities in the nineteenth century have drawn attention to the importance of the pre-existing structures of social, political and economic power in cities before the migrants arrived. Well-established elites were the least able to accommodate new migrant communities. Not only were such structures already well established in Belfast, but the predominantly poor and unskilled character of Catholic migrants merely confirmed Protestant notions about the baleful effects of Roman Catholicism on social and economic progress. Thus, while Catholicism had been no more than an unobtrusive minority denomination, the attitude of Belfast's secure and generally prosperous Protestants had been mainly tolerant. Munificent town-dwellers had expressed their liberality by contributing to the building of Belfast's first two Roman Catholic chapels in 1784 and 1815.[13] But the course of the '98 rebellion and subsequent political developments had led many Presbyterians to a distinctively anti-Catholic conservatism. Religious harmony in Belfast was now under threat, with the traditions of sectarian strife which rural dwellers brought with them grafted onto the tension generated by the political and religious polemics of the late 1820s and 1830s. These public demonstrations allowed the conservative and orthodox elements in both politics and religion to mount a serious challenge to liberalism in all its forms. Before 1830 religious riots in the town were still rare, but in the succeeding decades clashes became more frequent.[14] Competition for jobs, the popular and controversial exhortations of evangelical clergy, and the activities of the Orange Order were all contributory factors. But sectarian animosities, important though they were in shaping Belfast's development, were not the only outlet for religious energy. Religious experience, both formal and informal, was an integral aspect of everyday society and of the lives of those individuals who gave it its peculiar shapes and forms, and who were in turn affected by its demands. The efforts of the churches to meet the social and religious needs of Belfast society in the early nineteenth century were often prompted or tainted by competition either with the Roman Catholic Church or with other denominations, but this element must be set alongside other kinds of religious zeal.

In common with the situation in other British cities, official religious provision in Belfast in the early part of the nineteenth century was wholly inadequate for a growing population. The Church of Ireland parish church of St Anne's in High Street was supplemented only by a chapel-of-ease which opened for divine service in 1817, but 'though affording considerable accommodation [for subscribers], its capabilities as far as the poor were concerned, were very small; some half-dozen seats were set apart for them'.[15] Ballymacarrett, an area which underwent a dramatic industrial transformation in these years, and which was some distance from the parish church at Knockbreda, gained a small church in 1828 with the aid of the Board of First Fruits.[16] Since it catered for only 350 of a Church of Ireland population of 3,000, however, its benefits were minimal.[17] In the same period, Belfast had six Presbyterian churches. Two were connected with the Synod of Ulster, two with the Secession Synod and two with the Presbytery of Antrim.[18] Not only a lack of enthusiasm, but direct opposition to the creation of new congregations had prevented the extension of the Synod of Ulster's facilities for almost a century. Ministers of existing churches feared a reduction both in their numerical strength and in their financial remuneration. In the early 1820s, however, the persistence of concerned individuals resulted in the building of a new church at Fisherwick Place which was to become an important evangelical centre.[19] The opening of May Street Presbyterian Church in 1829 was also due, not to synodical concern for extending its outreach, but to lay pressure. In this case, influential citizens, anxious to align themselves with the political and religious views of Henry Cooke, erected the church especially for him.[20] While it seems that the Secession churches continued to have more appeal for those in humbler circumstances,[21] none of these dissenting churches was located in the new industrial areas where they were most needed.

The Methodists, more flexible in structure and functional in character, were in a better position to adapt to the rise of a new urban society. Always able to find a niche where the other churches were weak, Methodist societies in Belfast, once initial Calvinist opposition died down, took root in school-houses and meeting-houses borrowed or rented for the purpose. While perhaps lacking long-term stability, this arrangement did have the more important advantage of enabling missionaries and preachers to consolidate the interest of even a small group of adherents. These early buildings were of necessity inexpensive and, apart from being situated in the heart of the new communities, their more 'homely' structure appealed to the poorer classes who felt themselves inappropriately clad for the grandeur of the parish church.[22] By the early 1800s regular, well-attended services were under way in the industrial suburb of Ballymacarrett and in Cotton Court, and a larger, more central chapel was opened in Donegall Square in 1806.[23]

Methodism's greatest strength was in its response to the social and practical, as well as the spiritual needs of a community in transition.[24] Loose social bonds and the absence of welfare facilities created obvious needs which determined the direction of urban religious organizations. In 1816, for example, the Methodist Benevolent Society was formed to operate a clothing depository and a fund to ease the problems of food scarcities.[25] Home visitation was an important aspect of the Methodist outreach, and this close proximity with the lay membership, especially in times of fever, was simultaneously opportune, inspiring and, quite literally, deadly. Death and eternity were major themes of itinerating preachers, and everyday evidence of the imminence of judgement was clearly awe-inspiring. But the message was preached at great personal risk, with the death of preachers from fever frequently recorded.

By such temporal exertions Methodists helped to create a sense of community for new urban dwellers, offering them entertainment, encouragement and spiritual comfort. The growing importance of Belfast as a centre for northern Methodism was recognized by the holding of Conference there for the first time in 1827. By 1840 there were nine Methodist chapels in the town and its vicinity and the circuit was divided into two to accommodate the growing population of the outlying areas.[26] The Reverend Tackaberry, writing to a colleague in 1837, spoke of intensive work in the area through 67 classes comprising more than 900 members and a great many missionary outposts.[27] While the numbers seem unimpressive – a total of 1,386 on the Belfast circuits of the Primitive and Wesleyan organizations in a population of approximately 60,000 – it should be noted that the figures are for adult class members only. The number of adherents was probably at least double the recorded figure for class members. It is also clear that, once again, it was through their general influence, and the adaptation of their methods, rather than in their numerical strength that Methodists made the greatest impact on Ulster religion and society.

Not until the 1830s did the major denominations in Belfast make a concentrated effort to provide facilities for worship in the poorer areas of the town. By that stage the results of decades of neglect could no longer be ignored; 'our large towns are . . . growing into hordes of heathen, after whom no man is looking, and of whom nothing can reasonably be expected but aggravated and increased depravity'.[28] Insanitary conditions and irreligious behaviour were thus regarded as equally hazardous by Belfast's respectable middle class. Civic and religious leaders were particularly concerned about the degree of irreligion in what were rapidly becoming the slum areas of the town. A report from the early 1830s on the condition of the inhabitants around College Square North, where a Church of Ireland church was opened in 1833, reflects the degree of anxiety felt by concerned citizens as well as their conviction that provision of religious facilities would greatly alleviate other problems.

> The locality was notorious for drunken rows and unseemly brawls. An officer of the police informed the incumbent that for a long time before the erection of the church he could never pass a Saturday night in his own house, or enjoy a peaceful Sabbath, as he was required at such times to be constantly on duty, quelling the riots which habitually disgraced the district. He said, he soon perceived the happy influence exerted by the means of grace in the cessation of these disorders and the introduction of sobriety and peace. The country districts, though less marked by turbulence, were, perhaps, even in grosser darkness. No minister of religion sought out their inhabitants, they lived at a distance from the two churches in the town; and in them there was no provision for their accommodation. There were whole families which never sent one member to a place of worship; and in which no one had ever read a single chapter in the Bible. Many knew no better use of the Lord's Day than to spend the greater part of it in sleeping off the fatigue of the previous week.[29]

The churches were painfully out of touch with the needs of such a population, but were under increasing pressure to confront the manifold problems of irreligion. In Belfast, as with other British cities, the first step was to increase the number of sittings in areas of greatest need. Even where genuine zeal for improvement was present, however, ecclesiastical machinery was slow and cumbersome. Active participation and financial commitment on the part of the laity, and a high degree of clerical involvement were the additional prerequisites for a successful ecclesiastical building programme.[30]

The names of James Morgan and Henry Cooke, Thomas Drew and Bishop Mant are most closely associated with an intensive period of urban church extension in the 1830s and 1840s. The methods of James Morgan, a committed interdenominationalist, were informal but effective. He secured the support of Henry Cooke for the provision of a church with a low rate of seat rents in the Brown Street area. The two men then personally chose and secured a site and set up a fund-raising committee to make house-to-house collections.[31] The result of this bypassing of ecclesiastical bureaucracy was Townsend Street church, opened in 1833, and soon praised for introducing respectability as well as religion into an area formerly lacking both. The building of churches at Ballymacarrett (1836), York Street (1838) and College Square (1839) followed a similar pattern.[32] All were results of genuine attempts to accommodate the spiritual needs of the poor of the town by zealous clergy, materially and financially aided by generous laymen. At the same time, the Synod of Ulster, at its annual meetings, gave every encouragement to new buildings and asked for assurances from the government that all new congregations would be endowed.[33] As a result of the combined efforts of clergy, laity and synod, Belfast had a total of 15 churches connected with the Synod of Ulster by 1842.[34]

Within the Church of Ireland, Bishop Mant secured funds for the building of a church in College Square North, an area rapidly becoming a suburb without any of the necessary amenities. Christ Church with its 1,000 free sittings opened in July 1833, and the arrival of its new curate, Thomas Drew, proved a significant event in Belfast religion.[35] Intensely evangelical, energetic, innovative and often controversial, his efforts made the church into a centre for both religious fellowship and material aid.[36] While Mant may later have had cause to regret the outspoken zeal of this young clergyman, he proved an able champion of church extension. Drew, like Morgan, found that individual efforts and popular methods brought quicker results than formal procedures. After surveying the Belfast area with Archdeacon Mant, he began his campaign with a series of letters to the press. Appealing to those elements of Belfast society most concerned with social stability, he assured them that 'no town in Britain offers more abundant returns to minister, merchant and lawyer, for an outlay of prayer and contribution'.[37] His efforts resulted in a public meeting on the subject of church extension attended by leading clergy and laity in November 1838.[38] While the packed hall and the platform of dignitaries reflected general support for established institutions at a time of political tension, the participation of Methodist and Presbyterian clergy was typical of the shared concern occasioned by the sheer scale of urban problems throughout Britain at this time. The main beneficiary of this meeting was the newly formed Church Accommodation Society which made a significant contribution to episcopal church building during its short and controversial existence.[39]

In all denominations, the new religious fervour prompted an immense investment in human and material resources, reflected in additional Sabbath schools, prayer meetings, home visitations and the enlargement of churches. The augmentation of premises was also accompanied by an increase in the number of Sunday services offered to church-goers, and in the frequency of communion.[40] As urban society became more complex and concentrated, the churches were also able to fill an important, if transitional, social gap by attempting to meet the material as well as spiritual problems of their flocks. By offering charity and sociability – in the shape of loan funds, clothing funds, dispensaries and a proliferation of societies – churchmen hoped to make their facilities relevant and their theology meaningful.[41] A census of Christ Church's congregation in 1852 gives some evidence of the social groupings to which such endeavours appealed.[42] It suggests that the church catered for a large number of shoemakers, tailors, merchants and other small craftsmen, but not all were from the skilled elite of the working class. The attendance of millworkers, servants and labourers shows the success of Drew's evangelizing activities among the poorer inhabitants of the area. No doubt a large number of these adherents were attracted by the material benefits of Christ Church's various auxiliaries. Drew's methods had the advantage of involving the community more fully in the life of the church while also expressing the church's willingness to reach out to the everyday world of the people it served. Five years after its opening Christ Church had 400 regular attenders in its Sunday school and its dispensary received over 800 applications every year.[43]

Generally speaking, however, church attendance does not seem to have been a major priority of the lower classes, a tendency for which there were many reasons. Pride and tradition required potential church-goers to invest in at least a decent suit of clothes, and it seems that many of those who neglected public worship did so partly because poverty rendered them unable to meet the basic social demands of the occasion. It seems likely that those who did attend the churches were already trying to lift themselves to a position of social respectability. This suggestion is supported by clerical comments on the social and moral improvement consequent upon regular church attendance. In the church in Townsend Street, for example, Morgan claimed that the poor 'who went there rude and shabby . . . have so changed their habits under the power of the Word that they have become well dressed and well conducted, and have been turned from roughness to gentility'.[44] For a majority of slum dwellers, however, social distinctions, seating patterns and the cultural assumptions of those in control of the content of public worship, reinforced a sense of alienation which no amount of religious paternalism could hope to overcome.

MORAL REFORM AND SOCIAL REALITIES

The complex relationship between religious expression and popular culture suggests, however, that the full extent of religious influence cannot be measured purely in terms of church attendance or involvement in specifically religious functions. Thus, while the actual number of adherents to a committed evangelical life-style was always a minority in terms of percentage of population, its social creed penetrated deep into Ulster culture. In times of political insecurity and social stress, evangelicalism's strong emphasis on personal morality and its conservative social code came to be seen as major stabilizing factors. Against a background of rising Catholic nationalism, radical politics, secularization and industrialization, aristocrats, employers, clergy, churchmen and women, imbued with evangelical seriousness, attempted to propagate a scripture-based culture which upheld social and political stability. Spurred into action by a combination of missionary zeal and fear of an underclass of godless labourers, evangelical enthusiasm knew no limits. Its aim was the spiritual regeneration and 'moral elevation' of the lower classes of society and its weapons were temperance, education, sabbatarianism, charity and unrelenting moral campaigns. Through new agencies such as Sunday schools, temperance movements, town missions, tract and bible societies, as well as more traditional modes of control, evangelical leaders sought to promote 'higher and nobler ideals of life'. From pulpit and press, attacks were launched on a whole range of traditional leisure-time activities from drinking and dancing to theatre-going, cock-fighting and boxing. This pietistic campaign was thus a combination of cultural conflict and social control in which public respectability was generally interpreted as a reflection of personal morality. The extent to which these were in fact synonymous is highly debatable.

Motivated by evangelical zeal and social unease, tract distributors, city missioners, scripture readers and domestic visitors emerged to confront urban irreligion on its own squalid doorstep. In the busy dockside of the town, Bibles and tracts were distributed to emigrants and seamen by agents of the Belfast Religious Tract Society, founded in 1816.[45] Its publications supplied religious explanations for poverty and distress and sought to raise the religious and moral sentiments of the poor to a level beyond the excesses of drink and gambling in which so many sought comfort. Unfortunately, the impressive distribution figures tell us more about the industry of the society's agents than the effectiveness of the literature on its intended readers. It is unclear whether such titles as *The Danger of Delay*, *The Importance of Sobriety*, or *Honesty is the Best Policy* successfully competed with the cheap 'penny dreadfuls' which flooded the popular markets in the 1830s and 1840s.[46] In the effort to turn the hearts of rough working men to spiritual matters, women were frequently employed to visit labourers' homes and offer Bibles for sale at cheap weekly rates.[47] This ensured frequency of contact if not increased biblical knowledge.

More easy to measure, at least in terms of attendance, is the success of the Hibernian Sunday School Society in attracting young members. Not only ecclesiastical but the highest social and even commercial interests ardently supported a movement designed to promote respectable and morally uplifting habits among the uneducated.[48] Some idea of the response to these schools can be gleaned from the fact that in 1831 the proportion of Sunday scholars to population in Ulster was 1:14; in County Antrim it was 1:9.[49] Organizers in Belfast considered Sunday school work in terms of a mission and urged their agents to seek out children to swell their numbers. By 1820 Belfast had 20 schools associated with the Hibernian Sunday School Society, with 3,264 pupils and 274 teachers. Three years later, the Belfast Sunday School Union was formed to consolidate and extend Sunday school work in Belfast and the surrounding area. The reports of this organization indicate that the schools, which operated a regular system of visitation, were all situated in the town's most needy areas.[50]

All Protestant evangelicals agreed that Sunday schools were 'a means of eventually restoring political tranquillity to this long-distracted country'.[51] They worked for class harmony by stressing the 'mutual kindness and affection between rich and poor' exemplified in the bond of sympathy between the instructed and their (unpaid) teachers.[52] In addition to its specifically religious objects, the emphasis of the Sunday School Society was on instilling good manners, sound morals and respectable appearance.

While Sunday school managers had their own motives and expectations, however, they would not have achieved their outstanding degree of success if they had not been offering the lower orders something they needed and wanted in practical as well as spiritual terms. The utilitarian attributes of the Sunday school movement were particularly relevant to a society suffering the stresses of transition from rural to urban life. They offered educational and recreational facilities and a social substitute for the old rural relationships. Their educational provision, however rudimentary, was particularly important in the days before the establishment of a national system of elementary schools. With the mills and factories of the linen and cotton industries keeping many young people and even children in employment during weekdays, Sunday was often the only day in which any kind of educational pursuit was possible.[53] The Sunday schools, particularly in the early days, reached out to the very poorest elements in society. For listening to the scripture passages and the 'theology of poverty' preached by the teachers, the scholars received in return, warmth, shelter, education, sometimes material aid in the form of shoes or clothes, intermittent outings and entertainments, and – not least – a faith which helped them to cope with the vicissitudes of life.[54] The fact that many schools were initiated by those working and living in the community, further suggests that they were less a form of social manipulation than is commonly supposed. This matches the conclusions of English social historians who suggest that Sunday schools flourished because 'working-class parents wanted the education they provided, and generally endorsed the values that they taught'.[55] The benefits of literacy, cheapness and entertainment outweighed the obvious disadvantages of religious paternalism.

In wider social terms, Sunday schools made a distinctive contribution to working-class culture through their anniversary celebrations, street parades, Whitsun outings, book prizes and benefit societies. Moreover, these activities attracted a loyal band of activists whose lives were transformed by the weekly rhythms of preparation, prayer and planning. The extent to which Sunday schools recruited a new generation of committed church-goers is, however, less clear. The evidence suggests that religious allegiance fluctuated with age and situation. It does seem that in times of religious revival, evangelical efforts in the Sunday schools were rewarded by a significant rise in congregational numbers. W. R. Ward is nevertheless right to state that the 'Sunday school was the only religious institution which the nineteenth-century public in the mass had any intention of using'.[56]

Information on the beliefs and experiences of those who shunned official religious facilities is more difficult to find. The records of the Belfast Town Mission, 'a moral engine for the benefit of the poor, the untaught and neglected population of our town', offer valuable insights into popular urban religious attitudes in the first half of the nineteenth century.[57] The mission, formed as an interdenominational society in 1827 by the Presbyterian minister John Bryce, appointed agents to visit the poor in their own houses, to converse with them on religious matters, to read tracts or scripture portions and to issue invitations to churches and Sunday schools. The reports of the agents, as they went from house to house in the crowded back streets, reveal the pitiful degree of social and moral deprivation prevailing in these hovels. The society also established 'stations' which were visited by local clergy on two evenings a week for bible-reading and tract distribution. These meetings were held in the poorest and most overcrowded parts of the town in areas formerly deprived of any kind of religious enlightenment such as Brown Street, Sandy Row, Cromac Street, Little Donegall Street and Mill Row.

Believing that environment was responsible for spiritual and moral decline, responsible citizens presented the urban poor with 'higher and nobler ideals of life . . . compelling them, by persuasion and example, to live up to them'. However, the records of the mission's visitors suggest that the response was more complex. Although their efforts often met with opposition or hostility, they were frequently made welcome, and their conversations with the 'rough' working class often revealed a variety of religious experience, no less potent because of its informal nature. Many people who had been in the habit of attending religious venues in their youth gave up in middle age, either because of migration and lack of facilities or simply as a natural result of the ageing process. It was nevertheless evident that religion could retain its emotional hold while losing its institutional framework. Bible-reading and religious conversations offered instruction, nostalgia, diversion and comfort in the midst of bleak poverty. The mission agents had some success in persuading backsliders to attend the local 'stations' which organized religious services outside the rigid social milieu of the church. Many of those who retained a grasp of what they considered the 'essentials' of religion, however, displayed no interest whatsoever in doctrinal orthodoxy. Their vague belief that a generally well-intentioned life, lived free of the worst debaucheries, would be rewarded, was more prevalent than open scepticism or unbelief, and was also more difficult for the churches to counteract.[58]

It is in fact clear that, while the flexibility exercised by evangelical clergy of all denominations brought the gospel message to many overcrowded and destitute areas, these belated exertions ultimately failed to keep pace with both the growth of population and the separation of social classes. Thus the Reverend William O'Hanlon asked in 1853,

> How few of the church-going, orderly, affluent members of this city, have ever visited, or perhaps even heard of, such places as Brady's Row, Green-Court, Henry-Square, Johnny's-Entry, Poplar Court, Grattan Court . . . mostly crowded with human beings in the lowest stages of degradation.[59]

It would be a mistake to underestimate, therefore, the profound cultural gap between the 'respectable' religiosity of the middle and upper classes and the labouring poor. In a parallel study of London's City Mission Donald Lewis has highlighted contemporary awareness of 'the isolation of social classes one from another'.[60] Separated by urban geography, cultural values, social status, wealth and, at times, feelings of resentment, the urban working classes were not attracted by forms of religion which seemed to exacerbate, not diminish such distinctions. While ministers and scripture readers denounced the manifold distractions which kept the poor of the town from church, including theatre-going, gambling and drinking, it was equally likely that the difficulties of rearing a family in circumstances of extreme poverty left little time or inclination for a religious culture which demanded not only piety, but cleanliness, sobriety and respectability. The evangelical insistence on identifying and denouncing social and personal sin, therefore, alienated rather than attracted those with only limited opportunities for cheap entertainment and brief hours of escapism.

Determined to serve as the public conscience – whether the public liked it or not – the clergy of Belfast, with evangelical prompting, displayed an impressive commitment to the task of moral reform. Thomas Drew, in an appeal to the press signed by every clergyman of the established church in Belfast, stressed the importance of the press in the diffusion of ideas, and asked for a show of support in the cause of religion by the exclusion from the papers of notices referring to the stage, the boxing-room and the cockpit. Drew felt that drama in particular was

> the most dangerous part of our literature. Throughout the entire range of all plays an anti-Christian principle is maintained. Notwithstanding many splendid specimens of moral precepts, invitations to what is called virtue, and exhibitions of sin bringing forth death – yet among them all the leading principle is, that man

is, or may be, his own Saviour – But when these writings are transferred to the stage, there, indeed, do our objections become stronger a thousand fold. All the accompaniments are objectionable, the hours, the assembly, the excitement, the base language of the profligate portion of the audience, the indecent exposure of the persons of those called fashionable, the songs, the dancing, and the levity of conduct and dress of the figurantes. Nor are we to forget 'the poor players'; do we ever think of our being auxiliary to their spiritual destruction? How few escape privation and sin? How few of the female dramatis personae escape pollution of manner and life![61]

The Methodists, of course, consistently voiced their disapproval of 'frivolous' recreational activities and exhorted their members, with some degree of success, to refrain from such 'sinful amusements' as attending balls, plays and horse-races.[62] But of all the attacks on working-class diversion, that on drinking was perhaps the most sustained and ardent. Drunkenness was regarded as the prime cause of sexual immorality, gambling, broken homes, poverty and social strife, and was so prevalent that it was regarded as 'the national curse of Ireland'.[63] As with so many Ulster movements, the impetus for temperance societies originated in America, was taken up by local clergy of various denominations and, with the support of influential laymen, spread rapidly throughout the province.[64] By 1833, only four years after the first plans were published, there were 15,000 members of temperance societies in Ulster.[65] The emphasis of these societies was on moderation rather than total abstention.[66] The teetotal movement which began in 1834 was regarded as extremist, and middle-class fears of its radicalism appeared justified when Father Mathew's popular Roman Catholic crusade against 'all intoxicating liquors' became linked in the public mind with O'Connell's Repeal movement.[67]

While the records of churches and missions suggest a unified stance on the part of the religious versus the irreligious on the question of alcoholic consumption, there were several distinguishable approaches. The middle classes, while publicly supporting the values of sobriety, were not always keen to align themselves with the cause of temperance. The Reverend Dr John Edgar, an orator of some ability and founder of the movement in Ulster, found himself abused and ridiculed at his first campaign meetings.[68] The editor of *The Guardian* refused to print a public letter announcing the formation of the new society, and the members of Edgar's church declined the use of their meeting-house.[69] This indicates how the consumption of alcohol was considered acceptable by 'respectable' citizens. It should also be remembered that Ireland was the first European country to attempt such a venture, and that the element of novelty was itself a disincentive for conservative citizens.

Nor did all those who supported the temperance movement do so from purely religious motives. The basic underlying impulse, the idea of 'improvement', was central to evangelical ideology, but there were others who saw in the benefits arising from a more sober, industrious and thinking peasantry, the basis of political, as well as personal, advancement, and independence. Not only landlords and evangelicals, but employers, radicals and reformers in general supported the 'improving' movement, each viewing the advantages of a sober working class in a different light. The interests of employers in promoting the sobriety of their workforce is self-evident and in Belfast mill-owners, manufacturers and merchants promoted the cause.[70] Catholic nationalists were also convinced that the self-respect and self-esteem arising from sobriety would advance not only moral but political aspirations.[71] Self-denial was thus seen as the foundation of more than mere religious reform. The course of the temperance campaign shows how popular movements, particularly those with a religious basis, were drawn into wider Irish political concerns. Spokesmen of every colour and creed exploited the popular appeal of such reform movements without capitulating to their essentially religious intentions.[72]

But while a decline in the popularity of whiskey-drinking and general drunkenness was noted by many visitors and commissioners in this period, the problem of drunkenness in Ulster was by no means resolved. Many thousands remained unmoved by the crusade, while the resolutions of others were all too short-lived.[73] Nor should all the responsibility for the reported decline in alcoholic consumption be attributed to the endeavours of Edgar and Mathew. The introduction of revenue police and the reduction of duty on whiskey were undoubtedly significant factors in reducing the number of 'shebeens' and the local customs and festivities which surrounded them, while the increased supervision of 'improving' landlords and their agents was a further effective deterrent.[74] Evangelicalism with its network of aristocratic, gentry and clerical supporters exercised considerable social influence, built an organizational structure and offered an alternative subculture; but it was also a beneficiary of more specifically secular trends. Outside the polemics of religious reformers, the temperance movement can more realistically be seen as part of a wider process of adjustment to socioeconomic trends. Illicit distillation and periodic bouts of excessive drinking were aspects of Irish culture which were giving way to more legitimate and socially acceptable modes of behaviour. Visits to holy wells, the custom of the Irish Cry, cock-fighting, card-playing and dancing were also under pressure,[75] not only because of the vigilance of both Catholic and Protestant clergy, but because of increasing demands on time and money as the decline of the linen industry forced many rural dwellers to concentrate their energies on farming, while rapid urbanization changed the life-style of the town population.[76] Evangelicalism was then both the agent *and* the beneficiary of other changes in the Ulster economy and society in this period, but the latter was probably more important.

In an increasingly pluralistic and secular society, it was recognized that to engage successfully in competition with popular cultural activities it was necessary to offer not only morally, but socially acceptable alternatives. The success of the temperance movements – Catholic and Protestant – depended largely on their creation of alternative social outlets to the pubs or drinking-houses by providing an opportunity for social intercourse and recreational diversion, through tea-drinking, reading-rooms and participation in bands, dances and processions.[77] By the later nineteenth century the churches had established a formidable array of denominational improvement societies, which, along with a host of voluntary organizations such as the YMCA and the Boys' Brigade, offered a respectable alternative to the fleshly temptations of urban life.

The relation between the essentially 'religious' and 'traditional' aspects of popular culture is, of course, complex. The two were never completely separate, but interacted and merged at many points, particularly during the ritualized highlights of the personal and social calendar, over which the church claimed authority but which reached deep into folk history – birth, death, marriage, Easter and Christmas.[78] There was often a good deal of tension between clerical and popular attitudes to the celebration of these occasions. Easter Monday outings to Cavehill with drinking, dancing, eating and singing, for example, were the despair of religious leaders,[79] but when Thomas Drew and other Sunday school managers set out to promote a 'moral option', they wisely compromised by investing their religious celebrations with all the noise and colour of more traditional festivities.[80] Sunday school anniversaries and the opening of new churches were also celebrated in this way in an attempt to offer a lively alternative to the temptations of the new age. The process of modernization – in the shape of cheap Sunday railway excursions, for example – prompted a vigilance on the part of the clergy more suggestive of the urgency of the campaign than of its success.[81]

It is already clear that, despite evangelical intentions and claims, a series of compromises and mutual accommodations was a greater actuality than the supposed imposition of a code of behaviour on an unwilling but passive section of society. The complex interaction between belief and practice can most clearly be seen in the emergence of 'respectability' as a central feature in Protestant culture.[82] The desire for upward mobility on the part of the working classes is too often overlooked as an explanation for the encroachment of evangelical principles on popular culture. For many Ulster Protestants the temporal advantages of moral elevation were self-evident and personal ambitions were justified by the Puritan idea that worldly position was a reflection of divine approbation.[83] Religion and respectability were thus mutually reinforcing, and divisions between classes were perhaps less distinct than those between types of social behaviour and values which cut across class boundaries. The churches offered support for an orderly and self-respecting way of life which had tangible benefits. For wives and mothers, and for members of the lower and middle classes wishing to improve their situation, the virtues advocated by evangelical leaders – frugality, temperance and education – had temporal as well as religious advantages.[84]

For many Ulster Protestants Belfast's industrial expansion and relative prosperity were viewed as a direct consequence of its religious and ethnic base.[85] To what extent religion played a day-to-day role in the workplace is, however, particularly difficult to determine in this period. For many employers, whatever the depth of their personal religious conviction, evangelicalism supplied an ethic, based on scriptural principles, which dealt with the economic realities of life. Poverty was regarded as a warning to the rich and proud of the instability of life and a reminder of their social duties. The poor themselves would 'never cease out of the land', but would be rendered contented, if not rich, by biblical teaching.[86] Paternalistic practices were thus justified while attempts to assert class interests were seen not only as socially and politically radical, but as unscriptural and, indeed, immoral. Working Men's Combinations were therefore regarded as 'the greatest of all possible evils', not least because of the practice of holding meetings in taverns.

In the north, weavers were generally regarded as politically radical, but the decline of this class coincided with the rise of an urban workforce increasingly divided along sectarian lines.[87] The relation between sectarianism and trade unionism in the first half of the nineteenth century remains unclear. The traditional view is that with many trade unions tied to the Orange Order, workers, foremen, managers and factory owners were linked in a combination against Roman Catholicism which undermined the development of class-consciousness.[88] Modern economic historians see this as an oversimplification. Henry Patterson, for example, points to a variety of tensions existing within and between sections of the workforce, suggesting that religious and sectarian factors would 'at most, have exacerbated these problems at particular times of heightened political tension'.[89]

If sectarianism in the workforce undermined the development of class-consciousness so too did employer support for moral elevation as an antidote to social and industrial disharmony. Employers and manufacturers supported temperance, Sunday school, town mission and revival movements, and joined with workers in a variety of paternalistic and benevolent ventures. The Belfast Working Class Association for the Promotion of General Improvement, for example, sought to improve the character and conditions of working men by circulating 'useful, moral and entertaining' works and by stressing the benefits of temperance and thrift.[90] In its attention to the rights and duties between employer and employed it made the familiar link between personal morality and social harmony. The Protestant work ethic was likewise reaffirmed, with the assertion that 'idleness is the parent of crime and the forerunner of poverty'.[91]

The clergy of Belfast, similarly concerned to encourage the interdependence of the classes, united with the employers in these efforts. When a group of churchmen set out to develop an 'economic doctrine of religion' to deal with the commercial realities of nineteenth-century life, the scriptures once again offered inspiration and example. In a collection of essays entitled Gold and the Gospel, they reminded the material beneficiaries of industry of their social duties, stressing the responsibility of man as God's steward, and urging a more systematic exercise of benevolence.[92] To what extent evangelical theory was put into practice by employers is difficult to determine, though the great proliferation of voluntary societies concerned with social as well as spiritual problems in Belfast in the second half of the century suggests at least a nominal commitment to the principle of charity. [93] Nor is it easy to assess the extent to which paternalistic and benevolent movements influenced working men and women. A combination of deference, moral coercion, apathy and faith may have encouraged some within the lower classes to accept the inevitability of their place on a predetermined social scale. But there is hard evidence to suggest that neither religious paternalism nor appeals for religious solidarity were wholly successful in inducing the Protestant working class to know their place. In a series of Belfast elections before the first Home Rule Bill, for example, Belfast Conservatives had a hard job controlling the self-assertion of working-class Orangemen both in the selection of candidates and in subsequent voting behaviour. [94]

PROTESTANT AND CATHOLIC

While evangelical clergy perceived their role to be that of supporters of social and cultural cohesion, religion – particularly of the aggressive evangelical variety – could also be a divisive force, both in the family and the community. Rifts between parents and children and husbands and wives over the expression of their belief were common, and pious attitudes undoubtedly alienated a significant section of the working-class community. In wider social terms, the anti-Catholicism of Ulster's evangelical clergy ensured their prominence in the community's most enduring cultural conflict. A dispute in the early 1840s between Bishop Mant of Down and Connor and the evangelical clergy and laity of his diocese is revealing of local clerical attitudes to this more controversial aspect of evangelical faith.

The debate centred around accusations of the former's 'Puseyism', and must be seen within the wider framework of the ecclesiastical changes advocated by the clergy of the Oxford Movement which were regarded as popish by ultra-Protestants. None could deny that Mant had repeatedly spoken out against the doctrines of Rome; 'Against the Romish corruptions I have again and again raised my voice; from my Cathedral seat as well as in the pulpit, and by the press, in Charges to my clergy, as well as in sermons and other publications.' [95] However, his 'high church' sensibilities were equally evident. Critics denounced his 'prelacy', his insistence from the pulpit and in the press that 'nothing without the bishop was allowed', [96] and his unfortunate penchant for antagonizing Presbyterians. But it was the formation of the Church Architecture Society, 'hatched in secret and making its debut in a single day', in October 1842, on which evangelical opposition was most strongly focused. The new society appeared to Mant as a logical addition to the Church Accommodation Society by displaying a scholarly interest in architectural antiquity and by concerning itself with the style and furnishings of new buildings. [97] In the eyes of his parochial clergy, however, the new society was introducing, in what were already perilous times, 'Popish novelties, under the guise of antiquity'.[98] Mant was impeccably consistent in his high churchman-ship. His scholarly expertise was frequently exercised in defence of episcopacy, the liturgy and various aspects of public worship. His clergy, however, regarded his scholarly attributes and high-minded Anglican subtleties as inappropriate to the needs of the church in nineteenth-century Ulster. Their anti-Catholic convictions were grounded in local political and social realities rather than in architectural taste and liturgical nuances. To such men, Mant's views were suspiciously close to the polemics of the Oxford 'heretics'. Thomas Drew felt that Puseyism and Prelatism could 'damage Ireland and peril a conservative government'. In a letter to Emerson Tennent, Drew expressed the opinion that Mant should be restrained or translated.

> Bishop Mant is an Ultra, honest, learned, active in bookmaking and unsurpassed in letter-writing, but unnaturally timid and very accessible to flattery: he lives in a world of his own; chiefly of relatives and friends, who love him for his amicable private qualities and for his favours bestowed upon themselves. He and they go upon the error that Ireland is made up of churchmen or of such as ought-to-be churchmen. He judges of men from books and fulminates from his palace as securely as if there were no inflammatory elements around him.[99]

The Reverend William McIlwaine, vicar of St George's in Belfast, on whose recommendation Drew had been brought to the town, also regarded his bishop as 'weak and misguided, unable to distinguish between the coexisting and closely-allied Ultra-Churchmanship, and a tendency to the errors of Rome'.[100] McIlwaine launched an attack on Mant in the pages of the *Belfast Commercial Telegraph*. His opposition to the Church Architecture Society was supported by many local clergy and by a number of influential laymen. The affiliation of the society with the Cambridge Camden Society associated it, it was claimed, with the doctrinal errors of the Tractarians. This, and Mant's acceptance of the Camden Society's tracts – which offended by such details as calling the communion table an altar – were regarded as exhibitions of an 'heretical tendency'.

In February 1843, Mant was presented with a memorial from the clergy and laity of his diocese, expressing alarm at his activities and requesting him to withdraw from the Architecture Society.[101] The 1,300 signatures included the names of a peer of the realm, an MP, 11 deputy lieutenants, 40 JPs and representatives of the legal and medical professions, as well as private gentlemen, merchants, bankers, tradesmen, artisans and yeomen. The petition reflected the genuine concern of men who feared the steady encroachment of Catholicism in every aspect of political and social life. Mant based his reply, however, on the question of church discipline alone and refused to 'be placed under the ban of any of his clergy'.[102] The cultural distance between the bishop and his parochial clergy was great, and in the event it was not the Church Architecure Society but the highly successful Church Accommodation Society which was dissolved as a result of this clash between evangelical and high churchmanship. Mant's attempts to force the continuation of the Accommodation Society were to no avail. Its supporters felt that its name was blackened by Mant's chairmanship, and that lack of unity resulting from his activities 'impaired the efforts and impeded the further progress' of church extension work:

> the harmony and confidence exhibited at the great meeting in 1838 no longer existed. Since that year, the baneful influence of the Romanizing party in the Church of England had sadly increased to the perversion from the truth of many among both the clergy and the laity. It is not surprising, much less censurable, that earnest Christian men, alarmed at such detriment to the faith, should regard with suspicion, any approach to sentiment or practice which had wrought such evil.[103]

While this debate was little more than a hiccup in the continuing merger between evangelical and orthodox interests, it clearly showed the extent to which anti-Catholicism had taken a hold of Ulster's parochial clergy. It was perhaps this aspect of Ulster evangelicalism which gave it a real foothold in working–class culture, for in succeeding generations sectarian conflict kept religious issues, if not religious devotion, to the forefront of Belfast life.

Popular revivalism was institutionalized by this second generation of evangelical clerics who conceived of their duty as extending beyond the boundaries of their parish, and to include the conversion of erring papists. Henry Cooke retained his position as popular spokesman of Presbyterian conservatism, while Thomas Drew saw the Church of Ireland as a missionary church and himself as 'a missionary in his own field'.[104] He clearly expected all Protestants to unite against 'the fearful inroads which infidelity and Romanism are making upon the common truths and common cause'.[105] As a member of the Orange Order, Drew frequently invited the controversial preacher, the Reverend Mortimer O'Sullivan, to speak at fund-raising services in Christ Church. O'Sullivan, rector of Killyman, County Armagh from 1827, was endowed with all the 'furious bigotry' of the convert.[106] He called on the Protestants of Ulster to unite against the growing authority of the Roman Catholic Church in Ireland.[107] His appearances in Christ Church thus had a political as well as religious appeal and were sure to heighten local tension. Drew himself further popularized the Protestant cause by transforming religious occasions into community celebrations with flags flying and children singing as they marched in street processions.[108] In 1854, under his personal leadership, Christ Church Protestant Association was formed to regain all the ground lost by Protestantism since Catholic Emancipation. The association supported not only the repeal of this act, but the withdrawal of Maynooth grants, the abolition of nunneries and the dissolution of the National Education Board.[109]

Although often rebuffed by their fellow churchmen, Drew and Cooke represented a tradition of religious and political leadership which became an integral part of the Ulster tradition. In every generation, the anti-Catholic polemics of a vociferous minority of religious leaders had given a controversial cutting edge to Ulster Protestantism. Faced with an increasingly articulate Catholic presence, late eighteenth-century Methodists, the promoters of the Second Reformation, and – in the mid-nineteenth century – popular Belfast preachers such as Drew, 'roaring' Hugh Hanna, William McIlwaine and Thomas Roe, interpreted their religious duty in terms of direct confrontations with the 'Man of Sin'. Aggressively negative and socially divisive, this aspect of evangelicalism, deeply rooted in Puritan tradition, had a popular appeal and political significance which ensured its centrality in Ulster Protestant culture. The emotive rhetoric of open-air preachers played on traditional sectarian fears and frequently resulted in community friction. In the fields of south Ulster and the streets of Belfast, Protestants who never attended church were warned of imminent dangers to their heritage and supplied with a set of biblical symbols and images which raised their fears of Catholicism above the immediate local circumstances of jobs and housing. The perceived threat to traditional Protestant supremacy was presented not only in terms of seventeenth-century history, but as a crusade to uphold biblical truth against the onslaught of Rome and its agents in Ireland. Open-air sermons were, of course, designed to be more spontaneous and emotive than those addressed to pious church-goers on a Sunday morning. The congregation was also less easy to control. Those loitering on the streets, glad of a diversion and finding an immediate resonance in the preachers' message, responded directly and violently to its anti-Catholic content. Trouble-makers on both sides of the religious divide turned such occasions into riotous examples of evangelicalism's most pernicious influence.

The summer of 1857 was particularly noteworthy for this kind of populist quasi-religious activity. On this occasion it was a sermon preached by Thomas Drew which seemed to spark off the rioting, although since it was the 12th of July, and the traditional outlet for Orange celebration was banned by the Party Processions Act, feelings were undoubtedly running high even before he commenced his sermon.[110] Drew, Grand Chaplain of the Orange Order, and curate of a church situated between the Catholic Pound and Protestant Sandy Row, conceded nothing to the delicacy of the situation. It is difficult to view his sermon – a glorification of Protestantism and a vivid portrayal of popish persecutions – as anything other than inflammatory:

> Of old times lords of high degree, with their own hands, strained on the rack the limbs of the delicate Protestant women, prelates dabbled in the gore of their helpless victims. The cells of the Pope's prisons were paved with human gore and human hair. . . . The Word of God makes all plain; puts to eternal shame the practices of persecutors, and stigmatizes with enduring reprobation the arrogant pretences of Popes and the outrageous dogmata of their blood-stained religion.[111]

The effect of such graphic images on an uneducated congregation preparing for a day's celebration of their heritage requires little imagination. With

Catholics already expecting trouble, hostility and suspicion on both sides erupted in a week of violence, for which it was felt Drew carried at least some responsibility. When the Commissioners of Inquiry into the riot published their report a year later, they included his well-publicized sermon in their evidence and directed the attention of the Lord Lieutenant to its provocative nature.[112]

In mid-August, after weeks of tension, the Belfast Parochial Mission began a series of open-air services at the town's custom house steps, popular site for political and religious speech-makers. Open-air preaching was an innovation for Church of Ireland imcumbents and this particular project, instigated by Drew at Christ Church, proved short-lived but controversial.[113] Disturbances following Thomas Roe's sermon on 'Conversion' led to the cancellation of future meetings, but for the more militant spokesmen of Protestantism, this move smacked of a weak and dangerous defeatism. The *Belfast Newsletter* stated that

> The Romish mobs have triumphed in our town. The preaching of the Gospel in our streets to the destitute, ragged poor, is put down. Belfast now ranks with Kilkenny, or Cork, or Limerick. In these Romish cities, where priests are regnant and their mobs omnipotent and the authorities bow to their behest, no Protestant minister dare lift his voice in the streets or highways to proclaim the peaceful message of the Cross – he would be stoned or murdered.[114]

Hugh Hanna, minister of Berry Street Presbyterian church, and well-known for his outspoken anti-Catholicism, determined to assert the right of Protestants to preach the gospel. Despite requests from the Belfast Presbytery to avoid conflict, he preached to a large and excited crowd in Corporation Street on 6 September. Not surprisingly, this controversial act set alight the still smouldering resentments of both sections of the community, and resulted in renewed and bloody sectarian violence. Assertions of peaceful intention, accompanied by defiant and emotive rhetoric, had an ambiguity which was not lost on mobs of labouring men seeking both explanation and justification for a now traditional communal conflict. On such occasions anti-Catholicism was a major factor in forging relationship between churches and community in which more overtly 'religious' values played little part.

But while ethnic loyalty was no doubt important, it was never all pervasive. Competing and sometimes overlapping loyalties to denominations, employers, neighbourhoods and centres of recreation, though often neglected, were just as influential in creating the rich texture of working-class social relationships. For those who embraced it, evangelicalism's conservative social code provided a framework of stability in a period when the rapid progress of migration, urbanization and industrialization generated new tensions in the social structure of the northeast. Through moral agents, education, temperance, self-improvement societies, tract distribution, domestic visitation and a host of other devices this activist minority made a substantial contribution to the social and cultural life of Belfast in the first half of the nineteenth century.

But their relative success – not to be exaggerated – was due not only to their activism but to the social utility of such views for a society undergoing rapid transformation and in which religious and ethnic loyalties were strong, at least in times of crisis. Beyond that, evangelicalism was an important catalyst in the creation of a culture emphasizing voluntary organizations, mutual and self-improvement, religion and respectability, and Protestant identity. Ironically, but for some of the same reasons, Irish Catholicism was steaming on the same course.

Two problems dominated the Belfast Catholic community from at least the 1820s. The first was to make suitable religious provision for the fast-increasing Catholic population and the second was a settled conviction that right down the social scale, from wealthy merchants to unskilled labourers, Belfast Catholics were very much second-class citizens by comparison with their Protestant counterparts. Logistical problems of church building and parochial organization dominated the episcopates of William Crolly, Cornelius Denvir and Patrick Dorrian, who were successively bishops of Down and Connor and parish priests of Belfast from 1825 to 1885. Dorrian's career in particular as curate, coadjutor bishop and bishop is inextricably bound up with the growth and shape of the Catholic community in Belfast.[115] As a supporter of O'Connell and Parnell, and as a lifelong critic of Fenianism and violence, Dorrian was both a stout-hearted churchman and a vigorous constitutional nationalist who disliked Orangeism and evangelicalism in equal measure. The mission of the Catholic Church under his leadership was nevertheless in many respects a mirror image of the Protestant evangelicalism it opposed. More churches, more priests, more services, more confessions, more religious orders, more Sisters of Mercy, more temperance crusades, more self-improvement societies, more dispensaries and orphanages, more city missions, more religious tracts, and less craving subservience to the government, the Belfast corporation and the Protestant community. Thus in both Roman Catholic and evangelical Protestant communities there was a renewed emphasis on priests and ministers, a self-conscious reliance on female piety, a strong belief in the religious and social utility of education, an admirable commitment to holy charity and a relentless pursuit of religious respectability which almost certainly increased the gap between 'rough' and 'respectable' cultures.

Of more importance than shared themes for Protestant contemporaries was the way in which the growth of the Catholic community served to confirm Protestant stereotypes of the Roman Church. Since there were far fewer Catholic churches than Protestant ones per head of population the former were generally larger and more imposing. Moreover, because of the absence of a substantial mercantile community, the Catholic Church was unable to rely on middle-class beneficence for church-building and had to depend instead on more assiduous collections to finance building costs. Protestants interpreted the former as triumphalism and the latter as evidence of a ruthless church grinding down its humble adherents. In addition, the striking growth in the number of priests and religious orders fuelled the old fears of priestcraft, and the import of italianate devotional forms in the later Victorian period further persuaded evangelical puritans of the essentially foreign and superstitious nature of the Roman Church. Protestants thought they saw a growing, grasping, aggressive and intolerant church. Ironically, the correspondence of Catholic leaders in Belfast tells a rather different and more defensive tale. Preoccupied by high leakage rates, nervous of Protestant proselytism, burdened by huge debts, fearful of Orange excesses and often divided among themselves on issues of politics, strategy and aspiration, the Belfast Catholic leadership resembled anything but the aggressive monolith of Protestant imagination.

That these religious cultures had the capacity for conflict is self-evident, but it is the multi-layered nature of such conflict which made it such a recurring feature of Belfast life in the nineteenth century. Points of conflict were legion.[116] Open-air sermons, Orange parades, election hustings, funeral processions, the great Protestant protest meetings in the city's Botanical Gardens, Catholic festivals such as the feast day of the Assumption, celebrations of historical events and transferred tensions from the surrounding countryside, all contributed to riots at one time or another, especially in the years between 1857 and 1886. All came with their processions, effigies, slogans, party tunes, banners and rituals. To a remarkable extent clubs and processions became a way of life. There were already 32 Orange lodges in Belfast by the 1830s and parades in a special way marked out ethnic and religious territory. Where you could 'walk' you could control. Underpinning episodic outbreaks of riotous behaviour were irreconcilable disputes over government policy and seemingly interminable local wrangles over powers and privileges. Predominantly Protestant boards of guardians administered workhouses for predominantly Catholic paupers amid allegations of proselytism, a predominantly Protestant magistracy administered the law, a predominantly Protestant corporation allocated civic amenities and predominantly Protestant voters elected Protestant MPs. Even the allocation of graveyards occasioned sectarian animosity; Belfast was as much a divided city in death as it was in life.

Evangelical religion was not of course responsible for the demographic, social and political divisions which lay at the heart of popular disturbances in nineteenth-century Belfast, but it did supply a new generation of religio-political orators, an inherently competitive religious ideology, new occasions for conflict such as church parades and open-air preaching, and a powerful religious legitimation for more material conflicts. Part of this legitimation was a concentration on religious symbols and images dating back to the Reformation. One of the most interminable public controversies in Belfast, for example, was carried out between the evangelical rector of St George's, William McIlwaine, and the Roman Catholic Bishop of Down and Connor, Patrick Dorrian, over the alleged burning of a Bible by a Priest in a small Irish town.[117] In this case the incident's obvious triviality was massively overshadowed by the potent symbol of a burning Bible for Protestants already convinced of the pernicious influence of the Roman Church and its priests. What should not be underestimated is the sheer power of religious symbols, clerical rhetoric and crude stereotyping in further dividing communities already separated by urban geography and religious loyalties.

Although the ethnic and religious divisions of Belfast have come to be thought of as unique because of their persistence and longevity, they were by no means untypical of nineteenth-century cities in Britain, Europe and North America. Population migrations, challenges to *ancien régime* established churches and economic and social inequalities produced different configurations of religious conflict in scores of western cities in this period. It was not unusual, therefore, for religion to be a major component of the residential, occupational and ethnographic divisions of large cities, nor was it unusual for different religious traditions to keep alive separate heritages in their festivals and riots. Even Belfast's notorious 'Orange' and 'Green' disturbances were reproduced in recognizable forms in Glasgow, Liverpool and New York. In such cities the most avid practitioners of rioting, as in modern soccer riots, were commonly those with the least interest in the activity occasioning the dispute. Religious rioting in Belfast was essentially about tribal power not religious affiliations. But if Belfast was not unique in its violent divisions, a variety of circumstances made its problems particularly intractable. Not only was its population divided by ethnicity, religion, politics and national loyalty, but its economic power and social influence were unequally shared between its rival traditions. Moreover, Belfast was but a populous microcosm of the entire province of Ulster, and Ulster was itself a provincial anomaly in the island of Ireland. In addition, population movements in the eighteenth and nineteenth centuries ensured that Irish problems were given a global dimension. In short, not only was Belfast a divided city in the Victorian period, but its divisions were not easily confined to, or solved within, its own city boundaries. In one sense its difficulties were densely concentrated in the slums of its labouring poor, but in another they were diffused quite beyond manageable proportions. Belfast was not a uniquely divided nineteenth-century city, but the cumulative burdens of its people's histories made it peculiarly vulnerable to a long conflict.

[7]

'Born to serve': women and evangelical religion

. . . that women adorn themselves in modest apparel, with shamefacedness and
sobriety; not with broided hair, or gold, or pearls, or costly array; But (which
becometh women professing godliness) with good works. Let the woman learn
in silence with all subjection. (1 Timothy 2:9–11)

Rise up, ye women that are at ease. (Isaiah 32:9)

The patriarchal nature of mainstream religious organizations has, until
recently, been reflected in the exclusion of women from church government
and from playing all but a passive role in its most important rituals.
Paradoxically, attendance statistics suggest that, at congregational level at
least, female participation is predominant. Moreover, recent historical
studies, concerned to shift the focus from the institutional and political aspects
of religion to its broader social and cultural content, have drawn attention to
the variety of ways in which women experienced religion and have stressed
their important contribution to the religious community. While the growing
interest in the role of women in history generally has been impeded by the
deficiency and flaws of historical material, the prolific sources of denominations such as Methodism and the Society of Friends and the wealth of material
left by voluntary religious agencies, have proved irresistible to historians.
Although in terms of personal and social constraints, evangelicalism's
repression of sexuality, emphasis on domestic virtues and opposition to many
forms of popular entertainment, had a restricting effect on the contribution of
women to the wider secular society, there is much evidence to support the
suggestion that evangelical religion was more important than feminism in
enlarging women's sphere of action during the nineteenth century.

The purpose of this chapter is to offer some preliminary observations on
the role of women within eighteenth-century religious communities and to

show how they achieved a temporary position of influence in the early stages of the evangelical revival which was not sustained into the nineteenth century when male ministers, trustees and administrators regained full control. By that stage, however, a vast array of voluntary religious associations had opened up new opportunities for female endeavour which did not encroach on the activities of men. This was an important and largely uncontested qualification, for while the boundaries within which women's influence was permitted were stretched for essentially pragmatic purposes, they were neither redrawn nor discarded.

Predictably, it was not in the well-established denominations but in the new versions of popular, pietistic Protestantism which emerged throughout seventeenth- and eighteenth-century Europe that women's contribution became more visible. Although exhibiting considerable organizational and theological diversity, religious communities such as Quakers, Moravians and Methodists had some common attributes which both attracted and utilized female adherents. In their forms of worship, for example, there was more emphasis on emotion and experience than on tradition and formality. Moreover, with greater reliance placed on inner truth than on received dogma, the role of a mediatorial clergy was undermined as that of the laity was simultaneously enhanced. New organizational structures and, in the early stages at least, the lack of suitable meeting-places outside the home, also encouraged a degree of flexibility which gave women easier access to a range of religious functions. Thus, Keith Thomas states that 'women were numerically extremely prominent among the separatists' of the English Civil War period and that Quakers had 'more women than men among their recognized ministers'.[1] Similarly, Earl Kent Brown states that women were in a majority, 'perhaps a substantial majority', within eighteenth-century Methodism, an assessment confirmed by recent statistical surveys.[2] Surviving class membership lists of the Moravian community in Dublin in the 1740s tell a similar tale.[3]

Without having accurate information on the proportions of men and women within the established Protestant denominations in this period it is impossible to be certain that by comparison women were substantially over-represented within the smaller sects, but their presence was undoubtedly more important. Various interpretations have been offered to explain the importance of women in such movements. While eighteenth- and nineteenth-century commentators shared the underlying assumptions of Max Weber's statement that women were especially receptive to 'religious movements with orgiastic emotional or hysterical aspects to them',[4] recent studies have drawn attention to more tangible considerations. Some have suggested that women were attracted into the new sects by the wider scope of activity offered to them by the concept of spiritual equality, while others have shown how the moral values of the new religious movements, including temperance, frugality, fidelity and self-improvement, had a daily relevance to women who were concerned for the physical and moral welfare of their families.[5] Moreover, the search for motivation must also distinguish between characteristics based on wider cultural patterns and those specific to gender. For example, although accepted notions of what constituted 'natural' female behaviour helped to perpetuate ideal stereotypes, the characteristics upon which they were built, including zealous expressions of piety, excessive spirituality and emotional responses to evangelical sermons, were common to both men and women in this period. In addition, women are no more a cohesive social entity than men and a shared gender does not in itself produce a common experience. Criteria such as social status, age and personal circumstances shape religious behaviour as they do other areas of life.

At the topmost level of society, aristocratic patronage and benevolence made an important contribution to the support and diffusion of evangelical religion both inside and outside the churches.[6] Wives, widows and heiresses held strong positions of influence in their own locality – an influence frequently exercised on behalf of a strongly held personal faith. Their considerable financial and social advantages were often employed on behalf of their favourite religious organizations. Lady Sophia Ward, whose conversion led to conflict with her father, the Viscount of Bangor, bequeathed virtually her whole estate to religious and charitable organizations.[7] The financing of new churches or chapels of ease was an equally important outlet for aristocratic piety. In 1773 Lady Arabella Denny founded the Magdalene Chapel in Dublin which was frequented by persons of the highest social rank.[8] For some years this chapel provided an important venue for preachers connected to Selina, Countess of Huntingdon, one of the most prominent early patrons of Calvinistic Methodism. Converted during a serious illness, the countess joined with a 'select circle of women of high station' in prayer and scripture-reading meetings, appointed Whitefield as her chaplain and employed her resources to send 'popular preachers' on evangelistic trips throughout the country.[9] She also founded a chapel in Plunkett Street in Dublin which became an important centre for evangelical preaching.[10]

Lady Huntingdon thus played a significant role in establishing the links between British evangelicals and their Irish counterparts which made Dublin an important centre of evangelical enthusiasm in the late eighteenth century.[11] But though the Calvinist Methodists were dubbed 'the genteel Methodists' and despite testimonies of 'many of the higher orders' attending these preachers, some at least did not meet with the approval of high society.[12] The 'haranguing' to which some over-zealous preachers subjected their congregations offended the fine sensibilities of aristocratic church-goers. An important counterbalance to such difficulties and a significant factor in the spread of evangelical Protestantism, was the wide network of family ties which was particularly striking among evangelicals. Links between aristocratic evangelical families formed a compact but powerful unit which used its wealth, prestige and personal influence in the furtherance of a faith which promoted personal sobriety and social stability. Links between the Rodens of County Down and the influential Powerscourt family of Leinster extended over three generations. Lady Harriet Jocelyn married into the Massereene family at the end of the eighteenth century and the Farnhams and the Anneseleys were similarly connected. The Countess of Huntingdon's daughter married the Earl of Moira and the couple regularly opened their household to Calvinistic preachers.[13] The countess was also related to the Reverend Walter Shirley, rector of Loughrea, a Church of Ireland clergyman whose zealous evangelicalism brought him into conflict with his ecclesiastical superiors.[14] Thus, intermarriage in high society not only operated in the interests of wealth and property, but resulted in an extensive social and religious influence spanning the British Isles.

An even tighter set of social relations, based on a common ethnic identity, was evident in the Quaker movement. Although these seventeenth-century immigrants interacted widely with the wider Irish community – particularly in matters of commerce – their cultural assimilation did not extend to intermarriage.[15] Their distinctiveness was reinforced by strict rules of dress and behaviour in which an emphasis on simplicity was often taken to extremes. One young Quaker, for example, noted that her mother's objection to decoration extended to the display of images on china.[16] Some Quakers did live in humble circumstances,[17] and concern for the welfare of their poor was a central and recurring theme in monthly meetings, but their emphasis on literacy and education, the simplicity of their life-style and their renowned independence and industry characterized them as an upwardly mobile community which made 'a profound contribution to every aspect of commercial life in modern Ireland'.[18] The papers of Mary Leadbeater, poet, author and daughter of a Quaker schoolmaster, reveal a social, intellectual and religious network stretching across Britain and extending to North America.[19] The religious visits of travelling ministers, granted certificates of 'Unity and concurrence' by their local meeting, kept these groups in contact with each other. Such ministers could be of either sex, and Quaker women were also given their own separate spheres of responsibility in other areas as women's meetings at monthly, quarterly and provincial level paralleled those of the men.[20] However, while women dealt with social and disciplinary matters concerning their own sex including the relief of the poor, widows and orphans and the good behaviour, marriage plans and dress of women and girls, the men's meeting alone had executive authority. Nevertheless, interaction between meetings and the idea of spiritual, if not executive, equality gave women important roles to play in this distinctive community.

At all levels of society, women, either individually or as part of a wider network, played an important part in establishing links between religious groups and the communities in which they were situated. In the early days of a new religious movement, for example, success or failure was often determined by specifically practical considerations and this was an area in which respectable, pious and independent women were especially useful. Itinerant preachers needed an introduction into the community and a place to rest and hold meetings on their long and arduous circuits. Crookshank's

History of Methodism abounds with examples of the support given and initiatives taken by women in introducing Methodism into the towns and villages of Ireland. Mrs Alice Dawes, an evangelical widow and the principal supporter of Methodism in Belturbet, received the preachers and fitted up a room for their accommodation; the first preaching place in Armagh was rented by Mrs Russell, Mrs Isabella Maxwell and Mrs Jane Justice in 1762, and there are many examples of women inviting preachers to make use of their homes.[21] Such women gave moral support and encouragement as well as practical aid to preachers. They also served as links between rural societies and the Methodist central leadership. Some corresponded with Wesley, for example, to comment and advise on individual preachers. In 1769, Mrs Bennis's request to Conference for the appointment of an itinerant preacher to Limerick was noted by Crookshank as 'the earliest instance on record of the voice of the people being heard in connection with a preaching appointment'.[22]

Methodism's concern to draw in those on the periphery of society, the sick, the aged and the distressed, gave official recognition to traditional female duties and endowed them with a more tangible moral authority. Piety and respectability were more important attributes for sick visitors and class leaders than finance, property or social status. The dynamics of female classes, which often seemed more durable than their male counterparts, provoked comment from many visiting itinerants and kept the impetus going when initial enthusiasm had died down. Female prayer meetings were also noted as particularly successful examples of piety and devotion.[23]

One Methodist historian suggests that it was as class teachers and even preachers that women really 'transcended the stereotypical roles' of 'attendant and listeners to become active participants',[24] and it was as preachers that their activities proved most controversial. Although, in practical terms, this became the most contested area of women's contribution, it was not a new phenomenon. In the fifteenth century, the Lollards had proclaimed, 'Why should not women be priested and enabled to celebrate and preach like men',[25] and the religious radicalism of the Civil War period similarly gave encouragement to female preachers. The concept of spiritual equality was given most expression by the Quakers who employed women as the first Quaker preachers in London, Dublin and the American colonies.[26] Quakers were, however, an ethnically distinct community. It was with the advent of Methodism that female preaching became more widespread. Since most early Methodist local preachers were not ordained, there was no official ban or prohibitive qualifications to deter female enthusiasts.[27] Methodism's flexible structure and overriding concern to spread the gospel message gave rise to a pragmatism which deployed all methods in the interests of gospel proclamation. This was reflected in Wesley's advice to aspiring female preachers, which was cautious but no different in essence from that given to men.[28] He advised Alice Cambridge, when dealing with critics, to

> Give them all honour and obey them in all things, as far as conscience permits. But it will not permit you to be silent when God commands you to speak; yet I would have you give as little offence as possible; and therefore I would advise you not to speak at any place where a preacher is speaking near you at the same time, lest you should draw away his hearers. Also avoid the first appearance of pride or magnifying yourself.[29]

Women, like men, were therefore regarded as instruments of divine providence to meet exceptional circumstances, an interpretation confirmed by their popularity. Blind and emotional Margaret Davidson drew large crowds with the 'fervour and fluency of her witness',[30] and Alice Cambridge attracted numbers 'amounting to eight or ten thousand persons' on a tour of Ulster at the beginning of the nineteenth century.[31]

However, early acceptance, or at least tolerance, soon gave way to caution and then condemnation, as women's position within Methodism reflected its growing respectability and organizational stability. The 1802 Conference decreed it 'contrary both to scripture and to prudence that women should preach or should exhort in public'.[32] It seems that this decision was not entirely effective, but by the mid-nineteenth century female preaching had had its day both in Ireland and in England where it had been even more common.[33] In Ireland, it is plain that those preachers who most ardently supported their female counterparts were themselves 'enthusiasts' who frequently found themselves out of favour with an increasingly conservative Dublin leadership.[34] Those women who did continue the practice confined their activities to their own sex. Thus, while Alice Cambridge had addressed mixed congregations in the late eighteenth century, including a regiment of soldiers, together with their wives and children,[35] by the 1830s male followers of Anne Lutton were reduced to dressing in women's clothing in a vain attempt to hear her preach.[36]

Women's preaching should thus be seen as exceptional and transitional rather than officially sanctioned and accepted. Even at the peak of their influence women preachers were seen as itinerant supporters in virgin territory, as with the nineteenth-century overseas missionary movement, and were never accepted as regular preachers to settled congregations. The public activism of strong-willed individuals was possible only in periods of disruption or innovation. Female Ranters, Congregationalists and Baptists similarly took advantage of hierarchical breakdown in the Civil War period, but with the return to social and ecclesiastical stability these 'anomalies' were removed. In the early nineteenth century, the new generation of Methodists, with property considerations and growing, established congregations, was eager to defend itself from accusations of hysteria and sentimentality. As the movement became more institutionalized and respectable, a denomination rather than a voluntary association, men took over the dominant positions and women again assumed supportive and background roles.[37]

Even when female preaching was common women never succeeded in altering, nor indeed attempted to alter, the conventional relationships between men and women within religious communities.[38] For, while their opponents reviled them for casting off the virtues of their sex, their suppporters were equally careful always to refer to them in terms of their womanhood. Thus they were portrayed as either exemplifying or denying their 'nature'. Anne Preston, her supporters said, lived a 'life of feeling',[39] Alice Cambridge was neat, plain and greatly opposed to evil-speaking.[40] When speaking of Anne Lutton, the Victorian Methodist historian C. H. Crookshank felt it necessary to explain how such a woman, 'of respectable parents and trained in fear of the Lord', overcame her 'natural' female reticence.

> Called of God to proclaim to her fellow countrywomen the love of Christ, had she consulted her own feelings merely, her natural diffidence, deep humility and dislike to prominence would have presented an insurmountable barrier. But, believing that the Lord commanded, she dare not disobey and He crowned her labours with abundant blessing.[41]

Anne Lutton's correspondence suggests that she shared these sentiments.[42] The 'essential' nature of woman was thus accepted by both sides as determining the extent and nature of her activities. Modesty and humility precluded any prominent public role and the predominance of emotion over reason was regarded as a further limitation of the value of her contribution. Gideon Ouseley, although a known supporter of female preaching, remarked of a young woman preacher that while she was good at recounting her own experience and blessings, 'her knowledge was not equal to her zeal and some of her remarks were confused and incoherent'.[43] Wesley too felt that the exposition of texts was a male preserve, requiring logic, reasoning and sustained argument.

> With reference to women praying or giving short exhortations in public. He advises them to keep as far from preaching as they can, never to take a text and never to speak in a continued discourse without some break, above four or five minutes.[44]

These perceptions of male and female 'natural' attributes perpetuated the division of roles in areas other than the pastoral office. Despite the Quaker theory of equality, for example, men's meetings dealt with matters relating to property, including meeting-houses and burial grounds, and with negotiations with the state and the established church.[45] Generally speaking, matters of policy, the intricacies of doctrine and public debate were regarded as male concerns, while teaching, persuading and background supportive work were considered more appropriate for women. It was only with the rise of voluntary religious agencies at the beginning of the nineteenth century that new opportunities in these areas opened up.[46] Meanwhile, it was as wives and mothers that women's influence was most obviously disseminated through society, and through which undramatic but pervasive contributions were made to the vitality and spread of popular Protestantism. A member of the Methodist New Connexion indicated the way in which mothers could exercise their power in the interests of their family's moral welfare:

> We must take our children with us on the Sabbath day. All the meetings are needed – public worship, class meetings, the Sabbath school and the prayer meetings; to keep the children fully employed leaving them no time to serve the devil.[47]

Responsibility for the spiritual guidance of the young gave women a degree of moral authority which religious leaders have always stressed as an important element in their campaign for the regeneration of society. But appreciation of this fact has usually been modified by simultaneous assertions of women's inherent weakness and emotional vulnerability and this perception of the female sex also contributed to the growth of opposition to the Protestant sects. Those hostile to the popularity of itinerant preachers pointed derisively to the enthusiastic female response to their endeavours by suggesting both spiritual and physical exploitation.[48] Since it was almost always the woman of the house who first made contact with itinerants and consequently she who most often introduced the rest of the family to meetings, this was not simply an academic point. One orthodox minister was scathing about the 'opportunism' of itinerant Methodist preachers: 'Having a form of Godliness, they work on the minds of the unsteady and wavering and of all who are given to change, they creep into houses; they lead captive silly women.'[49] The mob violence which so often accompanied early Methodist activities was frequently related to their success among the women of a family or community. In Fermanagh in 1768 the Henderson family, with a large mob in tow, besieged the Methodist Armstrongs for two days to starve out two preachers who had converted their daughter.[50] There are many such examples of evangelical preachers taking advantage of feminine weakness and inevitably this was not always confined to mere persuasion.

The private minutes of the Methodist Conference suggest that relations between some itinerants and their female followers reached a degree of intimacy deemed 'unnatural' and unacceptable.[51] The connection between sexual and religious excitement was frequently made by contemporaries and there is no doubt that some revivalist preachers were charismatic, romantic figures whose rhetorical appeals for submission provoked a less than orthodox response. The emotional nature of conversions, particularly during periods of revival and the privacy and exclusiveness of class and band meetings added to local suspicions.[52] Dramatic conversion experiences, the intensity of religious ardour and the repentant sinner's subsequent change of life-style – all of which could be interpreted as 'unnatural' – also led to charges of madness, while the success of zealous preachers left them open to accusations of witchcraft.[53]

Clearly, in the context of the wider society, the ability of Protestant sects to attract large numbers of female adherents could have a negative as well as positive effect. Similarly, their emphasis on distinctiveness and separation from the world proved to be both their strength and their weakness. As already suggested, much energy was devoted to matters of dress and behaviour, with an emphasis on simplicity in the former and temperance and piety in the latter. Nor were the strictures of elders or of conferences merely advisory; failure to conform to strict discipline was closely investigated and could lead to expulsion from the Quaker, Methodist, or Moravian society.[54]

In theory at least, the sect's distinctiveness and separateness were maintained and the godly way of life was perpetuated, by encouraging members to marry only 'godly' persons or even by limiting personal relationships to within the sect itself. The Methodist Conference decreed that parents were 'forbidden to encourage children to marry 'unawakened persons',[55] while in Quaker society individuals took their marriage plans to both men's and women's meetings for approval.[56] The Moravians at Gracehill, as an enclosed community, were even stricter; marriage requests were brought before the elders before being submitted to the Lot.[57] Religious conformity thus took precedence over social or sexual compatability. Sexuality obviously created particular problems for these groups and awareness of the power of sex was met by strict separation of unmarried males and females. Classes for prayer and worship were sexually segregated and at Gracehill all casual intercourse between the sexes was strictly forbidden. One anecdote, referring to the admonition of a young boy in 1789, illustrates the extent to which this rule was enforced: 'The boy, John Carson, went to Mrs. O'Neill's himself to buy apples. He was called before the College of Overseers and told how sorry we were that he had taken such liberty without telling his labourer or room brother. Such steps lead to ruin.'[58] In this same community, single women (always a particularly dangerous and vulnerable group) were not permitted to be seen after dark. It is not difficult to see how such severe strictures could be counterproductive. Whereas between 1766 and 1770 the number of 'single sisters' necessitated the appointment of an extra official to look after their welfare, a year later it was noted that 'many sisters have gone to the world'.[59]

It is difficult to gauge the success or failure of those groups which did not physically remove themselves from the wider society. It is likely that demographic considerations and the vagaries of human nature made the imposition of their restrictions extremely difficult and there was consequently a gap between ideal and reality. Evidence suggests that within the family and the larger community religion could in fact be a divisive rather than a unifying factor, with the degree of conflict directly related to the intensity of faith. Alice Cambridge, following her conversion, reconsidered her relationship with a man 'to whom she was much attached, but who had not given his heart to Jesus . . . she at once ended an engagement which was contrary to the Word of God, and could not be accompanied with the Divine Blessing'.[60] A magistrate in Clara, who objected to his wife and daughter attending Methodist services, hired 24 Roman Catholics to beat up the itinerant preacher; his wife, not surprisingly, later left his household.[61] Similar examples of domestic discord abound, especially in the early stages of Methodist penetration into Irish localities.

For those whose religious commitment led to family conflict, however, the class and band meetings of the local Methodist society could offer solace and support. At these gatherings, established members and hesitant newcomers alike could benefit, both from confessing their doubts, fears and sins, and from hearing the experiences of others. These communal soul-barings offered a system of mutual support which enhanced their cohesiveness and strengthened their sense of solidarity as they battled against the values and sins of the wider world.[62] In a parallel study of East Cheshire, Gail Malmgreen suggests that the daily life of the chapel and its close network of 'brothers and sisters in Christ', helps explain its particular attraction for adolescents and young adults and those for whom family relationships were undergoing strain or change.[63] Recent oral evidence from a later period similarly highlights the importance of intimacy and the ethos of 'homeliness' in recreating family virtues in a religious setting.[64]

The intensification and diversification of evangelical activity in the nineteenth century greatly increased the opportunities for women's participation. Through the network of voluntary societies and organizations which clustered around the religious denominations, many women were given an opportunity to engage in social and administrative work in their communities. The domestic sphere widened to take in Sunday schools, foreign and domestic evangelistic missions, temperance, educational, bible and tract societies. The various reports indicate the areas in which it was felt women could be particularly successful – teaching, sponsorship, promotion and persuasion. Sunday school teaching rapidly became an acceptable occupation for women in many areas. It was a leadership role which offered an important outlet for piety as well as a position within the community, but one which could also be regarded as an extension of the traditional domestic duties of guidance and teaching. A handbook for Sunday school teachers announced that

> A woman's information influences the present comfort and future state of her family; if her house be well-ordered, the husband forsakes the ale-house and where there would have been want there is plenty. It is the mother who instructs the children, to her they look up for all they want and in general as she is, so are they.[65]

There was clearly a disproportionate number of females working in this area, and schools for female teachers were operational from the early nineteenth century. The Hibernian Bible Society noted that working-class men were much more open to persuasion from lady visitors when it came to buying Bibles[66] and the impressive distribution statistics recorded during these years owed much to the efforts of these voluntary labourers. The 1830 report of the Religious Tract and Bible Society noted the success of the Ladies' Association in promoting the circulation of tracts and books and in establishing libraries.[67] Similarly, the Ladies Society of the London Hibernian Society was by 1830 running 190 schools with some 8,000 scholars, and the Ladies Auxiliary to the Irish Society employed a small army of scripture readers.[68] Into this mixture of spiritual and practical work women brought their traditional domestic skills and applied them in a wider field. Their efforts did not go unappreciated, especially by those voluntary societies which struggled against the rigidity of ecclesiastical hierarchies. The records of the Church Missionary Society, for example, reveal the way in which women's auxiliaries were used to establish a base in Ireland, getting around the barriers imposed by the church on male-dominated societies which were regarded, especially in Anglican circles, as a threat to episcopal authority.[69] Ladies' auxiliaries also helped establish the ubiquitous penny-a-week subscription as the main resource of the evangelical religious societies. It was in the area of finance, in fact, that women proved themselves to be indispensable assets. By helping to unleash the 'power of the purse' in a systematic and regular fashion women were at the very heart of a remarkable Victorian industry of religious and moral campaigns in Britain and in Ireland.[70] Apart from direct, individual donations, the collectors of penny-a-week subscriptions were invariably either women or clergymen and they also acted as treasurers to local branches and as organizers of the more traditional fund-raising events such as bazaars and the sale of 'fancy work'.

Specifically female philanthropic societies, both evangelical and non-evangelical, also flourished in the mid-nineteenth century, and this type of involvement, while still largely secondary and supportive in nature, and still within the traditional arena of charity and benevolence, was important in offering an outlet to women's industry and talent outside the home and family circle. Women gave their time, commitment and local knowledge to the furtherance of these causes, and the result was a growing professionalism and a considerable broadening of physical and spiritual horizons. Closer involvement in charitable work, of whichever kind, certainly gave the upper and middle classes an opportunity to confront the realities of poverty and neglect and opened up direct contact with everyday social problems from which they had largely been protected. Ultimately this led to a social extension of their perception of Christian duty. Pious platitudes may often have been served up with the soup or administered with dressings, but there is at least some evidence of individuals going beyond the narrow constraints of proselytism. Societies such as the Belfast Ladies Relief Association may have been mainly concerned to 'imbue the minds of the scholars with the truth and spirit of the gospel', but the industrial schools they set up, supplied by lady teachers and superintendents, offered more concrete benefits to famine-stricken communities.[71] Frank Prochaska, in his study of women and philanthropy in England, speaks of the new range of opportunities opened up to women, as a 'crack in the door', and goes on to suggest that many early suffragettes reached their political radicalism through their experience of evangelical philanthropic work.[72] While there is insufficient evidence to make similar conclusions for Ireland, it undoubtedly was the case that Ulster women, through the evangelical voluntary societies, acquired skills and found interests outside the traditional boundaries of domestic life.

In the field of foreign missions, women were at first confined to supportive committees and auxiliaries and to fund-raising for male missionaries whose reports were generally designed to appeal to a maternal nature. However, the Zenana Mission, founded by the Presbyterian Church in 1873, promised women a more central and challenging role.[73] Under its full title, 'The Female Association for Promoting Christianity Among the Women of the East' sent out female missionaries. As well as offering traditional medical, educational and child-care facilities, this mission had a particular concern for the Zenana, that is, the part of the Indian household set aside for women, and to which men, including evangelical missionaries, had no access. While the setting up of the female mission was therefore essential to fulfil missionary objectives, it also gave local women the opportunity to consider the position of their eastern counterparts and to experience a different culture. Although the actual number of female missionaries leaving Ireland for Calcutta was small, home-based branches were kept well informed. By its second year the mission had 124 congregational auxiliaries in Ireland with over 6,000 members.[74] The idea of women missionaries became more acceptable as the century progressed; in 1887, the queen's Golden Jubilee year, it was reported that there were about 500 female missionaries in India attached to a variety of denominational societies.[75] The majority of these were native teachers and bible women taught by Europeans, but a door had been opened through which many women would pass in the following decades. The new venture required courage and assertiveness, and undoubtedly brought fulfilment. It was stressed, however, that their teaching of the gospel was secondary to the primary medical and educational functions of women missionaries, and thus they remained firmly within traditional female boundaries.

The annual reports of the Zenana Mission offer an intriguing glimpse into the respective roles of the sexes in late-Victorian religion. The first report confirmed that the mission had an all-female general committee, female secretaries and treasurer, and a committee of ministers available for consultation.[76] However, at the annual general meeting, all the speeches were made by men, and the images which the women held of themselves were often a pure reflection of those held by their male counterparts. 'We are born to serve the world' was the rallying cry offered by one Zenana missionary. So, although these particular women had to undertake arduous training, in a new language, in kindergarten methods and in medicine, and although their letters are suggestive of the difficult adjustment to the climate, food and culture in which they found themselves, the language in which their experiences are couched reaffirms their perception of women's subordinate role and their willing acceptance of male perceptions of their worth. The importance of language, imagery and symbolism in perpetuating conventional gender roles should not be overlooked. A male speaker at the Zenana annual general meeting stated that

> There is something about female piety that singularly adapts it to missionary enterprise. . . . Everyone knows that the graces which shone with perfect lustre in the character of Christ were mainly the feminine virtues. Submission, love, tenderness, self-sacrifice, devotement, sympathy, are characteristic features of the piety of women; and when joined with gifts, knowledge, and grace they make a model missionary. Without preaching, without descending to the lecture-room, or the arena of controversy, the Christian woman may go about doing good and to an extent that a seraph would envy.[77]

It is this continuing emphasis on traditional feminine virtues by the men who ran the evangelical voluntary organizations, and for whom the 'essential' nature of men and women predetermined religious as well as social roles, which most clearly emerges from a reading of the sources. The controversial nature of many religious meetings, with their emphasis on action and resolution, reinforced these perceptions, particularly in Ireland. In contrast to their own heated political debates, it was suggested that 'the religion of a woman ought to be an impassioned weakness, and that sweet spirit which was typified by the dove should spread its wings upon her'.[78] The *Belfast People's Magazine* also stressed the moral superiority of women, and the duties incumbent upon them.

> Let all females be persuaded, that God did not intend them, by any means, for mere servile purposes, but designed them to be truly helpmates to men; and, therefore, let them with a religious regard to the end of their creation, study by every winning grace, by every angel virtue, to lead those with whom they may be connected to happiness both here and hereafter.[79]

Women's power to influence men – for good or evil – was clearly recognized, but any evaluation of their worth placed them in a complementary and submissive relation, for 'upon the virtues of women much of that of man depended, and the religious habits of the sex could not fail to exercise a salutary influence'.[80] Similarly, while evangelicals encouraged the participation of women in many areas, it was clear that their moral authority was to be used not to erode traditional boundaries, but as an instrument in the regeneration of the wider society. Women provided much of the funding, the administrative expertise and the social skills necessary to maintain the popular status of evangelical societies, but men retained their official status and continued to exercise authority and determine policy. Traditional arrangements and traditional values were not only retained but upheld by evangelical theology, and the extension of women's influence was interpreted in purely spiritual terms. On the whole, women accepted, even welcomed, the cultural role conferred upon them by Ulster evangelicalism. They also picked out those aspects of Christ's personality with which to identify and unquestioningly drew upon the prevalent cult of evangelical domesticity, which after all offered tangible benefits when set alongside the domestic circumstances of women exposed to rougher and more irreligious households.

Women's contribution to popular Protestantism in this period is not easily reduced to facile categories. They certainly provided ammunition for critics, particularly in the early stages of evangelical enthusiasm, but as evangelicalism took on an aura of respectability, with congregations becoming more settled and the dignity of the pastoral office replacing the excitement of the circuit horse-rider, women became less controversial but more central to evangelicalism's social creed. Inevitably, the limits of women's actions were circumscribed by men, and the much-vaunted importance of female example in terms of piety, humility, and service was widely disseminated through family and social structures. But in these traditional areas women were not simply victims but willing participants in a campaign of moral reformation. It is, however, in the relation between popular Protestantism and home life that their presence was most significant. In a faith which relied strongly on idealized notions of domesticity, this should not be underestimated. It was not only that women enabled evangelists to establish a foothold in the family and the community, but that their activities ensured that religious values penetrated all aspects of everyday life in a way that institutionalized religion could not. Women's civilizing influence was evident too in the combination of holy charity and biblical education so common in the nineteenth century. The social events over which they presided – bazaars, teas, sales and Sunday school celebrations – tied the church or chapel closer to the community and established links which remain central to Ulster Protestant culture.

An over-concentration on the political aspects of Ulster religious history has diverted attention from less contentious aspects of its development. Personal, social and cultural values and the internal dynamics of religious faith, including the varieties of meanings and networks of relationships within which they are rooted, have fallen outside the mainstream of research. Women have too often been casualties of this historical bias. To incorporate their experiences and perceptions into this male-dominated history is to take an important step towards a more comprehensive understanding of the complexities of the past.

PART FOUR

From religious revival to provincial identity

[8]
Ulster awakened: the 1859 revival

And it shall come to pass in the last days, saith God, I will pour out of my Spirit upon all flesh: and your sons and your daughters shall prophesy, and your young men shall see visions, and your old men shall dream dreams. (Acts 2:17)

And the Lord added to the church daily such as should be saved. (Acts 2:47)

The phenomenon of religious revival, now that it scarcely troubles the Protestant churches of the northern hemisphere, has become an avid subject of inquiry for historians, sociologists and social anthropologists. Such intense study has thankfully improved our understanding of what are bewilderingly complex events. In the past social historians had a tendency to reduce explanations of revival to economic depression, political excitement, or chancy notions of societal modernization. Ecclesiastical historians responded by emphasizing the importance of theology, personal religious experience and the centrality of revivalistic preachers. Such explanations no doubt have their place, but they often fail to describe or interpret the process of religious revival in a way that would be recognizable to those who were revived. While admitting that human beings are not often the best judges of what is happening around them, it is surely churlish not to pay some attention to the human emotions, expectancy and experiences of those who engaged in the community rituals of religious revivalism. More recent work, by suggesting that religious revivals have an internal dynamic of their own, and by paying more attention to the laity and their religious experiences, has shed new light on old problems of explaining outbreaks of dramatic religious enthusiasm.[1] In particular, a number of studies of transatlantic revivals have drawn attention to the way in which vibrant community-based rituals, such as the Methodist love-feast and the Presbyterian communion season, have acted as focal points of intense emotion.[2] With expectations raised by cottage prayer meetings, vigorous preaching and hymn- and psalm-singing, such occasions were often the catalyst for the manifestation of striking religious phenomena, especially in the lives of young, unmarried women. In explaining the timing and extent of such revivals it is clearly appropriate to pay attention to the wider cultural environment in which they occurred, but such explanations in themselves do not do justice to the profound sense of sinfulness and unworthiness, and the ecstatic sense of forgiveness and release, which recur again and again in the personal accounts of revivalistic experiences. While it would be foolish to ignore the specific social, economic and political setting within which the Ulster revival was located, explanations of what happened in Ulster in 1859 have tended to reduce its religious significance because its interpreters have been largely ignorant of both a much wider tradition of transatlantic revivalism in the eighteenth and nineteenth centuries and an indigenous tradition of popular revivalism in Ulster stretching back a quarter of a millennium. Those who have studied transatlantic revivals on a much broader canvas conclude that

> The only stable factor amongst the whole complex of influences that operated at times of revival was the existence of a desire for and expectancy of revivals in the churches themselves. Essential to all revivals was a climate of opinion that regarded revivals as desirable, for a wide range of reasons that included the theological and the congregational . . . [and] the social and the economic. . . . Without economic depression and despite the excitement of politics, revivals were able to flourish; without an appropriate theological and congregational climate there could have been none.[3]

With that in mind, the purpose of this chapter is threefold: to address the problem of causation in the context of what had been happening in Ulster Protestantism over the previous century; to attempt to capture the flavour of the revival itself; and to assess its meaning within the Ulster Protestant community in the late nineteenth century.

The 1859 revival has been granted a special place in Ulster's religious history. It is most often portrayed as a spontaneous and dramatic outpouring of the Holy Spirit, leading to the conversion of many thousands of men and women and resulting in the moral and social reformation of a formerly sinful society. While this popular image requires a degree of modification in the interests of historical accuracy, the importance of the movement itself is not questioned. As Peter Gibbon has pointed out, 'the Ulster religious revival of 1859 involved larger numbers of people in sustained common activity than any movement in rural Ulster between 1798 and 1913'.[4] Its value to the historian is twofold. In the first place it shows the extent to which evangelical Protestantism had penetrated Ulster's religious culture by the late 1850s, and secondly it stands as a pivotal event within popular Protestantism itself. Before it happened it was longingly anticipated, after it happened it was nostalgically remembered, and ever after it became a litmus test of the spiritual vigour of evangelical religion. In the Ulster Protestant psychology the revival of 1859 was both a historical event and a supernatural encounter invested with almost mythical significance. The dramatic, visible and well-publicized nature of religious

Map 3   Places mentioned in chapter 8

activity in 1859 serves to highlight the more controversial aspects of evangelical faith, and indicates the degree of adjustment made by churchmen and laity to a movement which largely ignored conventional ecclesiastical and social boundaries. The term revival itself admits of no precise definition. It was probably first used by the American puritan Cotton Mather, who described religious revival as a situation in which religious matters became of primary and urgent importance to a whole community, and 'in which men and women experienced a deep sense of sin and an overwhelming desire for God's forgiveness'.[5] William McLoughlin goes one step further in his description of a religious awakening which he considers to be the effect of revival on the community at large, including those who are outside the Christian faith. He calls this a 'cultural revitalization' and explains that while 'revivals alter the lives of individuals; awakenings alter the world view of a whole people or culture'.[6] Whether *this* is what occurred in mid-nineteenth-century Ulster is rather more open to question.

Despite the frequency with which commentators have claimed that 'deadness, formality and indifference characterized the vast majority of the Church members' in the pre-revival period,[7] we have tried to show that there was a significant growth of evangelical religion among clergy and laity alike since the middle of the eighteenth century.[8] One explanation for this apparent paradox is suggested by James Walsh in his study of early eighteenth-century American revivals in which he observes that 'puritan ministers . . . deemed anything less than a revival a time of degeneracy'.[9] Just as religious converts are apt to exaggerate the change of outlook and life style occasioned by religious conversion, ecclesiastical interpreters of revival are prone to do the same thing with religious revivals. This tendency should be resisted in dealing with Ulster in 1859, for not only was the ground well cultivated for the bumper harvest of 1859, but ensuing crops were not very much different from what had come before.[10]

Periods of revivalistic growth were of course a common aspect of Methodism in both Britain and Ireland in the eighteenth and early nineteenth centuries.[11] But the significance of the 1859 Ulster revival is that it affected mostly – though by no means exclusively – the Presbyterian community. Conversionist evangelicalism, as we have seen, was not a new feature of Presbyterianism on the eve of the '59 revival, but its most important gains had been made in the previous three decades.[12] In these years troublesome doctrinal disputes had been largely eradicated by the campaign against Arianism spearheaded by Henry Cooke, the success of which opened the way to the union between the Synod of Ulster and the more strictly orthodox and evangelical Secession synod in 1840. This in turn resulted in a greater concentration on church extension movements, foreign and domestic missions, Sunday schools, and bible and tract distribution. By the mid-century an increased interest in personal conversion experiences and involvement in social and moral reform movements, such as the temperance campaign and the Belfast Town Mission, suggested the degree to which an activist evangelical theology had permeated both the General Assembly and, more importantly, the Presbyterian laity. A resolution to support open-air preaching, passed in 1853, gave fresh impetus both to a new style of preaching and to the attempt to reach those outside the church's jurisdiction.[13] With the number of Presbyterian ministers engaged in this activity growing from 8 in 1851 to 63 in 1857, 'popular' preachers such as Hugh Hanna and Tommy Toye became familiar, if sometimes controversial, figures on the streets of Belfast.[14] This 'popularizing' of religion by itinerant preachers and voluntary associations brought the gospel message to the forefront of many areas of life, and encouraged a more vigorous religious identity. The general background was thus conducive to revivalism, and the question of revival itself was specifically and consistently considered by the General Assembly throughout the 1840s and 1850s.[15]

By the mid-nineteenth century, therefore, Ulster had a tradition of revivalist enthusiasm upon which to draw. Presbyterians themselves could look back to the third decade of the seventeenth century when, in the same corner of County Antrim where the '59 revival originated, local minister Robert Glendinning initiated a 'bright and hot sun-blink of the Gospel'. The excitement generated by Glendinning spread rapidly through the locality of Sixmilewater, was channelled into a series of monthly meetings by a group of neighbouring ministers and resulted in numerous conversions.[16] As was made clear in chapter 1 the revivalistic fire of Ulster Presbyterianism did not die out entirely in 1625, but was kept flickering in the festivals surrounding the communion season. In the mid-eighteenth century John Cennick's itinerant preaching made a considerable impact in the same area. In the late eighteenth century south Ulster was the scene of a general Methodist revival, in which itinerant preaching and local social and economic pressures were the main ingredients.[17] The Armagh area witnessed a brief and more restrained variety of Presbyterian-inspired evangelical enthusiasm in the same period.[18] Although Methodist revivalism in Ireland, as in England, became less frequent in the nineteenth century, it was periodically rekindled by missionary enthusiasm and by intermittent outbreaks of cholera.[19] Religious revivalism was therefore by no means unique in Ulster society, and the endeavours of itinerant preachers, attached either to the Methodists or to any one of a variety of voluntary religious agencies, form a background of popular religious enthusiasm against which the dramatic events of 1859 should be set.

The importance of transatlantic influences has also been stressed in recent research into Irish religious life. With close links established by successive waves of emigrants, the Ulster-Scots community was particularly susceptible to the transmission of religious excitement generated by the American frontier experience. During the Second Great Awakening at the end of the eighteenth century, emigrant letters and visiting preachers had played an important role in inspiring local enthusiasm.[20] Similarly, when it was reported in 1858 that the churches of America had won a million converts during a revival of the previous two years, this 'good news' spread quickly through the Ulster Presbyterian community.[21] Numerous addresses from pulpits enlarged on the subject and tracts, eye-witness accounts and letters from emigrants made revivalism a popular conversational topic in religious circles.[22] Churches which had already been experiencing growth and some internal regeneration were greatly encouraged by this evidence of success. Many sent observers, and their published accounts of the American awakening added to the growing body of revivalist literature.[23]

With the *Presbyterian Missionary Herald* writing of 'the Vital transforming power of faith', the immediate result of this transatlantic stimulus was a significant increase in the number of local prayer meetings.[24] On both sides of the Atlantic the impetus for religious enthusiasm seems to have originated in such gatherings, indeed the American revival of the 1850s has been referred to as the 'Great Prayer Meeting Revival'.[25] Prayer perhaps helped to reconcile the contradiction in contemporary attitudes to revival which, on the one hand, was believed to be a spontaneous, unpredictable work of God – a supernatural phenomenon – yet also one which could be organized, or at least promoted, by human instrumentality. Since this paradox lies behind much of the subsequent controversy surrounding the revival, the part played by prayer meetings in its origin is worth noting. The intervention of the Holy Spirit, it could be claimed, ensured that there was 'less of man, more of God'. The American news had the effect of placing local revivalist activities in a more universal context. It appeared less disputable that the work was 'of the Lord' when it spanned continents.

All of these background factors are pertinent to the Ulster revival of 1859, described by Richard Carwardine as 'one of the most extraordinary of nineteenth-century revivals'.[26] Robert Jennings has pointed to the 'positive yearning for experiences similar to those at Sixmilewater', exhibited in sermons, addresses and religious literature within Presbyterianism in the years before the revival.[27] At the same time quiet, undramatic expressions of religious renewal were occurring in many different localities as a result of the growing strength of evangelical preaching. The origins of the revival proper are traced to Kells in the parish of Connor, where a group of young converts had set up prayer meetings of believers for the purpose of meditation and scripture-reading and to seek God's blessing.[28] News of the American revival transformed these occasions into active revival prayer meetings. Initial converts seem to have been made through family connections in Ahoghill and thus spread through the immediate neighbourhood in the winter months of 1858–9. The minister of the First Presbyterian Church in Ahoghill, the Reverend David Adams, was always insistent that a revival was not 'got up', but that preparations had been going on locally for some considerable time. As converts began to preach at specially convened meetings, it was in this area that the first real enthusiasm was witnessed. People fell 'prostrate under conviction of sin', and as many as 700 were reported as 'awakened'.[29]

Such reports were discussed at presbyteries and church meetings as the 'good news' spread rapidly through the counties of Antrim and Down in the spring and early summer of 1859. By July and August religious excitement had reached Counties Derry, Tyrone and Armagh. It affected not only rural villages but the seaside resorts of Portrush, Ballycastle, Donaghadee and Bangor, and major towns such as Belfast, Newry, Ballymena, Londonderry, Coleraine, Omagh, Lurgan, Portadown and Armagh. In the more southern and western counties of the province, however, its impact was much diminished. Generally speaking, it was most potent in areas of Presbyterian strength, weakest in Fermanagh, whose Protestants were mainly episcopalian and in the mainly Catholic areas of Cavan, Monaghan and Donegal.[30] Throughout the rest of Britain a wave of prayer meetings and revivalist activities was reported. The English response was muted, but the west of Scotland, closest to Ulster in religion and culture, also witnessed some revival excitement. In Wales, particularly in Cardiganshire, religious exuberance was already sweeping society under the leadership of Humphrey Jones and David Morgan.[31]

The 1859 Ulster revival, in common with some other revivals on the Celtic fringes of the British Isles in the nineteenth century, was not the work of professional revivalists.[32] Rather the initial impetus seems to have come from pious laymen operating in communities with at least a smattering of biblical knowledge and familiarity with basic Christian concepts of salvation and damnation. As the revival gathered momentum, however, both popular local preachers and more celebrated visitors from Britain and America such as Henry Grattan Guinness and Brownlow North were undoubtedly instrumental in spreading the word and generating excitement. The American Methodist evangelists Walter and Phoebe Palmer visited Ulster in July when the revival was at its height, and the latter's practice of urging penitents to come to the front of the church is an early example of what was to become a common feature in revivalist movements.[33] This externalized, public indication of the conversion experience was not only an important emotional outlet and an immediate expression of commitment for the individual involved, but an obvious means of impressing others. It is important to stress, however, that the Ulster revival was not an example of new-style technique revivalism imported from America, but was rather one of the last great folk revivals in the history of the British Isles.

One of the most effective methods of spreading the revival was through the preaching of new converts whose message, with all the fervour of new conviction, was obviously emotive and persuasive. The *Belfast Newsletter* reported on a revival meeting held at Great George's Street church in Belfast, to which the converts from Ahoghill were invited by the minister, the Reverend Tommy Toye. The church was crowded and many were turned away. The convert

> delivered a very impressive and touching discourse, characterised by considerable feeling and pathos, which appeared deeply to impress the minds of those present. He presented salvation as within the reach of all, that Christ died for all mankind, was willing and ready to save every sinner, was as willing to grant salvation to all at that meeting as he had been to him who addressed, and he knew that his Saviour had washed him from all sin and made him 'white as snow'. He urged on all present not to rest satisfied until they knew for themselves that all their sins were pardoned.[34]

Such raw popular emotion, however affecting and effective, was not universally well received within the churches. J. B. Armour, who was a theological student at the time, wrote that

> The revival is progressing in general very well but there are means used for its extension even by Presbyterian ministers which I think is very far from right, for example Mr. Thomas Toye's. They have prayer meetings I think every night and they have a penitent's form where those that are burned with sin kneel and groan over their sins and then the Reverend Thomas prays with them. If ever you were in a Methodist Chapel it is something of the same in Mr. Toye's.[35]

Church of Ireland clergy were even more critical of the introduction of preaching by the uneducated and unqualified, who were by definition beyond ecclesiastical control.[36]

Physical prostrations, which had been an important feature of late eighteenth-century revivals in England and America, but which had largely died out by the mid-nineteenth century, were the most controversial aspect of the Ulster revival in 1859. There were many descriptions of 'stricken' persons, in states of great weakness and partial stupor, calling upon God for mercy. The most extreme cases reported visions and some exhibited 'marks' on their body of supposedly divine origin. The local press played an important role in reporting these cases and highlighted sensational examples of individual conversions.

> A neatly attired young woman, apparently about 22 years of age, had been stricken an hour previously, and was supported in the arms of an elderly female, who was seated upon a low stool. The party impressed appeared to be in a state of very great prostration – a partial stupor, from which she was occasionally roused into a feeling of mental agony, depicted in heart-rending expressions of the countenance and uttered in deep, low wailings of terrible despair. Her face was deadly pale, and her eyelids closed, except when partially raised by a convulsive paroxysm, and even then no part of the eye was visible except a narrow line of white. Her pulse was intermittent and feverish, and her face and hands were covered with perspiration. Occasionally she extended her arms with an action as if groping in the air, and at other times they were elevated high over-head, where the hands were clasped, with startling energy, and her features became rigidly fixed into an expression of supplication of which no language could give an adequate idea.[37]

The reporter's struggle for adequate language to do justice to the experience he was describing was shared by all, including evangelical visitors from outside Ireland who came to witness events at first hand. Although most of the revival leaders claimed that such cases represented only a minority of converts, they were nevertheless disproportionately influential in generating the publicity upon which the revival thrived. Highly coloured reports were reprinted in newspapers and repeated in sermons, appeared in polemical pamphlets and were the subject of animated gossip in a wide range of social settings. Not only did the novelty element bring out the curious, but the apparently remorseless wave of physical prostrations gave rise to fear of being similarly afflicted, which encouraged many to examine the state of their own souls.[38]

Such physical manifestations posed profound problems of explanation for all concerned, but especially for those within the churches who acknowledged that the Holy Spirit *could* produce unusual experiences, but who were nevertheless unwilling to be cast in the role of gullible fanatics. Some clergy were prepared to accept them as genuine works of the Spirit, others thought the Holy Spirit used, but did not produce, physical prostrations,[39] and still others believed they were the counterfeit work of Satan designed to draw attention away from the genuinely spiritual fruits of the revival.[40] Among less impressionable sceptics, Armour thought them 'only imagination',[41] Frankfort Moore thought that the marks were due 'to the pinching and squeezing' of distressed females, while others blamed hysteria, contagion, or conditions in the factories.[42] Medical opinion pronounced 'physiological accidents' as the common diagnosis, which had the advantage of neither confirming nor denying the reality of the alleged spiritual changes in the sufferers and of avoiding the problem of causation altogether.[43] The most severe critic was the Reverend Isaac Nelson whose *Year of Delusion* was a savage indictment of the revivalists and their methods – full of accusations of 'imposture, pretence and falsehood'.[44] His contemporaries suggest that Nelson was personally embittered, but whatever his motivations, he was not alone in casting suspicion on the value of the revival movement.[45] There is little doubt, for example, that the cautious approach adopted by most English religious leaders to the revival in Ulster was due to its exotic manifestations of physical distress.

The nub of the problem was that the mid-nineteenth-century religious mind had reached an ambiguous phase of its development. It was sufficiently religious to grapple seriously with alleged spiritual phenomena, but was sufficiently rationalistic to be wary of abandoning the more secure explanations of the material world. Nor did it have the dubious advantage of being armed with modern explanations of the 'psychotherapeutic property of dissociative behaviour'. The result was a wide spectrum of opinion from the hotter evangelicals on one side to restrained liberals on the other. Historians are confronted with different problems of explanation, but they are no less difficult. Those who wish to see the paranormal events of 1859 as a reflection of the particular stresses and strains on Ulster society in that year will have to explain why similar expressions of religious enthusiasm were neither confined to this area nor to this period. During the Sixmilewater revival in the early seventeenth century, for example, an observer commented, 'I have seen them myself stricken and swoon with the Word, Yea, a dozen in one day carried out of doors as dead.'[46] Similar events occurred during the Great Yorkshire Revival between 1792 and 1796.[47] Examples of physical prostrations during Methodist revivals in Ireland are also numerous, particularly during the millenarian excitement of the 1790s.[48] While physical manifestations had been much less prevalent during the most recent American revivals in the 1850s, Ulster's experience was often compared with that of the Kentucky frontier revivalism at the turn of the century.[49] It could, of course, be argued that all such societies were experiencing stresses and strains, and that would no doubt be true, but not all vulnerable societies experience religious revivalism and physical prostrations. What is required here is both a sensitive appreciation of the psychological power of revivalistic expectancy in relatively small communities and a wider appreciation of the cultural vulnerabilities, both conscious and unconscious, of social groups.

Personal conversion is, of course, a more ubiquitous characteristic of religious revivals than physical prostration, but it presents no less of a challenge to historical analysis. No doubt there were some fraudulent, and many short-lived, conversions. That there was an element of hysteria also seems likely since very large numbers were often packed into church buildings and crowd psychology no doubt played a part in generating emotion. It would be a mistake to underestimate the religious content of these experiences, however, the number and intensity of which seem directly related to the urgency of the evangelical emphasis on the sinful state of humanity and the necessity for personal salvation. The simple fervent preaching of the gospel message could hold an immediate relevance, and suggest a degree of personal responsibility which seems to be central to these 'crisis conversions'. One young woman questioned about her experience explained that she had not been alarmed or terrified by the sermon, but 'I felt that they were my sins that had nailed the Saviour to the cross that he was wounded for my transgressions and bruised for mine iniquities, it was for this I grieved, and not from any fear of punishment.' With no intermediary between the penitent and the saviour, this personal confrontation could lead to an agony of self-loathing and self-debasement, before reaching the peace of submission. Such experiences closely parallel those of the well-documented conversions at Cambuslang in the 1740s. The conversion narratives collected by the local minister show that what particularly bothered converts 'was not the fear of damnation, but rather a sense of sin and dishonor that their convictions awakened in them, which they experienced as shame'.[50] It is not surprising that such a highly charged emotional experience should have a physical effect on the vulnerable, or a subduing effect on observers. It could also, of course, be self-generating, as listeners and observers, feeling the necessity of such experience, projected themselves into an emotional state. The centrality of the conversion experience to revival thus needs to be stressed. The intensity of the personal crisis, often followed by a change of life-style, was visible evidence to others of a real transaction having taken place and often led to expectancy in the community at large.

The resultant sense of urgency was perhaps the most compelling aspect of the revival movement. Such subjective and individualistic experiences gave it an impetus of its own. It was this momentum which determined the responses of the churches. Although they had not produced the revival, except in so far as it was a reaction against ecclesiastical alienation, they were concerned not to be marginalized by it. After initial hesitation and caution, it became clear to most religious leaders that they must take the initiative in channelling this spontaneous emotional movement into proper institutional frameworks. The Methodists were used to dealing with this kind of religious exuberance and encountered few problems. The Presbyterian General Assembly, having prepared itself for such an eventuality, pronounced itself satisfied that the revival was 'a great blessing from God' and recorded its 'sense of obligation to watch and pray and strive that the work of grace may be deepened and perpetuated among our people'.[51] The Bishop of Down and Connor and the Bishop and the Archdeacon of Derry were among Anglican supporters of the revival. Others gave a more cautious welcome, while many continued to withhold their approval.[52] N. D. Emerson neatly summarizes the attitudes of many Anglican clergy to the revival.

The main feature of the revival was that great numbers of people began to take their faith seriously. No doubt there is always something embarrassing about this; but the individual clergyman's task and privilege to guide, sympathetically and patiently, and to teach faithfully and charitably, must be the way to secure the genuine principles of spiritual revival and to discard the effervescent and the evanescent.[53]

The holding of interdenominational meetings at various stages of the revival was a stumbling-block for more orthodox clergy. Union prayer meetings were particularly popular since it was easier for the different denominations to unite for prayer than in more liturgical religious services. However, such interdenominational activities were intermittent and minor aspects of the evangelical movement as a whole, and their significance should not be exaggerated. Most of the churches responded to the general public enthusiasm for religious activities by opening their own churches for extra services, by setting up prayer meetings, by increasing their programme of visitation and by fully utilizing their own denominational resources.

What the churches were most interested in was translating temporary religious enthusiasm into long-term church attendance, but their success was strictly limited despite early encouragements. The Church of Ireland, for example, claimed 10,661 additional communicants in 307 congregations, and other churches also reported a significant growth in membership figures.[54] All too often, however, further research reveals that these increases were short-lived and fitted into a traditional revival pattern of a steady build-up, a spectacular climax and then a dramatic falling-off.[55] The Primitive Wesleyan Methodists, for example, having incurred losses in the previous three years, show a growth rate of between 2 and 9 per cent between 1856 and 1859 and a massive leap to 53.7 per cent in 1860, but recorded significant losses for more than a decade thereafter (Table 8.1). The same trend is evident in the statistics of the Wesleyan Methodists, but – not surprisingly in a more institutionalized denomination – is less dramatic. Presbyterian statistics are more difficult to quantify because the Assembly does not record individual members. The number of congregations nevertheless shows a similar pattern – steady increases from the 1830s, with a significant boost in the decade from 1850 to 1860, followed by a much slower rate of growth thereafter.[56] The Irish Evangelical Society also reported increased membership of the Congregational churches it supported, though it should be noted that this was again part of an already established trend.[57] Perhaps a more significant consequence of revivalism was the growth of those denominations which required a more visible and positive commitment from their adult members. The combination of independent organization, zealous preaching and strict piety led some new converts to forsake the older, more established denominations for the congregations of Baptists and Brethren for whom the period of revival proved particularly fruitful.[58]

Even the small and enthusiastic sects, however, found it difficult to maintain

Table 8.1   Methodist membership and growth rates in Ireland 1850–70

	Wesleyan Methodists			Primitive Wesleyan Methodists	
	Membership nos	Growth rate		Membership nos	Growth rate
1850	21,346		1850	10,420	
1851	20,232	−5.2	1851	10,357	− 0.6
1852	20,040	−0.9	1852	10,362	4.8
1853	19,608	−2.2	1853	10,077	− 2.8
1854	19,233	−1.9	1854	8,384	−16.8
1855	18,749	−2.5	1855	8,041	− 4.1
1856	18,952	1.1	1856	8,763	9.0
1857	19,287	1.8	1857	8,942	2.0
1858	19,406	0.6	1858	9,158	2.4
1859	19,727	1.7	1859	9,979	9.0
1860	22,860	15.9	1860	15,341	53.7
1861	23,351	2.2	1861	14,207	− 7.4
1862	22,741	−2.6	1862	12,852	− 9.5
1863	21,953	−3.5	1863	11,769	− 8.4
1864	20,996	−4.4	1864	10,580	−10.1
1865	20,031	−4.6	1865	9,805	− 7.3
1866	19,835	−1.0	1866	9,695	− 1.1
1867	19,657	−0.9	1867	9,416	− 2.9
1868	19,591	−0.3	1868	9,320	− 1.0
1869	19,659	0.3	1869	8,431	− 9.5
1870	19,963	1.5	1870	8,065	− 4.3

Membership numbers are taken from the annual minutes of Conference. Growth rates are calculated by expressing the annual net turnover of membership as a percentage of the total membership of the previous year.

their membership figures once the initial excitement of the revival had dissipated. By narrowing the focus to look at one church in particular a clearer picture emerges. In the Baptist church at Tobermore the membership of 269 in March 1860 was reduced to 223 by March 1865. By March 1869, when there was not a single addition to the congregation, the Reverend Carson said of the revival period that 'out of some 80 or 90 individuals received at that time, scarcely one remains to us at this moment. And what is worse than their exclusion or withdrawal, their evil conduct, or their spiritual apathy, did not fail to leave its mark behind.'[59] Much of the statistical success of the revival was therefore short-lived and some saw it as counterproductive.

With regard to the social status of those affected, there was again among contemporaries a general concentration on the most dramatic cases. Conversions of prostitutes, drunks and gamblers attracted attention out of all proportion to their actual number. It does seem, however, that the revival had a more immediate impact on poorer districts, and since physical prostrations were almost entirely confined to those of lower social status, the consequent excitement in densely populated areas was intense. Ewart's Row in Belfast, which was inhabited almost entirely by millworkers, and the back streets of Ballymena, were scenes of such religious frenzy.[60] Part of the problem in assessing the effect of revival on the lower classes is the difficulty of defining their religious experience in a way that can be measured. Church attendance is not a particularly sensitive barometer of belief. Hugh McLeod suggests that revivals, by generating excitement and by emphasizing experience over reason, played a part in filling the gap between official and folk religion.[61] American observers of revival also feel that they are most effective within this wider Christian subculture.[62] Thus in times of revival the simple, fervent, emotive message of the gospel, particularly when presented by uneducated preachers in an informal setting or by powerful professional evangelists, could have a direct – though usually transitional – appeal. This suggestion is supported by the evidence of the agents of the Belfast Town Mission who found that many of the poor of the town retained a belief in the general idea of a system of rewards and punishments and had an emotionally resonant, if doctrinally incoherent, religious faith.[63] Here was a foundation upon which popular preachers could build.

A close reading of events in the various localities suggests, however, that the most significant response to revivalist activity occurred among the 'respectable' working class rather than among the unemployed and destitute. This is further evidenced by the extension of religious practices from the home to the workplace. Meetings took place at lunch times in mills and in the shipyards.[64] Many employers were only too glad to encourage the clergy in offering this kind of service which, while uniting workers and employers at one level, was perhaps more significant in its support for a conservative and paternalistic regime. The provision of professional religious guidance would also presumably limit the kind of excesses which closed Ballygarvey bleachworks, Ewart's Mill, York Street Mill, Broughshane spinning mill and various other factories and warerooms, as prostrate workers succumbed to what had all the appearance of an epidemic.[65]

It also seems clear that a large proportion of those affected by the movement were already involved in the churches, often as Sunday school teachers or, in the case of Methodists, as class leaders, or simply as members of the congregation. Ministers' reports of conversions, for example, usually mentioned families they were accustomed to visiting in a pastoral capacity and who were therefore already oriented towards the churches and predisposed to accept the Christian gospel. Similarly, conversations with converts often revealed a general familiarity with the scriptures. There were those who stated that 'a new light was now thrown on passages of the Word of God, which were before dark and mysterious', or for whom 'a new meaning was given to Sunday school lessons', and those who declared their former professions 'all a worthless form'.[66] Such converts may have been less newsworthy, but they were probably more significant for the churches in the long term. In a similar vein, it has been suggested that the Sunday schools were the nurseries of the revival, and this helps explain some of the statistical trends, since once these resources had been tapped, potential converts were harder to find.[67]

Attention was also drawn to the disproportionate number of women and children converted, the suggestion being that they were more emotionally susceptible to the appeals of preachers. Converted children were also used to address adult gatherings.

> A little boy ten years old commenced to the astonishment of everyone, and he had not long begun when a poor woman, who had been under strong conviction for three months, came forward and shouted 'O Jesus', which she repeated again and again until she sank from exhaustion. A Mrs Hudson, converted about a fortnight before, commenced then with power to pray for her.[68]

John Kent states that within 'revivalist circles the converted child who saved his parents played as vital a role as did the Virgin Mary in contemporaneous Roman Catholic exhibitions of religious excitement'. Women were even more significant. Peter Gibbon finds an explanation for the preponderance of female converts in changing demographic patterns, leading to diminishing marriage prospects and a breakdown of traditional cultural expectations.[69] This tidy proposition is difficult to test. Gibbon stresses the revival's relative lack of impact in those areas where the 'marriage crisis' was weakest but, since these coincide with areas of Presbyterian weakness, it is difficult to be specific about cause and effect. Economic dislocation was nevertheless an important factor. For example, in Yorkshire and Wales, and in south Ulster in the eighteenth century, external tensions within the wider society can be seen to have played a part in generating religious excitement.[70] Stress and anxiety related to secular causes do seem to provoke a vulnerability which leads individuals to seek comfort and hope in religion. The most dramatic changes in the northeast's industrial growth had taken place in the textile industry, and women were most affected. Henry Patterson speaks of the predominance of females employed in the new mills, with women, young persons and children making up between 78 and 88 per cent of the workforce between 1835 and 1895.[71] The transition from domestic to factory production meant long hours of confinement in bad conditions, under a regime of harsh discipline. In general terms the revival may well have served as an outlet for frustration and anxiety for those confronted with such structural changes in their employment. The importance of women in popular religious movements has already been dealt with, but it does seem that young unmarried women in particular were disproportionately represented in the ranks of revival converts. The first converts in the Cambuslang revival were three young sisters, and thereafter young women, especially domestic servants, comprised a large group.[72] Of course female converts were welcomed by the churches because of their strategic role in influencing others. Henry Cooke's response to the question of female converts was purely pragmatic – 'God be praised', he exclaimed, 'they would in time be mothers.'[73]

The number of Roman Catholic converts reported was not large, but a good deal of publicity was given to them.[74] It has been pointed out that anti-Catholicism was a factor common to both American and Ulster Protestantism in the mid-nineteenth century, because both areas were undergoing a Roman Catholic resurgence. This may be one reason why the revival translated so easily from America to Ulster, and not so readily to other parts of Britain.[75] The politicization of the Roman Catholic community, and the revitalization of the Roman Catholic Church – parallelling Protestant evangelicalism – evidently posed problems for the Protestant community. Evangelicalism was itself assertive and inherently anti-Catholic, and the religious riots in Belfast of 1858 and 1859 were an indication of the growing breach between the two communities.[76] The Presbyterian General Assembly had begun to direct its attention more specifically to Roman Catholicism in the 1840s. Its frequent reports on the state of popery and its doctrinal errors prompted the remark in 1855 that 'The present is the hour for action.'[77] The revival was, however, a Protestant phenomenon. No deliberate proselytizing campaign was directed towards Catholics. But, while most participants stress that this outbreak of religious enthusiasm moderated, rather than exacerbated, sectarian feeling, other sources tell a different story. Frank Wright is probably correct to see the revival as yet another landmark in the religious differentiation between Protestants and Catholics which had become more marked over the bitter educational debates and the new exclusivity of the Roman Catholic hierarchy in Ireland.[78] For many Ulster Protestants, particularly in this period of increasing isolation from the rest of Ireland, the industrial expansion and relative prosperity of the northeast were viewed as a direct consequence of its religious and ethnic base. The rise of a more assertive Catholicism threatened that dominant religious ideology and the cultural identity which it embraced. During the seventeenth century predestinarian theology had facilitated the Protestant community's perception of itself as 'God's people in Ireland surrounded on all sides by antichristian idolatry and superstition'.[79] The rigidity of that doctrine was now in decline, but the interpretation of the revival as a divine visitation – which had little or no impact on Roman Catholic areas – provided a nineteenth-century alternative. The revival movement offered reaffirmation, justification and divine approval to a society which had undergone half a century of social, political and religious upheaval.

The revival's emphasis on moral reformation also reflected the cultural values of respectable Protestantism. Revivalists claimed a variety of beneficial social consequences for their campaign – from a decline in drunkenness to a fall in the crime rate – all of which were just as quickly refuted by the opposition.[80] While the drama and power of the revival movement may have had an immediate impact in some localities, long-term behavioural trends do not seem to have been much affected. Indeed, this whole debate must be placed in a wider pattern of changes in social behaviour in the first half of the nineteenth century, which have already been discussed, rather than looked at in isolation in 1859.[81]

What then emerges from a study of the Ulster revival in 1859? The great American revival of 1857–8 was undoubtedly an important stimulus, but with the soil of Ulster well prepared, the local experience took on a distinctiveness of its own. So many variables exist, however, that it is difficult to pinpoint specific causes – and why in any case did a local revival, not in itself a unique occurrence, become province-wide? The internal revitalization of the churches, the general feeling of expectancy and dramatic conversion experiences are important factors. To view the revival from a wider perspective, modern studies of popular revivalism suggest a direct relation between revival and societies whose identity or cohesion is perceived to be under threat.[82] Revivalist momentum, it is suggested, is sustained in opposition to the encroachment of external pressures on traditional culture – whether caused by industrialization, social dislocation, political progress or, in the case of Ulster, the emergence of a self-conscious and more powerful Roman Catholicism. Thus, Ulster, south Wales, Cornwall and parts of Scotland sought to maintain their distinctive identity through a common religious expression for which the tradition of a Bible-based, popular religious culture supplied the internal mechanism.

Numerically, the claims of the revival's supporters are difficult to substantiate. While huge open-air meetings focused attention upon the popular response, and some commentators considered 100,000 to be an underestimation of the number of converts,[83] church statistics suggest that the sudden rise in membership figures was transient and probably most effective within the church's existing constituency. Turning again to the definition of an awakening with which we started, it could be argued that the events of 1859 marked no fundamental upheaval in Ulster life. The revival was not a catalyst for change, but a kind of mid-century stepping-stone reflecting the consolidation of earlier evangelical enthusiasm. Its importance lies in the boost it gave to Protestant confidence, and its articulation of values perceived as central to the prosperity and unity of the province. But religious phenomena ought not to be reduced to mere sociological and cultural categories. Ultimately, revivalism has an internal dynamic of its own, and an elusive quality which all too often defies historical analysis. To the same extent as it heightened enthusiasm among its participants, it should evoke humility in its interpreters.

[9]
Home Rule and the Protestant mind 1860–90

Be ye not unequally yoked together with unbelievers: for what fellowship hath righteousness with unrighteousness? and what communion hath light with darkness? (2 Corinthians 6:14)

Come out from among them, and be ye separate, saith the Lord. (2 Corinthians 6:17)

The churches know by intimate neighbourhood with the people in every part of Ireland the true aims of those who clamour for separation. They see the effects of so-called Nationalism on morals, on character, on society, on the rights of property, and not least, on Christian institutions. Their estimate of Home Rule is the product of many influences. Observation, experience, intuition, historical facts, and facts of daily life – all contribute their part toward that fulness of conviction which they alike own and maintain. Such a solidarity of opinion does not exist on any other public question.[1]

The geographical distribution of Irish Protestantism was shaped initially not by a complex process of religious change, but by settlement patterns dating back to the sixteenth and seventeenth centuries. In particular, the migration of Scottish Presbyterians to the northeast of Ireland ensured that the province of Ulster had a higher density of Protestants than any other part of Ireland. The general effect of the evangelical revival, pioneered in the 1740s by the Methodists and the Moravians, was to reinforce that geographical pattern, despite repeated attempts to convert Roman Catholics in the south and west of the country. By the middle decades of the nineteenth century the growth of evangelicalism in all the major Protestant denominations had not only confirmed the geographical concentration of Protestantism in Ulster, but had contributed much to the distinctive religious, political and social ethos of the province. Ulster had also emerged as the most developed industrial and commercial part of the country and had experienced less population decline as a result of the famine. This cultural differentiation of Ulster from the rest of the island, though by no means complete, was a stumbling-block in the way of establishing political and religious structures acceptable to an increasingly potent Irish Catholic nationalism in the second half of the nineteenth century.

The religious problems associated with the governing of Ireland in this period were underpinned by those most inconvenient of historical facts, demographic statistics. Although the famine and resultant emigration took a savage toll of poorer Roman Catholics, the balance of denominational allegiances did not change all that much over the course of the century. In 1834 the division of population between Catholic, Anglican and Presbyterian was respectively 80.9 per cent, 10.7 per cent and 8.1 per cent. In 1861 the figures were 77.7 per cent, 12 per cent and 9 per cent and by 1901 they stood at 74.2 per cent, 13 per cent and 9.9 per cent. It was, however, the religious distribution of the population which most dramatically exposed the differences between Ulster and the rest of the country. The census of 1881 (Table 9.1), for example, not only showed that 75 per cent of Irish Protestants lived in Ulster, but that Ulster itself had almost equal numbers of Protestants and Catholics. A further breakdown into counties shows that Protestant strength was concentrated in the northeast of the province, including Belfast, and was weakest in the provincial border counties of Donegal, Monaghan and Cavan. The fact that Catholics outnumbered Protestants in five of Ulster's nine counties puts in perspective the religious equilibrium of so-called Protestant Ulster. Moreover, within Protestantism itself, the established church could boast only a bare majority of adherents. With the tide running against religious endowments throughout the British Isles, and with the Roman Catholic Church in Ireland under the leadership of Paul Cullen increasingly unwilling to acquiesce in state support for Protestantism, the future of the Church of Ireland seemed far from rosy.

By the 1860s the Church of Ireland was facing an unholy alliance of English and Welsh Nonconformists, Irish Catholics, Scottish voluntaries and utilitarian radicals, all lining up to disendow the Irish Church and remove state support for the Protestant religion in Ireland.[2] In the face of such an array of enemies the Irish Church began to fear that even its sister church, the Church of England, might not be strong enough to save it from serious damage. Irish Churchmen recognized that they had little defence on either moral or utilitarian grounds. As a 'Presbyterian Layman' pointed out in 1867, 'in 199 parishes there is not a single adherent of the established church, and 1,539 parishes, or nearly two-thirds of the whole, have not more than 100 adherents in each'.[3] The bitter pill which the Church of Ireland's defenders had to swallow is that, despite allegations to the contrary,[4] the church by 1869 was a more efficient, zealous and financially unexacting institution than it had been half a century earlier. As the church reformed its abuses to placate external criticism, external critics began to take the higher view that no amount of reform could possibly justify the state endowment of a minority church once the majority was no longer willing to put up with it. Irish Churchmen were not without arguments to defend their position, but in the political climate of

Table 9.1 Religious denominations, 1881, Ulster: provincial distribution
and numbers in counties and towns

Counties and towns	Roman Catholics	Church of Ireland	Presbyterians	Methodists	Others
Antrim	51,590	45,212	116,813	3,427	10,687
	(22.7%)	(19.8%)	(51.3%)	(1.5%)	(4.7%)
Armagh	75,909	53,390	26,077	4,884	3,117
	(46.4%)	(32.7%)	(16.0%)	(3.0%)	(1.9%)
Belfast	59,975	58,410	71,521	9,141	9,075
	(28.8%)	(28.1%)	(34.4%)	(4.4%)	(4.3%)
Carrickfergus	1,169	1,746	5,525	435	1,134
	(11.7%)	(17.4%)	(55.2%)	(4.4%)	(11.3%)
Cavan	104,685	19,022	4,396	1,088	285
	(80.9%)	(14.7%)	(3.4%)	(0.8%)	(0.2%)
Donegal	157,608	24,759	20,784	2,014	870
	(76.5%)	(12.0%)	(10.1%)	(1.0%)	(0.4%)
Down	76,690	56,514	99,301	3,894	11,791
	(30.9%)	(22.8%)	(40.0%)	(1.6%)	(4.7%)
Fermanagh	47,359	30,874	1,708	4,863	75
	(55.8%)	(36.4%)	(2.0%)	(5.7%)	(0.1%)
Londonderry	73,274	31,596	54,727	938	4,456
	(44.4%)	(19.1%)	(33.2%)	(0.6%)	(2.7%)
Monaghan	75,714	13,623	12,213	544	654
	(73.7%)	(13.3%)	(11.9%)	(0.5%)	(0.6%)
Tyrone	109,793	44,256	38,564	3,597	1,509
	(55.5%)	(22.4%)	(19.5%)	(1.8%)	(0.8%)
Summary of religious denominations by provinces					
Connacht	783,116	32,522	3,059	2,239	721
	(95.3%)	(3.9%)	(0.4%)	(0.3%)	(0.1%)
Leinster	1,094,825	157,522	12,059	7,006	7,577
	(85.6%)	(12.3%)	(0.9%)	(0.6%)	(0.6%)
Munster	1,249,384	70,128	3,987	4,769	2,847
	(93.8%)	(5.3%)	(0.3%)	(0.4%)	(0.2%)
Ulster	833,566	379,402	451,629	34,825	43,653
	(47.8%)	(21.8%)	(25.9%)	(2.0%)	(2.5%)

Statistics are taken from Vaughan and Fitzpatrick, *Irish Historical Statistics*, pp. 58–9.

the 1860s they were not very convincing. Obscurantist and antiquarian claims about being 'the Old Catholic Church of Ireland'[5] cut no ice, and it soon became clear that there were only two possible defences. The first revolved around the implications Irish disestablishment would have for the Church of England[6] and the second was based on the need to preserve Protestant truth against Romish error in Ireland. Unfortunately the former had two edges to it, and it was a pity from the Church of Ireland's point of view that Gladstone became persuaded that vigorous treatment of the Irish Church was the best means of preserving religious establishments elsewhere. The second argument was both more plausible in Ireland and less persuasive in the rest of Britain. The Bishop of Ossory, Ferns and Leighlin, no doubt forgetting that politicians of all people least like to be reminded of their inconsistencies, tried the dubious tactic of quoting younger Gladstone to older Gladstone.

> The Government, as a Government, was bound to maintain that form of belief which contained the largest portion of truth with the smallest admixture of error. Upon that ground the Government of this country maintained the Protestant, and declined to maintain the Catholic religion.[7]

Gladstone was too much of a moralist not to be troubled by such discrepancies, and since he had already given his support to the endowment of Maynooth in 1845, he was, in 1868, prepared to consider a scheme of concurrent endowment of all the major religious denominations in Ireland.[8] English bishops thought this was the best that could be done for the Church of Ireland, but Irish bishops, the Irish Catholic hierarchy and Nonconformist voluntaries all repudiated it, and Gladstone was left with little alternative but to press on with disestablishment. All that remained to be settled were the terms, and the English bishops secured a better deal for their Irish counterparts than could have been achieved by their own efforts.[9]

The established church was not the only Protestant church in Ireland to be affected by disendowment, because it had implications for both the Presbyterians' *regium donum* and the future of Protestantism in Ireland. Whereas both the Presbytery of Antrim and the Remonstrant Synod of Ulster quickly and unanimously welcomed the dismantling of Anglican privileges, the debates within the General Assembly were more convoluted and acrimonious.[10] Many regretted the end of a special relationship with the state spanning two centuries and feared that Protestantism in Ireland would be rendered more vulnerable by a repudiation of the state's responsibility to 'endow the truth'.[11] On the other hand, Presbyterians had suffered too much from Anglican exclusivity and privilege to be much cast down by disendowment of the Church of Ireland. In the event, the assembly decided to confine its negotiations with the government to the issue of Presbyterian endowments alone and a compromise was agreed by which the *regium donum* was commuted for a lump sum. The Presbyterian laity promised to augment the commutation fund to ensure that their ministers were adequately remunerated.[12] While the General Assembly largely confined itself to the general principles and immediate issues confronting it in 1869, the situation outside the walls of its learned debates was more volatile. In 1867 an ageing Henry Cooke once more defended the principles of a common Protestantism at one of the first great public meetings convened to protest about disestablishment.

> It is because I recognize in her a noble branch of the great Protestant tree planted in Europe by the hands of the Reformers; because I hear in her the living voice of the primitive evangelical teachers, and the dying testimony of that glorious company of martyrs and confessors, by whom liberty of conscience, the right

of private judgment, and unrestricted access to the Sacred Scripture have been asserted, recovered and secured.[13]

The former moderator's speech was made during a particularly emotive display of Protestant solidarity in Hillsborough, when he was joined by other Protestant leaders on a united platform of episopalian, Methodist and Presbyterian spokesmen.[14] As in 1834, Cooke was speaking as an individual, not as a representative of the General Assembly, but in 1869 the point that 'the churches of the Reformation are all of one family' was taken up by other Presbyterian evangelicals in great popular demonstrations at which doctrinal and ecclesiological differences were temporarily set aside in the interests of Protestant solidarity.[15]

Anti-Catholicism was the most common unifying feature of evangelical Protestantism, and with this reinforced by census evidence of its demographic weakness and by increasing nationalist pressure, Protestant spokesmen stressed the need for state protection and support of their religion in the face of 'a powerful and well-organized opponent'.[16] The centrality of anti-Catholicism was further highlighted by its ability to bridge both pro- and anti-disestablishment pressure groups. Whereas evangelical supporters of the established church viewed it as a bulwark against Catholicism, its evangelical critics condemned it for being 'a nursery and training school for Rome'.[17] Most evangelicals and ultra-Protestants nevertheless opposed disestablishment as both a danger to the prosperity of the present and a betrayal of the sacrifices of the past.[18] 'Conciliation', it was claimed, aroused arrogance and aggression in Roman Catholics and endangered the Protestant community.[19] In the crusade against 'a tyrant majority and . . . a government supported by Radicals, Infidels and Sceptics', there was seen to be no room for neutrality.[20] Disestablishment was interpreted as the surrender of an important strategic position on the part of a powerful ally, and those who had been to the fore in the campaign against Catholic Emancipation now spoke alongside a new generation of popular religious leaders whose presence served to reinforce the ongoing nature of the struggle. While the prefacing of speeches by prayers and hymn-singing stressed the essentially religious nature of the opposition to the government, the substantial presence of the Orange Order, represented as 'carrying out the spirit of Bible Christianity',[21] heightened the populist, militant atmosphere, and indicated the extent to which 'religious' values pervaded the wider culture. But perhaps most serious of all for conservatives both in and outside the church, and on both sides of the Irish Sea, were the wider political implications of the Irish Church Act. For those who interpreted its passage as a breach of the Act of Union, its repercussions not only endangered the constitution, but threatened the integrity of the empire.

> The Bill of Mr. Gladstone violates the solemn compact on which the integrity of the United Kingdom depends, and is perilous to the peace and unity of Empire. . . . If this Bill be carried, with all its confiscating and sacrilegious enactments, seven years will not elapse until the next onslaught will be on the property of the country, which will necessarily lead to civil war.[22]

This prophecy turned out to be incorrect, but disestablishment did not take Irish religion out of the realm of political conflict in the way that was hoped. As Parsons states, 'by 1871 the government had thus *constitutionally* withdrawn from involvement in religion in Ireland more thoroughly than it had in Wales, Scotland or England yet in the twentieth century religion and politics have remained interconnected in Ireland in a manner which had already ceased in the rest of Britain by the 1920s'.[23]

While the disestablishment issue was rich in complexities for the Presbyterian community, the question of land reform was, for most of the nineteenth century, a more straightforward matter. The strength of Presbyterianism among tenant farmers was evidenced by the continued support of its governing body for improved tenant rights and by the presence of both clerical and lay Presbyterian spokesmen at campaign meetings.[24] The land question was seen to be Ireland's central problem: 'the main part of the public interest was the land, then and always. Upon its possession, its tenure, its treatment, and its rent, all questions turned. Even the furious tithe war was nothing but a branch of the agrarian difficulty.'[25]

The campaign against the privileges of landlordism superficially united Presbyterians and Catholics in opposition to the Anglican ascendancy. In true liberal tradition, the common interests of farmers, north and south, were pursued in the face of the 'tyranny' of a small minority, and the Gladstonian policy of legislative reform was encouraged.[26] But although Catholics and Presbyterians shared common grievances, there were ominous signs of disharmony beneath the surface. Differing perceptions of the origin of the Ulster custom, for example, based on opposing views of history, indicated a significant ideological divide.[27] Nationalist determination to unite the land and religion platforms brought tensions to the surface, and though spokesmen proclaimed the 'necessity for continued agitation and co-operation with the South', 'the sectarian tocsin had been sounded, and as usual the material interests of the people suffered'.[28] Traditional Presbyterian support for Liberal causes in the nineteenth century, including tenant-right and reform of the franchise, became increasingly squeezed between Irish nationalism in all its forms on the one hand, and the growing sectarianism inspired by Orangeism and Catholic reaction on the other. In the countryside the Land League 'reinforced the politicization of rural Catholic nationalist Ireland, partly by defining that identity against urbanization, landlordism, Englishness and – implicitly – Protestantism'.[29] Ironically, however, the most anti-Protestant speeches made by Land League leaders in Ulster were made by Protestants.

In Belfast, Liberalism had largely melted under the white heat of repeated sectarian riots, the emergence of a distinctly Orange popular Protestantism and organizational atrophy. By 1880 Ulster Liberalism had indeed become a rural party. A detailed analysis of voting behaviour in the County Down by-election of 1884, for example, shows that Presbyterian Liberalism was overwhelmingly stronger in rural areas with few Catholics, than in urban areas or in districts with a substantial Catholic population.[30] In such circumstances

Liberalism was more a consequence of distance from conflict than a benign attitude towards it. The election of 1885 further demonstrated that 'even before Gladstone's turn to Home Rule, Liberalism was a minority presence among the enlarged electorate' and that 'the greater part of the Catholic population was clearly within the nationalist camp'. Even before Home Rule cast its shadow 'the unmistakeable drift of Protestant political expressions was away from conventional politics, whether Liberal or Conservative, towards a Conservatism in which plebeian militancy had a growing place, especially in the urban context'.[31] In the countryside, however, Presbyterian support for tenant-right and Liberalism lasted longer in County Antrim than in the south and west of Ulster. Liberalism after all was a tenant farmer's creed, and one reason for the electoral success of the Conservatives in 1885 and later was the enfranchisement of the agricultural labourers who were both more receptive to the appeal of militant Protestantism and hostile to the Liberals as the party of their farmer employers. The fact that County Antrim was also a particularly strong centre of revivalism in 1859 shows that no simple connection can be made between religious enthusiasm and political expression without taking into account peculiarities of social status, occupation, region and political personality.

By 1885, before Gladstone experimented with Home Rule, Ulster Protestants, despite long-standing political and denominational differences, had been thrown together by a formidable range of pressures. Disestablishment of the Irish Church, educational competition, the 'invasion of Ulster' by the Irish National League after 1883, agrarian violence, Cullen's anti-Protestant leadership of the Catholic Church, sectarianism in Belfast and the perceived economic superiority of the Lagan valley over the rest of Ireland, all coalesced to persuade Ulster Protestants that they were facing a Catholic-inspired nationalist threat to their entire way of life. Evangelical Protestantism, which had helped create some of the pressures it professed to abhor, supplied many of the symbols, much of the religious legitimacy and not a few of the prejudices which were pressed into service the following year.

Since neither the disestablishment of the Irish Church nor various attempts at land reform had quietened Ireland, Gladstone reached the conclusion that only a well-considered measure of self-government offered any prospect of long-term peace and stability. Not surprisingly, such a bold constitutional proposal helped crystallize the differences between Irish Catholics and Protestants, and between Ulster and the rest of the country, despite the insistence of those opposed to Home Rule that Gladstone's scheme would bear heavily on the population as a whole. Nevertheless, in a remarkable way the Home Rule crisis brought into sharp focus an Irish Protestant mentality, centred in Ulster, which had been forged over a quarter of a millennium of turbulent history. Moreover, the resistance to Home Rule in Ulster in the period 1885–1920 cemented a Protestant identity which subsequent events have done nothing to undermine. The inability of either the British state or Irish nationalism to coerce or accommodate this sturdy and peculiar minority has resulted in one of the most intractable problems in the modern world. The purpose of this chapter is to use the Home Rule crisis of 1886 as a window through which to view the Irish Protestant tradition at a decisive moment in its history. This will be accomplished in two parts. First, there will be an assessment of how the main Protestant churches in Ireland – episcopalian, Presbyterian and Methodist – responded to Gladstone's proposals within the setting of a wider British Protestantism. Second, there will be an attempt to explore the Ulster Protestant mind from the standpoints both of those within the tradition and of those Irish Protestants who vigorously repudiated it.

Most members of the Church of Ireland had regarded the disestablishment of the church in 1869 as the end of a cycle of concessions to Irish Roman Catholics which had begun with Catholic Emancipation in 1829. All legitimate grievances had been met, a position of religious equality had been reached and the Church of Ireland had been painfully reconstructed to suit its new circumstances.[32] Within this mental framework all subsequent agitations on behalf of Irish Catholics – educational, agrarian or constitutional – were viewed not as legitimate attempts to secure fair treatment but as unjustified actions designed to take advantage of Irish Protestantism's relative weakness. In his presidential address to the special meeting of the General Synod in March 1886 the Archbishop of Dublin stated:

> I have carefully considered the statements put forward by those who advocate Home Rule, and I cannot for the life of me discover where the grievance is to be found. If any of our fellow-countrymen were still living under the tyranny of the penal laws, as they were, unfortunately, some years ago, if Catholic emancipation had not become a fact, if they were able even to complain of the ascendancy in this land of a State Church, or if they were able to persuade us that, owing to some fault in the limits of the franchise . . . they have not a voice in the Imperial Parliament upon questions such as education or the land. . . I would look at the matter in an entirely different light. It is no use trying to trample out a real grievance. But if there be no grievance, then we must trace these demands for Home Rule to one of two causes . . . sentiment or . . . ulterior aims. . . . Undoubtedly, behind the claim for Home Rule – and we should be fools if we did not believe it – there lurks the demand for entire separation, and for a very advanced form of socialism.[33]

What lies behind this speech is the sincere conviction that the old pattern of agitation, coercion and concession had come to an end; what was therefore at stake in 1886 was the future destiny of the nation, and who was to have the power to shape it.

An examination of the voluminous pamphlet literature of the Church of Ireland between disestablishment and the Home Rule crisis shows that just under half (over 200) were devoted to Prayer Book revision and ritualist controversies, a further third (130) were concerned with educational debates and about a fifth (80) addressed matters of finance and property.[34] This reflects the determination of many within the church to maintain its essential Protestantism, to resist Catholic educational encroachments and to protect the church's remaining endowments. As a result of the structural changes consequent upon disestablishment the northern laity, who were generally speaking more evangelical, had achieved more representation, if not necessarily more power, owing to the checks and balances in synodical voting arrangements. The requirement of a two-thirds majority of each order – bishops, clergy and laity – present and voting, subjected the church, according to the Protestant Defence Association (PDA), to the 'absolute control of a minority, whose Romanising tendencies are patent to all men'.[35] Ritualism, the PDA contended, had corrupted the Church of England, damaged the Protestant missionary movement through its influence on the Society for the Propagation of the Gospel, and, if unchecked, would ruin Protestantism in Ireland.[36] The theology of the Irish High Church Party was, of course, anything but Roman, 'but the simple fact that it moved away from an evangelical position, settling upon more sacramentarian thought, was enough to stir a fear of Rome's potential presence in the Church's fold'. The campaign for the revision of the Prayer Book on more Protestant lines was therefore the 'defensive reaction of a Church which knew the enemy to be without, and to be formidable and aggressive. It was that of a Church which feared that the enemy on the outside might enter through even what the Prayer-Book permitted, and that in the process everything would be lost.' As it turned out, the Prayer Book revision was achieved relatively agreeably due to the fear of schism, the openness of the debates and the voting system of the church which put a brake on hasty legislation. But the recurring ritualistic controversies within the church put episcopalian evangelicals on their guard against the 'murky whirlpool of superstition' which threatened to deliver them into the hands of Rome.[37]

For many within the church, Home Rule threatened to do the same thing by another route. Even the normally controlled *Irish Ecclesiastical Gazette* in the midst of the crisis detected a conspiracy of 'a foreign and Ultramontane Church, worked by the Jesuits' to overthrow the Protestant religion in Ireland: 'If we and Rome cannot live together on terms of peace, we must do so with the sword in our hands. No surrender!'[38] Despite such opinions the leadership of the Church of Ireland was slower to respond to the possibility of Home Rule than the other churches. Resolutions against a separate Parliament from the ultra-Protestant Dr Craig at the Dublin Synod in 1885 had been ruled out of order on the grounds that it was a political matter outside the competence of the church.[39] The situation in Ulster was rather different. There were reports in the *Gazette* of sermons against Home Rule in the diocese of Down and Connor and of enthusiastic episcopalian contributions to the meetings surrounding the visit to Belfast of Lord Randolph Churchill.[40] There was considerable pressure from the north for the bishops to do something and they agreed to convene a special synod of the church to debate the issue in late March 1886. Debate is a slight misnomer, for despite the Archbishop of Dublin's assurances that the Church of Ireland was one of the most representative bodies in the world, and despite his political disclaimers, the resolutions against Home Rule were prepared in advance and were moved by the bishops and other dignitaries within the church. The resolutions were predictable enough, with imperial themes close to the surface.[41]

Although Irish episcopalians opposed Home Rule on essentially the same grounds as the other Protestant churches, a number of distinctive themes do emerge from the Church of Ireland's records. As befitted the only Protestant church in Ireland with a considerable amount of its property and personnel located outside Ulster, there was an understandable reluctance to allow that Ulster was a distinct entity which might require special treatment. Indeed Leinster episcopalians argued a similar case as Ulster Protestants in suggesting that the Protestant parts of the south of Ireland, notably the old Pale, were wealthier and more progressive than the Catholic west, and were therefore specially worth listening to by British politicians.[42] The Church of Ireland's opposition to Home Rule also reflected its social status. In terms of social class the established church had the most eclectic membership of any of the churches, but it also had a higher percentage of the gentry and the landed aristocracy.[43] The landed lay leadership of the church was more at home with the more sophisticated tactics of the Irish Loyal and Patriotic Union[44] or the Irish Unionist Alliance[45] than with the more populist styles of urban Orangeism, but there was still an old paternalist, aristocratic and crypto-militarist tradition which saw it as its duty to muster the troops in a national emergency.[46] There was also more hard-headed talk within the Church of Ireland over the precise impact Home Rule would have on episcopalian endowments, investments, loans and bonds.[47] There was a general consensus that the church's wealth would be alarmingly reduced and there was also unease about what a nationalist parliament would do to the church's more attractive endowments such as Trinity College. These fears introduced an element of *realpolitik* into many churchmen who were concerned to conduct opposition to Home Rule in a manner not too prejudicial to their vested interests should they be defeated. Generally speaking, then, the Church of Ireland tried to lead with a high hand and had nothing but contempt for the riotous element within Ulster Protestantism who acted like 'fools and madmen'.[48]

The Church of Ireland was also glad to have the numerical support of other Irish Protestants in resisting Home Rule.[49] In Ulster, common cause was made with Presbyterians and Methodists in the great protest rallies,[50] but traditional animosities were not entirely forgotten. The fact that the Church of Ireland insisted on retaining its old name, despite disestablishment, was a constant thorn in Presbyterian flesh.[51] This superficially trivial contention was symbolic of more substantial grievances. There was, for example, an overwhelming preponderance of episcopalians in official positions in law and local government. Moreover, the Church of Ireland took a particularly tough stand on agrarian outrages, which many Presbyterians regarded as more of a reflection on the behaviour of Irish landlords than on Catholic criminality. The Church of Ireland was also less enthusiastic about the Evangelical Alliance than the other churches, especially the Methodists.[52] As a church organized in territorial units it felt itself peculiarly vulnerable to the conversionist ideology of the smaller evangelical churches. Allegations of poaching were common and the Church of Ireland was prone to dismissive comments on 'tasteless evangelicalism'. The Salvation Army, for example, was condemned as 'ribald sanctimoniousness'.[53] One similarity between the Church of Ireland and the other churches is the speed with which opposition to Home Rule became the badge of true churchmanship. At the General Synod Richard Bagwell stated that 'there are some Protestant MPs who have taken the oath of allegiance to Mr Parnell; but they in no way represent Protestant feeling. Not one of them. . . would have the slightest chance of election by any Synod, or any council or vestry, of the Church of Ireland, throughout the length and breadth of the country.'[54] By the time of the second Home Rule Bill in 1893, 1,190 vestries out of 1,218 gave their approval to a protest against the measure.[55] Those who were out of step were regarded either as weak in faith or strong in self-interest.

Gladstone could not be regarded as the Church of Ireland's most respected politician. Episcopalians were the least troubled of any Irish Protestants by residual loyalty to the Grand Old Man. In 1886 they repudiated Home Rule and got on with their business of repairing glebes, overseeing church investments, protecting church education and endowing the Clergy Good Service Fund. But they derived particular pleasure from planning the enthusiastic Jubilee celebrations for Queen Victoria in 1887.[56] The imperial crown still mattered, regardless of the perceived abominations of distrusted politicians confusing justice for Ireland with concessions to Catholic nationalism.

The long struggle for political, religious and social equality with episcopalians had endowed Ulster Presbyterians with a heightened perception of their prominence in the liberal-dissenting tradition. They were therefore concerned to articulate their opposition to Home Rule within the wider forum of British Nonconformity, and were well represented on the liberal-unionist platform. However, like other denominations influenced by evangelicalism, nineteenth-century Presbyterianism's understanding of progress in Ireland was intricately bound up with its resistance to an increasingly ultramontane Catholicism. Evangelical missions to Roman Catholic areas marked a change of policy from the earlier period,[57] while annual reports on the state of popery, resolutions on the invalidity of papal ordinances, and expressions of concern over persecutions in Spain indicated awareness of the wider dimensions of the Catholic threat.[58] Throughout this period anxiety over Romish influences at home and abroad continued to preoccupy the General Assembly. Its most prolonged and contentious internal controversy, for example, was the debate about instrumental music which paralleled the anti-ritualist campaign within the Church of Ireland in the same period. Although the essence of the debate was about traditional and modern forms of worship, more fervent evangelicals were able to represent instrumental music as 'owing its admission into Christian worship to the innovating spirit of Popery in the dark ages, when altars, images, prayers for the dead, and Latin masses were introduced'.[59] Such preoccupations boded ill for the reception of Home Rule in 1886, which was all too easily dismissed as Rome rule.

This new crisis once more provoked a reaction based on the perception that political, religious and social concerns were inextricably interwoven. The immediate response therefore was the calling of a special meeting of the General Assembly, 'to consider the present serious state of the country'. While there was general agreement that the land question needed to be settled equitably, proposals for 'a separate parliament for Ireland, or an elective National Council, or any legislation tending to imperil the legislative union between Great Britain and Ireland' were seen as 'disastrous to the best interests of our country'.[60] While proclaiming their continued support for civil and religious equality, Ulster Presbyterians feared that, given demographic realities, a Home Rule government would lead to 'the ascendancy of one class and creed in matters pertaining to religion, education, and civil administration', leaving no satisfactory safeguards for minorities.[61] Thus anti-Catholic and anti-Home Rule arguments were not seen to mark any departure from traditional Presbyterian liberalism. On the contrary, the bill was thought to be giving in to forces which were themselves illiberal – namely the Irish parliamentary party and agrarian outrage. To submit to such extremes would, it was feared, produce a denominational system of education and threaten Protestant freedoms.[62]

The main priority of the General Assembly was to circulate these views throughout Britain so that the basis of its opposition was clearly understood and kept separate from the more visible and alarming actions of the 'Orange' populace. This was the main thrust of the annual meeting, convened three months later. By presenting Gladstone's latest proposals as out of step with British Nonconformist liberalism and placing themselves firmly in the reforming tradition, Ulster Presbyterians claimed the support of liberal dissenters on the mainland. Copies of the assembly's resolutions were sent to MPs and to Scottish and English Presbyterian ministers, and a deputation was sent to London to canvass other influential figures.[63] Dissent from this majority view was strictly limited, in official reports at least, but it was by no means absent. A 'sturdy' minority of the General Assembly supported the second Home Rule bill in 1893 and its supporters were able to present Gladstone with a petition signed by a 'cross-section of society', containing 3,535 signatures, in favour of its passage.[64] The papers of the Reverend J. B. Armour, converted to the Home Rule side in the late 1880s, make it clear that, apart from the small minority prepared to articulate their opposition, many more ministers supported the assembly resolutions only because of congregational pressure.[65] With boycotts and exclusions resulting from failure to comply with majority opinion, it is certainly conceivable that some ministers would opt to set aside their political views in the interests of congregational harmony. While this qualification serves to modify the view of a united ministerial front against Home Rule, however, it also illustrates the strength of community pressure which was both more pervasive and ultimately more effective.

Representing the voice of the professions and of trade and commerce, and with the nucleus of their support in Belfast itself, Presbyterians formed a powerful interest group which linked their relative prosperity with their religious identity. The Reverend R. M. Edgar of Dublin, editor of the *Presbyterian Churchman*, stated in 1886 that

> Ulster, least favoured of the provinces by nature, has become the leading province, mainly through Presbyterian industry and energy. It is our Presbyterian base of operations, and we who occupy the advanced posts beyond Ulster, hope to hold them and extend our pickets and do our best to transform the people into an integral and loyal portion of the greatest Protestant Empire that has as yet existed in the world.[66]

His article on 'Catholic versus Protestant Nations! A Contrast for the Times' clearly reflected the widely held view that the choice was between imperial Protestant glory and a tyrannical impoverished Catholic state. A survey of the material, mental and moral status of the nations of the world suggested that 'all the Protestant countries march at the head'. Thus, one of the central arguments of anti-Home Rulers was that a Dublin government's protectionist policies would 'empty their mills, clear their rivers and shipyards, would stop their looms, would make the voice of their spindles silent and would cause a complete destruction of the industry that has made the province so prosperous'.[67]

With such fears easily converted into discrimination and job losses, there were violent sectarian street riots in Belfast in the summer of 1886, and the fiery preaching of some evangelical Presbyterians, such as Hugh Hanna, further inflamed local tensions.[68] One particular sermon, preached to his congregation on Sunday 13 June 1886, after a period of rioting, was critical of the part played by the police force and plainly asserted the right of resistance.

> We stand for right and truth and liberty against the forces of error and tyranny, and we are resolved to resist them in whatever form they may appear. Our safety for every interest that is dear to us lies in the union existing with the sister kingdom – with our kith and kin across the narrow seas that separate us from our Scottish and English brethren. We shall enter into no political partnership with the apostles of sedition and outrage, in Ireland or anywhere else, and we shall defend ourselves against all domination of such kind.[69]

This sermon was reprinted in local newspapers and Hanna's words, as in 1857, were subject to close questioning from the commissioners sent to Belfast to investigate the riots. Claiming to represent the opinions of 'practically the whole Protestant community', Hanna's defence was vigorous. Loyalist resistance to the triumph of the separatists had to be seen in the light of a province on the 'brink of civil war', the authorities' 'gross mismanagement' of the crisis and the actions of a constabulary which had 'changed its front along with Gladstone'. His exhortations to his congregation were, he claimed, 'not only true but expedient', and the sermon as a whole 'social, ethical and pacific'.[70] Hanna clearly felt that it was the duty of the clergy to give counsel in times of trouble, and that it should be appropriate to the seriousness of the threat posed to Ulster Protestantism, however irresponsible it might seem to outsiders. Such zealous language was rarely heard within the calmer confines of the General Assembly, and the meeting on the morning following the riots was held behind closed doors.[71] Nevertheless, whether proclaimed from the platforms of Liberal-Unionist meetings, or expounded from Belfast pulpits, the strength of Presbyterian resistance to Home Rule was undoubted. The Reverend Edgar quite rightly judged that 'the agitators have reckoned without their host'.[72]

The response of Irish Methodists to Home Rule has to be seen in the light of their attitudes throughout the nineteenth century to demands from the Roman Catholic Church and its alleged political representatives.[73] With near unanimity Irish Methodists had opposed in turn Catholic Emancipation, national education, the Repeal campaign, the Maynooth grant and the disestablishment of the Church of Ireland. The ideology behind such opposition was based not so much on political partisanship or economic self-interest as on a settled religious conviction that the Roman Catholic religion was the primary cause of all other Irish problems. Thus, political remedies whose effect was to undermine the Protestant foundations of church and state could only perpetuate the very evils they were designed to remove. Only religious conversion from Catholicism to evangelical Protestantism, however implausible that had become by the late Victorian period, offered the prospect of long-term peace and stability in Ireland. The anti-Catholic strand in Irish Methodism, however, was not simply a product of its evangelical theology, but arose naturally from the peculiarities of its own history. Methodism in Ireland had taken strongest root in areas settled by English episcopalians and had always regarded itself as culturally integrated into British Protestantism.[74] It was, moreover, the sister church of England's largest Nonconformist denomination and was held to have a special place in the worldwide missionary contest, or so it was perceived, between Irish Catholicism and British Protestantism. As late as 1883 the British Methodist Conference stated that Irish Methodists were in a 'position of danger and of supreme importance' because 'Irish Romanism supplies the main strength of the Papacy in every English-speaking nation'. With undisguised self-interest it went on to suggest that 'our chief political, municipal, and social difficulties would become far less serious if the Irish race were Protestantized. Few things could so materially promote the highest and best intentions of England and Scotland as the conversion of Ireland to the pure Christianity of the New Testament.'[75] Irish

Methodism was of course in no position to effect this transformation, not least because it had become by the 1880s as much an Ulster-based denomination as its Presbyterian Nonconformist counterpart (Table 9.1),[76] but its religious diagnosis of Ireland's miseries remained as unimpaired as its commitment to the union between Britain and Ireland.

In an officially endorsed letter to the queen in 1881 the Irish Methodist Church had already condemned agrarian terrorism and deprecated any attempt to dissolve the union as a palliative to militant nationalism.[77] It came as no surprise therefore that the *Christian Advocate*, the denominational newspaper, entered 1886 in a determined mood. 'Home Rule for Ireland', it stated in the first of many uncompromising editorials, 'means not only war against the Crown rights of England, but war against the Crown rights of Christ. . . its inspiration is religious antipathy, its methods plunder, its object Protestant annihilation.'[78] Apart from reflecting the hostility of Irish Methodists to Home Rule the *Advocate* gave more attention to the forging of a united Protestant front than any of the other denominational periodicals. It gave extensive coverage to the anti-Home Rule activities of the episcopalian, Presbyterian, Moravian and Secession churches[79] and through its advocacy of the Evangelical Alliance it envisaged not only a pan-Protestant resistance to Home Rule but a pan-Evangelical campaign as well.[80] Home Rule was thus seen not as a debatable political strategy for the government of Ireland, but as an attack on the whole Protestant way of life.[81] Part of the Protestant way of life, according to the *Advocate*, was a stake in Britain's imperial greatness to which the Methodists were particularly entitled as a result of their heroic contribution to the international missionary movement.[82] The *Advocate*'s editorials bemoaned the corrupting political influence of Romanism in American cities, extolled the benefits of English government and culture in India (in crudely racial terms) and claimed that 'where missionaries go education goes, and the extent to which our English language with all its glorious freightage of terms for liberty, purity, honour and humanity, has been spread among the nations, is a cause for profound gratitude to every enlightened and far-seeing mind'.[83] With such benefits in mind the *Advocate* stated quite categorically that 'Ulster will not submit to anything even seeming to be connected with the tactics of those who would dismember the Empire'.[84]

The most interesting aspect of the *Advocate*'s editorials in 1886 is not so much the ideology behind its opposition to Home Rule, predictable as it was, but its reflection of the obvious tensions within Methodism in the British Isles caused by Gladstone's Irish policy.[85] The paper was at least open enough to print letters from Irish Methodists, mostly from outside Ulster, who either supported Home Rule or regretted that the official agencies of the church, including the Committee of Privileges, should take such an uncompromising position on a purely political matter.[86] This dissident minority alleged that its interests were being ignored and that there was both subtle and not so subtle pressure exerted on Methodist Home Rulers to either keep quiet or come into line. In response the *Advocate* stated that it was better to lose anyone, better to 'lose any number than at such a crisis be false to our country, our posterity, our Church and our God'.[87] One particular thorn in the *Advocate's* flesh was the Methodist MP for West Clare, Jeremiah Jordan, who was a rural merchant of tenant farming origins. In his maiden speech in the House of Commons in a debate on Home Rule, Jordan delivered a blistering attack on landlordism, clericalism and Orange bigotry. Of Ulster Protestants, he stated that 'property is very largely their religion' and that although they claimed to put their faith in providence they relied just as much on 'powder and ball'. According to Jordan the nub of the problem was that 'these people have been pampered all their lives up to the present time; they have been in the ascendancy and they have monopolized power in the country. What they fear is that they will now have to be placed on an equality with other people.'[88] The *Advocate's* response to Jordan was not to discuss his opinions but to cast doubts on his Methodism.[89]

A more serious problem confronting Irish Methodists in 1886 was the stance taken on Home Rule by their English brethren. The *Methodist Times* under the editorship of Hugh Price Hughes supported Gladstone's proposals as did much of the rest of English Nonconformity, despite having no history of sympathy for the cause of Home Rule. By 1886 English Nonconformity's commitment to Gladstonian Liberalism was more important than its loyalty to Protestantism in Ireland, though for many the Home Rule episode occasioned a painful choice between the two.[90] Had anyone other than Gladstone sponsored the Home Rule cause the position taken by English Nonconformists would have been very different. Their loyalty was primarily to the man not the issue. This was cold comfort to Irish Methodists whose estimation of Gladstone's statesmanship fell as rapidly as had their support for Peel during the Maynooth crisis forty years earlier. For them the issue was immeasurably more important than the man or his party. Irish Methodists were acutely aware that 1886 witnessed an important change in their relationship with the rest of British Protestantism. The *Christian Advocate* saw it as the culmination of a new 'English Revolution' in which, for a period of 25 years, English Protestants had gone soft on Romanism: 'The old safeguards of legislation have been demolished one by one. Act after Act has been effaced, which had been regarded as essential to the Protestant character of the empire, and this has gone on until the Protestant succession to the throne is scarcely safe. The duty of opposing Rome has altogether disappeared from quarters where it used to be paramount.'[91] In their address to the British Methodist Conference in 1886 the Irish Conference tried to maintain the old relationship by appealing to a shared history. 'In 1802', the address stated, 'your fathers challenged our loyalty to a united Methodism by referring to "the new and glorious compact" by which the British Isles had just been united. We hold you to that challenge.' The response of the British Conference was, however, an impeccably bland mixture of providentialism, spiritual sympathy and pious words.[92]

The events of 1886 had come as a shock to Irish Methodists, not only in the sense of having to come to terms with Home Rule, but also in having to accept that English Nonconformist opinion was less reliable than they had supposed. Gladstone's defeat in parliament and at the polls brought some comfort, as did their view that English Methodist opinion had been unduly influenced by the 'dictatorial centralization' of Hugh Price Hughes and his supporters.[93] In the years ahead many Irish Methodists made the trip to England to re-educate English Nonconformist opinion on the unchanging character of Irish Catholicism. Within Ireland only a tiny minority of Methodists repudiated the official opposition of the church to Home Rule, and for some of the preachers life was made deliberately uncomfortable by their congregations.[94] Generally speaking support for Home Rule came from Methodists in the south and west for whom landlordism was regarded as the real cause of their misery and from those whose commercial security had been based on good relations with their Catholic neighbours and who consequently had little to fear from Home Rule.[95] The older, more evangelical, Ulster-based Methodists, and those with little contact with the land, were the most implacable opponents of Home Rule. By 1888 Dr Evans, an eminent Irish Methodist, was able to tell his London audience that the Vice-President of Conference (the highest office in Irish Methodism), the Secretary, all the District superintendents, the presidents of the Methodist colleges, all Irish members of the Legal Hundred and the overwhelming majority of the preachers had signed a declaration against Home Rule.[96] The official position had been established and would not easily be changed. All that remained was to determine the tactics of opposition.

Dr Evans's speech on Methodist solidarity against Home Rule was made at a banquet hosted by the Nonconformist Unionist Association to present Lord Salisbury and Lord Hartington with an address against Home Rule signed by Irish Nonconformist ministers. The Whitehall Rooms of the Hotel Metropole were specially decorated for the occasion with a harp and crown over the chair and underneath these symbols were the inscriptions *Tria Juncta in Uno; Quis Separabit?* and *Libertus in Legibus.* Apart from serving the interests of the Nonconformist Unionist Association, the aim of the banquet was to persuade influential British politicians that Gladstone's estimation of the views of Irish Protestants was badly mistaken and that Irish Nonconformists were united in opposition to Home Rule on more noble grounds than mere Orange bigotry. The event was highly stage-managed and had been meticulously planned over a period of six months by W. E. Ball, the secretary of the Nonconformist Unionist Association.[97] Ball's unlikely chief contact and political adviser in Ireland was the Duke of Abercorn, an episcopalian landowner and member of the Irish Loyal and Patriotic Union.[98] He wrote letters of introduction for Ball to Irish political and religious leaders and defended his position by stating:

Fancy if I in my humble position in the north of Ireland, instead of bringing all parties together, had taken a different course and had proclaimed the Presbyterian Ministers to be a Radical class of men not worth relying upon – why, it would have made every Body hostile to each other and would have done no end of mischief.[99]

Abercorn canvassed opinion among Presbyterian and Methodist ministers and personally invited R. J. Lynd, the Presbyterian Moderator and 'most ardent defender of the Union', to the London banquet.[100] On the eve of the great day Ball's brother wrote to him with pardonable fraternal enthusiasm.

> There is no doubt that your political strategy is admirable, I seem to perceive a touch of genius in it. You will have perceived from the G.O.M.'s [Gladstone's] speech at the Bingley Hall here that your Association galls him bitterly. There can be no question that it strikes him on a side where he had hitherto seemed impregnable, but where in fact he is most vulnerable. I was not at the Bingley Hall, but those who were present say that his references to the Nonconformist ministers of Ulster were much more passionate than the newspaper reports would lead you to suppose. His face, gestures, and voice added an intensity of vitriolic hatred that evaporated in the process of reporting. I enclose a letter printed in the Birmingham Daily Post which will indicate the sort of effect which Gladstone's speech is having upon Nonconformists generally. I imagine all this will greatly strengthen your Association. Surely Nonconformists ought to perceive that this man is more interested in Irish Roman Catholics than in them.[101]

The aim of the banquet was not to persuade Gladstone to think again, but to convince wavering English Nonconformists that their loyalty to Gladstone had led them to ignore the unanimously expressed wishes of their Irish co-religionists. The tone of the meeting was all-important. Episcopalians were discreetly urged not to attend, Orangeism was not to appear and opposition to Home Rule was to be expressed in liberal humanitarian, not sectarian, terms. All went to plan.[102] The leaders of the Irish Presbyterian, Methodist, Congregational and Baptist churches took it in turn to show why 864 out of 990 Nonconformist ministers throughout Ireland had signed an address against 'a separate Parliament for Ireland, or any legislation tending to imperil the Legislative Union between Great Britain and Ireland, or to interfere with the unity and supremacy of the Imperial Parliament'.[103] Lynd, on behalf of Irish Presbyterians, denied that their rejection of Gladstone was a rejection of Liberalism and stated that Presbyterian support for tenant farmers, for the civil and religious liberties of Roman Catholics and for a well-thought-out measure of local government remained undiminished. In a clear appeal to English Nonconformist values he stated that Home Rule would lead to the effective endowment of the Roman Catholic religion and the end of the principle of united secular and separate religious education and would require coercion on an unprecedented scale against the loyal Protestant minority.[104] Evans, who had clearly been stung by Gladstone's disparaging remarks about Irish Nonconformists in his Bingley Hall speech, repeated the Irish Methodist appeal to the loyalty of the English connexion and stated that Home Rule would accelerate the speed of Protestant emigration which had eroded Methodist strength throughout the nineteenth century. The Congregationalist and Baptist spokesmen came closest to importing Protestant religious prejudices into the debate and, according to the printed record, the audience was less impressed with this approach than with the others. McCaig, the Baptist representative, denied that there was coercion in Ireland, stated that the priests would be the real beneficiaries of Parnellism in Ireland and accused nationalists of desecrating the Sabbath. 'Sunday is the great day for League meetings,' he stated, 'members of Parliament choose that day for displaying their oratorical powers, with the accompaniment of bands playing political and party tunes – often to the annoyance and disturbance of worshipping Protestants.'[105] All the speakers were at pains to point out that Irish Protestants of whatever party or creed were united in their hostility to Home Rule. Protestant Home Rulers were dismissed as an insignificant minority whose genuine Protestantism – in the religious sense – was suspect and whose principles were regarded as thinly disguised self-interest. Zealous Christianity and worthy citizenship were thought to be incompatible with Gladstone's version of Liberalism.

The banquet of November 1888 was an encouragement to those English Nonconformist leaders such as Spurgeon, Dale and Newman Hall, who had doubted the wisdom of Gladstone's Irish policy, but it was only one aspect of the work of the Nonconformist Unionist Association in Ireland. W. E. Ball was equally keen to exploit the electoral potential of using Irish Noncon-formist ministers as platform-speakers in English constituencies.[106] Fiery Irish orators had been doing this throughout the nineteenth century, but by the late Victorian period English provincial Nonconformity required rather more sensitive nurturing. Ball found it difficult to attract men of the 'right calibre' at the right price and the whole scheme was littered with disputes over the cost of hospitality and recriminations about unsatisfactory speakers.[107] The educated leadership of the Irish Nonconformist churches were either too busy with church affairs or too unwilling to become political preachers to be of much use to the Nonconformist Unionist Association. The less able were both more willing to be of service and more likely to appeal to religious prejudice than political economy. Despite these teething troubles, Irish ministers appeared frequently during British elections to urge Protestant solidarity and imperial unity in the period after 1886. Anti-Catholicism was well capable of transferring Nonconformist voters into the unionist camp particularly in the Methodist strongholds of Lincolnshire and the southwest, and in areas with a significant Irish Catholic population such as Lancashire. Generally speaking, the more evangelical and theologically conservative wings of British Nonconformity were the most susceptible to appeals from their Irish co-religionists. Thus Bebbington concludes that many Nonconform-ists deserted Gladstonian Liberalism not because their economic prosperity weakened their chapel allegiances, but because they had a genuine religious motive for voting unionist: 'Those who responded to unionist appeals for solid-arity with protestant Irishmen were not allowing their own interests to prevail over their chapel loyalties: their very chapel loyalties drove them to consider the unionist appeals. This, then, was a populist, classless style of politics.'[108]

The coming together of Irish Nonconformist churches against Home Rule was significant within both Ireland and Britain. In Ireland it offered an apparently more worthy medium of expressing opposition to Gladstone than either Ulster Orangeism or mere economic self-interest.[109] It was also a way of tapping into the strong Presbyterian liberal tradition which could nevertheless still claim to be true to its dissenting and liberal heritage. But it also had the unintended effect of Ulsterizing Protestant resistance to Home Rule by concentrating on the geographical area in which Nonconformity was strong. Moreover, the coming together of the churches on an agreed platform further marginalized those who had an alternative vision of Ireland's future. Opposition to Home Rule had become, within the space of a few years, the test of the virility of an Irishman's Protestantism. The effect of the Home Rule issue on British Nonconformity was equally important. It introduced a fierce partisanship into Nonconformist politics which divided churches and damaged old friendships.[110] Within Methodism Hugh Price Hughes and Sir George Chubb sniped relentlessly at each other while other churches tried unsuccessfully to draw boundaries between religion and politics. The trouble with the Irish Question was that no such boundary existed. Over the longer term the initial Nonconformist support for Gladstone's policy weakened. Parnell's moral frailties and the educational objectives of English Roman Catholics were unexpected bonuses for the unionist cause. Under such relentless pressure the English Nonconformist press sometimes gave way to the crudest forms of anti-Catholicism that would not have been out of place half a century earlier. Ireland had once again shown that there were limits to the liberality of liberalism.

The response of the Irish Protestant churches to Home Rule was no mere example of institutional posturing, for their opposition rested on a cultural bedrock of Protestant assumptions and values which were central to the emergence of a Protestant identity in Ulster. A recent survey of some 30 Ulster Unionist speeches against Home Rule in 1886, for example, shows that in descending order of priority the arguments employed were as follows: the representatives of an ascendant Roman Catholicism would persecute the Protestant community; Ulster Protestants would be deprived of their imperial heritage and would thus have a reduced status in the world; Catholic nationalists had no respect for law and order and would deliver Ulster into social and economic ruin; Home Rule was a betrayal of loyalism; and Ulster would be forced to shoulder the fiscal and economic burden of Ireland under Home Rule.[111] The disproportionate number of reported speeches from Protestant ministers may partly account for the high profile given to religious fears in this survey, but there can be no doubt that the above issues were indeed dominant in the manifold pamphlets, speeches and meetings against Home Rule.[112] What is striking about this Ulster Protestant *Weltanschauung* is the extent to which it was a self-referentially coherent ideology, embracing past, present and future as well as religion, politics and society. The only chink in its armour was its perceived inability to sustain itself against an imperialistic Catholic nationalism without the continued support of the rest of the United Kingdom. That was precisely the frailty exposed by Home Rule, and it was made harder to bear by Gladstone's and Parnell's persistent but erroneous belief that the eighteenth-century Patriot tradition was a stronger force in Irish Protestantism than Ulster loyalism.[113] The belief persisted, against formidable evidence to the contrary, because both men wished it were so.

Ulster Protestants had an alternative view of Irish history which was relentlessly rehearsed at Orange, church and political meetings throughout the nineteenth century. The Great Protestant Meeting in Belfast against the Irish Church Bill in 1869 is a good example of its kind.[114] A huge crowd, optimistically estimated at 100,000 people, crammed into the Botanic Gardens on a bright summer's day. The platform dignitaries were in their place, the music was played by the Conservative Amateur Band and the catering was in the able hands of Miss Johnson of the Abercorn Arms Hotel. At the heart of the day's entertainment were the speeches, many of which were populist history lectures about the struggles and triumphs of Irish Protestants against an unchanging and disloyal Catholicism. As events and heroes were recalled to the cheers of the crowd, the virtues most admired were staunchness and unchanging principles, the evils most railed against were betrayal and accommodation. These appeals to forefathers, faith and the settlement of the land not only foreshortened the past, but helped even the most impious to believe that they were part of a tradition protected by divine providence for a quarter of a millennium. Here was a memorial and celebratory culture resonant with providential turning-points and rich in symbols. The most expert platform orators knew exactly how to manipulate their audience for the maximum applause and the crowd knew exactly how to manipulate platform orators to tell them what they most wanted to hear. It was not only a great day out for all, but soon took its place in the tradition it was called to celebrate. As with many such meetings since the passage of Catholic Emancipation in 1829, it was a protest against British government policy, and that characteristic also became central to the tradition. But in making their protests Ulster Protestants were not so much giving expression to a contractual view of their relationship with the rest of the United Kingdom as demonstrating their belief that the pragmatic liberalism of much government policy in Ireland in the Victorian period was based on mistaken assumptions about the real causes of Ireland's difficulties.[115] Hence the suggested remedies, culminating in Home Rule, were not only betraying Irish Protestantism, but were guaranteed to perpetuate the very problems they were designed to solve. In such circumstances the right to resist depended upon the seriousness of the threat to Protestant life, liberty and property.

The part played by evangelical religion in stiffening the resolve of Ulster Protestants against Home Rule should not be underestimated. For over a century old Reformation polarities had been given new social meanings in a province sufficiently divided on grounds of religion to sustain the crudest forms of stereotyping sanctified by theological principles. Protestants believed that having access to the 'Open Bible', being free from priestcraft and superstition and adhering to a progressive and enlightened faith were at the heart of Ulster's cultural and economic superiority over the rest of Ireland, and, equally important, of Protestant Ulster's superiority over Catholic Ulster.[116] The hotter the Protestantism, in terms of its evangelical zeal, the firmer was this belief and the sharper the antagonism against the 'whole system' of Roman Catholicism. In assessing the power of evangelical religion in Ulster Protestant ideology, Frank Wright perceptively notes that 'defence of the socialization process of evangelical protestantism is more of a universal concern than an actual belief in evangelicalism itself'.[117] He means by this that Ulster Protestants, in the mass, have been more committed to the *right* to preach the reformed religion and to maintain its influence in education, culture and society than to the essence of religious belief itself. Hence the religious heroes of Ulster Protestantism have not been theologians or pietists, but rather those who have most resolutely defended the rights of Ulster Protestants to adhere to the reformed faith against the unwelcome encroachments of the Roman Church. From this perspective any concession made to Roman Catholics was by definition a weakening of historic Protestantism. The one could make progress only at the expense of the other.[118]

One of the great strengths of evangelical ideology in Ulster was the way in which it could simultaneously narrow the focus to a contest between reformed religion and Catholic superstition in Ireland and widen it to an international conflict of major proportions. This was facilitated by the late Victorian expansion of the British Empire and by the post-famine migrations of Irish Catholics. Here was a clash of two world empires, one of commerce, Christianity and civilization as exported by Great Britain and the other a sordid, embittered and disloyal Irish Catholic migration, particularly to the United States, where it created another culture in its own image. The corruptions of Tammany Hall and the ill-fated invasion of Manitoba merely confirmed the unchanging character of the Catholic Irish even when thousands of miles from home. 'The Home Rule movement', stated the Reverend Gilbert Mahaffy to the YMCA, 'has been, from first to last, a movement hostile to British rule. And fostered as it has been on American soil, and supported by American dollars, it is essentially republican.'[119] Thus, depending on circumstances, Ulster Protestants could think of themselves either as a faithful remnant of righteousness in a pagan land or as part of a great and civilizing world empire. These were equally comforting and culturally reinforcing ideas. The Reverend Thomas Ellis, for example, told the loyal Orangemen of Portadown in 1885: 'We have sacrificed our duty to God and to each other too often on the altar of Popish compromise, worldly expediency and carnal selfishness.' He called upon them, as 'the faithful few among the faithless many – the loyal Sons of Judah amid the faithless men of Israel', to abandon their lax Protestantism and follow in the steps of their glorious forefathers.[120] Others, more impressed by Ulster's commercial vitality than depressed by its religious worldliness, simply wanted protection against a Roman Catholic ascendancy so that 'we shall be allowed to continue our triumphant march of Prosperity under the protection of the British flag, a United Parliament, and the Imperial Crown'.[121] Such a framework was watertight. Ulster's success was due to the blessings of providence and the energy of its people, its failures were attributable to enemies on all sides pressing in on a loyal but vulnerable remnant. It is perhaps surprising that such ideas did not give rise more often than they did to racial notions of the inherent superiority of Ulster Protestants to Irish Celts. It is, of course, possible to find references to such arguments, but they appear mostly in academic journals not in popular speeches.[122] The reason for this is that the ethnic stereotyping indulged in by most Ulster Protestants was based more on religious and cultural assumptions than on scientific or racial observations. Irish Catholics were economically and culturally inferior, not primarily because of their racial pedigree, but because of their religion. Thus, some of the greatest heroes of the Protestant missionary movement in Ireland were converted Catholics. The Irish did not choose the Catholic religion, therefore, because they were racially inferior, they became inferior because they followed the Catholic religion, as was the case with many other European nationalities. The extent to which the undeniably common ideas of Anglo-Saxon racial superiority contributed to diagnoses of the Irish problem has probably been exaggerated in both Britain and Ireland. Tom Dunne has shown, for example, that even intensely nationalistic English intellectuals resorted not so much to full-blown race theories about Irish Celts as to historical and cultural arguments for the retarded growth of Irish civilization.[123] Since Gaelic society had bequeathed the political instincts and habits of tribesmen, not citizens, the Irish were simply not ready for the responsibilities of self-government. Hence stereotypes based on impressions and chauvinistic historical comparisons were probably more influential in shaping attitudes than the kind of race theories prevalent in the United States where the problems were more urgent.

Ultimately, the most important contribution of evangelicalism to Ulster Protestant ideology was the sheer vigour of its anti-Catholicism. The Roman Catholic Church in Ireland was regarded as all pervasive in influence, monolithic in scope, imperialist in intention, persecuting in its essential nature and impoverishing in its social effects. No state in which its representatives were in control could offer any credible safeguards for the rights of religious minorities. Faced with such a possibility Ulster Protestant theology had the capacity to adapt to new circumstances. The view that all Christian citizens had a sacred duty to support lawfully constituted authorities was capable of being transformed into a sacred duty to resist religious tyranny. As with English Puritanism on the eve of the Civil Wars, the anti-Catholicism of Ulster Protestants was a potentially radical force, and was, of course, more capable of mass realization than was sacrificial piety. It was propagated by a resurgent Orangeism whose rank and file of agricultural labourers and urban workers was led by the Fermanagh gentry and baptized by the churches. Depending upon the seriousness of the crisis, Orange excesses, including pseudo-military drilling, came to be less feared than Protestant apathy. Even the licence of the Belfast Protestant mobs was defended by some religious leaders who apparently saw no incongruity between this and their earlier attacks on Fenian agrarian outrages.

Evangelicalism also helped to build bridges between denominations, between clergy and laity and between churches and voluntary associations. It sustained links between Irish and British organizations, from the staunchly Protestant, such as the Scottish Protestant Alliance and the Protestant Institute of Great Britain, to the politically mild such as the Evangelical Alliance and the YMCA. Although most of the prolific evangelical societies devoted to Christian morality and self-improvement operated a 'no politics' principle, their very ethos contributed much to an Ulster Protestant identity. When addressing itself to the issue of Home Rule, for example, the YMCA journal stated that

> The bulletin is not a political journal, but a grave national crisis such as this concerns young men, as well as other. It concerns Christian young men very specially. If carried, this bill would change the entire character of our national life. It would alter the prospects of many of us who are preparing for trades, or commercial life, or for the professions. It would have the most material influence on the religion of the nation . . . but perhaps the worst feature of the proposed measure is the tremendous leverage it would give to Romanism – the curse of Ireland for generations.[124]

The formidable array of both denominational and inter-denominational improvement societies in late nineteenth-century Ulster helped create an ethos of godliness and good citizenship which was inextricably bound up with loyalty to the British way of life. When the Home Rule crisis awakened the slumbering unionist associations in provincial Ulster, therefore, they found themselves lying on an easily politicized bed of respectable Protestant culture.[125] By then evangelical religion had thrown up successive generations of political preachers who unashamedly used their clerical influence on behalf of popular Protestant causes. Their contribution further united religion and politics in a way that boded ill for statesmen called upon to disentangle the threads. As the Reverend Thomas Ellis told the Portadown Orangemen, he had never been able to understand how any man 'with the Bible in his hands and who believed in the moral government of the World by God' could separate religion from politics. Ironically, Gladstone, who provoked much breast-beating among Ulster Protestants, was one of a dwindling number of English statesmen to put much store on such sentiments.[126]

Important though the influence of evangelicalism was in forging an Ulster Protestant identity, it would be misleading to present late nineteenth-century Irish Protestantism in crudely monolithic terms. Not only were there important denominational and class differences, but there was also a Protestant nationalist tradition which supported Home Rule. Mainly religious moderates and liberal reformers, the Protestant Home Rulers were not ideologically committed to any specific Home Rule proposal. Their major unifying factor was the desire to dissociate themselves from the bigotry of the majority Protestant community. Regarding a Protestant Home Rule movement as the 'outcome and true essence of true liberalism', these Gladstonian loyalists were committed to a political rather than a religious tradition.[127] Their tolerance towards those of other religions reflected their lack of commitment to the more dogmatic varieties of Protestant faith, thus ensuring that the antagonism of their less forbearing co-religionists followed well-worn channels of attack upon their alleged religious and political apostasy.

For a Protestant minister, of whatever denomination, active support of Home Rule in the 1880s carried consequences of varying seriousness. The hostility of congregations, colleagues, or superiors was expressed both verbally and physically and could mean preaching to an empty church hall, or the termination of a budding clerical career.[128] Such pressures, apart from the hardships caused to the individuals concerned, made it difficult for activists to rally public support and this has probably led to an underestimation of the extent of Protestant support for Home Rule. Even with this in mind, however, any readjustment would simply be to the size of a minority, which was never in any position to make its influence felt. In general terms the Protestant Home Rulers thought of themselves as an enlightened minority whose traditional opposition to landlordism and episcopalian ascendancy helped forge a bond with their Catholic counterparts. Confident of Gladstone's ability, from which they had benefited in the past, and given the alternatives of coercion or minority domination, they believed Home Rule would have beneficial effects for both religious communities in Ireland. A democratically based self-government, it was felt, would not only bring material gains, but end sectarianism and diminish the role of priests in Roman Catholic culture.[129] Such views were shaped, as were those of their opponents, both by experience and by a particular interpretation of Irish history in which the Presbyterian reformers of the late eighteenth century were accorded a prominent position.

It is clear that most members of the Irish Protestant Home Rule Association (IPHRA) represented the more urbane and prosperous side of Protestantism, and there was undoubtedly an element of pragmatism in their political opinions. Merchants, shopkeepers, barristers, doctors and members of parliament scattered throughout rural Ireland were after all dependent on the patronage and goodwill of their Roman Catholic neighbours. And while they were aware of their religious isolation, their position as an integrated minority determined that their perception of Catholic Ireland would differ from that of more cohesive Protestant communities in the northeast. It was also, of course, because they were in such a minority that these individuals felt they could most legitimately speak to the fear of Catholic intolerance which in their opinion had been scurrilously magnified by Orange bigots in Ulster. They were, nevertheless, completely unrepresentative of mainstream Protestant opinion. Despite claims of its growth and influence, the reality of the IPHRA's ineffectiveness was reflected in its predilection for caution and compromise, and while such vagueness facilitated the membership of liberal reformers, it militated against the active involvement of ardent Home Rulers. Anxiety not to antagonize Protestants on the one side or Roman Catholics on the other had a negative influence on strategy. Plans to hold public lectures were rejected for fear of rousing the anger of Catholic clergy and visits of Liberal cabinet ministers were viewed as 'inexpedient'. Perhaps more serious in the long run, the divergence between the Belfast and Dublin branches of the movement revealed basic differences in the interpretation of a nationalism which was only slowly developing a cohesive ideology.[130] The emerging distinctions between the general political liberalism of the north and the more robust southern nationalism reflected inherently different cultural experiences and expectations. The optimism which comes across in the correspondence is therefore more an expression of the liberal outlook of prosperous, forward-looking individuals than of a united political party, and was not in any case unconditional. The unacceptably violent tactics employed by some nationalists, for example, eroded their belief in the capacity of Irishmen to accommodate their traditional differences without bloodshed.

From the mid-nineteenth century, according to Professor Ward, churches and their theologians in the British Isles, western Europe and North America struggled to construct a social policy which took account of market forces and national aspirations while maintaining the Christian ethic of love and self denial.[131] As state support for religious establishments inexorably waned, Christian socialism, Tory paternalism and liberal individualism were all tried and found wanting in region after region. Churches could neither win the ear of governments nor establish a secure foothold in the world of labour and were thus condemned to enter the twentieth century in search of ever more desperate and futile remedies for a disease they had never properly diagnosed. In the nineteenth century such social policy as there was was developed by voluntary associations who forced moral and social issues together and campaigned unremittingly for a more godly and hence more prosperous society. But ultimately this was not so much a social policy as an unsuccessful tug of war against the mighty forces of industrialization, class consciousness and secularism. While some sought in vain for ways of maintaining Christian values in a *laissez-faire* world, Ulster Protestants, who scarcely thought about these matters had a solution thrust upon them. Persuaded by the revival of 1859 that God was still on their side, forced to accept in 1869 that the state would no longer shore up Irish Protestantism and faced with the defeat of their national and cultural aspirations in 1886, Ulster Protestants dug deep into their historical tradition and once again found strength in adversity. Their remarkable unity of purpose has confounded the British and Irish states for over a century and was constructed with unlikely materials. The sheer vigour of Irish Ultramontanist Catholicism provided them with a far more visible and comprehensible enemy than mere secularism. The concessionary policies of successive British governments persuaded them that the state itself offered no ultimate guarantees at the same time as utilitarians and socialists in Britain placed hopelessly unrealistic faith in the capacity of the state to bring in their millennium. Evangelicalism, which in Britain had undermined the old denominational order, but which had little else to offer after its own religious zeal had declined, in Ulster strengthened denominational cooperation on the big, if not the little, issues, and offered a perfect theological rationalization of Ulster Protestants' innate sense of their own superiority. At the same time that many theologians and intellectuals became aware that expanding market forces threatened the traditional framework of Christian ethics, Ulster Protestants claimed the market as their own, not only as beneficiaries of the greatest market in the world, the British Empire, but in response to the protectionist noises made by Catholic nationalists.

The Protestant solidarity effected by such forces transcended – but did not entirely eliminate – the denominational, class and urban/rural tensions which helped undermine the churches in the rest of western Europe. In Ulster the platforms of the great Protestant 'Monster meetings' were dominated by men of landed and commercial property, the clergy and the educated professionals. They played oratorical games with their hearers safe in the knowledge that any excesses of the mob would be directed not against them but against their shared religious enemy. Relatively safe from erosion from within, and reinforced by enemies from without, Ulster Protestantism, by comparison with many other religious communities in the late nineteenth-century world, was in a good position to maintain its religious identity, even if its political future was still contested territory. The price paid for this religious success was considerable, not least in terms of the nature of religion itself, but apart from in the writings of a small band of Protestant idealists the cost was scarcely ever considered. There were simply far more urgent matters to address.

[10]

Conclusion

One generation passeth away, and another generation cometh: but the earth abideth for ever. (Ecclesiastes 1:4)

The thing that hath been, it is that which shall be; and that which is done is that which shall be done: and there is no new thing under the sun. (Ecclesiastes 1:9)

The path from the origins of pietism and revivalism among the displaced and persecuted Protestant minorities in central Europe in the early eighteenth century to evangelical Protestantism in late nineteenth-century Ulster is full of twists and turns, but it is still recognizable as a path. From Wesley's early contacts with Moravians and Bohemians to those sober Wesleyan gentlemen who stood silently in mass protest against Home Rule in Belfast in 1886 there is a century and a half of turbulent history. The part played by evangelical religion in cementing a provincial identity substantially different from the rest of Ireland is really a story within a story. The original plot has to do with the settlement patterns and religious conflicts stirred up by the Reformation and the complex political and social relationship between Britain and Ireland. Not only was Ulster different in important respects from other parts of Ireland before the mid-eighteenth century, but early evangelicals could not have foreseen the way in which their religious enthusiasm was to be confined, more or less, to the northern part of the island. The original intentions of Wesley and Cennick, the voluntary religious societies and the 'second Reformation' were to take the gospel to the whole country and, as time went on, to work for the conversion of Catholic Ireland. Demographic realities and increased religious conflict determined otherwise. By the mid-nineteenth century only the most optimistic evangelicals considered the conversion of Ireland to be a realistic proposition. As missionary objectives became circumscribed by realism, evangelical Protestants began to fear that history was working against them. Not only was Catholic Ireland unconverted, but it dared press for an apparently inexhaustible set of political and religious concessions, including self-government and the repeal of the Union. Politics offered little hope of a final defence, because those with the power did not have to live with the problem. Religion fared no better. When at last the great revival came, it awakened the Protestant faithful and bypassed the Catholic population altogether. If God was not going to deliver the enemy into their hands, Ulster Protestants felt they at least had the right to defend their own small corner. Slowly but inexorably a garrison mentality began to replace the old conversionist activism. An evangelical defensive mentality, which is noticeable in the southern counties of Ulster in the 1780s and 1790s, came more into view in the decades following Catholic Emancipation. Peel's first great concession was indicative of the fact that English statesmen, however tardily and inconsistently, could no longer govern Ireland on principles enshrined in the Protestant Constitution.

What the preceding chapters make clear is that eighteenth- and nineteenth-century evangelicalism was a broad church, transcending boundaries of gender, religious denomination and social class. Moreover its adherents are not easily reduced to a particular religious typology. They included bellicose pulpit politicians as well as pious dispensers of manifold charities. Some were ardent Calvinists while others were equally ardent Arminians. Most were less devoted to a theological system than to a religious life-style based on obedience to the Word and the cross, and commitment to evangelism and social action. The centrality of religious conversion to evangelicalism, however, led inexorably to a more competitive religious climate in which evangelical Protestants and Roman Catholics came into more regular conflict. Evangelical enthusiasm thus reinforced an older tradition of anti-Catholicism which combined elements of ethnicity, culture, civilization and colonialism to produce a powerful and multifaceted ideology. 'No Popery' not only has a remarkably luxuriant literature in Ireland, but it often displays a surprising eclecticism and complexity. As with most popular ideologies it had both crude populist expressions and more sophisticated rational defences. Its appeal stretched from the street corner to the tea rooms of the House of Commons. Nevertheless evangelicalism carried with it no inevitable political consequences. Its constituency in both England and Ireland was not politically monochrome. But just as in England and Wales evangelicalism's cutting-edge was most clearly represented in Free Church liberalism, in Ireland it became more closely identified with the desire of Ulster Protestants to maintain their way of life against Catholic and nationalist pressure. Evangelicalism alone did not create these powerful religiopolitical configurations, but it played an important part in furnishing them with religious legitimacy and in uniting different social classes in pursuit of the same objectives.

Notes

ABBREVIATIONS USED IN THE NOTES
AND BIBLIOGRAPHY

ADV   Association for the Purpose of Discountenancing Vice and Promoting the
           Practice of Virtue and Religion
BFBS   British and Foreign Bible Society Mss
CMS   Church Missionary Society
HCMS   Hibernian Church Missionary Society Papers
IPHRA   Irish Protestant Home Rule Association Mss
IWHS   Irish Wesley Historical Society
LMS   London Missionary Society Mss
MARC   Methodist Archives Research Centre
MMSA   Methodist Missionary Society Archives
NIPRO   Northern Ireland Public Records Office
NLI   National Library of Ireland, Dublin
NUA   Nonconformist Unionist Association Papers
RCB   Representative Church Body Library
SOAS   School of Oriental and African Studies
TCD   Trinity College, Dublin

1   THE RISE OF EVANGELICAL RELIGION 1740–80

1   A. Hume, 'Miscellaneous essays on topography, ethnology, language, etc.',
    Ulster Journal of Archaeology 7 (1859), p. 5.
2   R. D. Edwards, *Atlas of Irish History* (London: 1973), p. 165.
3   J. G. Simms, *The Williamite Confiscation in Ireland, 1690-1703* (London: 1956).
4   See, for example, the correspondence of Richard Mant, Bishop of Down and
    Connor (1823–48) in W. B. Mant, *Bishop Mant and his Diocese* (Dublin: 1851), p. 158.
5   W. H. Crawford, 'Economy and society in eighteenth-century Ulster', PhD
    thesis, Queen's University, Belfast, 1983, p. 26.
6   I. Grubb, *Quakers in Ireland 1654–1900* (London: 1927); D. Hempton, 'Religious
    minorities', in P. Loughrey (ed.), *The People of Ireland* (Belfast: 1988), pp. 155–68.
7   M. J. Westerkamp, *Triumph of the Laity: Scots-Irish Piety and the Great Awakening
    1625-1760* (Oxford: 1988).
8   S. O'Brien, 'A transatlantic community of saints: the Great Awakening and the

first evangelical network, 1735–1755', *American Historical Review* 91, 4 (October, 1986), pp. 811–32.

9   W. R. Ward, 'The relations of enlightenment and religious revival in Central Europe and in the English-speaking world', *Studies in Church History* subsidia 2 (1979), pp. 281–305; W. R. Ward, 'Power and piety: the origins of religious revival in the early eighteenth century', *Bulletin of the John Rylands University Library of Manchester* 63, 1 (1980), pp. 231–52; J. L. Kincheloe, Jr, 'European roots of evangelical revivalism: Methodist transmission of the pietistic socio-religious tradition', *Methodist History* 18 (July, 1980), pp. 262–71.

10 W. R. Ward, 'The renewed unity of the brethren: ancient church, new sect or interconfessional movement?', *Bulletin of the John Rylands University Library of Manchester* 70, 3 (1988), pp. 77–92.

11 ibid., pp. 91–2.

12 F. Baker (ed.), *The Works of John Wesley*, Vol. 26, *Letters II 1740–1755* (Oxford: 1982), pp. 281–98.

13 Moravian Church House, London, John Cennick, 'An account of the most remarkable passages relating to the Awakening in Dublin in Ireland from the beginning to the settlement of the congregation'. Transcript of his journal.

14 ibid., p. 35.

15 D. N. Hempton, 'Methodism and the law, 1740–1820', *Bulletin of the John Rylands University Library of Manchester* 70, 3 (1988), pp. 93–107.

16 Moravian Church House, John Cennick's Journal, p. 43.

17 S. G. Hanna, 'The origin and nature of the Gracehill Moravian settlement 1764–1855, with special reference to the work of John Cennick in Ireland 1746–1755', MA thesis, Queen's University, Belfast, 1964, pp. 35–40.

18 R. H. Hutton, *A History of the Moravian Church* (London: 1909), p. 328.

19 Hanna, 'The Gracehill Moravian settlement', plate IV.

20 F. M. Harris, 'John Cennick in Ireland', *Irish Baptist Historical Society Journal* 15 (1982–3), pp. 21–9.

21 S. Madden, *Memoir of the Life of the Late Reverend Peter Roe, A. M. . . .* (Dublin: 1842), p. 243.

22 R. Haire, *Wesley's One-and-Twenty Visits to Ireland* (London: 1947).

23 W. R. Ward and R. P. Heitzenrater (eds), *The Works of John Wesley*, Vol. 18, *Journals and Diaries, I* (1735–1738) (Nashville, Tenn.: 1988), p. 56.

24 ibid., p. 76.

25 ibid., p. 77.

26 T. E. Warner, 'The impact of Wesley on Ireland', PhD thesis, University of London, 1954, pp. 323–4.

27 D. Hempton, *Methodism and Politics in British Society 1750–1850* (London: 1984), pp. 34–43.

28 *John Wesley, Journal*, 14 August 1747, 25 April 1758.

29 ibid., 3 June 1758, 24 June 1760.

30 ibid., 3 April 1748, 10 April 1748, 25 June 1756, 4 July 1756, 22 May 1760.

31 ibid., 26 April 1778.

32 Ward and Heitzenrater, *Journals and Diaries*, p. 74.

33 Hempton, 'Religious minorities', pp. 155–68.

34 *Wesley, Journal*, 19 July 1756.

35 Ward and Heitzenrater, *Journals and Diaries*, p. 66.

36 Haire, *Wesley's Visits to Ireland*, p. 49.

37   D. N. Hempton, 'Methodism in Irish society, 1770–1830', *Transactions of the Royal Historical Society* 5th series 36 (1986), pp. 117–42.

38   *Minutes of the Methodist Conference in Ireland,* Vol. 1, 1744–1819 (Dublin: 1864), p. 11.

39   E. P. Thompson, *The Making of the English Working Class* (London: 1963) and W. R. Ward, *Religion and Society in England, 1790–1850* (London: 1972).

40   A. Everitt, *The Pattern of Rural Dissent: the Nineteenth Century* (Leicester: 1972); E. P. Thompson, 'Anthropology and the discipline of historical context', *Midland History* 1 (1972), pp. 41–55; J. Rule, 'Methodism, popular beliefs and village culture in Cornwall, 1800–50', in R. D. Storch (ed.), *Popular Culture and Custom in Nineteenth-Century England* (London: 1982), pp. 48–70

41   C. D. Field, 'The social structure of English Methodism: eighteenth–twentieth centuries', *British Journal of Sociology* 28 (1977), pp. 199–225.

42   D. W. Bebbington, *Evangelicalism in Modern Britain: a History from the 1730s to the 1980s* (London: 1989), pp. 20–74.

43   R. E. Davies, *Methodism* (London: 1963).

44   H. A. Snyder, *The Radical Wesley and Patterns for Church Renewal* (Downers Grove, Ill.: 1980).

45   W. Arthur, *The Life of Gideon Ouseley* (London: 1876); W. G. Campbell, *'The Apostle of Kerry', the Life of the Rev. Charles Graham* (Dublin: 1868); F. J. Cole, *The Cavalry Preachers* (Belfast: 1945); Crook, *Sketch of the Life and Character of the Late Rev. William Crook by his Son* (Dublin: 1863); C. H. Crookshank, *A Methodist Pioneer: the Life and Labours of John Smith . . .* (London: 1881); R. H. Gallagher, *John Bredin* (Belfast: 1960), and R. H. Gallager, *Pioneer Preachers of Irish Methodism* (Belfast: 1965); A. Stewart and G. Revington, *Memoirs of the Life and Labours of the Rev. Adam Averell* (Dublin: 1848).

46   R. Smith, *The Life of the Rev. Mr. Henry Moore* (London: 1844), pp. 58–65.

47   SOAS, MMSA, boxes 1–3 and 74–5. Additional correspondence of itinerant missionary preachers is to be found in NIPRO, IWHS and the Ouseley Collection, CR6/3, ACC 13019, 28 folders of paginated Mss collected and transcribed by J. O. Bonsall and enlarged by John Hay.

48   S. W. Christophers, *Class-Meetings in Relation to the Design and Success of Methodism* (London: 1873), p. 78, and G. Alley, *Our Class Meeting* (Dublin: 1868).

49   E. Smyth, *The Extraordinary Life and Christian Experience of Margaret Davidson* (Dublin: 1782); C. H. Crookshank, *Memorable Women of Irish Methodism in the Last Century* (London: 1882); J. J. McGregor, *Memoir of Miss Alice Cambridge* (Dublin: 1832).

50   R. L Cole, *Love-Feasts: a History of the Christian Agape* (London: 1916), p. 279.

51   *Methodist Magazine* 25 (1802), pp. 37–40.

52   J. Baxter, 'The great Yorkshire revival 1792–6: a study of mass revival among the Methodists', in M. Hill (ed.), *A Sociological Yearbook of Religion in Britain* 7 (1974), pp. 46–76; T. Shaw, *A History of Cornish Methodism* (Truro: 1967), p. 65.

53   L. Dow, *Works: Providential Experience of Lorenzo Dow in Europe and America,* 3rd edn (Dublin: 1806), p. 142. Also, NIPRO, IWHS, L. Dow to G. Ouseley, 7 May 1819. For more on Dow see R. Carwardine, *Trans-Atlantic Revivalism, Popular Evangelicalism in Britain and America, 1790–1865* (Westport, Conn.: 1978), and J. Kent, *Holding the Fort: Studies in Victorian Revivalism* (London: 1978).

54   Smith, *Life of Moore,* p. 87.

55 C. H. Crookshank, *History of Methodism in Ireland*, 3 vols (London: 1885–8), Vol. 2, pp. 90–1.

56 Thompson, 'Anthropology and historical context', pp. 41–55. See also D. Clark, *Between Pulpit and Pew: Folk Religion in a North Yorkshire Fishing Village* (Cambridge: 1982), pp. 145–60.

57 Rule, 'Methodism, popular beliefs and village culture', pp. 48–70; J. Rule, *The Experience of Labour in Eighteenth-Century Industry* (London: 1981), pp. 207–8.

58 Arthur, *Life of Ouseley*, pp. 165–70.

59 NIPRO, IWHS, A. Clarke to G. Ouseley, 6 December 1806.

60 D. Bowen, *The Protestant Crusade in Ireland 1800–1870* (Dublin: 1978); A. R. Acheson, 'The evangelicals in the Church of Ireland 1784–1859', PhD thesis, Queen's University, Belfast, 1967.

61 NIPRO, Methodist Mss, Minutes of Conference, 1792–1813, CR6/3. Although the official minutes were published each year, this volume contains private minutes on sensitive subjects such as cases of spiritual discipline and relations with other churches.

62 S. J. Connolly, *Priests and People in Pre-Famine Ireland (1780-1845)* (Dublin: 1982), pp. 74–134.

63 Linenhall Library, Belfast, W. Gregory, 'Extracts of a tour through the north of Ireland . . . in the summer of the year 1800' (typescript). See also G. Hamilton, *The Great Necessity of Itinerant Preaching: A sermon delivered in the new meeting-house in Armagh at the formation of the Evangelical Society of Ulster, on Wednesday 10th of October, 1798* (Armagh: 1798); M. Lanktree, *Biographical Narrative* (Belfast: 1836); and *The Report of a Deputation of the London Hibernian Society, respecting the Religious State of Ireland* (London: 1808), p. 18.

64 Acheson, 'Evangelicals in the Church of Ireland'; J. Liechty, 'Irish evangelicalism, Trinity College Dublin, and the mission of the Church of Ireland at the end of the eighteenth century', PhD thesis, St Patrick's College, Maynooth, 1987; M. Hill, 'Evangelicalism and the churches in Ulster society, 1770–1850', PhD thesis, Queen's University, Belfast, 1987, pp. 19–27.

65 Bebbington, *Evangelicalism*, pp. 1–19.

66 Ward and Heitzenrater, *Journals and Diaries*, pp. 75–7.

67 Liechty, 'Irish evangelicalism', pp. 40–182.

68 A. C. H. Seymour, *The Life and Times of Selina, Countess of Huntingdon*, 2 vols (London: 1844), p. 169.

69 ibid., p. 207.

70 Madden, *Life of Roe*, p. 67.

71 T. W. Moody, *The Social History of Modern Ulster: Ulster since 1800*, 2nd series (London: 1958), p. 231.

72 P. Brooke, *Ulster Presbyterianism: the Historical Perspective 1610–1970* (Dublin: 1987); R. F. Holmes, *Our Irish Presbyterian Heritage* (Belfast: 1985).

73 C. Vane (ed.), *Memoirs and Correspondence of Viscount Castlereagh*, 12 vols (London: 1848–53), Vol. 3, pp. 161–3.

74 Westerkamp, *Triumph of the Laity*, pp. 74–135; Holmes, *Presbyterian Heritage*, ch. 3.

75 C. G. Brown, *The Social History of Religion in Scotland since 1730* (London: 1987), pp. 30–8.

76 N. Landsman, 'Evangelists and their hearers: popular interpretation of revivalist preaching in eighteenth-century Scotland', *Journal of British Studies* 28, 2 (1989), pp. 120–49.

77   J. Thompson, 'The inter-relationship of the Secession Synod and the Synod of Ulster', PhD thesis, Queen's University, Belfast, 1980; W. D. Killen, *History of the Presbyterian Church* (London: 1880), Vol. 3, p. 364; D. Stewart, *The Seceders in Ireland, with Annals of their Congregations* (Belfast: 1950). See also NIPRO, The Seceders, Minutes of the Secession Synod, D1759/1F/3.

78   A. Gailey, 'The Scots element in North Irish popular culture: some problems in the interpretation of an historical acculturation', *Ethnologia Europea* 3 (1975), pp. 2–22.

79   A. Loughridge, *The Covenanters in Ireland: a History of the Reformed Presbyterian Church of Ireland* (Belfast: 1984).

80   P. Brooke, 'Controversies in Ulster Presbyterianism 1790–1836', PhD thesis, University of Cambridge, 1981.

81   J. M. Barkley, *The Eldership in Irish Presbyterianism* (Belfast: 1963), p. 49.

82   NIPRO, Session Minute Books, CR3. See also J. Stevenson, *Two Centuries of Life in Down 1600–1800* (first published 1920; this edn Belfast: 1990), pp. 169–202.

83   Barkley, *Eldership*, p. 52.

84   NIPRO, Session Minute Book for Ballycarry, County Antrim, 1704–80, CR3/31/1.

85   D. Miller, 'Presbyterianism and "modernization" in Ulster', *Past and Present* 80 (1978), pp. 66–90.

86   ibid., p. 73.

87   P. Corish, *The Irish Catholic Experience: a Historical Survey* (Dublin: 1985), p. 150.

2   REBELLION AND REVOLUTION: *c*. 1780–1800

1   E. R. R. Green, *The Lagan Valley: 1800–1850. A Local History of the Industrial Revolution* (London: 1949), p. 26. See also W. H. Crawford, 'Landlord-tenant relations in Ulster 1609–1820', *Irish Economic and Social History* 2 (1975), pp. 5–21; W. H. Crawford, *Domestic Industry in Ireland* (Dublin: 1972); C. Gill, *The Rise of the Irish Linen Industry* (Oxford: 1964, first published 1925).

2   W. A. McCutcheon, *The Industrial Archaeology of Northern Ireland* (Belfast: 1980), p. 283; W. A. Maguire, *The Huguenots in Ulster 1685–1985* (Lisburn: 1985); S. Smile, *The Huguenots, their Settlements, Churches and Industries* (London: 1876).

3   W. H. Crawford and B. Trainor, *Aspects of Irish Social History 1750–1800* (Belfast: 1969), p. 74; A. Young, *A Tour in Ireland with general observations . . . in the years 1776, 1777 and 1778* (Belfast: 1983), p. 44; W. H. Crawford, 'The evolution of Ulster towns 1750–1850' in P. Roebuck (ed.), *Plantation to Partition . . .* (Belfast: 1981), pp. 140–56; T. W. Freeman, *Ireland: Its Physical, Historical, Social and Economic Geography* (London: 1950), pp. 238–9.

4   M. Beames, *Peasants and Power: the Whiteboy Movements and their Control in Pre-Famine Ireland* (London: 1983).

5   D. W. Miller, *Queen's Rebels: Ulster Loyalism in Historical Perspective* (Dublin: 1978), p. 145.

6   D. W. Miller, 'The Armagh troubles', in S. Clark and J. S. Donnelly (eds), *Irish Peasants: Violence and Political Unrest 1780–1914* (Manchester: 1983), pp. 155–91; M. Elliott, *Partners in Revolution: the United Irishmen and France* (London: 1982); Beames, *Peasants and Power*, p. 30.

7   Elliott, *Partners in Revolution*, p. 42; Miller, 'The Armagh troubles', p. 179.

8   H. Senior, *Orangeism in Ireland and Britain 1795–1836* (London: 1966), p. 18.

9   M. Wall, 'The Whiteboys', in T. D. Williams (ed.), *Secret Societies in Ireland* (Dublin: 1973) (pp. 13–25), p. 25.

10 J. Kelly, 'The genesis of "Protestant ascendancy": the Rightboy disturbances of the 1780s and their impact on Protestant opinion', in G. O'Brien (ed.), *Parliament, Politics and People* (Dublin: 1989), pp. 93–127.

11 P. Livingstone, *The Monaghan Story: a Documented History of the County Monaghan from the Earliest Times to 1976* (Clogher: 1980), p. 239.

12 T. Bartlett, 'Select documents XXXVIII: defenders and defenderism in 1795', *Irish Historical Studies* 24, 95 (May, 1985) (pp. 373–94), p. 389.

13 *Rules and Regulations for the Use of all Orange Societies, Revised, Corrected and Adopted by the Grand Orange Lodge of Ireland. Assembled at Dublin in January 1820* (Dublin: 1820).

14 Miller, *Queen's Rebels*, p. 56.

15 W. R. Ward, *Religion and Society in England 1790–1850* (London: 1972), p. 1. See also R. A. Soloway, *Prelates and People: Ecclesiastical Social Thought in England, 1783–1852* (London: 1969); G. F. A. Best, *Temporal Pillars: Queen Anne's Bounty, the Ecclesiastical Commissioners, and the Church of England* (Cambridge: 1964); N. Murray, 'The influence of the French Revolution on the Church of England and its rivals, 1789-1802', PhD thesis, University of Oxford, 1975; V. Kiernan, 'Evangelicalism and the French Revolution', *Past and Present* 1 (February, 1952), pp. 44–56.

16 *Ireland's Mirror, or A Chronicle of the Times*, 2 vols (Dublin: 1804–5), preface to Vol. 1, p. iii.

17 R. Woodward, *The Present State of the Church of Ireland: Containing a Description of its Precarious Situation and Consequent Dangers to the Public*, 6th edn (Dublin: 1787).

18 *Fortescue Mss*, Vol. IV (1905), pp. 55–6, Rev. C. M. Warburton to the Marquis of Buckingham, 12 January 1798, Loughgilly.

19 Soloway, *Prelates and People*, p. 48.

20 Still the most useful source is A. T. Q. Stewart, 'The transformation of Presbyterian radicalism in the north of Ireland, 1792–1825', MA thesis, Queen's University, Belfast, 1956.

21 For the closely knit economic and family networks of the Belfast radicals see Stewart, 'Transformation of Presbyterian radicalism', pp. 5–7.

22 ibid., pp. 16–47; P. Brooke, 'Controversies in Ulster Presbyterianism 1790–1836', PhD thesis, University of Cambridge, 1981, pp. 20–6.

23 R. F. G. Holmes, 'Eighteenth-century Presbyterian radicalism and its eclipse', *Bulletin of the Presbyterian Historical Society of Ireland* 3 (January, 1973), pp. 7–15; R. F. G. Holmes, *Our Irish Presbyterian Heritage* (Belfast: 1985); P. Brooke, *Ulster Presbyterianism: the Historical Perspective 1610–1970* (Dublin: 1987), ch. 6.

24 For the course of the United Irish Rebellion see Elliott, *Partners in Revolution*. For the problems within Presbyterianism see also, R. F. G. Holmes, 'Ulster Presbyterianism and Irish nationalism', *Studies in Church History* 18 (1982), pp. 535–48; D. Miller, 'Presbyterianism and "modernization" in Ulster', *Past and Present* 80 (1978), pp. 66–90; Brooke, 'Controversies in Ulster Presbyterianism', pp. 26–36.

25 *Records of the General Synod of Ulster, 1691–1820*, Vol. III, p. 208.

26 Brooke, 'Controversies in Ulster Presbyterianism', pp. 71–109.

27 Miller, 'Presbyterianism and "modernization" ', pp. 76–80.
28 A. Loughridge, *The Covenanters in Ireland: a History of the Reformed Presbyterian Church of Ireland* (Belfast: 1984), p. 28; NIPRO, Acts and Proceedings of the Associate Synod of Ireland, D1759/1F/1.
29 M. Lanktree, *An Apology for what is called Lay-Preaching, in a Series of Letters: addressed to the Rev. James Huey, Presbyterian Minister of Ballywillan . . .* (Newry: 1815).
30 A. Haldane, *The Lives of Robert Haldane of Aithrey and of his Brother, James Alexander Haldane*, 7th edn (Edinburgh: 1860), p. 210.
31 A. C. H. Seymour, *The Life and Times of Selina, Countess of Huntingdon*, 2 vols (London: 1844), p. 169.
32 M. Hill, 'Evangelicalism and the churches in Ulster society: 1770–1850', PhD thesis, Queen's University, Belfast, 1987, pp. 108–9.
33 See, for example, T. L. Birch, *Physicians Languishing under the Disease* (Belfast: 1791); Rev. H. Henry, *An Address to the People of Connor, Containing a Clear and Full Vindication of the Synod of Ulster: From the Aspersions of the People called Covenanters* (Belfast: 1794); Anon., *An Account of the Trial of Edward Smyth, Late Curate of Ballyculter* (Dublin: n.d.).
34 P. E. Sangster, 'The life of the Reverend Rowland Hill (1744–1833) . . .', PhD thesis, University of Oxford, 1964, p. 67; Murray, 'The influence of the French Revolution', p. 216.
35 J. Walker, *Church in Danger* (Dublin: 1796); A. R. Acheson, 'The evangelicals in the Church of Ireland, 1784–1859', PhD thesis, Queen's University, Belfast, 1967; J. Liechty, 'Irish evangelicalism, Trinity College Dublin, and the mission of the Church of Ireland at the end of the eighteenth century', PhD thesis, St Patrick's College, Maynooth, 1987.
36 P. Berger, *The Social Reality of Religion* (London: 1967); J. F. C. Harrison, *The Second Coming: Popular Millenarianism: 1780–1850* (London: 1979).
37 Brooke, 'Controversies in Ulster Presbyterianism', pp. 26–35; Miller, 'Presbyterianism and "modernization" ', pp. 80–4.
38 Brooke, 'Controversies in Ulster Presbyterianism', pp. 26–35.
39 Union Theological College, Belfast, Minutes of the Associate Synod of Ireland (Burgher), 1799–1814, p. 65; NIPRO, Records of the Reformed Presbytery of Antrim, 1803–11, CR5/5A/1/2A.
40 Many examples could be given. See M. Lanktree, *Biographical Narrative* (Belfast: 1836); *Belfast Newsletter*; C. H. Crookshank's *History of Methodism in Ireland*, 3 vols (London: 1885–8); and the minutes of the various synods and the Methodist Conference.
41 *The Manuscripts and Correspondence of James, first Earl of Charlemont*, 2 vols (London: 1891–4), p. 303.
42 *Memoirs of Francis Dobbs, also Genuine Reports of His Speeches in Parliament on the Subject of a Union, and his Prediction of the Second Coming of the Messiah* (Dublin: 1800).
43 Murray, 'The influence of the French Revolution', p. 193. See also, R. E. Davies and E. G. Rupp (eds), *A History of the Methodist Church in Great Britain* (London: 1965), Vol. 1, pp. 299–302.
44 T. L. Birch, *A Letter from an Irish Emigrant to His Friend in the United States . . .* (Philadelphia, Pa:. 1799).
45 S. Neill, *A History of Christian Missions* (London: 1973), ch. 9.

46 MARC, T. Coke to T. Morrell, Downpatrick, 23 June 1790, PLP 28.7.4.
47 For discussions on this aspect of Methodism, see J. Obelkevich, *Religion and Rural Society: South Lindsey 1825–1875* (Oxford: 1976); D. Hempton, *Methodism and Politics in British Society 1750–1850* (London: 1984), pp. 26–9; H. McLeod, *Religion and the People of Western Europe 1789–1970* (Oxford: 1981), p. 39.
48 Quoted in Lanktree, *Biographical Narrative*, p. 70.
49 Irish Address to British Conference, 1799, in *Minutes of the Methodist Conferences in Ireland*, Vol. I, 1744–1819 (1799), p. 117.
50 D. N. Hempton, 'Methodism in Irish society: 1770–1830', *Transactions of the Royal Historical Society*, 5th series, 36 (1986), pp. 117–42.
51 C. H. Crookshank, *A Methodist Pioneer: the Life and Labours of John Smith . . .* (London: 1881); W. H. Crawford, 'Economy and society in south Ulster in the eighteenth century', *Clogher Record* 7, 3 (1975), pp. 26, 71–2.
52 *Minutes of the Methodist Conferences in Ireland*, Vol. I, p. 113.
53 T. Coke, *Copies of Letters from the Missionaries who are Employed in Ireland for the Instruction in their own Language, and for the Conversion of the Native Irish . . .* (London: 1801). The output of letters by Irish Methodist missionaries in this period was prolific. Regrettably they are not yet catalogued, nor even collected in one place. The main collections are as follows: SOAS, London, MMSA, Irish folders; MARC, the John Rylands University Library of Manchester, papers of Joseph Butterworth, Adam Clarke, Thomas Coke and Gideon Ouseley; NIPRO, IWHS, and the Ouseley Collection.
54 *Methodist Magazine* 25 (1802), pp. 40–2.
55 NIPRO, Ouseley Collection, Charles Graham and Gideon Ouseley to Dr Coke, 8 April 1800.
56 NIPRO, Ouseley Collection; J. O. Bonsall left a transcription of Ouseley's journal beginning in April 1803. See also *Methodist Magazine* 25 (1802), pp. 225–6; 26 (1803), pp. 375–7; 27 (1804), pp. 381–2; 28 (1805), p. 383; 29 (1806), pp. 90–4.
57 NIPRO, Ouseley Collection, Ouseley's journal, 10 October 1803.
58 NIRPO, Ouseley Collection, Charles Graham and Gideon Ouseley to Dr Coke, 6 January 1800.
59 Moreover, the region itself became less prosperous in the early nineteenth century, especially after 1815. It was a latecomer to the linen industry and one of the earliest regions to contract. See McCutcheon, *Industrial Archaeology*, pp. 283–324.
60 W. R. Ward, 'The religion of the people and the problem of control, 1790–1830', *Studies in Church History* 8 (1972), pp. 237–57, and Ward, *Religion and Society in England*, pp. 75–85; Hempton, *Methodism and Politics in British Society*, pp. 92–6.
61 W. J. Green, *Methodism in Portadown* (Belfast: 1960); R. H. Gallagher, *Methodism in the Charlemont Circuit* (Belfast: 1961); J. M. Lynn, *A History of Wesleyan Methodism on the Armagh Circuit*, 3rd edn (Belfast: 1887); R. Gillespie, *Wild as Colts Untamed. . .* (Lurgan: 1977).
62 Crookshank, *History of Methodism in Ireland; Minutes of the Methodist Conference in Ireland*, Vol. 1, 1744–1819 (1801), p. 137; Lanktree, *An Apology for what is called Lay-Preaching*. See also, J. R. Binns, 'A history of Methodism in Ireland from Wesley's death in 1791 to the re-union of Primitives and Wesleyans in 1878', MA thesis, Queen's University, Belfast, 1960.
63 For similar problems within English Methodism see Hempton, *Methodism and Politics in British Society*, ch. 3; Murray, 'The influence of the French Revolution', pp. 215–66.

64   Even then a sizeable remnant remained within the established church. See R. A. Ker, 'The origins of Primitive Wesleyan Methodism in Ireland', *Proceedings of the Wesley Historical Society* 43, part 4 (May, 1982), pp. 77–85.
65   Crookshank, *History of Methodism in Ireland*, Vol. II, p. 132; see also letters on Methodist loyalty, MARC, MAM. PLP. 28.
66   MARC, Anon., *A Reply to Mr. John Johnson's Remarks, on an Address Lately Published and Signed by 30 Men in Office amongst the Methodists: To which is Added an Affectionate Address to the People called Methodists living in Ireland*, pamphlet; Binns, 'Methodism in Ireland', p. 49.
67   E. Thomas, *Irish Methodist Reminiscences. Being Mainly Memorials of the Life and Labours of the Rev. S. Nicholson* (London: 1889); G. E. Orr, *Lisburn Methodism* (Belfast: 1975).
68   Thomas, *Irish Methodist Reminiscences*, p. 59.
69   G. Ouseley to *Dublin Evening Mail*, 10 April 1825.
70   G. Hamilton, *Introductory Memorial Respecting the Establishment and First Attempt of the Evangelical Society of Ulster. 10 October 1798* (Armagh: 1798).
71   SOAS, Correspondence of agents, box 1, folder 6; Cooper to LMS, 20 June 1799; ibid., Cooper to LMS, 18 July 1799; ibid., George Hamilton, Armagh to Rev. J. Eyre, London, 2 January 1799.
72   Linenhall Library, Belfast, W. Gregory, 'Extracts of a tour through the north of Ireland . . . in the summer of the year 1800' (typescript).
73   ibid.; Union Thelogical College, Belfast, Minutes of the Associate Synod of Ireland (Burgher), 1779–1814, pp. 120–1, 130, 136–7; NIPRO, Acts and Proceedings of the Associate Synod of Ireland, D1759/1F/1, pp. 24–5.
74   *Records of the General Synod of Ulster, 1691–1820*, Vol. 3 (Belfast: 1898), p. 279, p. 298; Gregory, 'Extracts of a tour through the north of Ireland'.
75   Lanktree, *Biographical Narrative*, pp. 156–7; NIPRO, Ouseley Collection, CR6/3, Ouseley to Lanktree, March 1805.
76   D. N. Hempton, 'Gideon Ouseley: rural revivalist, 1791–1839', *Studies in Church History* 25 (1989), pp. 203–14.
77   NIPRO, Ouseley Collection, II, fols 1–10; III, fols 1–3; IV, fols 1–7.
78   ibid., XXVI, fol. 4.
79   The importance of the military in the early dissemination of Irish Methodism is deserving of more attention. See ibid., fol. 10. See also IX, fol. 29; XII, fols 3–5; XIII, fol. 16.
80   ibid., V, fols 1–24; VI, fols 1-20; XXVIII, fol. 3.
81   ibid., XXVIII, fol. 4. See also NIPRO, IWHS, Gideon Ouseley to Mathew Tobias, 14 June 1820.
82   NIPRO, Ouseley Collection, VII, fol. 10.
83   ibid., XI, fol. 23; XII, fols 16–17; XX, fol. 19.
84   ibid., XXVIII, fol. 9.
85   D. N. Hempton, 'The Methodist crusade in Ireland 1795–1845', *Irish Historical Studies* 22 (March, 1980), pp. 33–48.
86   NIPRO, Ouseley Collection, XII, fols 30–5.
87   *The Report of a Deputation from the London Hibernian Society Respecting the Religious State of Ireland* (Dublin: 1808), p. 26.
88   Hempton, *Methodism and Politics in British Society*, ch. 5; SOAS, Correspondence of agents, home correspondence, box 1, folder 6, W. Cooper to LMS, 20 June 1799.

89   D. Bowen, *The Protestant Crusade in Ireland 1800–1870* (Dublin: 1978); I. M. Hehir, 'New lights and old enemies: the Second Reformation and the Catholics of Ireland, 1800–1835', MA thesis, University of Wisconsin, 1983.

90   D. H. Akenson, *The Church of Ireland: Ecclesiastical Reform and Revolution 1800–1885* (London: 1971); E. Brynn, *The Church of Ireland in the Age of Catholic Emancipation* (London: 1982); Holmes, *Our Presbyterian Heritage*, pp. 110–24.

91   D. Hempton and M. Hill, 'Godliness and good citizenship: evangelical Protestantism and social control in Ulster 1790–1850', *Saothar* 13 (1988), pp. 68–80.

3   EVANGELICAL EXPANSION: COOPERATION AND CONFLICT

1   R. Rouse and S. C. Neill, *A History of the Ecumenical Movement 1517–1948*, 2nd edn (London: 1967), p. 310.

2   cf. Ruth Rouse's definition of voluntaryism: 'By voluntary movements are understood those movements or organisations initiated not by a church as such, but by a group of Christians or by some Christian individual'; ibid., p. 309. See also F. K. Brown, *Fathers of the Victorians: the Age of Wilberforce* (Cambridge: 1961); S. Yeo, *Religion and Voluntary Organisations in Crisis* (London: 1976).

3   W. T. Whitley, *A History of British Baptists* (London: 1923), pp. 211–41. For general histories of foreign missions, see G. Warneck, *History of Protestant Missions* (Edinburgh: 1884); S. Neill, *A History of Christian Missions* (London: 1973).

4   R. H. Martin, 'The pan-evangelical impulse in Britain 1795–1830: with special reference to four London societies', PhD thesis, University of Oxford, 1974, p. 74. See also P. E. Sangster, 'The life of the Reverend Rowland Hill (1744–1833) and his position in the evangelical revival', PhD thesis, University of Oxford, 1964, pp. 189–97; D. W. Lovegrove, 'The practice of itinerant evangelicalism in English Calvinistic dissent', PhD thesis, University of Cambridge, 1980; F. E. Bland, *How the Church Missionary Society Came to Ireland* (Dublin: 1935), p. 42.

5   D. M. Thompson, *Denominationalism and Dissent: 1795–1835* (London: 1985), pp. 15–16.

6   E. Stock, *The History of the Church Missionary Society . . .* , 4 vols (London: 1899–1916).

7   News of the loss of the missionary ship of the LMS, the *Duff*, was reported to have increased zeal among all who heard of it; SOAS, Correspondence of agents, home correspondence, box 1, folder 8, John Lowry, Tyrone to LMS, 10 October 1799. See also ibid., box 3, folder 7, Rogers to LMS, 13 June 1819.

8   *Records of the General Synod of Ulster, 1691–1820*, Vol. III (Belfast: 1898), p. 386; Union Theological College, Belfast, Minutes of the Associate Synod of Ulster (Burgher), 1799–1814. No mention is made of the deputation in the minutes of the Anti-Burgher Synod.

9   R. H. Boyd, *Couriers of the Dawn: the Story of the Missionary Pioneers of the Presbyterian Church in Ireland* (Belfast: 1938), p. 17.

10   For Church of Ireland support see SOAS, Correspondence of agents, box 5, folder 2, R. J. Edmonds to LMS, 1 August 1827, and box 5, folder 3, J. Philips, report from Ireland, 12 July 1828. For later opposition, see ibid., box 7, folder 2,

G. Gorgerley (?) to LMS reporting many Presbyterian pulpits closed to him and blaming the 'coldness and opposition' of both major churches on attacks on them from Independents, 21 August 1837. R. Knill on the other hand blamed the voluntaryism of the LMS; ibid., box 7, folder 4, 29 June 1839; while J. Smith listed the poverty of the LMS, the Arian controversy and Presbyterians' own missionary efforts as reasons for declining support, in box 7, folder 9, home correspondence, 4 June 1841.

11 Boyd, *Couriers of the Dawn*, p. 17.

12 See the correspondence between Irish evangelicals and the CMS, in University of Birmingham, CMS Archives, G/AC3. This series of incoming correspondence within the British Isles is arranged chronologically, with an index of names. See also the correspondence of the HCMS and minutes of committee proceedings, held in the RCB, Dublin.

13 ibid., and *Annual Report of the Hibernian Church Missionary Society* (Dublin: 1825).

14 N. Taggart, 'The Irish factor in world Methodism in the eighteenth and nineteenth centuries', PhD thesis, Queen's University, Belfast, 1981, p. vii; Anon., *Resolutions on the Formation of the Methodist Missionary Society of the Dublin District* (Dublin: 1814).

15 University of Birmingham, CMS Archives: G/AC 3, J. Hewitt to CMS, 27 April 1814, Account of the Formation of the Hibernian Church Missionary Society, 6 June 1814; and D. Wilson, Notes of a Journey to Armagh, 23 June 1814; Bland, *How the Church Missionary Society Came to Ireland*, p. 107.

16 Brown, *Fathers of the Victorians*, p. 250.

17 The early policy of the CMS was to encourage the individual sponsoring of the education of a named child; see RCB, HCMS Annual Reports, 1805–21.

18 ibid., Reports of Deputation Meetings, 1828–9; HCMS abstract letter book, Rev. H. Wolsey to HCMS, 1 September 1820. It was stated, for example, that ladies needed to be sent regular missionary reports or they would lose interest; abstract letter book, Viscount Lifford to HCMS, 24 August 1818.

19 *Report of the Committee of the London Hibernian Society, 1810* (Dublin: 1810).

20 Linenhall Library, Belfast, W. Gregory, 'Extracts of a tour through the north of Ireland . . . in the summer of the year 1800', p. 7 (typescript).

21 For this discussion we are indebted to Irene Hehir who generously made available to us her thesis and her opinions. See I. M. Hehir, 'New lights and old enemies: the Second Reformation and the Catholics of Ireland, 1800–1835', MA thesis, University of Wisconsin, 1983.

22 T. Coke, *Copies of Letters from the Missionaries who are Employed in Ireland for the Instruction in their own Language, and for the Conversion of the Native Irish, with a Short Address to the Generous Public* (London: 1801). See a letter asking that the Archbishop of Tuam be recommended to promote the use of Irish catechisms and bibles (172?), Bodleian Library, Oxford, papers of Henry Newman, secretary of the Society for Propagating the Gospel, MS. Rawl. D839 13,606. For early Presbyterian missions to the Irish see R. F. G. Holmes, *Our Irish Presbyterian Heritage* (Belfast: 1985), p. 59; Cambridge University Library, BFBS Mss, account of translations, Vol. 5.

23 ibid., extract of a letter from the Rev. Robert Shaw, Kilkenny, 24 October 1850; Rev. J. Jebb, Tipperary, 10 November 1804.

24 ibid., committee report, 1 December 1806.

25 J. Liechty, 'Irish evangelicalism, Trinity College Dublin, and the mission of the

Church of Ireland at the end of the eighteenth century', PhD thesis, St Patrick's College, Maynooth, 1987.

26 Cambridge University Library, BFBS Mss, account of translations, from Dr Stokes, 4 May 1807. For the most recent assessment of the state of the Irish language in this period, see G. Fitzgerald, 'The decline of the Irish language 1771–1871', in M. Daly and D. Dickson (eds), *The Origins of Popular Literacy in Ireland: Language Change and Educational Development 1700–1920* (Dublin: 1990), pp. 59–72.
27 Cambridge University Library, BFBS Mss, account of translations from ADV, 7 May 1807.
28 ibid., from A. Clarke, 9 November 1807.
29 C. Anderson, *Memorial on Behalf of the Native Irish with a view to their Improvement in Moral and Religious Knowledge through the Medium of their own Language* (London: 1815); Hehir, 'New lights,' pp. 106–8.
30 Cambridge University Library, BFBS Mss, account of translations, from Reverend Dr Thorpe, January 1815, 14 November 1823.
31 ibid.
32 *Annual Report of the Baptist Society for Promoting the Gospel in Irish by Establishing Schools for teaching the Native Irish, for Itinerant Preaching, etc.* (London: 1815). See also J. Thompson, 'Baptists in Ireland 1792–1922: a dimension of Protestant dissent', PhD thesis, University of Oxford, 1988.
33 Irish classes remained only a minority concern for the London Hibernian Society and were exclusively for children. The 1830 report states that there were 3 Irish schools in Munster, 8 in Ulster and 42 in Connaught; *Report of the Annual General Meeting of the London Hibernian Society, 1830* (Dublin: 1830).
34 TCD, Committee minutes of the Irish Society, 22 October 1818, ms. 7644.
35 In its first year the Hibernian Bible Society was granted £100 by the BFBS which promised goodwill and assistance; *Annual Report of the Hibernian Bible Society for the year 1808* (Dublin: 1808).
36 Anon., *The Unfinished Task: the Story of the Hibernian Bible Society* (Dublin: n.d.), p. 5.
37 *Annual Report of the Hibernian Bible Society for the year 1808* (Dublin: 1808).
38 Cambridge University Library, BFBS Mss, misc. book no. 33, Mathias and Thorpe to the Reverend Owen, 19 April 1806.
39 *Records of the Synod of Ulster*, Vol. III, p. 311.
40 ibid., p. 357. See also Cambridge University Library, BFBS Mss, letter from B. McDowell, Synod of Ulster to BFBS, 2 August 1809, thanking them for generous support, but requesting Bibles and testaments to be sent in sheets, so they can insert the psalms.
41 *Records of the Synod of Ulster*, Vol. III, pp. 367–8.
42 *Annual Report of the Belfast, Antrim, Ballymena and Ballymoney Branches of the Hibernian Bible Society, for the year ending April 1814* (Belfast: 1815).
43 *Annual Report of the Hibernian Bible Society for the year 1822* (Dublin: 1823); Cambridge University Library, BFBS Mss, correspondence bk. II, pp. 56–9, R. Stevens to J. Tarn, 12 October 1821; 9th Annual General Meeting of the Religious Tract and Book Society, quoted in *Primitive Wesleyan Magazine*, Vol. I (Dublin: 1823); NIPRO, Bible Society, Cookstown, T. Millar to J. Stewart, 8 March 1812 and 24 April 1812, D1367/2/224 and D1367/2/226; W. Canton, *The Story of the Bible Society* (London: 1904), p. 114.

44   *Annual Report of the Hibernian Church Missionary Society, 1820* (Dublin: 1821).
45   Cambridge University Library, BFBS Mss, correspondence bk II, p. 34, R. Newenham to Lord Teignmouth, 30 July 1821.
46   J. K. L., *Letters on the State of Ireland* (Dublin: 1825), p. 119. See also *Two Reports of the Committee of Education, appointed by the Association for Discountenancing Vice . . . of the Dioceses of Armagh and Dromore* (Dublin: 1800); D. H. Akenson, *The Irish Education Experiment* (London: 1970), pp. 86–94.
47   *The Report of a Deputation from the London Hibernian Society, Respecting the Religious State of Ireland, to which is annexed a plan of the Society*, 2nd edn (London: 1808).
48   For comment on this change of policy see J. Thompson, 'Baptists in Ireland 1792–1922: a dimension of Protestant dissent', PhD thesis, University of Oxford, 1988, p. 48.
49   Rev. D. Stuart, *A Sermon Preached by Appointment of the Irish Evangelical Society in the Scots Church, Mary's Abbey, Dublin, with Appendix and Description* (Dublin: 1818).
50   *24th Report of the London Hibernian Society, 1830* (Dublin: 1830).
51   *Annual Report of the Irish Society, 1830* (Dublin: 1830).
52   J. G. MacWalter, *The Irish Reformation Movement in its Religious, Social and Political Aspects* (Dublin: 1852), p. 153.
53   TCD, ms 7644, Irish Society committee minutes, December 1818.
54   *Two Reports of the Committee of Education, 1800.* See also Anon., *Reflections on the Spirit etc. of Religious Controversy* (London and Dublin: 1806).
55   Rev. M. C. Motherwell, *Memoir of Albert Blest . . .* (Dublin: 1843), pp. 230–1. See also D Bowen, *The Protestant Crusade in Ireland 1800–1870* (Dublin: 1978) and Hehir, 'New lights'.
56   *24th Report of the London Hibernian Society.*
57   TCD, ms 7645, Irish Society committee minutes, February 1827.
58   ibid., ms 7644, Irish Society committee minutes, November 1818.
59   For some examples, see ibid., ms 7645, Irish Society committee minutes, November 1826, and 23 February 1827.
60   *The Report of a Deputation from the London Hibernian Society Respecting the Religious State of Ireland* (Dublin: 1808).
61   *12th Annual Report of the London Hibernian Society* (Dublin: 1818).
62   *Report of the London Hibernian Society, 1837* (Dublin: 1837).
63   *21st Report of the Irish Society* (Dublin: 1839).
64   H. Clayton, 'Societies formed to educate the poor in Ireland in the late eighteenth century and early nineteenth century', MLitt thesis, Trinity College, Dublin, 1981, p. 86.
65   RCB, *Report of the Sunday School Society for Ireland, 1810* (Dublin: 1811); H. Clayton, *To School without Shoes: a Brief History of the Sunday School Society of Ireland, 1809–1979* (Dublin: 1979); RCB, Records of the Sunday School Society for Ireland, 1809–1971, ms 182.
66   Anon., *Hints for Conducting Sunday Schools, Useful also for Day Schools and Families . . .* , 2nd edn (Dublin: 1819).
67   For a wider discussion of the impact of Sunday schools, see W. T. Laqueur, *Religion and Respectability: Sunday Schools and Working-Class Culture* (London: 1976), p. 172; H. McLeod, *Religion and the Working Class in Nineteenth-Century Britain* (London: 1984); W. R. Ward, *Religion and Society in England, 1790–1850* (London: 1972), p. 13; D. Hempton, *Methodism and Politics in British Society, 1750–1850* (London: 1984), pp. 86–92.

68 W. Urwick, *Biographical Sketches of the Late James Digges La Touche* (Dublin: n.d.), pp. 149–51.

4 THE CHURCHES: SCHISM AND CONSOLIDATION

1 University of Birmingham, CMS, Archives G/AC3, report of visit to Ireland of Revs J. Pratt, D. Wilson and W. Jowett, June 1814.
2 D. H. Akenson, *The Church of Ireland: Ecclesiastical Reform and Revolution, 1800–1885* (London: 1971).
3 *Primitive Wesleyan Magazines* (1827–8), p. 375. Henry Cooke attributed 'a large proportion of the advance of orthodoxy and the decline of Arianism in the Presbyterian Church to a visible and increasing improvement in the established clergy . . . I am speaking of those in the the the north, with whom I have been acquainted'; First Report of the Commission of Enquiry into Irish Education, H.C. XII (1825) (400).
4 Stuart was here opposing the translation of George La Poer Beresford to the diocese of Kilmore, making strong objections to his moral character; E. Brynn, *The Church of Ireland in the Age of Catholic Emancipation* (London: 1982), pp. 46–8.
5 NIPRO, Redesdale Papers, T3030/4/3, T3030/4/4, Wickham to Redesdale, 18 February 1803, 15 July 1803.
6 This point is made by Brynn, *Church of Ireland* p. 399.
7 Akenson, *Church of Ireland*, pp. 120, 123, 128–9.
8 NIPRO, Beresford Papers, T2772/2/1, vol. XI, Stopford to Beresford, n.d.
9 Akenson, *Church of Ireland*, pp. 167–77.
10 W. B. Mant, *Bishop Mant and His Diocese* (Dublin: 1857), p. 289.
11 NIPRO, Beresford Papers, T2772/1, vol. V, Bishop of Killala to Archbishop Beresford, 10 March 1833.
12 ibid., T2772/2/9 (this bundle contains many letters on the plight of the lower clergy and the need to raise funds); Akenson, *Church of Ireland*, p. 151; *Report of the Proceedings of a Public Meeting Held at Freemason's Hall, 3 December 1835* (Dublin: 1835).
13 Akenson, *Church of Ireland*, p. 167.
14 NIPRO, Correspondence of Lord Downshire, D607/C/12, Lord Roden to Rev. C. Close, 22 August 1834.
15 See ibid., D607/C/12/448; D607/C/12/449; D607/C/12/510; D607/C/12/520: correspondence between Downshire and Roden.
16 H. Senior, *Orangeism in Ireland and Britain: 1795–1836* (London: 1936), p. 237.
17 J. Liechty, 'The popular Reformation comes to Ireland: the case of John Walker and the foundation of the Church of God, 1804', in R. V. Comerford, M. Cullen, J. Hill and C. Lennon (eds), *Religion, Conflict, and Coexistence in Ireland* (Dublin: 1990), pp. 160–88; A. Acheson, 'The evangelicals in the Church of Ireland', PhD thesis, Queen's University, Belfast, 1967, p. 123.
18 Liechty, 'The popular Reformation', p. 178.
19 University of Birmingham, CMS Archives, G/AC3, report of Revs Pratt, Wilson and Jowett.
20 F. E. Bland, *How the Church Missionary Society Came to Ireland* (Dublin: 1935), p. 100.

21 H. Cnattigius, *Bishops and Societies: a Study of Anglican Colonial and Missionary Expansion 1698–1850* (London: 1952), p. 58.

22 RCB, HCMS, abstract letter book, Rev. S. Oliver, Loughall, 17 November 1814.

23 ibid., minutes of committee proceedings, 1818–24, letter to the bishops and archbishops of Ireland, 22 December 1814. See also ibid., abstract letter book and minutes of committee proceedings; abstract letter book, 1814–23, Rev. O'Bierne to HCMS, 25 May 1819.

24 Rev. A. O'Callaghan, *Thoughts on the Tendency of Bible Societies as Affecting the Established Church and Christianity itself as a 'Reasonable Service'* (Dublin: 1816).

25 Anon., *The Danger of Disseminating the Scriptures without Note or Comment* (Dublin: 1818).

26 See, for example, Rev. J. E. Jackson, *Reasons for Withdrawing from the Hibernian Bible Society* (Dublin: 1822).

27 J. D. Sirr, *A Memoir of Power Le Poer Trench, Last Archbishop of Tuam* (Dublin: 1845), p. 461.

28 Lord Teignmouth, *Letter to Rev. C. Wordsworth, D.D., in Reply to his Strictures on the British and Foreign Bible Society* (Dublin: 1810); S. P. Kerr, 'The Church of Ireland in Belfast, 1800–1870', MPhil thesis, University of Edinburgh, 1978, p. 140.

29 NIPRO, Beresford Papers, T2772/1, Stoppard to Beresford, 30 September 1828; ibid., T2772, D. Donaldson to Beresford, December 1830.

30 Mant, *Bishop Mant*, pp. 121, 159.

31 For example, see Archbishop of Dublin, *Letter to Archdeacon of Dublin and Archdeacon of Glendalough from the Archbishop of Dublin* (Dublin: 1836); Anon., *Letter to one of the deputation who waited on the Archbishop of Dublin with a Memorial on Wednesday 7 December 1836* (Dublin: 1836); Kerr, 'The Church of Ireland', p. 140; Acheson, 'The evangelicals in the Church of Ireland'; Mant, *Bishop Mant*, p. 373.

32 ibid., pp. 121, 159.

33 *Christian Examiner*, preface to vol. IX (July–December, 1829).

34 *Christian Examiner* VI (May, 1828).

35 *Christian Examiner* VII (October, 1828).

36 Mant, *Bishop Mant*, p. 312.

37 See for example, Rev. J. McGhee, *Episcopal and Clerical Duty and Responsibility Considered in a Letter respectfully addressed to the Right Rev. the Lord Bishop of Down and Connor on his Lordship's Charge v the E.C.H.M* (Dublin: 1835).

38 NIPRO, Beresford Papers, T2772/1/8/208, vol. I, 'The Home Mission'.

39 NIRPO, Annals of Christ Church, Belfast, T2159, pp. 25–8.

40 Included in ibid., 'Account of the first meeting of the Clergy Aid Society', 11 September 1838, pp. 39–40.

41 ibid., 'Account of the formation of the Additional Curates Fund for Ireland', 27 March 1838.

42 Anon., *Dioceses of Down and Connor: the Bishop's Charge . . .* (Belfast: 1839).

43 Union Theological College, Belfast, Minutes of the Associate Synod of Ireland (Burgher), 1779–1814; NIPRO, Acts and Proceedings of the Associate Synod of Ireland, 1747–1818, D1759/1F/1; NIPRO Minutes of the Secession Synod 1818–40, D1759/1F/2.

44 ibid.

45 Rev. D. Stuart, *Sermon Preached in the New Meeting-House, Cookstown, at the Opening of the Presbyterian Synod of Ireland, distinguished by the name of Seceders, Tuesday, July 4th, 1820* (Dublin: 1820).

46 P. Brooke, 'Controversies in Ulster Presbyterianism: 1790–1836', PhD thesis, University of Cambridge, 1981, p. 68.

47 J. Jamieson, 'The influence of the Reverend Henry Cooke on the political life of Ulster', MA thesis, Queen's University, Belfast, 1950, p. 65; *Ireland's Mirror, or a Chronicle of the Times* (Dublin: July, 1804), pp. 525–6; R. J. Rodgers, 'James Carlile: 1784–1854', PhD thesis, Queen's University, Belfast, 1973, p. 57; *Records of the General Synod of Ulster, 1691–1820*, Vol. III (Belfast: 1898), p. 131; Cambridge University Library, BFBS Mss, misc. bk no. 3, and Instructions for Depositories to BFBS, 1808; SOAS, Correspondence of agents, home correspondence, box 5, folder 5, J. Hands, Letterkenny to LMS, 1830.

48 *Records of the General Synod of Ulster*, Vol. III, pp. 33, 369.

49 Fourth Report of the Commission of Enquiry into Irish Education, H.C. 1826–7, (89) XIII, pp. 151–67; J. Morgan, *Recollections of My Life and Times* (Belfast: 1874).

50 Brooke, 'Controversies in Ulster Presbyterianism', p. 178.

51 J. Thompson, 'The inter-relationship of the Secession Synod and the Synod of Ulster', PhD thesis, Queen's University, Belfast, 1980, p. 377.

52 R. F. G. Holmes, *Henry Cooke* (Belfast: 1981). See also J. L. Porter, *The Life and Times of Henry Cooke, D.D.* (Belfast: 1875).

53 Holmes, *Henry Cooke*, pp. 6, 21.

54 See NIPRO, Correspondence of the second Baron Dufferin, D1071/B/C/41/4–5, two letters from A. H. Rowan, 7 and 21 December 1817; W.H. Drummond, *Autobiography of Archibald Hamilton Rowan* (Dublin: 1840).

55 J. M. Barkley, 'The Arian schism in Ireland, 1830', *Studies in Church History* 9 (1972), pp. 323–40.

56 ibid., p. 323; Brooke, 'Controversies in Ulster Presbyterianism'; Holmes, *Henry Cooke*, ch. 3.

57 NIPRO, Foster-Massereene Papers, D207/26/23, history of *regium donum* payments, 21 February 1805; J. S. Reid, *History of the Presbyterian Church in Ireland* (London: 1853), Vol. III, p. 159; Holmes, *Henry Cooke*, p. 16.

58 W. D. McEwen, lecturer in elocution at the academy, was one of those who had supported Smethurst on his tour; Holmes, *Henry Cooke*, p. 23.

59 Porter, *Henry Cooke*, p. 68.

60 *Minutes of the Synod of Ulster* (1824), p. 31, (1825), p. 25.

61 Minutes of Evidence taken before the Select Committee of the House of Lords, H.C. 129 (1825), viii.

62 NIPRO, Records of the Presbytery of Antrim, T1053/1, 17 August 1783–18 May 1834, entry for 6 June 1825.

63 ibid.

64 *Minutes of the Synod of Ulster* (1826), p. 31.

65 Porter, *Henry Cooke*, p. 65; Holmes, *Henry Cooke*, pp. 93–4; A. Haldane, *The Lives of Robert Haldane of Aithrey and of his Brother, James Alexander Haldane*, 7th edn (Edinburgh: 1860), p. 469.

66 *Constitution and Discipline of the Presbyterian Church, with a Directory for the Celebration of Ordinances and the Performance of Ministerial Activities* (Belfast: 1825); *Remonstrance of Persons Connected with the General Synod of Ulster, Against Certain of the Late Proceedings of that Body* (Belfast: 1828).

67   H. Cooke, *Authentic Report of the Speech of the Reverend Henry Cooke, Delivered at the General Synod of Ulster held at Cookstown, July, 1828* (Belfast: 1883 edn).

68   'It was clear that there were agencies at work in Strabane which were neither theological nor Christian. Self-interest, the will to win, political prejudice, displays of popular feeling, all played their part. "The pressure from without, as well as the vital doctrines within, forbade neutrality", admitted Cooke's friend, James Morgan'; Holmes, *Henry Cooke*, p. 51; *Minutes of the Synod of Ulster* (1827), p. 22.

69   *Remonstrance of Persons connected with the General Synod of Ulster.*

70   Cooke, *Authentic Report of the Speech of the Rev. Henry Cooke.*

71   ibid.

72   Liberals in the synod protested that the committee appointed to examine the candidates for the ministry would be usurping the rights of the Presbyterians; Cooke, *Authentic Report of the Speech of the Rev. Henry Cooke*. See also *Belfast Newsletter*, 6 July 1827; Anon., *The Thinking Few: a Poem dedicated to the Right Worshipful Grand Master of the New Arian Lodge No. 666* (Belfast: 1828); and reports of the trial at Carrickfergus Record Court on two men charged with assault during a brawl between those on opposing sides during a heated contest for a vacancy in the pastoral charge of Killyead, *Belfast Newsletter*, 3 April 1827.

73   Reid, *History of Presbyterianism*, p. 487; *Minutes of the Synod of Ulster* (1829), pp. 1–8, (1830), pp. 1–6. See NIPRO, Records of the Presbytery of Antrim, T1053/1, for its comments on the meeting-house at Clough, which was the subject of a lengthy dispute.

74   Jamieson, 'The influence of the Reverend Henry Cooke', p. 17; Holmes, *Henry Cooke*, p. 81.

75   Reid, *History of Presbyterianism*, p. 492.

76   'Report of the Presbyterian Missionary Society for Ireland in connection with the Synod of Ulster, presented to the Synod at their Annual General Meeting in Cookstown, 1833', *Minutes of the Synod of Ulster* (1833), p. 8.

77   Morgan, *Recollections*, pp. 59–66; *Minutes of the Synod of Ulster* (1831), pp. 28–9, 32, (1832), p. 7.

78   Special Meeting of the Synod at Belfast, 8 April 1840; *Minutes of the General Assembly, 1840–1850*, Vol. I.

79   J. Noble, *An Address to the Methodists of Ireland Respecting the Sacrament of the Lord's Supper* (Newry: 1814).

80   'A correct statement of the question respecting the ordinances', *Minutes of the Methodist Conferences in Ireland*, Vol. I (1744–1819), pp. 364–5. See, for example, W. Stewart, *A Plea for Original Methodism: a Letter Addressed to the Methodist Preachers of Ireland* (Dublin: 1814); C. Knox, *Two Sermons on Schism* (Dublin: 1814); M. Lanktree, *An Apology for what is called Lay-Preaching . . .* (Newry: 1815).

81   ibid.; M. Lanktree, *Biographical Narrative* (Belfast: 1836). Unfortunately, letters dealing with the schism have been suppressed in Gideon Ouseley's papers, but his support for the pro-sacrament party was evident in the aftermath of the dispute at least. 'Letter to the societies who have petitioned for the sacraments, etc.', *Minutes of the Methodist Conference in Ireland*, Vol. II (1814), p. 365; C. H. Crookshank, *History of Methodism in Ireland*, 3 vols (London: 1885–8), Vol. II, p. 402.

82   Lanktree, *Biographical Narrative*, p. 246.

83 *Minutes of the Methodist Conference*, Vol. II (1828), pp. 390–1, 429–30.

84 NIPRO, Primitive Wesleyan Minutes, CR6/3, General Principles of the Methodist Constitution, agreed upon in Dublin, 1818.

85 J. R. Binns, 'A history of Methodism in Ireland from Wesley's death in 1791 to the re-union of Primitives and Wesleyans in 1878', MA thesis, Queen's University, Belfast, 1960.

86 *Printed Report of Case Submitted to the Rt. Hon. the Attorney General . . . Together with Saurin's replies, dated 7 July, 1816, and 14 July, 1816* (Dublin: 1816); S. Steele, *Five Letters Addressed to the Rev. Adam Averell, Occasioned by his Coalition with the Clones Association* (Dublin: 1818); Anon., *The Conference Reviewed, Embracing a Summary of Some Late Occurrences among the Methodists of Ireland and Exhibiting a defence of the Primitive Wesleyan Methodists Attached to the Established Church . . .* (Dublin: 1819); SOAS, MMSA, file 1818–1820, James Bell, Downpatrick, 7 April 1819, 29 September 1819, A. Noble, Antrim, 12 May 1819, M. Lanktree, Comber, 24 February 1824, R. Wilson, Letterkenny, 26 May 1819; ibid., MMSA, file 1823–5, R. Bailey, Rathmullan Mission, 6 January 1824; MARC, John Rylands Library, Manchester, Butterworth Papers, Butterworth to S. Wood, Dublin, 22 May 1819, MAM PLP 21.36.24.

87 MARC, John Rylands Library, Manchester, H. Moore to the Methodist Preachers in Great Britain, 1824, and R. Newton, circular letter to the Preachers and Stewards; SOAS, MMSA, box 75; ibid., box 74, C. McCord, Tyrone, 27 June 1823.

88 ibid., A. Sturgeon, 13 October 1818, R. Bailie, Derry and Antrim, 10 October 1820, 30 December 1820, R. Reilly, Ballinasloe, Answer to Questionnaire, J. Wiggins, Cootehill, 22 June 1822; MARC, J. Bell, Dublin, 2 July 1819, correspondence with London Committee, MAM PLP 8–3; NIPRO, Ouseley Papers, CR6/3, particularly letters relating to Charles Graham; Lanktree, *Biographical Narrative*, p. 273.

89 *Minutes of the Methodist Conference*, Vol. II (1828).

90 Missionaries reported that the north of Ireland was a field well worth cultivating, though its people were inclined to be 'cautious' and conversions were less spectacular than in the south; SOAS, MMSA, box 74, R. Bailie, Ballymena Mission House, 4 January 1820.

91 *Hansard*, 2nd series, Vol. XX, 19 March 1829, p. 1311.

92 For example, see G. Ouseley, *Letters in Defence of the Roman Catholics of Ireland . . .* (London: 1829); NIPRO, Ouseley Papers, CR6/3, letter dated 12 May 1819, Ouseley to Conference, 8 June 1825.

93 SOAS, MMSA, box 74, draft report on Irish Missions 1806; ibid., T. Coke, Lisburn to the Missionary Committee, 31 July 1806.

94 MARC, Butterworth Papers, PLP 21.36.01, *Protestant Union Meeting, formed 22 January 1813, London Tavern 17 April 1819. (For the Defence and Support of the Protestant Religion and the British Constitution as established at the Glorious Revolution 1688)*; ibid., Allan Collection, box 7, file 3.

95 ibid., box 8, file 1, Deery to Butterworth, 13 May 1820.

96 MARC, Andrew Hamilton to Joseph Butterworth, 19 May 1820.

97 MARC, John Stuart to Joseph Butterworth, 29 May 1820; see also William Stewart to Joseph Butterworth, 12 May 1820.

98 NIPRO, IWHS, Matthew Tobias to Jabez Bunting, 28 November 1828.

99 ibid., Tobias to Bunting, 17 March 1829.

100   SOAS, T. Bewley, Banagher, reports on Wesleyan Mission Schools, 2 July 1823
      and 22 October 1824; SOAS, MMSA, box 74, Bewley, extract from journal,
      July 1825; ibid., box 75, T. Edwards, Dublin, 1 January 1828.

5   RELIGION AND SOCIETY: CONVERSIONS AND CONTROVERSY

1   D. Bowen, *The Protestant Crusade in Ireland 1800–1870* (Dublin: 1978); I. M.
    Hehir, 'New lights and old enemies: the Second Reformation and the Catholics
    of Ireland, 1800–1835', MA thesis, University of Wisconsin, 1983.
2   Amicus Hibernicus, *The Letters of Amicus Hibernicus of Roman Catholic Affairs and
    the State of Ireland, as they appeared in The Instructor, London Newspaper, and
    Christian Guardian: Also Two Letters to the Secretary of the Protestant Union: with a
    Preface, containing a few observations on 'Faction Unmasked' by the same Writer*
    (Dublin: 1816).
3   NIPRO, Ouseley Collection, CR6/3, G. Ouseley to *Dublin Evening Mail*, 10
    April 1825.
4   *The Report of a Deputation from the London Hiberianian Society Respecting the
    Religious State of Ireland* (Dublin: 1808).
5   Rev. M. C. Motherwell, *Memoir of Albert Blest* . . . (Dublin: 1843), p. xii.
6   P. Livingston, *The Monaghan Story: a Documented History of County Monaghan
    from the Earliest Times to 1976* (Clogher: 1980), p. 241.
7   P. Corish, *The Irish Catholic Experience: an Historical Perspective* (Dublin: 1985),
    p. 158.
8   J. Duffy, *Clogher Record Album: a Diocesan History* (Monaghan: 1975); S. J.
    Connolly, 'Catholicism in Ulster 1800–1850', in P. Roebuck (ed.), *Plantation to
    Partition* . . . (Belfast: 1981), pp. 157–72.
9   Corish, *The Irish Catholic Experience*, p. 172 and Hehir, 'New lights', p. 256.
10 K. Whelan, 'The rise of the Sweetman family, 1700–1900', paper read at the
    Irish Religious History Society Conference at Queen's University, Belfast,
    May 1981.
11 R. B. McDowell, *Public Opinion and Government Policy in Ireland, 1801–1846*
    (London: 1952), p. 98.
12 J. A. Reynolds, *The Catholic Emancipation Crisis in Ireland, 1823–9* (New Haven,
    Conn.: 1954), p. 16.
13 See, for example, the pamphlets of Gideon Ouseley, held in MARC, especially
    Letters in Defence of the Roman Catholics of Ireland (London: 1829); also Petition of
    the Presbyterian Congregation at Clare, County Armagh, *Belfast Newsletter*, 24
    February 1827.
14 NLI, Farnham Papers, ms. 18,630, Beresford to Farnham, 1827; ibid., ms. 18,604
    (3), [name illegible] to Farnham; ibid., ms. 3504, notebook of Henry Maxwell.
15 Anon., *Protestant Union for the Defence and Support of the Protestant Religion and the
    British Constitution as established at the Glorious Revolution in 1688* (London: 1813).
16 *Benevolent and Religious Orange Reporter*, no. 1 (October, 1826).
17 F. O'Farrell, *Catholic Emancipation: Daniel O'Connell and the Birth of Irish
    Democracy* (Dublin: 1985), p. 133.
18 Select Committee on Orange Lodges, H.C. XVI (1835), p. 189.

19   P. O'Farrell, 'Millennialism, messianism and utopianism in Irish history', in *Anglo-Irish Studies* 2 (1976), pp. 45–67; S. Clarke and J. S. Donnelly (eds), *Irish Peasants: Violence and Political Unrest 1780–1914* (Manchester: 1983).

20   NIPRO, Ouseley Collection, CR6/3, vol. 1, p. 35.

21   J. Doyle, pastoral letter addressed to the Roman Catholic clergy of the deanery of Kilrock, to be read to their respective flocks, quoted in W. J. Fitzpatrick, *The Life, Times and Correspondence of the Right Reverend Dr. Doyle, Bishop of Kildare and Leighlin*, 2 vols (Dublin: 1890), Vol. 2.

22   G. Ouseley, *The Awful Adoration* (Dublin: 1825).

23   Dublin Castle, State of the Country Papers, March 1823, 2375/8, 2375/10, 2622.

24   O'Farrell, *Catholic Emancipation*, p. 39.

25   G. Broeker, *Rural Disorder and Police Reform in Ireland, 1812–1936* (London: 1970), pp. 1–19.

26   An example of the attitude of a local magistrate towards a Protestant evangelist is given by Methodist missionary C. McCord in a letter to London headquarters in January 1828. While he was preaching to a large crowd at a market, 'a man, greatly agitated, came forward, touched the Bible in my hand, and said What Book is that. For this small offence a magistrate would have committed him to prison, but for my interference. The magistrate said to me, "you need not be afraid we would suffer you to be opposed or insulted".' SOAS, MMSA, box 75.

27   J. K. L., *Letters on the State of Ireland* (Dublin: 1825), pp. 89–90.

28   *Clogher Record* 2 (1958) quotes various instances recorded in the *Dublin Weekly Register*; for example, on Saturday 27 March 1824, two Orangemen prosecuted for burning the hair off the head of a young married woman were let off; on 23 July 1825, in Clones, magistrates failed to prevent the erection of flags and arches by 'disruptive Orange ruffians'; J. Verner wrote to Lord Downshire about his unhappiness at expressions of Orangeism by magistrates in County Down, NIPRO, Correspondence of Lord Downshire, D607/C/12/110, Verner to Downshire, 10 December 1811.

29   Reformers were hampered by fears of offending 'loyal Protestant interest'; it was pointed out that even to suggest the necessity of reforms would be 'very wounding to the feelings of many loyal good men'; E. Brynn, *Crown and Castle: British Rule in Ireland, 1800–1830* (Dublin: 1978), pp. 124–5.

30   *Clogher Record* 2 (1958); Select Committee on Orange Lodges, H.C. XVI (1835). It was reported that at a Letterkenny demonstration, 'the Catholics (awed by military force) were obliged to become quiet spectators of the Orange processions; they were much irritated and will certainly take the first opportunity to proceed to some acts of violence'.

31   Select Committee on Orange Lodges, H.C. XV (1835), evidence of H. R. Baker, p. 201.

32   ibid., H. C. XVI (1835), p. 189.

33   ibid., H. C. XV (1835), evidence of James Christie, p. 388.

34   ibid., H.C. XVI (1835), p. 189.

35   G. O'Tuathaigh, *Ireland Before the Famine: 1798–1848* (Dublin: 1972), pp. 87–8.

36   For the most recent analysis of the composition and discipline of the nineteenth-century police, see S. H. Palmer, *Police and Protest in England and Ireland 1780–1850* (Cambridge: 1988).

37   ibid., p. 332.

38   ibid., pp. 360–2.

39   Hehir, 'New lights and old enemies', pp. 196–200; G. Ensor, *Letters Showing the Inutility and Showing the Absurdity of what is rather fantastically termed 'The New Reformation'* (Dublin: 1828), p. 14.

40   Lord Farnham, *A Statement of the Management of the Farnham Estates* (Dublin: 1830).

41   'Drivers' were the men paid to visit the tenantry in order to collect arrears. Their authority to impound livestock, etc., and their exploitation of the situation in their own interests – for example, by charging extra fees for the release of stock – made them highly unpopular figures.

42   J. R. R. Wright, 'An evangelical estate, *c.*1800–1825: the influence on the Manchester estate, County Armagh, with particular reference to the moral agencies of W. Loftie and H. Porter', PhD thesis, Northern Ireland Polytechnic, 1982. Wright points out that the term 'moral agent' was new, and finds no evidence of its use in England.

43   Advertisements for men of high moral character can be found in most contemporary newspapers. See also NIPRO, Correspondence of Lord Anneseley, D1854/6/1, Moore to Porter, 4 March 1839.

44   C. S. Stanford, *Memoir of the Late Reverend W. H. Krause . . .* (Dublin: 1854).

45   See, for example, the Rev. C. White, *Sixty Years Experience as an Irish Landlord: Memoirs of John Hamilton* (London: n.d.).

46   Wright, 'An evangelical estate'.

47   Report of the Commissioners appointed to Enquire into the Occupation of Land in Ireland, H.C. XIX (1845), pp. 18–19; J. S. Donnelly, *Landlord and Tenant in Nineteenth-Century Ireland* (Dublin: 1973), p. 22.

48   ibid., pp. 22–3.

49   For example, see evidence regarding Lord Mountcashel's lands in County Antrim, p. 573 and appendix B, no. 14, Report of the Commissioners appointed to Enquire into the Occupation of Land in Ireland (1845).

50   Lord Farnham, *The Substance of a Speech Delivered by the Rt. Hon. the Lord Farnham, at a Meeting held in Cavan on Friday, 20 January 1828, for the Purpose of Promoting the Reformation in Ireland* (Dublin: 1827).

51   Reports of the 1827 meeting went through various editions, to which were added appendices, notes, etc. The progress of the Reformation was also regularly reported in northern newspapers such as the *Belfast Newsletter* as well as the *Christian Examiner, The Watchman* and the *Primitive Wesleyan Magazine*.

52   *The Watchman or Protestant Guardian: A Weekly Paper* II (1827), p. 400.

53   Ensor felt that the Ulster response was 'insipid', *The Reformation*, p. 68. He recorded two conversions in County Tyrone and six in County Armagh, p. 53. Published reports of the meetings, however, note that they were very well attended.

54   A Primitive Wesleyan missionary, noting the great interest and improvement in religion in Ballyjamesduff, commented, 'The chief cause of our society improving so much at present, is the great Reformation going on in such a glorious manner in this country'; *Primitive Wesleyan Magazine* 5 (1827–8).

55   Ensor, *The Reformation*.

56   Farnham, *The Substance of a Speech Delivered by the Rt. Hon. the Lord Farnham*.

57   Ensor, *The Reformation*, p. 14. He also drew attention to the frequency of relapses.

58   ibid. See also, 'Fintona Farnhamites' in *Clogher Record*, 9 February 1827; Anon., *Correspondence between the Rev. Doctor Logan, Roman Catholic Bishop of Meath, and*

the Rev. *Robert Winning, Superintendent of Irish Schools in the Kingscourt District with the Resolutions of 125 Teachers therein* (Dublin: 1827); Anon., *Specimens of the Conversions at Cavan by Bible Saints Submitted to the Common Sense of the People of England* (Dublin: 1827); Rev. T. Maguire, *False Weights and Measures of Protestant Curate of Cavan Examined and Exposed* (Dublin: 1833).

59 Bowen, *The Protestant Crusade*, pp. 95–6; Hehir, 'New lights and old enemies', p. 208.

60 Ensor, *The Reformation*, p. 17.

61 J. Madden, *Farnham Hall or The Second Reformation in Ireland: a Poem* (Dublin: 1827).

62 Disturbances are recorded for this period in the States of the Country Papers at Dublin Castle, the Reports of the Irish and London Hibernian Societies, and the Methodist minutes. The Irish Society seemed particularly problematic. A letter from the Reverend Winning who went to Cavan to represent the Irish Society at a trial against a man called Moore, for firing at the Irish masters, is included in the Farnham manuscripts. Winning asserted the need for 'justice' to be done, pointing out the recurrent threats and intimidation to which teachers were subjected. He reminded Farnham, whose support he solicited, of three murders so far committed; see NLI, Farnham Papers, ms. 18,612 (6).

63 Anon., *The Protestant Colonization Society* (Dublin: 1830). A Wesleyan Methodist missionary reported from Cavan in 1831 an increase in the number of emigrants as a result of murders and fears of the political situation; see SOAS, MMSA, box 75. See also NLI, Farnham Papers, ms. 28,608, Beresford to Farnham, 26 March 1829.

64 NIPRO, Beresford Papers, T2772/2/4, vol. XI. See also NLI, Farnham Papers, ms. 18,604 (2), G. Moore to Farnham, 4 January 1829.

65 D. Bowen, *Souperism: Myth or Reality* (Cork: 1970).

66 See, for example, J. E. Gordon, *The Church of Ireland Considered in her Ecclesiastical Relation to the Roman Catholic Part of the Population* (London: 1849).

67 E. Nangle, *The Achill Mission and the Present State of Protestantism in Ireland . . .* (London: 1838); Earl of Roden, *Progress of the Reformation in Ireland . . .*, 2nd edn (Dublin: 1852).

68 T. W. Freeman, *Pre-Famine Ireland . . .* (Manchester: 1957), pp. 145–6.

69 Bowen, *The Protestant Crusade*, pp. 194–225.

70 Rev. J. McHale, *Second Letter of Right Rev. J. McHale, Bishop of Moronia to Lord Farnham* (Dublin: n.d.).

71 NLI, Farnham Papers, ms. 18,608, M. G. Beresford to Farnham, 9 July 1834.

72 ibid.

73 MARC, MAM PLP 80.46.13, Ouseley to Bunting, 1 April 1829 and 5 December 1835.

74 G. Ouseley, *Old Christianity Defended* (Dublin: 1820); Ouseley, *The Awful Adoration*; Anon., *Supplement to the Roman Catholic Expositor and Friend of Ireland . . .* (1825); Anon., *Appeal to Members of the Church of Rome Residing in Randalstown and its Vicinity*, 2nd edn (Belfast: 1827); Anon., *Protestants' Reasons for Not Worshipping Saints and Images* (Dublin: 1827).

75 *The Watchman* (1827).

76 Anon., *Authentic Report of the Discussion at Downpatrick* (Belfast: 1829).

77 *Christian Enquirer* (Strabane: 1828).

78 Anon., *Authentic Report of the Discussion at Downpatrick*.

79   Anon., *Address of the Committee of the Protestant Association to the People of England*, 3rd edn (1839).

80   Anon., *Authentic Report of the Discussion at Derry Between Six Roman Catholic Priests and Six Church of Ireland Clergy* (Dublin: 1828).

81   *Christian Enquirer* I, Strabane, 1828.

82   Alexander Carson to Plunkett, quoted by Lord Farnham in his speech in Cavan in January 1827, under the auspices of the Cavan Reformation Society.

83   Bowen, *The Protestant Crusade*, pp. 83–113.

84   Hehir, 'New lights and old enemies', p. 249.

85   Ensor, *The Reformation*, p. 41.

86   For an example of the reaction to Catholic Emancipation, and what was seen as an upsurge of 'Roman aggression', see 'Protestantism placed on the defensive in Ireland', *Christian Examiner* (1831), in which the loss of Protestant power over politics and education is lamented. See also NLI, Farnham Papers, especially letters from T. Lefroy on the need to protect Protestant interests in 1830, ms. 18,611 (1).

87   D. W. Bebbington, *Evangelicalism in Modern Britain: a History from the 1730s to the 1980s* (London: 1989), pp. 84–6.

88   I. S. Rennie, 'Evangelicalism and English public life: 1823–1850', PhD thesis, University of Toronto, 1962.

89   Rennie notes the evidence of the Continental Society (1819) as a contributory factor in evangelical pessimism. Tours on behalf of this society were undertaken in Ireland by popular leaders in 1822 and again in 1828.

90   Krause to his sister, 29 November 1831, quoted in Stanford, *Memoir*, p. 163.

91   A. L. Drummond, *Edward Irving and his Circle* (London: n.d.); S. C. Orchard, 'English evangelical eschatology 1790–1850', PhD thesis, University of Cambridge, 1969.

92   D. N. Hempton, 'Evangelicalism and eschatology', *Journal of Ecclesiastical History* 31, 2 (April, 1980), pp. 179–94.

93   H. H. Rowden, *The Origins of the Brethren* (London: 1967).

94   T. C. F. Stunt, 'Evangelical cross-currents in the Church of Ireland, 1820–1833', *Studies in Church History* 25 (1989), pp. 215–22.

95   T. Rea, *The Life and Labours of David Rea, Evangelist* (Belfast: 1917); J. G. Hutchinson, *Sowers, Reapers, Builders: a Record of over Ninety Irish Evangelists* (Glasgow: 1984); H. Pickering, *Chief Men among the Brethren* (London: 1931).

96   Rennie, 'Evangelicalism and English public life'.

97   Wright, 'An evangelical estate', p. 25.

98   *Primitive Wesleyan Magazine* (March 1834). Matthew Lanktree wrote from Donaghadee in the same period, 'pressed by the messenger of death, and unknowing who next might be summoned to the cholera house or the grave, a general concern for eternal life pervaded the community'; see M. Lanktree, *Biographical Narrative* (Belfast: 1836), p. 381. Contemporary sermon titles reflect alarm and fear, and the evangelical 'cure': 'Pestilences arrested by Prayer', 'Blessed Turf v Cholera', 'Cholera', 'God's Judgment Considered' – all are dated 1832.

99   D. H. Akenson, *The Irish Education Experiment* (London: 1970).

100 J. K. L., *Letters*, pp. 119–221.

101 Akenson, *The Irish Education Experiment*, ch. 3.

102 Reports on the Select Committee to which the Reports on the Subject of Education were Referred, H.C. IV (1828).

103 This was advocated in the major recommendations of the First Report of the Commission of Enquiry into Irish Education, H.C. XII (1825), pp. 97–101.

104 H. Cooke, *National Education: a Sermon Preached in the Presbyterian Church, May Street, Belfast, January, 1832* (Belfast: 1832).

105 Akenson, *The Irish Education Experiment*, p. 191.

106 Address at the formation of the Down and Connor Diocesan Society, 1838; see NIPRO, Correspondence of Lord Downshire, D671/C/188/37. Bishop Mant's views are well expressed in *A Churchman's Apology, or Clerical Pledges Stated with Reference to National Education in a Justificatory Letter to the Rt. Hon. Sir Robert Peel* (Dublin: 1844).

107 C. R. Elrington to Beresford, stating that funds are exhausted, 23 November 1842; see also J. L. Crosthwaite to Beresford, 6 December 1842, in NIPRO, Beresford Papers, T2772/2, vol. XI; Anon., *Appeal of the Church Education Society for Funds* (Dublin: 1842).

108 W. R. Ward, *Early Victorian Methodism, the Correspondence of Jabez Bunting 1830–1858* (Oxford: 1976), p. 16. For the reaction of the Irish Methodist Missions see SOAS, Methodist Mission House mss., Elijah Hoole to John James, 18 January, 9 July, 12 July and 29 October 1832.

109 D. Hempton, *Methodism and Politics in British Society 1790–1850* (London: 1984).

110 See the comments made by the Buntingite James Dixon, *The Present Position and Aspects of Popery and the Duty of Exposing the Errors of Papal Rome, a lecture first delivered in Sheffield, 12 December 1839* (London: 1840).

111 R. J. Rodgers, 'James Carlile, 1784–1854', PhD thesis, Queen's University, Belfast, 1973, p. 176.

112 ibid.; Anon., *Address of the General Synod of Ulster to the People under their Care on the Subject of Education* (Belfast: 1838).

113 Anon., *A Full and Authentic Report of the Important and Interesting Proceedings of the Great Meeting of the Friends of Education and the Whole Bible* (Dublin: 1832).

114 W. B. Mant, *Bishop Mant and His Diocese* (Dublin: 1857), p. 347; G. Ouseley, *Letters on Topics of Vast Importance to All Roman Catholics and the State . . .* (Dublin: 1832), stressing that it would be totally hypocritical 'for Protestants to stand by and watch children being taught "Romish errors"'. Ouseley went on to claim that the new plan 'enjoins upon Protestants, not merely to permit, but absolutely to encourage the teaching of *Popery, Unitarianism,* and every possible form of Apostacy and infidelity'; *Report of the Proceedings of the 21st Annual General Meeting of the Society for Promoting the Education of the Poor in Ireland* (Dublin: 1833); G. Miller, *The Present Crisis of the Church of Ireland Considered* (Dublin: 1844); *Education in Ireland: the Scriptural and the National Systems Contrasted; Vast Expenditure of the British State in Teaching the Youth of Ireland the Errors of Popery* (Dublin: 1854).

115 Viscount Lifford, *Ireland and the Irish Church: Its Past and Present State and Future Prospects* (London: 1844).

116 Akenson, *The Irish Education Experiment*, p. 199.

117 J. L. Porter, *The Life and Times of Henry Cooke, D.D.* (Belfast: 1875), pp. 246–7.

118 Anon., *The Substance of an Address to the Irish Clergy at the Rotunda* (Dublin: 1836).

119 Porter, *Life of Cooke*, p. 201.

120   *The Irish Protestant containing the Most Important Speeches Delivered at Conservative Meetings* . . . I, 1 (Belfast: 1835).

121   R. F. G. Holmes, *Henry Cooke* (Belfast: 1981), p. 115; Porter, *Life of Cooke*, p. 229.

122   'Great Protestant Down Meeting', *Irish Protestant* I, IX.

123   Porter, *Life of Cooke*, p. 242. See also *Irish Protestant* I, XI–XIII.

124   T. Allan to his son Thomas, 9 March 1829, mentioning the anxiety of Lord and Lady Farnham for Methodist support in the Cavan area; see MARC, Allan Collection.

125   D. N. Hempton, 'Methodism and anti-Catholic politics, 1800–1846', PhD thesis, University of St Andrews, 1977, pp. 112–41.

126   G. Ouseley, 'The tranquillity of Ireland', an article in the *Sligo Journal*, 21 May 1823; see SOAS, MMSA, box 74.

127   G. Ouseley, *An Easy Mode of Securing Ireland's Peace. Letter to P. G. Crampton, Solicitor-General, 12 April 1833* (Dublin: 1833).

128   NIPRO, Ouseley Collection, CR6/3, Ouseley, 17 December 1835.

129   *Methodist Magazine* (1833), p. 873.

130   O'Farrell, *Catholic Emancipation*, p. 212. The State of the Country Papers in Dublin Castle report that in September 1828, Brunswick clubs embraced nearly the entire population as a result of Lawless's visit.

131   H. Senior, *Orangeism in Britain and Ireland: 1795–1836* (London: 1966), pp. 245– 6. For a report on the formation of a Brunswick club, see Anon., *Report of the Speeches Delivered at a Very Numerous and Respectable Meeting of Protestants Held at Churchill, County Armagh* (Dublin: 1828).

132   Anon., *Protestant Conservative Society: a Plan for the Protection of Landed Proprietors, Magistrates and the Lower Orders, Against the Combinations with which they are Assailed, and to Secure the Interests of Property and Religion at the Ensuing General Election* (Dublin: 1832); NLI, Farnham Papers, ms. 18,610 (7), Cottingham to 5th Lord Farnham, 17 June 1832.

133   R. M. Sibbett, *Orangeism in Ireland and throughout the Empire*, 2 vols (Belfast: 1939), Vol. II, p. 89. See also Rev. J. McGhee, *A Letter to the Protestants of the United Kingdom, Exhibiting the Real Principles of the Roman Catholic Bishops and Priests in Ireland* (London: 1835).

134   C. E. Tonna, *Letters from Ireland* (London: 1837), pp. 292–3.

135   J. C. Colquhoun, *The Object and Uses of Protestant Associations*, 2nd edn (London: 1839), p. 9.

136   Hempton, 'Methodism and anti-Catholic politics', pp. 269–303.

137   Bowen, *The Protestant Crusade*, p. 197.

138   RCB, ms. 17, minutes of 'Protestant Alliance' 1845–8, 17 November 1845.

139   ibid., letter from Dean of Dromore to Protestant Alliance, 5 January 1846.

140   ibid., objects of the Protestant Alliance, 17 December 1845.

6   RELIGION IN THE CITY:
EVANGELICALISM IN BELFAST 1800–60

1   For a wider discussion of the relation between religion and class see E. Halevy, *A History of the English People in the Nineteenth Century*, 4 vols (London: 1949– 51); E. S. Itzkin, 'The Halevy thesis – a working hypothesis?', *Church History* 44,

1 (1975), pp. 47–56; A. D. Gilbert, 'Methodism, dissent and political stability in early industrial England', *Journal of Religious History* 10 (1978–9), pp. 381–99; D. N. Hempton, 'Evangelical revival and society: a historiographical review of Methodism and British society c.1750–1850', *Themelios* 8, 3 (April, 1983), pp. 19–25; E. J. Hobsbawm, *Primitive Rebels* (Manchester: 1959); E. J. Hobsbawm, *Labouring Men: Studies in the History of Labour* (London: 1964); E. P. Thompson, *The Making of the English Working Class* (London: 1963); J. Foster, *Class Struggle and the Industrial Revolution: Early Industrial Capitalism in Three English Towns* (London: 1974); P. Joyce, *Work, Society and Politics: the Culture of the Factory in Later Victorian England* (Brighton: 1980); H. McLeod, 'Recent studies in Victorian religious history', *Victorian Studies* 21, 2 (1978); H. McLeod, *Religion and the Working Class in Nineteenth-Century Britain* (London: 1984); H. McLeod, 'New perspectives on working-class religion: the oral evidence', *Oral History* 14, 1 (1986), pp. 31–49; J. Rule, 'Methodism, popular beliefs and village culture in Cornwall, 1800–50', in R. D. Storch (ed.), *Popular Culture and Custom in Nineteenth-Century England* (London: 1982), pp. 48–70; E. Yeo and S. Yeo (eds), *Popular Culture and Class Conflict, 1500–1914* (Brighton: 1982).

2 D. J. Owen, *History of Belfast* (Belfast: 1921); NIPRO, *Belfast: Problems of a Growing City* (Belfast: 1973); J. Bardon, *Belfast: an Illustrated History* (Belfast: 1982).

3 W. H. Crawford, 'Economy and society in eighteenth-century Ulster', PhD thesis, Queen's University, Belfast, 1983, p. 48; *Clogher Record* 3 (1975).

4 Crawford, 'Economy and society', pp. 135, 161.

5 For the most recent analysis of Belfast's 'brief flirtation with cotton', see F. Geary, 'The Belfast cotton industry revisited', *Irish Historical Studies* 26, 103 (May, 1989), pp. 250–67 and 'The rise and fall of the Belfast cotton industry: some problems', *Irish Economic and Social History* 3 (1981), pp. 30–49. See also Owen, *History of Belfast*, p. 297; E. R. R. Green, 'Early industrial Belfast', in J. C. Beckett and R. E. Glassock (eds), *The Origin and Growth of a City* (London: 1967), pp. 78–87; I. Budge and C. O'Leary, *Belfast: Approach to Crisis* (London: 1973), p. 21.

6 R. E. Glassock, 'The growth of the port', in Beckett and Glassock, *The Origin and Growth of a City*, pp. 98–108.

7 'Between 1820 and 1836 there was a tenfold increase in the number of shoemakers, stockingmakers, and dressmakers involved in the provisions trade': Budge and O'Leary, *Belfast*, p. 22.

8 W. A. Maguire, *Living Like a Lord: the second Marquis of Donegall 1769–1844* (Belfast: 1984), p. 75.

9 E. Jones, *A Social Geography of Belfast* (London: 1960), p. 36.

10 Rev. W. O'Hanlon, *Walks among the Poor of Belfast and Suggestions for their Improvement* (Belfast: 1853); P. Froggatt, 'Industrialisation and health in Belfast in the early nineteenth century', in D. Harkness and M. O'Dowd (eds), *The Town in Ireland* (Belfast: 1979); Report from Select Committee on the State of the Poor in Ireland (1830), vol. VII, p. 4; NIPRO, *Belfast*, pp. 152–63.

11 S. E. Baker, 'Orange and green: Belfast, 1832–1912', in H. J. Dyos and M. Wolff (eds), *The Victorian City . . .*, Vol. 2 (London: 1973), pp. 789–814.

12 A. C. Hepburn and B. Collin, 'Industrial society: the structure of Belfast, 1901', in P. Roebuck (ed.), *Plantation to Partition . . .* (Belfast: 1981), pp. 210–28; L. A. Clarkson, 'Population change and urbanisation, 1821–1911', in L. Kennedy and P. Ollerenshaw (eds), *An Economic History of Ulster 1820–1939* (Manchester: 1985), pp. 137–57.

13   P. Corish, *The Irish Catholic Experience: a Historical Survey* (Dublin: 1985), p. 169.
14   See Budge and O'Leary, *Belfast*.
15   T. Drew, 'The church in Belfast', quoted in W. B. Mant, *Bishop Mant and his Diocese* (Dublin: 1857), pp. 230–1.
16   NIPRO, Correspondence of Lord Downshire, D607/C/188/5, printed circular on a project for a church or chapel-at-ease at Ballymacarrett, 1824.
17   *Fourth and Final Report of the Down and Connor Church Accommodation Society . . .* (Belfast: 1843).
18   Rev. J. McConnell, *Presbyterianism in Belfast* (Belfast: 1912), p. 18.
19   J. Morgan, *Recollections of My Life and Times* (Belfast: 1874), p. 74.
20   McConnell, *Presbyterianism*, p. 73.
21   ibid., p. 69.
22   This point is reiterated in much of the correspondence, and in the biographies of the period.
23   J. Adams, *A Brief History of Belfast Methodism, 1805–1809* (Belfast: 1890), p. 17.
24   For a wider discussion of Methodism and urban life, see A. D. Gilbert, *Religion and Society in Industrial England . . .* (London: 1976).
25   M. Lanktree, *Biographical Narrative* (Belfast: 1836), p. 274.
26   *Minutes of the Methodist Conference in Ireland* (1840).
27   Quoted in Adams, *Belfast Methodism*.
28   R. M. Sibbett, *For Christ and Crown: the Story of a Mission* (Belfast: 1926), p. 52.
29   NIPRO, Annals of Christ Church, Belfast, T2159, A. Dawson, 'The annals of Christ Church, Belfast', pp. 10–11.
30   For the importance of the laity in the affairs of religious organizations, see S. Yeo, *Religion and Voluntary Organisations in Crisis* (London: 1976).
31   Morgan, *Recollections*, pp. 67–9. For the importance of hymn-singing to evangelicals, see A. R. Acheson, 'The evangelicals in the Church of Ireland, 1784–1859', PhD thesis, Queen's University, Belfast, 1967, pp. 235–9.
32   McConnell, *Presbyterianism*, pp. 82, 87, 89.
33   *Minutes of the Synod of Ulster, 1831–1840*, 1833, pp. 18, 48.
34   McConnell, *Presbyterianism*, p. 28.
35   NIPRO, Dawson, 'The annals of Christ Church', p. 8.
36   ibid., p. 51. See also Stephen Kerr, 'The Church of Ireland in Belfast', MPhil, University of Edinburgh, 1978.
37   *Belfast Chronicle*, 8 September 1838.
38   A full account is given in NIPRO, Dawson, 'The annals of Christ Church'.
39   *Fourth and Final Report of the . . . Church Accommodation Society . . .*
40   *Minutes of the Synod of Ulster 1831–40*, 1832, pp. 6–16; NIPRO, Armagh Visitation Records, 1839, DI04/29/1/14.
41   Morgan, *Recollections*, p. 82; NIPRO, Dawson, 'The annals of Christ Church', p. 59.
42   NIPRO, The State of the District of Christ Church, Belfast, with Regard to the Ministers of the Established Church in the year 1852, CR1/13/D1.
43   NIPRO, Dawson, 'The annals of Christ Church', p. 30.
44   Morgan, *Recollections*, pp. 59–66.
45   Rev. W. Carr, *The Conversion of Seamen* (Belfast: n.d.).
46   J. R. R. Adams, *The Printed Word and the Common Man: Popular Culture in Ulster, 1700–1900* (Belfast: 1987).
47   *Annual Report of the Hibernian Bible Society, 1822* (Dublin: 1822).

48 H. Clayton, *To School Without Shoes: a Brief History of the Sunday School Society for Ireland 1809–1979* (Dublin: 1979).

49 RCB, Records and Annual Reports of the Sunday School Society for Ireland, 1809–1971, ms. 182.

50 *9th Report of the Belfast Sunday School Union* (Belfast: 1831).

51 Cambridge University Library, BFBS Mss, miscellaneous book 2, Adam Averell to BFBS, 6 August 1807.

52 RCB, Records and Annual Reports of the Sunday School Society for Ireland, *Hibernian Sunday School Society Report, 1826* (Dublin: 1826); Anon., *Hints for Conducting Sunday Schools . . .*, 2nd edn (Dublin: 1819).

53 H. Clayton, 'Societies formed to educate the poor in Ireland in the late eighteenth and early nineteenth century', M.Litt thesis, Trinity College, Dublin, 1981.

54 Anon., *Hints for Conducting Sunday Schools*; letters from teachers indicate that responses were largely dependent on local conditions; see letter from Lisburn, 3 November 1811, and from Castledawson, 14 February 1811, RCB, *Hibernian Sunday School Report, 1812* (Dublin: 1812).

55 T. W. Laqueur, *Religion and Respectability: Sunday Schools and Working-Class Culture* (London: 1976); McLeod, *Religion and the Working Class*.

56 W. R. Ward, *Religion and Society in England, 1790–1850* (London: 1972), p. 13; D. Hempton, *Methodism and Politics in British Society, 1750–1850* (London: 1984), pp. 86–92.

57 The major source of information for the Belfast City Mission is Sibbett, *For Christ and Crown*.

58 For parallels in English cities see H. McLeod, *Class and Religion in the late Victorian City* (London: 1974); J. Cox, *The English Churches in a Secular Society: Lambeth 1870–1930* (Oxford: 1982), pp. 90–128; Yeo, *Religion and Voluntary Organisations*, pp. 117–62; J. Kent, 'Feelings and festivals', in H. J. Dyos and M. Wolff (eds), *The Victorian City* (London: 1973), Vol. 2, pp. 855–71; E. R. Wickham, *Church and People in an Industrial City* (London: 1964).

59 O'Hanlon, *Walks Among the Poor*, p. 3.

60 D. Lewis, *Lighten their Darkness: the Evangelical Mission to Working-Class London, 1828–1860* (London: 1986).

61 NIPRO, Dawson, 'The annals of Christ Church', p. 48; see also *Hibernian Evangelical Magazine* 14 (September, 1816), p. 407.

62 *Minutes of the Methodist Conferences in Ireland*, Vol. 1, 1744–1819.

63 Sibbett, *For Christ and Crown*, p. 35.

64 P. T. Winskill, *The Temperance Movement and Its Workers: a Record of Social, Moral, Religious and Political Progress* (London: 1892), p. 50; *Report of the Committee of the Ulster Temperance Society, 1838* (Belfast: 1838).

65 *Address of the Ulster Temperance Society, 1833* (Belfast: 1833).

66 *Address of the Ulster Temperance Society, 1829* (Belfast: 1829); W. D. Killen, *Memoir of John Edgar, D.D., L.L.D.* (Belfast: 1867), p. 94.

67 See NIPRO, Correspondence of Lord Downshire, D607/C/12/131, D607/C/12/831, for the correspondence between Downshire and Father Mathew, and D607/C/12/821, Downshire to Dr John Shaw; J. G. Kohl, *Travels in Ireland* (London: 1844), pp. 93–113.

68 W. D. Killen, *Reminiscences of a Long Life* (London: 1901), p. 188.

69 C. E. Crookshank, *History of Methodism in Ireland*, 3 vols (London: 1885–8), Vol. III, p. 134.

70 'In Belfast twenty-seven firms in the provision trade, with Messrs. John and Thomas Sinclair at their head, and twenty millowners and manufacturers, proclaimed their determination, in a published resolution, "to furnish their workmen with no spirituous liquor as refreshment, but to substitute, when necessary, some wholesome beverage"', Killen, *Memoir of John Edgar*, p. 63.

71 C. G. Duffy, *My Life in Two Hemispheres*, 2 vols (Dublin: 1969), Vol. 1, p. 54; Kohl, *Travels in Ireland*, pp. 93–113; *Feudal Slavery Broken and Ireland Freed by Temperance* (Belfast: 1840); C. Kerrigan, 'The social impact of the temperance movement, 1839–1845', *Irish Economic and Social History* 14 (1987), pp. 20–38; E. Malcolm, *Ireland Sober, Ireland Free: Drink and Temperance in Nineteenth-Century Ireland* (Dublin: 1986).

72 Despite early optimism that the temperance crusade would unite Catholics and Protestants, two separate movements emerged in Ireland; see Rev. P. Rogers, *Father Theobald Mathew: Apostle of Temperance* (Dublin: 1943); for a wider discussion of nineteenth-century temperance see B. Harrison, *Drink and the Victorians* (London: 1971).

73 B. Noel, *Notes of a Short Tour through the Middle Counties of Ireland, in the Summer of 1836, with observations on . . . the peasantry* (London: 1837), p. 78.

74 C. E. Tonna, *Letters from Ireland* (London: 1837), p. 28; H. D. Inglis, *A Journey Throughout Ireland During the Spring, Summer and Autumn of 1834*, Vol. II (London: 1835), notes that legal whiskey was becoming as cheap as illicit, because of the reduction on Irish spirits, therefore the illegal trade was greatly reduced, pp. 109–10; see also NIPRO, Ordnance Survey memoirs, Mic. 6, for numerous reports on reductions in illicit distillation and in alcoholic consumption itself.

75 Ordnance Survey memoirs for the parishes of Layd, Cushendall, Mallusk, Ardclinis, Ballyclugg, Derrykeighan, and Culfreightrin provide examples.

76 J. Binns, *The Miseries and Beauties of Ireland*, 2 vols (London: 1837), p. 82.

77 For a vivid description of a procession by a local temperance band, see Sibbett, *For Christ and Crown*, p. 37.

78 For a discussion of the definition of popular religion and its relation to official Christianity, see J. Obelkevich, *Religion and Rural Society: South Lindsey 1825–1875* (Oxford: 1976), p. 261, and Rule, 'Methodism, popular beliefs and village culture'; for the Roman Catholic parallel see Sean Connolly, *Priests and People in Pre-Famine Ireland, 1780–1845* (London: 1982).

79 J. Gray, 'Popular entertainment', in J. C. Beckett (ed.), *Belfast: the Making of the City, 1800–1914* (Belfast: 1983), pp. 98–111; NIPRO, Ordnance Survey memoirs, Mic. 6/13, p. 157.

80 NIPRO, Dawson, 'The annals of Christ Church', pp. 87–93.

81 'One minister declared that the railway was sending souls to the Devil at the rate of 6d a head', Bardon, *Belfast*, p. 89.

82 Hugh McLeod comments on the changing usages of the term 'respectability', which by mid-century denoted moral worth, regardless of position, and was thus a status to which all could aspire; *Class and Religion in the Late Victorian City*, p. 13.

83 R. H. Tawney, in the introduction to M. Weber, *The Protestant Ethic and the Spirit of Capitalism* (London: 1930).

84 H. McLeod, *Religion and the People of Western Europe, 1789–1979* (Oxford: 1981), p. 32; G. Malmgreen, 'Domestic discords . . .', in J. Obelkevich, L. Roper and R. Samuel (eds), *Disciplines of Faith . . .* (London: 1987).

85 For a typical example of this perception see *Irish Intelligence: the Progress of the Irish Society of London* (London: 1848), Vol. 1, pp. 92–5; see also S. J. Connolly, 'Religion, work-discipline and economic attitudes: the case of Ireland', in T. M. Devine and D. Dickson (eds), *Ireland and Scotland, 1600–1850* (Glasgow: 1983), pp. 235–60.

86 *Lecture on the Connection between Religion and Industry delivered in the Music Hall, Belfast on Tuesday evening, 2 December 1851 to members of the Working Classes Association, by the president of the Queen's College, Belfast* (Belfast: 1852); T. Drew, 'The rich and the poor', in *The Irish Pulpit: a Collection of Original Sermons by Clergymen of the Established Church* (Dublin: 1839), pp. 251–69.

87 Bardon, *Belfast*, p. 69.

88 P. Devlin, *Yes, We Have No Bananas: Outdoor Relief in Belfast, 1920–39* (Belfast: 1981), p. 27.

89 H. Patterson, 'Industrial labour and the labour movement, 1920–1914', in Kennedy and Ollerenshaw (eds), *An Economic History of Ulster 1820–1939*, p. 176; R. Munck, 'The formation of the working class in Belfast, 1788–1881', *Saothar* 11 (1986), pp. 75–89; Connolly, 'Religion, work-discipline', p. 243.

90 *Belfast People's Magazine* I (1847).

91 *Lecture on the Connection between Religion and Industry.*

92 J. Garnett, 'Gold and the gospel', in W. J. Sheils and D. Wood (eds), *Studies in Church History* 24 (1987), pp. 158–83.

93 S. Kerr, 'Voluntaryism within the established church in nineteenth-century Belfast', in ibid., 23 (1986), pp. 347–62; A. Jordan, 'Voluntary societies in Victorian and Edwardian Belfast', PhD thesis, Queen's University, Belfast, 1989.

94 B. Walker, *Ulster Politics: the Formative Years, 1868–86* (Belfast: 1989), pp. 122–3, 148–9, 188–90.

95 Mant, *Bishop Mant*, p. 423. For a wider discussion of the Oxford Movement, see G. Rowell (ed.), *Tradition Renewed: the Oxford Movement* (London: 1986).

96 Anon., *Ecclesiologism Exposed: Being the Letters of 'Clericus Connorensis' as Originally Published in the Belfast Commercial Chronicle . . .* (Belfast: 1843).

97 Mant, *Bishop Mant*, pp. 425–6.

98 Anon., *Ecclesiologism Exposed*, letter 1.

99 NIPRO, Correspondence between Emerson Tennent and Thomas Drew, 19 July 1842, D2922/C/12/1–6.

100 Anon., *Ecclesiologism Exposed*, letter 2.

101 ibid., appendix.

102 ibid., XIX.

103 *Fourth and Final Meeting of the Down and Connor Church Accommodation Society*, 19 January 1843.

104 *Report of the Clergy Aid Society 1839* (Belfast: 1839).

105 NIPRO, Dawson, 'The annals of Christ Church', pp. 76–86.

106 D. Bowen, *The Protestant Crusade in Ireland 1800–1870* (Dublin: 1978), p. 117.

107 Select Committee on Orange Lodges, H.C. XV (1835), evidence of M. O'Sullivan, p. 37.

108 See Dawson's account of the Easter celebrations in Christ Church, in his 'The annals of Christ Church', pp. 87–93.

109 ibid., p. 160.

110 A. Boyd, *Holy War in Belfast* (Belfast: 1969).

111   Bardon, *Belfast*, p. 107.
112   Boyd, *Holy War*, p. 44.
113   NIPRO, Dawson, 'The annals of Christ Church', p. 208.
114   Quoted in Boyd, *Holy War*, p. 39.
115   A. Macauley, *Patrick Dorrian, Bishop of Down and Connor 1865–1885* (Dublin: 1987).
116   Baker, 'Orange and green'.
117   Macauley, *Patrick Dorrian*, pp. 133–5.

7 'BORN TO SERVE': WOMEN AND EVANGELICAL RELIGION

1   K. Thomas, 'Women and the Civil War sects', *Past and Present* 13 (April, 1958), pp. 42–62.
2   E. K. Brown, 'Women in church history: stereotypes, archetypes and operational modalities', *Methodist History* 18 (1980), pp. 109–32; G. Malmgreen, 'Domestic discords: women and the family in East Cheshire Methodism, 1750–1830', in J. Obelkevich, L. Roper and R. Samuel (eds), *Disciplines of Faith: Studies in Religion, Politics and Patriarchy* (London: 1987), pp. 55–70; and N. F. Cott, 'Young women in the Second Great Awakening', *Feminist Studies* 3 (1975), pp. 14–29.
3   Moravian Church House, London, John Cennick, 'An account of . . . the Awakening in Dublin . . .'.
4   M. Weber, *Sociology of Religion* (London: 1966).
5   Thomas, 'Women and the Civil War sects', p. 44; H. McLeod, *Religion and the People of Western Europe 1789–1970* (Oxford: 1981), pp. 28–35. See also C. Cross, 'He-goats before the flocks', *Studies in Church History* 8 (1972), pp. 195–202. For a wider study of this aspect see G. F. Moran, '"Sisters" in Christ: women and the church in seventeenth-century New England', in J. W. James (ed.), *Women in American Religion* (Philadelphia, Pa: 1980), pp. 47–65; J. Rendall, *The Origins of Modern Feminism in Britain, France and the United States 1780–1860* (London: 1985).
6   F. K. Brown, *Fathers of the Victorians . . .* (Cambridge: 1961), p. 3.
7   C. H. Crookshank, *Memorable Women of Irish Methodism in the Last Century* (London: 1882), pp. 151–60.
8   A. C. H. Seymour, *The Life and Times of Selina, Countess of Huntingdon*, 2 vols (London: 1884), Vol. 2, p. 196.
9   A. Stevens, *The Women of Methodism: Memoirs of Its Three Founders* (London: n.d.).
10   Seymour, *Life and Times of Selina*, Vol. 2, pp. 169, 202–27. See also Rev. M. C. Motherwell, *Memoir of Albert Blest, for Many Years Agent and Secretary for the London Hibernian Society* (Dublin: 1843), p. 40.
11   F. E. Bland, *How the Church Missionary Society Came to Ireland* (Dublin: 1935), ch. 5; A. R. Acheson, 'The evangelicals in the Church of Ireland, 1784–1859', PhD thesis, Queen's University, Belfast, 1967; RCB, Proceedings of the Association for the Purpose of Discountenancing Vice and Promoting the Practice of Virtue and Religion, ms. 174.
12   Seymour, *Life and Times of Selina*, p. 197.
13   We are grateful to I. M. Hehir for helping to establish these connections.
14   Seymour, *Life and Times of Selina*, p. 183.

15   O. Goodbody, *Guide to Irish Quaker Records 1654–1860* (Dublin: 1967); I. Grubb, *Quakers in Ireland 1654–1900* (London: 1927). For an interesting discussion of Quakerism and early Methodism, see G. F. Nuttall, 'Early Quakerism and early Primitive Methodism', *Friends' Quarterly* 7 (1953), pp. 179–87.

16   *Leadbeater Papers: a Selection from the Mss and Correspondence of Mary Leadbeater* (London: 1862), Vol. 1, p. 128.

17   D. E. C. Eversley, 'The demography of the Irish Quakers, 1650–1850', in J. M. Goldstrom and L. A. Clarkson (eds), *Irish Population, Economy and Society* (Oxford: 1981), pp. 57–88. See also A. Gailey, 'The Ballyhagan inventories 1716–1740', *Folklife* 15 (1977), pp. 37–64, esp. p. 62.

18   D. N. Hempton, 'Religious minorities', in P. Loughrey (ed.), *The People of Ireland* (Belfast: 1988), pp. 155–68, 164.

19   *Leadbeater Papers*, Vol. 1.

20   NIPRO, Quaker Records, Mic. 16.

21   C. H. Crookshank, *History of Methodism in Ireland*, 3 vols (London: 1885–8), Vol. I, pp. 25, 58, 180, 203, 362; see also R. Haire, *Wesley's One-and-Twenty Visits to Ireland* (London: 1947), pp. 87, 117.

22   Crookshank, *History of Methodism*, Vol. 1, p. 229.

23   ibid., Vol. 1, pp. 189, 290–1, 383–4; Vol. 2, pp. 53, 296; Vol. 3, p. 138; and many examples in Crookshank's *Memorable Women of Irish Methodism*.

24   E. K. Brown, 'Women of Mr Wesley's Methodism', *Studies in Women and Religion*, Vol. II (New York: 1983); see also Brown, 'Women in church history', pp. 109–32.

25   R. M. Haines, 'Wild wittes and wilfulness: John Swetsock's attack on those poyswunmongers, the Lollards', *Studies in Church History* 8 (1972) (pp. 143–53), p. 152.

26   Thomas, 'Women in the Civil War sects', p. 47.

27   While some Methodist preachers were ordained Anglican ministers, the ordination of its preachers did not become general Methodist policy until 1816. An indication of the difficulties caused by their ambiguous relationship to the established church can be found in M. Lanktree, *Biographical Narrative* (Belfast: 1836), p. 136.

28   E. K. Brown, 'Women of the word', in H. F. Thomas and R. Skinner (eds), *Women in New Worlds* (Nashville, Tenn.: 1981), pp. 69–87.

29   Crookshank, *History of Methodism*, Vol. 2, p. 31.

30   Crookshank, *Memorable Women of Irish Methodism*, p. 67; see also E. Smyth, *The Extraordinary Life and Christian Experience of Margaret Davidson* (Dublin: 1782).

31   Crookshank, *Memorable Women of Irish Methodism*, pp. 191–203; see also J. J. McGregor, *Memoir of Miss Alice Cambridge* (Dublin: 1832).

32   *Minutes of the Methodist Conferences in Ireland*, Vol. 1, 1744–1819, p. 152.

33   D. Valenze, *Prophetic Sons and Daughters: Female Preaching and Popular Religion in Industrial England* (Princeton, NJ: 1985), and W. F. Swift, 'The women itinerant preachers of early Methodism', *Proceedings of the Wesley Historical Society* 28 (1951–2), pp. 89–94; and 29 (1953–4), pp. 76–83.

34   See NIPRO, Ouseley Collection, CR6/3, letter from Zachariah Taft to Gideon Ouseley, 15 February 1823.

35   Crookshank, *History of Methodism*, Vol. 2, p. 153.

36   E. Thomas, *Irish Methodist Reminiscences: Memorials of the Life and Labour of the Late Reverend S. Nicholson* (London: 1889), p. 10.

37 D. N. Hempton, 'Methodism in Irish society: 1770–1830', *Transactions of the Royal Historical Society*, 5th series, 26 (1986), pp. 117–42.

38 Although dealing with a different profession and period, an interesting analysis on the gap between women's access to a profession, and equal opportunities within it, is provided in an essay by J. K. Conway, 'Politics, pedagogy and power', *Daedalus* (1987), pp. 137–52.

39 H. Bingham, *The Life Story of Ann Preston* (Toronto: 1907), p. 33.

40 Crookshank, *History of Methodism*, Vol. 2, p. 31.

41 ibid., p. 405.

42 Letters of Anne Lutton of Moira; a volume of original letters of 'Holy Anne' Lutton, *c*.1810–1840. We wish to thank Mr J. Gamble for making this available from his private collection.

43 NIPRO, Ouseley Collection, CR6/3, Ouseley, 22 September 1802. See also D. N. Hempton, 'Gideon Ouseley: rural revivalist 1791–1839', *Studies in Church History* 25 (1989), pp. 203–14.

44 N. Curnock (ed.), *The Journal of John Wesley . . .* 8 vols (London: 1909), Vol. V, p. 306.

45 Goodbody, *Irish Quaker Records*, p. 4.

46 The best general assessment of women's involvement in voluntary religious agencies in this period is provided by F. Prochaska, *Women and Philanthropy in Nineteenth-Century England* (Oxford: 1980).

47 Thomas, *Irish Methodist Reminiscenses*, p. 12. For a parallel American example see N. F. Cott, *The Bonds of Womanhood: 'Woman's Sphere' in New England 1780–1835* (New Haven, Conn.: 1977), pp. 46–7.

48 J. Walsh, 'Methodism and the mob in the eighteenth century', *Studies in Church History* 8 (1972), pp. 213–37.

49 *An Address to the Clergy of the United Church in Ireland on the Present Crisis, by an Aged Minister of the Gospel* (Dublin: 1800).

50 Crookshank, *History of Methodism*, Vol. 1, pp. 218–19.

51 NIPRO, Methodist Mss, private minutes of the Methodist Conference in Ireland, CR6/3.

52 Walsh, *Methodism and the Mob*, p. 224.

53 C. H. Crookshank, *A Methodist Pioneer: the Life and Labours of John Smith . . .* (London: 1881).

54 Goodbody, *Irish Quaker Records*, pp. 16–17; 'The Large Minutes according to the Last Edition, published during the Life of Mr. Wesley', in *Minutes of the Methodist Conferences in Ireland*, Vol. 1, 1744–1819, p. xiv; S. G. Hanna, 'The origin and nature of the Gracehill Moravian settlement 1764–1855, with special reference to the work of John Cennick in Ireland 1746–1755', MA thesis, Queen's University, Belfast, 1964, p. 109.

55 *Minutes of the Methodist Conferences in Ireland*, Vol. 1, 1744–1819, p. 152.

56 Goodbody, *Irish Quaker Records*, p. 10.

57 Hanna, 'The Gracehill Moravian settlement', p. 109.

58 ibid., p. 168.

59 ibid., pp. 167–8.

60 Crookshank, *History of Methodism*, Vol. 1, pp. 353–4.

61 ibid., p. 340.

62 S. W. Christophers, *Class-Meetings in Relation to the Design and Success of Methodism* (1873); for specific illustrations of the importance of class meetings to hesitant

newcomers, see NIPRO, Ouseley Collection, CR6/3, 'Early history of Gideon Ouseley', by J. Bonsall, p. 13, and Crookshank, *History of Methodism*, Vol. 2, p. 14.

63 Malmgreen, 'Domestic discords'.

64 H. McLeod, 'New perspectives on Victorian working-class religion: the oral evidence', *Oral History* 14, 1 (1986), pp. 31–49.

65 Anon., *Hints for Conducting Sunday Schools, Useful also for Day Schools and Families* . . ., 2nd edn (Dublin: 1819).

66 *Report of the Hibernian Bible Society, 1822* (Dublin: 1822).

67 *Religious Tract and Bible Society, 16th Report* (Dublin: 1830).

68 *24th Annual Report of the London Hibernian Society* (Dublin: 1830); TCD, see Annual Reports of the Irish Society for Promoting the Education of the Native Irish through the Medium of their Own Language, especially 1834 and 1836.

69 F. E. Bland, *How the Church Missionary Society Came to Ireland* (Dublin: 1935); RCB, HCMS, auxiliary letter book, Report of the Deputation to the North, 26 September 1820.

70 Prochaska, *Women and Philanthropy.*

71 W. D. Killen, *Memoir of John Edgar, D.D., L.L.D* (Belfast: 1867), p. 249.

72 Prochaska, *Women and Philanthropy*, p. 23. For a wider discussion of the political activity of women engaged in religious sects see C. M. Prelinger, 'Religious dissent, women's rights and the Hamburger Hochschule fuer das weibliche Geschlecht in mid-nineteenth century Germany', *Church History* 45 (1976), pp. 42–55; N. A. Hardesty, *Women Called to Witness: Evangelical Feminism in the 19th Century* (Nashville, Tenn.: 1984); O. Banks, *Faces of Feminism* (Oxford: 1981).

73 The printed reports of the Female Association for Promoting Christianity among the Women of the East are held in Presbyterian Church House, Belfast.

74 *Report of the Female Association, 1876* (Belfast: 1876).

75 *Report of the Female Association, 1877* (Belfast: 1877).

76 *Report of the Female Association, 1875* (Belfast: 1875).

77 *Report of the Female Association, 1876.*

78 *Report of the Debates which took place at the Two Meetings of the Ladies Auxiliary to the London Hibernian Society, held at Cork, 8th and 9th September, 1824* (Dublin: 1824).

79 *Belfast People's Magazine* 1 (1847).

80 *Report of the Debates . . . at Cork . . .*

8 ULSTER AWAKENED: THE 1859 REVIVAL

1 N. Landsman, 'Evangelists and their hearers: popular interpretation of revivalist preaching in eighteenth-century Scotland', *Journal of British Studies* 28, 2 (1989), pp. 120–49.

2 L. E. Schmidt, *Holy Fairs: Scottish Communions and American Revivals in the Early Modern Period* (Princeton, NJ: 1989).

3 R. Carwardine, *Trans-Atlantic Revivalism: Popular Evangelicalism in Britain and America, 1790–1865* (Westport, Conn.: 1978), p. 56.

4 P. Gibbon, *The Origins of Ulster Unionism: the Formation of Popular Protestant Politics and Ideology in Nineteenth-Century Ireland* (Manchester: 1975), p. 44.

5 R. F. G. Holmes, *Our Irish Presbyterian Heritage* (Belfast: 1985), p. 121.

6   W. McLoughlin, *Revivals, Awakenings and Reform: an Essay on Religion and Social Change in America, 1607–1977* (Chicago: 1978), p. xiii.

7   I. R. K. Paisley, *The 'Fifty-Nine' Revival* (Belfast: 1958), pp. 11–12.

8   See also A. R. Scott, 'The Ulster revival of 1859', PhD thesis, Trinity College, Dublin, 1962; M. Hill, 'Evangelicalism and the churches in Ulster society, 1770–1850', PhD thesis, Queen's University, Belfast, 1987.

9   J. Walsh, 'The Great Awakening in the First Congregational Church of Woodbury, Connecticut', *William and Mary Quarterly*, 3rd series, 28 (1971), pp. 543–62.

10 See the 'Reports of the Committee on the State of Religion' published in the *Irish Presbyterian Missionary Herald* from the 1840s.

11 J. Baxter, 'The great Yorkshire revival 1792–6: a study of mass revival among the Methodists', in M. Hill (ed.), *A Sociological Yearbook of Religion in Britain* 7 (1974), pp. 46–76; D. N. Hempton, 'Methodism in Irish society, 1770–1830', *Transactions of the Royal Historical Society*, 5th series, 36 (1986), pp. 117–42; T. Shaw, *A History of Cornish Methodism* (Truro: 1967).

12 D. Miller, 'Presbyterian and "modernization" in Ulster', *Past and Present* 80 (1978), pp. 66–90.

13 *Minutes of the General Assembly, 1840–50*, Vol. I, p. 204; *8th Annual Report on Open-Air Preaching by Ministers of the General Assembly of the Presbyterian Church in Ireland 1858* (Belfast: 1859).

14 J. M. Barkley, 'Tommy Toye – revivalist preacher', *Bulletin of the Presbyterian Historical Society of Ireland* 8 (November, 1978), pp. 2–15; A. Boyd, *Holy War in Belfast*, 2nd edn (Belfast: 1970), pp. 10–44.

15 *Minutes of the General Assembly, 1840–50*, Vol. I, pp. 327–8, 484–5, 585, 672; *Minutes of the General Assembly, 1851–60*, Vol. II, pp. 48–9, 185, 274, 364–7, 447.

16 W. D. Bailey, *The Six Mile Water Revival of 1625* (Newcastle: 1976); R. S. Jennings, 'The origins of Ulster Presbyterian revivalism in the mid-nineteenth century', MTheol, Queen's University, Belfast, 1985; M. J. Westerkamp, *Triumph of the Laity: Scots-Irish Piety and the Great Awakening 1625–1760* (Oxford: 1988), pp. 15–42.

17 Hempton, 'Methodism in Irish society'; M. Hill, 'Popular Protestantism in Ulster in the post-rebellion period *c.*1790–1810', *Studies in Church History* 25 (1989), pp. 191–202.

18 G. Hamilton, *The Great Necessity of Itinerant Preaching, Introductory Memorial to the Evangelical Society of Ulster* (Armagh: 1798); Linenhall Library, Belfast, Wm Gregory, 'Extracts of a tour through the north of Ireland . . . in the summer of the year 1800' (typescript).

19 C. H. Crookshank, *History of Methodism in Ireland*, 3 vols (London: 1885–8); D. Luker, 'Revivalism in theory and practice', *Journal of Ecclesiastical History* 37, 4 (October 1986), pp. 603–19.

20 S. O'Brien, 'A transatlantic community of saints: the Great Awakening and the first evangelical network, 1735–1755', *American Historical Review* 91, 4 (October, 1986), pp. 811–32; J. E. Orr, *The Light of Nations: Evangelical Renewal and Advance in the Nineteenth Century* (Devon: 1965).

21 J. E. Orr, *The Second Evangelical Awakening in Britain* (Edinburgh: 1949), p. 17.

22 *Minutes of the General Assembly, 1840–50*, Vol. I; Orr, *The Second Evangelical Awakening in Britain*, p. 39; Carwardine, *Transatlantic Revivalism*, pp. 170–4.

23 *Minutes of the General Assembly, 1840–50,* Vol. I, p. 678; J. Thompson, 'Irish Baptists and the 1859 revival', *Irish Baptist Historical Society Journal* 17 (1984–5), pp. 4–10.
24 *Irish Presbyterian Missionary Herald* (September, 1858).
25 McLoughlin, *Revivals, Awakenings and Reform,* p. 141.
26 Carwardine, *Transatlantic Revivalism,* p. 172.
27 Jennings, 'The origins of Ulster Presbyterian revivalism'.
28 Rev. D. Adams, *The Revival at Ahoghill. Its Narrative and Nature* (Belfast: 1859); Rev. W. Richey, *Connor and Coleraine; or Scenes and Sketches of the Last Ulster Awakening* (Belfast: 1870).
29 Adams, *The Revival at Ahoghill;* Orr, *The Second Evangelical Awakening,* p. 40.
30 ibid.; W. Gibson, *The Year of Grace: a History of the Ulster Revival of 1859,* 2nd edn (Belfast: 1903). For details of the spread of the revival in Counties Cavan and Monaghan see L. T. Brown, 'The Presbyterians of Cavan and Monaghan: an immigrant community in south Ulster over three generations', PhD thesis, Queen's University, Belfast, 1986, vol. 1, pp. 326–69.
31 Carwardine, *Transatlantic Revivalism,* pp. 172–4; J. Kent, *Holding the Fort, Studies in Victorian Revivalism* (London: 1978), pp. 71–131; Rev. H. M. MacGill, *The Present Revival of Religion in Scotland: a Paper read at the Conference of the Evangelical Alliance, held at Nottingham, October 1860 . . .* (1860); Rev. J. Venn, *The Revival in Wales: a paper . . .* (1860).
32 Luker, 'Revivalism in theory and practice'; C. B. Turner, 'Revivalism and Welsh society in the nineteenth century', in J. Obelkevich, L. Roper and R. Samuel (eds), *Disciplines of Faith . . .* (London: 1987), pp. 309–23.
33 Gibson, *The Year of Grace,* p. 82; Scott, 'The Ulster revival', pp. 98, 209; Orr, *The Second Evangelical Awakening,* p. 43; J. T. Carson, *God's River in Spate* (Belfast: 1958), pp. 63, 67, 124; Carwardine, *Transatlantic Revivalism,* p. 172.
34 *Belfast Newsletter,* Monday 30 May 1859.
35 NIPRO, Armour Papers, D1792, J. B. Armour to J. Megaw, Ballyboyland, 14 September 1859.
36 RCB, ms 77, letters of Rev. E. Stopford on the Belfast Revival, 15, 18, 21 July 1859; Rev. E. Maguire, *Fifty Eight Years of Clerical Life in the Church of Ireland* (Dublin: 1904), p. 22; N. D. Emerson, *The Church of Ireland and the 1859 Revival* (Belfast: 1959), p. 6; Orr, *The Second Evangelical Awakening,* pp. 184–5.
37 Reprinted in *Belfast Newsletter,* 30 May 1859.
38 Gibson, *The Year of Grace,* p. 100; *Belfast Newsletter,* 6 June 1859; Rev. J. Weir, *The Ulster Awakening: Its Origin, Progress and Fruit with Notes of a Tour of Personal Observation and Inquiry* (London: 1860), p. 93.
39 Adams, The Revival at Ahoghill; Rev. J. Morgan, *Thoughts on the Revival of 1859* (Belfast: 1859); A. McCann, *The Strikings Down and the Marks Vindicated* (Belfast: 1859).
40 Rev. E. Hincks, *God's Works and Satan's Counter-Works, as now carried on in the North of Ireland . . .* (Belfast: 1859); Rev. W. McIlwaine, *Revivalism Renewed* (Belfast: 1859); Rev. J. Montgomery, *The Holy Spirit: Its Nature and Work: with a Special Reference to the Movement now going on around us, called a Revival of Religion* (Belfast: 1859).
41 NIPRO, Armour Papers, Armour to Megaw, 14 September 1859.
42 F. Moore, *The Truth about Ulster* (London: 1914), p. 188.
43 Rev. J. McCosh, *The Ulster Revival and Its Physiological Accidents . . .* (Belfast:

1860); Rev. E. Stopford, *The Work and the Counter-Work; or the Religious Revival in Belfast, with an explanation of the Physical Phenomena*, 4th edn (Dublin: 1859); Weir, *The Ulster Awakening*.

44 I. Nelson, *The Year of Delusion: a Review of the Year of Grace*, 2nd edn (Belfast: 1860), p. 25.

45 Rev. W. Hamilton, *An Inquiry into the Scriptural Character of the Revival of 1859* (Belfast: 1866); T. MacNeece, *Words of Caution and Counsel on the Present Religious Revival Addressed to his Parishioners* (Belfast: 1859).

46 Rev. T. Hamilton, *History of the Irish Presbyterian Church* (Edinburgh: 1887), p. 43.

47 Baxter, 'The great Yorkshire revival', pp. 53–5.

48 Crookshank, *History of Methodism*, Vol. II.

49 See letter from McIlvaine, Bishop of Ohio, to the Bishop of Down and Connor, quoted in Gibson, *The Year of Grace*, p. 218.

50 Landsman, 'Evangelists', pp. 138–9; *Missionary Herald of the Presbyterian Church in Ireland*, 1 July 1859, p. 342.

51 *Minutes of the General Assembly, 1851–60*, Vol. II, p. 868.

52 See note 36.

53 N. D. Emerson, *The Church of Ireland and the 1859 Revival* (Belfast: 1959).

54 Gibson, *The Year of Grace*, p. 112; Orr, *The Second Evangelical Awakening*, pp. 184–207.

55 R. Currie, A. Gilbert and L. Horsley, *Churches and Churchgoers: Patterns of Church Growth in the British Isles since 1700* (Oxford: 1977), pp. 38–45.

56 *Minutes of the Presbyterian General Assembly*.

57 J. M. Henry, 'An assessment of the social, religious and political aspects of Congregationalism in Ireland in the nineteenth century', PhD thesis, Queen's University, Belfast, 1965.

58 Thompson, 'Irish Baptists and the 1859 revival'; H. D. Gribbon, 'Irish Baptists in the 19th century: economic and social background', *Irish Baptist Historical Society Journal* 16 (1983–4), pp. 4–18; R. Coad, *A History of the Brethren Movement*, 2nd edn (Exeter: 1976), pp. 170–2.

59 D. P. Kingdon, 'Irish Baptists and the revival of 1859 with special reference to Tobermore', *Irish Baptist Historical Society Journal* 1 (1968–9), pp. 19–30.

60 *Belfast Newsletter*, 1 June 1859; Rev. D. McMeekin, *Memories of '59*, p. 43; Gibson, *The Year of Grace*, p. 75.

61 H. McLeod, *Religion and the People of Western Europe, 1789–1970* (Oxford: 1981), p. 39.

62 Kent, *Holding the Fort*, pp. 362–3.

63 R. M. Sibbett, *For Christ and Crown: the Story of a Mission* (Belfast: 1926), p. 61.

64 W. E. Allen, *The '59 Revival in Ireland, the United States of America, England, Scotland and Wales* (Belfast: 1955); Gibson, *The Year of Grace* p. 75.

65 *Belfast Newsletter* 30 May, 3 June, 8 June, 28 June 1859; McMeekin, *Memories of '59*, p. 71.

66 *Presbyterian Missionary Herald*, 1 July 1859.

67 Carwardine, *Transatlantic Revivalism*, p. 197.

68 *Wesleyan Times*, 11 July 1859; for other examples see *Belfast Newsletter*, 13 June 1859; Orr, *The Second Evangelical Awakening*, p. 49; Carson, *God's River in Spate*, p. 120.

69 Gibbon, *The Origins of Ulster Unionism*, pp. 45–65.

70 Turner, 'Revivalism and Welsh society'; Baxter, 'The great Yorkshire revival'; Hempton, 'Methodism and Irish society'.
71 H. Patterson, 'Industrial labour and the labour movement, 1820–1914', in L. Kennedy and P. Ollerenshaw (eds), *An Economic History of Ulster 1820–1939* Manchester: 1985), pp. 158–83.
72 H. McLeod, *Religion and the Working Class in Nineteenth-Century Britain* (London: 1984); D. Valenze, *Prophetic Sons and Daughters* . . . (Princeton, NJ: 1985); F. Prochaska, *Women and Philanthropy in Nineteenth-Century England* (Oxford: 1980).
73 *Belfast Newsletter*, 14 June 1859.
74 Orr, *The Second Evangelical Awakening*, p. 205; Gibson, *The Year of Grace*, pp. 37, 196.
75 Kent, *Holding the Fort*, p. 72.
76 Boyd, *Holy War in Belfast*.
77 *Minutes of the General Assembly, 1851–60*, Vol. II, pp. 364–7.
78 F. A. Wright, 'Developments in Ulster politics, 1843–86', PhD thesis, Queen's University, Belfast, 1989, pp. 291–306. See also letters and news-cuttings dealing with riots in Belfast, 1857–8, in NLI, Larcom Papers, mss 7623–4; Haire, *The Story of the '59 Revival*, p. 7; Orr, *The Second Evangelical Awakening*, p. 205.
79 A. Ford, 'The Protestant Reformation in Ireland', in C. Brady and R. Gillespie (eds), *Natives and Newcomers: the Making of Irish Colonial Society 1534–1641* (Dublin: 1986), pp. 50–74.
80 Weir, *The Ulster Awakening*, pp. 48–50; *Buick's Ahoghill* (Antrim: 1987), p. 81; W. Reid, *Authentic Records of Revival* (Belfast: 1860), pp. 161–73; Orr, *The Second Evangelical Awakening*, p. 179; Gibson, *The Year of Grace*; Carson, *God's River in Spate*, pp. 96–9, 21; Scott, 'The Ulster revival', p. 402.
81 L. Kennedy, 'The rural economy, 1820–1914', in Kennedy and Ollerenshaw, *An Economic History of Ulster 1820–1939*, pp. 1–61; L. A. Clarkson, 'Population change and urbanisation, 1821–1911', in Kennedy and Ollerenshaw, *An Economic History of Ulster, 1820–1939*, pp. 137–57.
82 Baxter, 'The great Yorkshire revival', p. 59; McLoughlin, *Revivals, Awakenings and Reforms*, p. 10.
83 Paisley, *The 'Fifty-Nine' Revival*, p. 137.

9 HOME RULE AND THE PROTESTANT MIND 1860–90

1 *Christian Advocate*, 15 January 1886.
2 G. Parsons, 'Irish disestablishment', in *Religion in Victorian Britain*, Vol. II, *Controversies* (Manchester: 1988), pp. 124–46.
3 A Presbyterian Layman, *Facts and Figures Regarding the Irish Church* (Belfast: 1867).
4 ibid.; W. M. Brady, *Facts or Fictions? Seven Letters on the 'Facts Concerning the Irish Church' Published by the Church Institution* (Dublin: 1867).
5 A. T. Lee, *Facts respecing the Present State of the Church in Ireland* (Dublin: 1868), p. 10; An Irish Protestant, *The Established Church in Ireland in Relation to Other Religious Bodies in that Country* (London: 1868), pp. 9–10.
6 *Speeches Delivered at the Great Meeting held in St. James' Hall on Wednesday afternoon,*

May 6, 1868 . . . (London: 1868). See also G. A. Denison, *The Churches of England and Ireland One Church* . . . *a Paper read at a Special Meeting of the Irish Church Society, Dublin, Wednesday, September 30th, 1868* (Dublin: 1868); Rev. J. Briggs (ed.), *A Historical Survey of the Relations which have Subsisted between the Churches of England and Ireland and the See and Court of Rome* . . . (London: 1868); J. Jebb, *The Rights of the Irish Branch of the United Church of Ireland and England* (London: 1868); J. J. Murphy, *An Irish Churchman's View of Irish Politics* (Belfast: 1869), p. 4.

 7   J. T. O'Brien, *The Case of the Established Church in Ireland*, 2nd edn (London: 1867), p. 53.

 8   G. I. T. Machin, *Politics and the Churches in Great Britain*. Vol. I, *1832 to 1868* (Oxford: 1977), p. 363.

 9   Parsons, 'Irish disestablishment'.

10   An Irish Protestant, *The Established Church*, pp. 28–9; *Minutes of the General Assembly 1861–70*, Vol. III (1869).

11   ibid., p. 1239.

12   R. F. G. Holmes, *Our Irish Presbyterian Heritage* (Belfast: 1985), pp. 132–3.

13   J. L. Porter, *The Life and Times of Henry Cooke D.D.* (Belfast: 1875), pp. 451–3.

14   Anon., *The Great Protestant Demonstration at Hillsborough, October 30, 1867* (Belfast: 1867).

15   Professor R. Dill and the Reverend H. Henderson, speaking at the monster meeting at the Ulster Hall on 29 April 1869, Anon., *The Great Presbyterian Demonstration in Belfast* . . ., *April 29 1869* (Belfast: 1869), pp. 11, 37.

16   Lee, *Facts*, p. 5; *Report of the Proceedings of the Synod of Aberdeen at its Meeting of October 13 1868 in reference to the Protestant Church of Ireland* (Aberdeen: 1868); J. C. Colquhoun, *The Progress of the Church of Rome towards Ascendancy in England traced through the Parliamentary History of Nearly Forty Years* (London: 1868).

17   R. Knox, *Plain Truths and Stern Facts for Honest Men* (Belfast: 1868), pp. 7–9.

18   An Irish Clergyman, *The Irish Church* (London: 1868), p. 6. This pamphleteer focused upon 'what our Protestantism in church and state has cost us', referring to the 'martyrs' blood shed at the Reformation and the soldiers' blood at the Revolution, and at Boyne, Aughrim, and Limerick . . . to make England, and the Established Church of England and Ireland thoroughly Protestant, and Protestant for all future times'.

19   Anon., *The Great Protestant Demonstration in Belfast*, pp. 59–60. See also the evidence of Hugh Hanna, Report by the Commissioners of Inquiry (1886) Respecting the Origins and Circumstances of the Riots of Belfast . . . 1886, H.C. 18 (1887), p. 21.

20   *Proceedings of the Great Presbyterian Demonstration*, p. 8.

21   Wm Johnston, MP, *The Great Protestant Demonstration at Botanic Gardens*, p. 21.

22   ibid., 4th resolution, proposed by J. W. Fulton, p. 47. See also Rev. R. Oulton, *The Repeal of the Union* (Dublin: 1868). A London Rector, *A Letter to the Rt. Hon. W. E. Gladstone, M.P. on his Proposal to Abolish the Irish Branch of the United Church of England and Ireland* (London: 1868), p. 2.

23   Parsons, 'Irish disestablishment', p. 140.

24   Letter from J. Rutherford, Banbridge, *Banner of Ulster*, 29 June 1840; S. C. McElroy, *The Route Land Crusade* (Coleraine: n.d.); J. R. B. McMinn, *Against the Tide: J. B. Armour, Irish Presbyterian Minister and Home Ruler* (Belfast: 1985), p. xxviii.

25   An Irish Presbyterian, *Ulster and Home Rule* (Belfast: 1886), p. 11.

26 *Banner of Ulster*, 16 July 1850.
27 Holmes, *Our Presbyterian Heritage*, pp. 130–1; D. W. Miller, *Queen's Rebels: Ulster Loyalism in Historical Perspective* (Dublin: 1978), pp. 76–7.
28 Quoted in a letter appearing in the *Whig*, 2 October 1853; McElroy, *Land Crusade*, p. 19.
29 R. F. Foster, *Modern Ireland 1600–1972* (London: 1988), p. 415.
30 F. A. Wright, 'Developments in Ulster politics, 1843–86', PhD thesis, Queen's University, Belfast, 1989.
31 ibid., pp. 652–3.
32 The standard treatments of the Church of Ireland in this period are D. H. Akenson, *The Church of Ireland: Ecclesiastical Reform and Revolution, 1800–1885* (London: 1971) and R. B. McDowell, *The Church of Ireland, 1869–1969* (London: 1975). See also A. J. Megahey, 'The Irish Protestant churches and social and political issues: 1870–1914', PhD thesis, Queen's University, Belfast, 1969.
33 *Journal of the General Synod of the Church of Ireland* (Dublin: 1886), Special Meeting (23 March), pp. liv–lxii.
34 Calculations are based on the rich pamphlet collection of the Representative Church Body Library, Dublin.
35 The Protestant Defence Association of the Church of Ireland, *Revision of the Prayer-Book* (Dublin: 1875), pp. 3–4.
36 See the *Reports of the Protestant Defence Association of the Church of Ireland* which were published annually in Dublin. There is a voluminous collection of pamphlets on ritualism and prayer-book revision. See, for example, W. H. Ferrar, *The Christian Sacrifice, Remarks on a Sermon with the above Title preached in St. George's Church Dublin on Feb. 16th 1866 by the Rev. A. Dawson* (Dublin: 1866); A Lay Representative, *Thirty-Four Reasons why a Revision of the Book of Common Prayer is Imperatively Called For* (Dublin: 1870); *Documents and Correspondence on the Subject of the Services in the Cathedral of St. Fin Barre, Cork* (Cork: 1872); L. F. S. Maberly, *The Introduction and Spread of Ritualism in the Church of Ireland under His Grace Archbishop Trench* (Dublin: 1879); *Ritualism in the Diocese of Dublin . . .* (Dublin: 1889); Whitehall Review, *Rome's Recruits: A List of Protestants who have become Catholics since the Tractarian Movement* (London: 1878). Less polemical contributions may be found in the columns of the *Irish Churchman*, a monthly periodical, which ran from 22 February 1868 to 21 August 1869.
37 P. J. Fahey, 'Ritualism, the revision movement and revision theology in the Church of Ireland 1842–1877', 2 vols, Doctor of Sacred Theology, Rome, 1976, pp. 31–3, 59.
38 *Irish Ecclesiastical Gazette*, 27 March 1886.
39 *Irish Church Records* (compiled and collected by Robert Walsh D.D.), Vol. VIII, p. 110.
40 *Irish Ecclesiastical Gazette*, 16 January and 27 February 1886.
41 *Journal of the General Synod of the Church of Ireland*, 1886, p. lxiii.
42 *Irish Church Records*, Vol. VIII, pp. 122–3, 130.
43 Megahey, 'The Irish Protestant churches', ch. 1.
44 See the Irish Loyal and Patriotic Union, *The Real Dangers of Home Rule* (Dublin: 1887) and *Union or Separation?* (Dublin: 1888).
45 NIPRO, Irish Unionist Alliance Mss (1887–1914), D989A/8/1/1–33.
46 D. C. Savage, 'The origins of the Ulster unionist party, 1885–6', *Irish Historical Studies* 12, 47 (March 1961), pp. 185–208.

47 *Irish Ecclesiastical Gazette*, 23 January 1886.
48 ibid., 12 June 1886.
49 *Irish Church Records*, Vol. VIII, p. 132.
50 *Irish Ecclesiastical Gazette*, 27 February 1886.
51 *Irish Church Records*, Vol. VIII, p. 43; *Minutes of the General Assembly*, Vol. IV (1871), p. 134.
52 *Irish Ecclesiastical Gazette*, 16 October 1886.
53 ibid., 25 September 1886.
54 *Irish Church Records*, Vol. VIII, p. 131.
55 McDowell, *The Church of Ireland*, p. 99.
56 *Journal of the General Synod of the Church of Ireland*, 1887.
57 *Minutes of the General Assembly, 1851–60*, Vol. II (1860), p. 891.
58 *Minutes of the General Assembly, 1861–70*, Vol. III (1861), p. 52; (1862), p. 178.
59 A. Robinson, *Facts for Irish Presbyterians* (Broughshane: n.d.). See also *Purity of Worship Defence Association in connection with the Irish Presbyterian Church. An Address presented to the Ministers, Elders, and Members of the Church* (Belfast: 1875).
60 *Minutes of the General Assembly*, Vol. VII (1886), pp. 12–13.
61 ibid.
62 ibid. See also An Irish Presbyterian, *Ulster and Home Rule*, p. 23; Rev. D. Manderson, *How an Irish Nonconformist Views the Question of Home Rule with Regard to the Peace and Prosperity of Ireland* (Dungannon: 1893); Rev. R. J. Lynd, *The Present Crisis in Ireland . . .* (Belfast: 1886).
63 *Minutes of the General Assembly, 1886–90*, Vol. VII (1886), pp. 105, 146.
64 NIPRO, Armour Papers, D1792/A2/25, J. B. Armour to W. E. Gladstone, July 1893. The letter accompanied copies of the Protestant Home Rule Address.
65 ibid., Rev. D. Houston to J. B. Armour, 3 August 1892. See also McMinn, *J. B. Armour.*
66 *Presbyterian Churchman* (1886), p. 96.
67 Quoted in Holmes, *Our Irish Presbyterian Heritage*, p. 134. See also *Presbyterian Churchman* (1886), p. 95 and Sir R. Anderson, *Sidelights on the Home Rule Movement* (London: 1906), p. 218.
68 See, for example, A. Boyd, *Holy War in Belfast* (Belfast: 1969), ch. 8.
69 Report by the Commissioners of Inquiry (1886) Respecting the Origins and Circumstances of the Riots in Belfast . . . 1886, appendix D, p. 587.
70 ibid., pp. 345–61; 'Speeches delivered at the meeting of Belfast Constitutional Club 17 August 1886', reported in *Belfast Newsletter*, 18 August 1886.
71 'The General Assembly', *Presbyterian Churchman* (1886), pp. 193–7.
72 ibid., p. 96.
73 D. N. Hempton, 'The Methodist crusade in Ireland 1795–1845', *Irish Historical Studies* 22, 85 (March, 1980), pp. 33–48.
74 D. N. Hempton, 'Methodism in Irish society 1770–1830', *Transactions of the Royal Historical Society*, 5th series, 36 (1986), pp. 117–42.
75 *Minutes of the Methodist Conference in Ireland* (1883).
76 Megahey, 'The Irish Protestant churches', ch. 1.
77 *Minutes of the Methodist Conference in Ireland* (1881).
78 *Christian Advocate*, 8 January 1886.
79 ibid., 12 March, 4 June and 18 June 1886.
80 ibid., 19 February 1886.
81 ibid., 15 January 1886.

82 See N. W. Taggart, *The Irish in World Methodism 1760–1900* (London: 1986).
83 *Christian Advocate*, 19 March, 9 April and 4 June 1886.
84 ibid., 11 June 1886.
85 ibid., 22 January 1886.
86 ibid., 22 January, 29 January and 5 February 1886.
87 ibid., 4 June 1886.
88 *Hansard*, 3rd series, CCV, cols 651–61.
89 *Christian Advocate*, 26 February 1886.
90 The resultant divisions disturbed English Methodism at least until the end of the century. See, for example, *Methodist Times*, 8 July 1886; *New Review* 7, 38 (July, 1892); *St Stephen's Review* 31, 3 September 1892. For a more general analysis, see D. W. Bebbington, *The Nonconformist Conscience: Chapel and Politics, 1870–1914* (London: 1982), pp. 84–105; and D. W. Bebbington, 'Nonconformity and electoral sociology, 1867–1918', *Historical Journal* 27, 3 (1984), pp. 633–56.
91 *Christian Advocate*, 7 May 1886.
92 *Minutes of the Methodist Conference in Ireland* (1886).
93 *Christian Advocate*, 18 June 1886.
94 NIPRO, IWHS, W. Nicholas to C. Crookshank, 25 February 1889. See also NIPRO, Papers of Jeremiah Jordan, D2073/2/1/13, A. Duncan to J. Jordan, 4 May 1886.
95 Jeremiah MacVeagh, *Religious Intolerance under Home Rule. Some Opinions of Leading Irish Protestants* (London: 1911).
96 *Irish Nonconformists and the Unionist Leaders: Speeches of the Irish Protestant Ministers on Home Rule, 14 November 1888* (London: 1888), p. 14.
97 NIPRO, NUA, D2396/1/1–24 and D2396/5/1–3, S. K. McDonnell to W. E. Ball, 3 August, 14 August and 30 October 1888; Lord Wolmer to W. E. Ball, 25 July, 7 August, 10 August, 5 November, 6 November and 9 November 1888.
98 ibid., D2396/3/1–13, Duke of Abercorn to P. E. W. Sykes, 30 April, Abercorn to W. E. Ball, 23 June, R. Ross to Abercorn, 26 June, Abercorn to W. E. Ball, 28 June, R. J. Lynd to Abercorn, 30 June, Abercorn to Mr Cox, 29 August, Abercorn to Mr Henderson, 29 August, Abercorn to Sir Thomas Butler, 29 August, Abercorn to Mr Patterson, 29 August, Abercorn to W. E. Ball, 14 November, Abercorn to W. E. Ball, 2 December, and Abercorn to W. E. Ball, 4 December 1888.
99 ibid., D2396/3/11, Duke of Abercorn to W. E. Ball, 2 December 1888.
100 ibid., D2396/3/3–5, R. Ross to the Duke of Abercorn, 26 June, Abercorn to W. E. Ball, 28 June, R. J. Lynd to Abercorn, 30 June 1888.
101 ibid., D2396/5/10, J. L. Ball to W. E. Ball, 13 November 1888.
102 ibid., D2396/5/5, D2396/5/8, D2396/5/14, Charles Adeane to W. E. Ball, 22 November and 24 November 1888, Lord George Hamilton to W. E. Ball, 10 December 1888.
103 *Irish Nonconformists*, pp. 4–5.
104 ibid., pp. 7–12.
105 ibid., p. 21. For the Baptist position, see Joshua Thompson, 'Baptists in Ireland 1792–1922: a dimension of Protestant Dissent', PhD thesis, Oxford 1988.
106 NIPRO, NUA, D2396/1/1–24, Lord Wolmer to W. E. Ball, 20 September, 24 September, 9 October, 10 October, 22 October, 23 October (two letters) 1888. English Liberal Unionists also spoke against Home Rule on national platforms and in local constituencies; see G. J. Goschen and Lord Hartington, *The*

Disruption Bill (London: 1886); G. J. Goschen, *The Cry of 'Justice to Ireland'* (London: 1886); G. J. Goschen, *Address to the Electors of the Eastern Division of Edinburgh* (London: 1886); Lord Hartington, *Address to the Electors of the Rossendale Division of Lancashire* (London: 1886).

107   NIPRO, NUA, D2396/3/13 and D2396/1/1–24, W. E. Ball to Lord Wolmer, (n.d.) October 1888, and Lord Wolmer to W. E. Ball, 3 November, 5 November, 27 November 1888.

108   Bebbington, 'Nonconformity and electoral sociology', pp. 633–56.

109   For the range of Irish Nonconformist arguments against Home Rule see W. Arthur, *Shall the Loyal be Deserted and the Disloyal Set over Them? An Appeal to Liberals and Nonconformists* (London: 1886); T. Webb, *Ipse Dixit or the Gladstonian Settlement of Ireland* (Dublin: 1886); R. MacGeogh, *Ulster's Apology for Being Loyal* (Belfast: 1888); A Member of the Society of Friends in Ireland, *The Society of Friends in Ireland and Home Rule* (Dublin: 1893); Rev. D. Manderson, *How an Irish Nonconformist views the Question of Home Rule*; A. McCaig, *Reasons Why Nonconformists Should Oppose Home Rule* (Dublin: 1886); *Irish Baptist Magazine* (May, 1887), pp. 70–1.

110   *Methodist Times*, 8 July 1886; D. W. Bebbington, 'Gladstone and the Baptists', *Baptist Quarterly* 26 (1975–6), pp. 224–39; Bebbington, *The Nonconformist Conscience*, pp. 84–105. For a revealing insight into the confusions of English Liberalism occasioned by Gladstone's Irish policy, see Liberatis, *The Pilot Balloon: a Calm Exposé of the 'Manchester Guardian'. Consisting of Verbatim Extracts from the Editorial Columns 1884 to 1886, on the Home Rule Question* (Manchester: 1889).

111   J. Loughlin, *Gladstone, Home Rule and the Irish Question 1882–93* (Dublin: 1986), appendix 2, pp. 295–6.

112   For other interpretations of early Ulster Unionism see P. Buckland, *Ulster Unionism and the Origins of Northern Ireland 1886–1922* (Dublin: 1973); J. F. Harbinson, *The Ulster Unionist Party 1882–1973* (Belfast: 1973); A. Jackson, *The Ulster Party: Irish Unionists in the House of Commons, 1884–1911* (Oxford: 1989).

113   Loughlin, *Gladstone*, pp. 123–52.

114   Anon., *The Irish Church Bill: the Great Protestant Demonstration in Belfast* (Belfast: 1869). For similar events, albeit on a smaller scale, see Anon., *The Great Protestant Demonstration at Hillsborough, October 30, 1867* and Anon., *Proceedings of the Great Presbyterian Demonstration in Belfast in favour of Protestant Endowments in Ireland . . .*

115   The notion of a contractual relationship between Ulster loyalists and the United Kingdom is developed by Miller, *Queen's Rebels*, pp. 65–80.

116   *The Home Rule 'Nutshell', examined by an Irish Unionist* (Belfast and Dublin: 1912).

117   F. Wright, 'Protestant ideology and politics in Ulster', *Archives Européennes de Sociologie* 14 (1973), pp. 213–80.

118   For the survival of this view into contemporary Ulster fundamentalism see S. Bruce, *God Save Ulster! The Religion and Politics of Paisleyism* (Oxford: 1985).

119   G. Mahaffy, *The Attitude of Irish Churchmen in the Present Political Crisis . . .*, 3rd edn (Dublin: 1886), p. 12.

120   T. Ellis, *God and the Nation. A Sermon preached to the Orangemen of the District of Portadown in St. Mark's Church Portadown* (Armagh: 1885).

121   *The Home Rule 'Nutshell'*, p. 99.

122   Loughlin, *Gladstone*, p. 160.

123　T. Dunne, "'La trahison des clercs": British intellectuals and the first home-rule crisis', *Irish Historical Studies* 23, 90 (1982), pp. 134–73.

124　YMCA, *Bulletin* (Belfast, 1885).

125　D. Hempton and M. Hill, "'Godliness and good citizenship": evangelical Protestantism and Social Control in Ulster, 1790–1850', *Saothar* 13 (1988), pp. 68–80. See also, R. Johnston, *The Story of the Central Presbyterian Association, Belfast 1882–1932* (Belfast: 1932); N. McNeilly, draft history of the Church of Ireland Young Men's Society (CIYMS); *Church of Ireland Young Men's Society Centenary Souvenir Handbook* (Belfast: 1950); C. Binfield, *George William and the YMCA. A Study in Victorian Social Attitudes* (London: 1973); W. E. Dornan, *One Hundred Years: the Story of the City of Belfast Y.M.C.A.* (Belfast: 1950); *Proceedings of the Irish Conference of Representatives of Young Men's Christian Association* (Dublin: 1868).

126　Ellis, *God and the Nation*.

127　NLI, IPHRA, ms. 3657, press cutting from the *Freeman*, 23 June 1886.

128　NLI, Minutes of IPHRA committee, 13 October 1886. See J. Loughlin, 'The Irish Protestant Home Rule Association and nationalist politics', *Irish Historical Studies* 24, 95 (May, 1985), pp. 341–60.

129　NLI, Minutes of IPHRA committee, 20 October 1886; MacVeagh, *Religious Intolerances Under Home Rule*.

130　NLI, Minutes of IPHRA committee, 5 June 1886 and [no day given] July 1887. See also Loughlin, 'Irish Protestant Home Rule Association', p. 343.

131　W. R. Ward, 'The way of the world: the rise and decline of Protestant social Christianity in Britain', *Kirchliche Zeitgeschichte* 1, Heft 2 (1988), pp. 293–305.

Bibliography

(1) Primary sources

    (a) Manuscripts
    (b) Printed sources

        (i) Minutes, reports, etc.
        (ii) Parliamentary material

    (c) Newspapers and periodicals
    (d) Pamphlets

(2) Secondary sources

    (a) Nineteenth-century books
    (b) Twentieth-century books
    (c) Articles

        (i) In books
        (ii) In journals

    (d) Unpublished theses

(1) PRIMARY SOURCES

(a) Manuscripts

Bodleian Library, Oxford
Papers of Henry Newman, secretary of the Society for Propagating the Gospel, MS. Rawl. D839 13,606.

British Museum
Correspondence of Bishop Percy, Ad. Mss 32,335.
Memorial against Tithes Bill, Ad. Mss 37,300, fols 325–6.

Cambridge University Library
British and Foreign Bible Society (BFBS) Mss, account of translations and misellaneous books 2–3.

Dublin Castle
State of the Country Papers, 2375/8, 2375/10, 2622.

Linenhall Library, Belfast
Gregory, W. Extracts of a tour through the north of Ireland engaged under the patronage of the Evangelical Society of Ulster, in the summer of the year 1800. Transcript.

Methodist Archives Research Centre (MARC), John Rylands Library, Manchester
Allan Collection. Butterworth Papers. Correspondence of Thomas Allan, Jabez Bunting, Joseph Butterworth, Adam Clarke, Thomas Coke, Henry Deery, Gideon Ouseley, Charles Prest.

Moravian Church House, London
Cennick, John. An account of the most remarkable passages relating to the Awakening in Dublin in Ireland from the beginning to the settlement of the congregation. Transcript of his journal. Moravian Historical Society, British Province.

National Library of Ireland, Dublin (NLI)
Diary of Lady Anne Jocelyn, ms 18,430.
Farnham Papers, mss 18602–30.
Larcom Papers, Minutes and Papers of the Irish Protestant Home Rule Association (IPHRA), mss 3657.
Notebook of Henry Maxwell, ms 3504.
Religious journal in two volumes of John Saunderson, Methodist preacher, County Cavan, ms 21 156–7.
Summary of account of First Fruits, 1743–90, ms 2017.

Northern Ireland Public Record Office, Belfast (NIPRO)
Acts and Proceedings of the Associate Synod of Ireland, 1747–1818, copied by D. Stewart, D1759/1F/1.
Annals of Christ Church, Belfast, T2159.
Armagh Visitation Records, 1839, DIO4/29/1/14.
Armour Papers, D1792.
Beresford Papers, T2772.
Bible Society, Cookstown, mss, D3167/2/221–6.
Correspondence of the second Baron Dufferin with Archibald Hamilton Rowan, D1071B/C/41/4–5.
Correspondence between Emerson Tennent and Thomas Drew, D2922/C/12/1–6.
Correspondence of James Murphy, Bishop of Clogher, DIO (R.C.) 1/4A–B.
Correspondence of Lord Annesley, D1854/6.
Correspondence of Lord Downshire, D607.
Correspondence of the third Earl of Roden, Mic. 147/5.
Diary of John Galt, D561.
Elegy of the Death of William Staveley, D2013/1/3.
Foster-Massereene Papers, D207.
Irish Unionist Alliance Mss, D989A/8/1/1–33.
Irish Wesley Historical Society (IWHS) Mss.
Lists of Sunday schools in Counties Antrim, Derry and Down, D2784.

Methodist Mss, Minutes of Conference, 1792–1813, CR6/3.

Minutes of the Secession Synod, 1818–40, D1759/1F/2.

Nonconformist Unionist Association (NUA) Papers, D2396.

Ordnance Survey Memoirs, Mic. 6.

Ouseley Collection, CR6/3 ACC 13019, 28 folders of paginated mss collected and transcribed by J. O. Bonsall and enlarged by John Hay in preparation for a biography.

Papers of Jeremiah Jordan, D2073/2/1/13.

Papers of Thomas Sinclair, D3002.

Primitive Wesleyan Minutes, CR6/3.

Quaker Records.

Records of the Presbytery of Antrim, 17 August 1783–18 May 1834, T1053.

Records of the Reformed Presbytery of Antrim, 1803–11, CR5/5A/1/2A.

Redesdale Papers, T3030.

The Seceders, Burgher and Anti-Burgher, Being Extracts from the Original Minutes of Both Synods, Now Deposited in Edinburgh, prior to the Erection of the Two Synods in Ireland in 1779 and 1798 Respectively, D1759/1F/3.

Session Minute Books, CR3.

The State of the District of Christ Church, Belfast, with Regard to the Ministers of the Established Church in the year 1852, CR1/13/D1.

Representative Church Body Library, Dublin (RCB)

Hibernian Church Missionary Society (HCMS), minute books and abstract letter books, 1814–58, and Annual Reports.

Journal of the General Synod.

Proceedings of the Association for the Purpose of Discountenancing Vice and Promoting the Practice of Virtue and Religion.

Records and Annual Reports of the Sunday School Society for Ireland, 1809–1971, ms 182.

School of Oriental and African Studies, London (SOAS)

Correspondence of agents of the London Missionary Society (LMS) in connection with Ireland, home correspondence, boxes 1–7.

Methodist Missionary Society Archives (MMSA); correspondence between London Missionary Committee and Irish missionaries, boxes 74 and 75.

Trinity College, Dublin (TCD)

Annual Reports of the Irish Society for Promoting the Education of the Native Irish through the Medium of their Own Language.

Proceedings of the Committee of the Irish Society, 1818–32, mss 7644–5.

Union Theological College, Belfast

Minutes of the Associate Synod of Ireland (Burgher), 1779–1814. Typescript.

University of Birmingham

Church Missionary Society (CMS) Archives: Account of the Formation of the Hibernian Church Missionary Society, 6 June 1814; committee minutes, G/C1; series of incoming correspondence within British Isles, G/AC3; Wilson, Rev. J., Notes of a Journey to Armagh, 23 June 1814.

(b) Printed sources

(i) Minutes, reports, etc.
Minutes of the Methodist Conferences in Ireland. Vol. I, 1744–1819. Dublin: 1864.
Thereafter annual *Minutes of the Methodist Conference in Ireland.*
Minutes of the General Assembly. Vols I–VII. 1840–90.
Records of the General Synod of Ulster, 1691–1820, 3 vols. Vol. III, 1778–1820. Belfast: 1898.
Minutes of the Synod of Ulster, 1821–30, 1831–40.

A History of the Congregations in the Presbyterian Church in Ireland 1610–1982. Belfast: 1982.
The Manuscripts and Correspondence of James, first Earl of Charlemont, 2 vols. London: 1891–4.

Annual Reports of the Baptist Society for Promoting the Gospel in Irish by Establishing Schools for teaching the Native Irish, for Itinerant Preaching, etc.
Annual Reports of the Belfast Sunday School Union.
Annual Reports of the Church Education Society. (RCB.)
Annual Reports of the Female Association for Promoting Christianity among the Women of the East.
Annual Reports of the Hibernian Bible Society.
Annual Reports of the Hibernian Church Missionary Society, 1805–21. (RCB.)
Annual Reports of the London Hibernian Society.
Annual Reports of the Irish Evangelical Society.
Annual Reports of the Irish Society. 1833–45. (TCD.)
Annual Reports of the Protestant Defence Association of the Church of Ireland.
Annual Reports of the Sunday School Society for Ireland. 1810–67. (RCB.)

Charge of the Bishop of Raphoe at the Primary Visitation of that Diocese, 17 October 1821. Dublin: 1822.
Constitution and Discipline of the Presbyterian Church, with a Directory for the Celebration of Ordinances and the Performance of Ministerial Activities. Belfast: 1825.
Correspondence on the Formation, Objects and Plan, of the Roman Catholic Bible Society. London: 1813.
Fourth and Final Report of the Down and Connor Church Accommodation Society, 19 January 1843. Belfast: 1843.
Rules and Regulations for the Use of all Orange Societies, Revised, Corrected and Adopted by the Grand Orange Lodge of Ireland. Assembled at Dublin in January 1820. Dublin: 1820.
The Bishop's Charge; with Statement of the Proceedings of the Several Diocesan Societies, for 1839. Belfast: 1839.
The Report of a Deputation from the London Hibernian Society, Respecting the Religious State of Ireland, to which is annexed a plan of the Society, 2nd edn. London: 1808.
Two Reports of the Committee of Education, appointed by the Association for Discountenancing Vice and Promoting Religion and Virtue, of the Dioceses of Armagh and Dromore. Dublin: 1800.

(ii) Parliamentary material
Parliamentary Papers Relating to the Established Church in Ireland. Ordered to be Printed, 29 July 1807, H.C. 1807 (78) V.

First Report of the Commission of Enquiry into Irish Education, H.C. XII (1825).

Minutes of Evidence taken before the Select Committee of the House of Lords, H.C. 129 (1825), viii.

Reports on the Select Committee to whom the Reports on the Subject of Education were Referred, H.C. IV (1828).

Select Committee on Orange Lodges, H.C. XV (1835).

Select Committee on Orange Lodges, H.C. XVI (1835).

Report of the Commissioners appointed to Enquire into the Occupation of Land in Ireland, H.C. XIX (1845).

Report by the Commissioners of Inquiry (1886) Respecting the Origins and Circumstances of the Riots of Belfast in June, July, August and September 1886, H.C. XVIII (1887).

(c) Newspapers and periodicals

Arminian Magazine
Banner of Ulster
Belfast Newsletter
Belfast People's Magazine
Benevolent and Religious Orange Reporter
Bulletin, YMCA
Christian Advocate
Christian Enquirer
Christian Examiner, vols 6–11 (1828–31)
Clogher Record
Hibernian Evangelical Magazine
Ireland's Mirror, or A Chronicle of the Times, 2 vols (Dublin: 1804–5)
Irish Baptist Magazine
Irish Church Records
Irish Churchman (1868–9)
Irish Ecclesiastical Gazette
Irish Presbyterian Missionary Herald
Irish Protestant
Methodist Times
Presbyterian Churchman
New Review Primitive Wesleyan Magazine, vol. 1 (1823), vol. 11, (1834)
St Stephen's Review
The Watchman

(d) Pamphlets

A Lay Representative. *Thirty-Four Reasons why a Revision of the Book of Common Prayer is Imperatively Called For*, Dublin: 1870.

A London Rector. *A Letter to the Rt. Hon. W. E. Gladstone, M.P. on his Proposal to Abolish the Irish Branch of the United Church of England and Ireland*. London: 1868.

A Member of the Society of Friends in Ireland. *The Society of Friends in Ireland and Home Rule*. Dublin: 1893.

A Presbyterian Layman. *Facts and Figures Regarding the Irish Church*. Belfast: 1867.

Adams, Rev. D. *The Revival at Ahoghill. Its Narrative and Nature*. Belfast: 1859.

Amicus Hibernicus. *The Letters of Amicus Hibernicus on Roman Catholic Affairs and the State of Ireland, as they appeared in The Instructor, London Newspaper, and Christian Guardian: Also Two Letters to the Secretary of the Protestant Union: with a Preface, containing a few observations on 'Faction Unmasked' by the same Writer.* Dublin: 1816.

An Irish Clergyman. *The Irish Church.* London: 1868.

An Irish Presbyterian. *Ulster and Home Rule.* Belfast: 1868.

An Irish Protestant. *The Established Church in Ireland in Relation to Other Religious Bodies in that Country.* London: 1868.

Anderson, C. *Memorial on Behalf of the Native Irish with a view to their Improvement in Moral and Religious Knowledge through the Medium of their own Language.* London: 1815.

Anderson, Sir R. *Sidelights on the Home Rule Movement.* London: 1906.

Anon. *An Account of the Trial of Edward Smyth, Late Curate of Ballyculter.* Dublin: n.d.

Anon. *A Reply to Mr. John Johnson's Remarks, on an Address Lately Published and Signed by 30 Men in Office amongst the Methodists: To which is Added an Affectionate Address to the People Called Methodists living in Ireland.* n.d.

Anon. *The Unfinished Task: the Story of the Hibernian Bible Society.* Dublin: n.d.

Anon. *The Pedlar's Letter to the Bishops and Clergy of Ireland.* Dublin: 1760.

Anon. *Extracts of a Letter from a Gentleman in Ireland to Mr. Wm. Thompson.* London: 1798.

Anon. *Reflections on the Spirit etc. of Religious Controversy.* London and Dublin: 1806.

Anon. *The Monstrosities of Methodism, Being an Impartial Examination into the Pretensions of Modern Sectaries to Prophetic Inspiration, Providential Interferences, and Spiritual Impulse.* Dublin: 1808.

Anon. *Protestant Union for the Defence and Support of the Protestant Religion and the British Constitution as established at the Glorious Revolution in 1688.* London: 1813.

Anon. *Resolutions on the Formation of the Methodist Missionary Society of the Dublin District.* Dublin: 1814.

Anon. *The Danger of Disseminating the Scriptures without Note or Comment.* Dublin: 1818.

Anon. *Hints for Conducting Sunday Schools, Useful also for Day Schools and Families, compiled by the Committee of the Sunday Schools Society for Ireland,* 2nd edn. Dublin: 1819.

Anon. *The Conference Reviewed, Embracing a Summary of Some Late Occurrences among the Methodists of Ireland and Exhibiting a Defence of the Primitive Wesleyan Methodists Attached to the Established Church, Humbly Recommended to the Consideration of the Established Church.* Dublin: 1819.

Anon. *A Statement of the Proceedings of the Anti-Biblical Meeting, New Ross, November 23.* Wexford: 1824.

Anon. *Arrogance and Fanaticism Combatted.* Dublin: 1824.

Anon. *A Report of the Proceedings of Three Public Meetings, Cork, in Opposition to the General Use of the Scriptures, Together with Arguments which were Advanced in Defence of the Same.* Dublin: 1825.

Anon. *Supplement to the Roman Catholic Expositor and Friend of Ireland, published under the Direction of the Society for Promoting Religious Inquiry in Ireland.* 1825.

Anon. *Appeal to Members of the Church of Rome Residing in Randalstown and its Vicinity,* 2nd edn. Belfast: 1827.

Anon. *Correspondence between the Rev. Doctor Logan, Roman Catholic Bishop of Meath, and the Rev. Robert Winning, Superintendent of Irish Schools in the Kingscourt District, with the Resolutions of 125 Teachers therein.* Dublin: 1827.

Anon. *Protestants' Reasons for Not Worshipping Saints and Images.* Dublin: 1827.

Anon. *Specimens of the Conversions at Cavan by Bible Saints Submitted to the Common Sense of the People of England.* Dublin: 1827.

Anon. *Authentic Report of the Discussion at Derry Between Six Roman Catholic Priests and Six Church of Ireland Clergy.* Dublin: 1828.

Anon. *Remonstrance of Persons Connected with the General Synod of Ulster, Against Certain of the Late Proceedings of that Body.* Belfast: 1828.

Anon. *Report of the Speeches Delivered at a Very Numerous and Respectable Meeting of Protestants Held at Churchill, County Armagh.* Dublin: 1828.

Anon. *The Thinking Few: a Poem Dedicated to the Right Worshipful Grand Master of the New Arian Lodge No. 666.* Belfast: 1828.

Anon. *Authentic Report of the Discussion at Downpatrick.* Belfast: 1829.

Anon. *The Protestant Colonization Society.* Dublin: 1830.

Anon. *A Full and Authentic Report of the Important and Interesting Proceedings of the Great Meeting of the Friends of Education and the Whole Bible.* Dublin: 1832.

Anon. *Protestant Conservative Society: a Plan for the Protection of Landed Proprietors, Magistrates and the Lower Orders, Against the Combinations with which they are Assailed, and to Secure the Interests of Property and Religion at the Ensuing General Election.* Dublin: 1832.

Anon. *Report of the Proceedings of a Public Meeting Held at Freemason's Hall, 3 December 1835.* Dublin: 1835.

Anon. *The Position of the Church of Ireland and the Duty of Presbyterians in Reference to it at the Present Crisis.* Belfast: 1835.

Anon. *The Signs of the Times: In which the Evils and Dangers of the Present System of Tithes and Regium Donum are Exposed, and Some Late Improvements in Church and State pointed out: By the Eastern Presbytery of the Reformed Presbyterian Church in Ireland,* 2nd edn. Belfast: 1835.

Anon. *Letter to one of the deputation who waited on the Archbishop of Dublin with a Memorial on Wednesday 7 December 1836.* Dublin: 1836.

Anon. *The First and Second Blast of the Trumpet against the Monstrous Union of Presbytery and Prelacy by a Member of the Synod of Ulster.* Belfast: 1835.

Anon. *The Substance of an Address to the Irish Clergy at the Rotunda.* Dublin: 1836.

Anon. *The Voluntaries in Belfast: a Report of the Discussion on Civil Establishments of Religion, held in Belfast, upon the Evenings of 16th and 17th March, 1836.* Belfast: 1836.

Anon. *The Substance of a Speech Delivered at the Meeting of the Protestants of Ireland at the Mansion House.* Dublin: 1837.

Anon. *Address of the General Synod of Ulster to the People under their Care on the Subject of Education.* Belfast: 1838.

Anon. *Address of the Committee of the Protestant Association to the People of England,* 3rd edn. 1839.

Anon. *Dioceses of Down and Connor: the Bishop's Charge with statements of the Proceedings of the Several Diocesan Societies for 1839.* Belfast: 1839.

Anon. *John Knox and the Reverend Thomas Drew.* Belfast: 1840.

Anon. *The Plea of Presbytery on Behalf of the Ordination, Government, Discipline and Worship of the Christian Church as Opposed to the Unscriptural Character and Claims of Prelacy,* 2nd edn. Belfast: 1841.

Anon. *Appeal of the Church Education Society for Funds.* Dublin: 1842.

Anon. *Ecclesiologism Exposed: Being the Letters of 'Clericus Connorensis' as Originally Published in the Belfast Commercial Chronicle, with Introductory Remarks and an Appendix.* Belfast: 1843.

Anon. *The Great Protestant Demonstration at Hillsborough, October 30, 1867*. Belfast: 1867.

Anon. *Proceedings of the Great Presbyterian Demonstration in Belfast in favour of Protestant Endowments in Ireland, Monster Meeting at the Ulster Hall, April 29, 1869*. Belfast: 1869.

Anon. *The Irish Church Bill: the Great Protestant Demonstration in Belfast*. Belfast: 1869.

Arthur, W. *Shall the Loyal be Deserted and the Disloyal Set over Them? An Appeal to Liberals and Nonconformists*. London: 1886.

Bickersteth, Rev. E. *The Substance of an Address made to about 260 of the Irish Clergy (after an early breakfast together) at the Rotunda in Dublin, April 15 1836*. London: 1836.

Birch, T. L. *Physicians Languishing under the Disease*. Belfast: 1791.

Birth, T. L. *Sermon Preached before the Very Reverend, the General Synod of Ulster, Lurgan, June 26, 1793*. Belfast: 1793.

Birch, T. L. *A Letter from an Irish Emigrant to His Friend in the United States Giving an Account of the Rise and Progress of the Commotions in Ireland of the United Irish and Orange Societies*. Philadelphia, Pa: 1799.

Birmingham Gazette, *Ireland as It Is and as It Would Be under Home Rule: Sixty-Two Letters Written by the Special Commissioner of the Birmingham Daily Gazette between March and August, 1893*. Birmingham: 1893.

Boggs, R. *Alexander Carson of Tobermore*. Belfast: 1969.

Brady, W. M. *Facts or Fictions? Seven Letters on the 'Facts Concerning the Irish Church' Published by the Church Institution*. Dublin: 1867.

Briggs, Rev. J. (ed.). *A Historical Survey of the Relations which have Subsisted between the Churches of England and Ireland and the See and Court of Rome, from the Norman Conquest to the Present Time*. London: 1868.

Buck, C. *The Close of the Eighteenth Century Improved. A Sermon Preached at Princes Street Chapel, December 28, 1800*. London: 1800.

Calderwood, Prof. and Prof. Butcher. *Speeches Delivered at a Meeting Held in Queen Street Hall, Edinburgh on Wednesday February 17, 1886, to Uphold the Legislative Union between Great Britain and Ireland*. Dublin: 1886.

Carr, Rev. W. *The Conversion of Seamen*. Belfast: n.d.

Clancy, J. M. *The Orange Bogey*. Dublin: 1886.

Clayton, H. *To School Without Shoes: a Brief History of the Sunday School Society for Ireland, 1809–1979*. Dublin: 1979.

Cloncarty, Earl of. *Remarks on the Past History and Present Position and Responsibilities of the Church of Ireland*. Dublin: 1871.

Coke, T. *Copies of Letters from the Missionaries who are Employed in Ireland for the Instruction in their own Language, and for the Conversion of the Native Irish, with a Short Address to the Generous Public*. London: 1801.

Colquhoun, J. C. *Ireland: Popery and Priestcraft the Cause of Her Misery and Crime*, 2nd edn. Glasgow: 1836.

Colquhoun, J. C. *The Object and Uses of Protestant Associations*, 2nd edn. London: 1839.

Colquhoun, J. C. *The Progress of the Church of Rome towards Ascendancy in England traced through the Parliamentary History of Nearly Forty Years*. London: 1868.

Cooke, H. *National Education: a Sermon Preached in the Presbyterian Church, May Street, Belfast, January, 1832*. Belfast: 1832.

Cooke, H. *Authentic Report of the Speech of the Reverend Henry Cooke, Delivered at the General Synod of Ulster Held at Cookstown, July, 1828*. Belfast: 1883.

Cooke, H. 'Strikes'. A Lecture Delivered at the Request of the Y.M.C.A., Belfast. Belfast: 1854.
Cooper, W. Letters on Various Religious Subjects. London: 1806.

Denison, G. A. The Churches of England and Ireland One Church. By Identity of Divine Trust: a Paper read at a Special Meeting of the Irish Church Society, Dublin, Wednesday, September 30th, 1868. Dublin: 1868.
Dickson, W. S. Sermon on the Coming of the Son of Man: Preached Before the Particular Synod of Belfast, at their Annual Meeting, November 4, 1777. Belfast: 1777.
Dixon, James. The Present Position and Aspects of Popery and the Duty of Exposing the Errors of Papal Rome, a lecture first delivered in Sheffield, 12 December 1839. London: 1840.
Dobbs, F. Memoirs of Francis Dobbs, also Genuine Reports of His Speeches in Parliament on the Subject of an Union, and his Prediction of the Second Coming of the Messiah. Dublin: 1800.
Documents and Correspondence on the Subject of the Services in the Cathedral of St. Fin Barre, Cork. Cork: 1872.
Dublin, Archbishop of. Letter to Archdeacon of Dublin and Archdeacon of Glendalough from the Archbishop of Dublin. Dublin: 1836.

Ellis, T. God and the Nation. A Sermon preached to the Orangemen of the District of Portadown in St. Mark's Church Portadown. Armagh: 1885.
Ensor, G. Letters Showing the Inutility and Showing the Absurdity of what is rather fantastically termed 'The New Reformation'. Dublin: 1828.

Farnham, Lord. The Substance of a Speech Delivered by the Rt. Hon. the Lord Farnham, at a Meeting held in Cavan on Friday, 20 January 1828, for the Purpose of Promoting the Reformation in Ireland. Dublin: 1828.
Farnham, Lord. A Statement of the Management of the Farnham Estates. Dublin: 1830.
Ferrar, W. H. The Christian Sacrifice, Remarks on a Sermon with the above Title preached in St. George's Church Dublin on Feb. 16th 1866 by the Rev. A. Dawson. Dublin: 1866.
Fleming, R. The Rise and Fall of Anti-Christ. Dublin: 1800.

Gordon, J. E. The Church of Ireland Considered in her Ecclesiastical Relation to the Roman Catholic Part of the Population. London: 1849.
Goschen, G. J. Address to the Electors of the Eastern Division of Edinburgh. London: 1886.
Goschen, G. J. The Cry of 'Justice to Ireland'. London: 1886.
Goschen, G. J. and Lord Hartington. The Disruption Bill. London: 1886.
Gwynn, S. The Ulster Revival: a Strictly Natural and Strictly Spiritual Work of God. Belfast: 1859.

Hamilton, G. Introductory Memorial Respecting the Establishment and First Attempt of the Evangelical Society of Ulster, 10 October 1798. Armagh: 1798.
Hamilton, G. The Great Necessity of Itinerant Preaching. A sermon delivered in the new meeting-house in Armagh at the foundation of the Evangelical Society of Ulster, on Wednesday 10th of October 1798. Armagh: 1798.
Hamilton, Rev. W. An Inquiry into the Scriptural Character of the Revival of 1859. Belfast: 1866.
Hartington, Lord. Address to the Electors of the Rossendale Division of Lancashire. London: 1886.

Henry, Rev. H. *An Address to the People of Connor, Containing a Clear and Full Vindication of the Synod of Ulster: From the Aspersions of the People Called Covenanters.* Belfast: 1794.
Hincks, Rev. E. *God's Works and Satan's Counter-Works, as now carried on in the North of Ireland, a sermon preached in Killyleagh church on Sunday 31st July 1859.* Belfast: 1859.
Hume, Rev. A. *Results of the Irish Census of 1861, with a Special Reference to the Church of Ireland.* London: 1864.

Irish Loyal and Patriotic Union. *The Real Dangers of Home Rule.* Dublin: 1887.
Irish Loyal and Patriotic Union. *Union or Separation?* Dublin: 1888.
Irish Nonconformists and the Unionist Leaders: Speeches of the Irish Protestant Ministers on Home Rule, 14 November 1888. London: 1888.

Jackson, Rev. E. *Reasons for Withdrawing from the Hibernian Bible Society.* Dublin: 1822.
Jebb, J. *The Rights of the Irish Branch of the United Church of Ireland and England.* London: 1868.
J. K. L. *Letters on the State of Ireland.* Dublin: 1825.
Journal of the General Synod of the Church of Ireland. Dublin: 1886, 1887.

Killen, W. D. *Why Should Prelacy Dominate?* Belfast: 1868.
King, Rev. R. G. S. *Ulster's Refusal to Submit to a Roman Catholic Parliament, stated and justified by the Rev. R. G. S. King.* Londonderry: n.d.
Knox, A. *Remarks on an Expostulatory Address to the Members of the Methodist Society.* Dublin: 1802.
Knox, C. *Two Sermons on Schism.* Dublin: 1814.
Knox, R. *Plain Truths and Stern Facts for Earnest Men.* Belfast: 1868.

Lanktree, M. *An Apology for what is called Lay-Preaching, in a Series of Letters: Addressed to the Rev. James Huey, Presbyterian Minister of Ballywillan, near Coleraine, Occasioned by his Sermon on the Divine Appointment of a Gospel Ministry.* Newry: 1815.
Lecture on the Connection between Religion and Industry delivered in the Music Hall, Belfast, on Tuesday evening, 2 December 1851 to members of the Working Classes Association, by the president of the Queen's College, Belfast. Belfast: 1852.
Lee, A. T. *Facts respecting the Present State of the Church in Ireland.* Dublin: 1868.
Liberatis. *The Pilot Balloon: a Calm Exposé of the 'Manchester Guardian'. Consisting of Verbatim Extracts from the Editorial Columns 1884 to 1886, on the Home Rule Question.* Manchester: 1889.
Lifford, Viscount. *Ireland and the Irish Church: Its Past and Present State and Future Prospects.* London: 1844.
Lockett-Ford, Rev. A. (ed.). *The Official Report of the Church Conference held at Armagh, September, 1892.* Belfast: 1892.
London Hibernian Society. *A Report of the Debates which took Place at 2 Meetings of the Cork Ladies' Auxiliary to the L.H.S.* Dublin: 1824.
Lynd, Rev. R. J. *The Present Crisis in Ireland, a Lecture Delivered at a Meeting of the May Street Literary Association: January 5, 1886.* Belfast: 1886.

Maberly, L. F. S. *The Introduction and Spread of Ritualism in the Church of Ireland under His Grace Archbishop Trench.* Dublin: 1879.
McCaig, A. *Reasons Why Nonconformists Should Oppose Home Rule. Dublin: 1886.*

McCann, A. *The Strikings Down and the Marks Vindicated.* Belfast: 1859.

McCarthy, J. G. *A Plea for the Home Government of Ireland.* London: 1871.

McCosh, Rev. J. *The Ulster Revival and Its Physiological Accidents: a Paper read before the Evangelical Alliance, September 22nd, 1859.* Belfast: 1860.

McCrea, Rev. J. *Protestant Poor: a Conservative Element of Society: Being a Sermon Preached in Ebenezer's Church, Dublin for the Protestant Colonization Society of Ireland.* Dublin: 1830.

MacGeogh, R. *Ulster's Apology for Being Loyal.* Belfast: 1888.

McGhee, Rev. J. *A Letter to the Protestants of the United Kingdom, Exhibiting the Real Principles of the Roman Catholic Bishops and Priests in Ireland.* London: 1835.

McGhee, Rev. J. *Episcopal and Clerical Duty and Responsibility Considered in a Letter respectfully addressed to the Right Rev. the Lord Bishop of Down and Connor on his Lordship's Charge v the E.C.H.M.* Dublin: 1835.

McGill, Rev. H. M. *The Present Revival of Religion in Scotland: a Paper read at the Conference of the Evangelical Alliance held at Nottingham, October 1860, with subsequent additions.* 1860.

McHale, Rev. J. *Second Letter of Right Rev. J. McHale, Bishop of Moronia to Lord Farnham.* Dublin: n.d.

McIlwaine, Rev. W. *Revivalism Renewed.* Belfast: 1859.

McIlwaine, Rev. W. *On Physical Afflictions in Connection with Religion, as Illustrated by 'Ulster Revivalism'.* Belfast: 1860.

McKnight, J. *Persecution Sanctioned by the Westminster Confession of Faith, Addressed to the Clergy, Eldership and Laity of the Synod of Ulster.* Belfast: 1836.

MacNeece, T. *Words of Caution and Counsel on the Present Religious Revival Addressed to his Parishioners.* Belfast: 1859.

MacVeagh, J. *Religious Intolerance under Home Rule. Some Opinions of Leading Irish Protestants.* London: 1911.

MacVeagh, J. *The Ulster Bogey.* Dublin: 1911.

MacVeagh, J. *'Home Rule or Rome Rule'. The Truth About Religious Intolerance in Ireland.* London: 1912.

Madden, J. *Farnham Hall or The Second Reformation in Ireland: a Poem.* Dublin: 1827.

Maguire, Rev. T. *False Weights and Measures of Protestant Curate of Cavan Examined and Exposed.* Dublin: 1833.

Mahaffy, G. *The Attitude of Irish Churchmen in the Present Political Crisis: Address to Monkstown Y.M.C.A.,* 3rd edn. Dublin: 1886.

Manderson, Rev. D. *How an Irish Nonconformist Views the Question of Home Rule with Regard to the Peace and Prosperity of Ireland.* Dungannon: 1893.

Mant, R. *The Church, the Guide of Her Ministers' Conduct and Teaching. A Charge Delivered at the Ordinary Visitation at Lisburn, Wednesday, September 7th, 1836.* Dublin: 1836.

Mant, R. *A Churchman's Apology, or Clerical Pledges Stated with Reference to National Education in a Justificatory Letter to the Rt. Hon. Sir Robert Peel.* Dublin: 1844.

Miller, G. *The Present Crisis of the Church of Ireland Considered.* Dublin: 1844.

Montgomery, Rev. J. *The Holy Spirit: Its Nature and Work: with a Special Reference to the Movement now going on around us, called a Revival of Religion.* Belfast: 1859.

Morgan, Rev. J. *Thoughts on the Revival of 1859.* Belfast: 1859.

Murphy, J. J. *An Irish Churchman's View of Irish Politics.* Belfast: 1869.

Nangle, E. *The Achill Mission and the Present State of Protestantism in Ireland. Being the*

Statement delivered by the Rev. Edward Nangle at a Meeting of the Protestant Association, in Exeter Hall, December 28 1838. London: 1838.

Nangle, E. *The Pastoral of the Roman Catholic Bishops and Archbishops of Ireland. Dissected in Seven Letters to Dr. McHale*. Dublin: 1859.

Napper, Rev. W. *A Narrative of the Principal Proceedings of the British and Foreign Bible Society*. Dublin: 1813.

Newland, Rev. H. *An Apology for the Established Church in Ireland Being an Attempt to Prove that its Present State is More Pure than in any Period since the Reformation, in a Series of Letters addressed to the Earl of Mountcashel*. Dublin: 1829.

Noble, J. *An Address to the Methodists of Ireland Respecting the Sacrament of the Lord's Supper*. Newry: 1814.

O'Brien, J. T. *The Case of the Established Church in Ireland*, 2nd edn. London: 1867.

O'Callaghan, Rev. A. *Thoughts on the Tendency of Bible Societies as Affecting the Established Church and Christianity itself as a 'Reasonable Service'*. Dublin: 1816.

O'Christian, P. *An Important Review of the State of the Curates of Ireland, with a Demonstration of the Expediency and Absolute Necessity of Treating them in a Manner more Consistent with Religion and Humanity*. Cork: 1797.

Oulton, Rev. R. *The Repeal of the Union*. Dublin: 1868.

Ouseley, G. *The Substance of Two Letters to the Rev. John Thayer, once a Presbyterian Minister, but now a Roman Catholic Priest and Missionary. In Consequence of his Public Challenge to all Protestants*. Dublin: 1814.

Ouseley, G. *The Substance of a Letter to the Rev. Mr. Fitzsimmons, Roman Catholic Priest on some Chief Pillars or Principal Articles of his Faith*. Glasgow: 1815.

Ouseley, G. *Old Christianity Defended*. Dublin: 1820.

Ouseley, G. *Five Letters in reply to the Rev. Michael Branaghan PP*. Dublin: 1824.

Ouseley, G. *Letters to Dr. Doyle on the Doctrines of his Church with an easy effectual plan to obtain Immediate Emancipation*. Dublin: 1824.

Ouseley, G. *The Divine Right of All to Read the Holy Scriptures*. Dublin: 1824.

Ouseley, G. *The Awful Adoration*. Dublin: 1825.

Ouseley, G. *Three Letters to Doctor Doyle on Roman Catholicism*. Dublin: 1826.

Ouseley, G. *Error Unmasked. Priest Walsh's Attack on Protestantism and its Clergy defeated, his Professions proved vain, and his faith deeply erroneous*. Dublin: 1828.

Ouseley, G. *Letters in Defence of the Roman Catholics of Ireland, in which is Opened the Real Source of their Many Injuries, and of Ireland's Sorrows*, 3rd edn. London: 1829.

Ouseley, G. *Review of a Sermon preached by Dr. Peter Baynes, Roman Catholic Bishop, at the opening of the R. Catholic Chapel, in Bradford, Yorkshire*. Dublin: 1829.

Ouseley, G. *Calvinism-Arminianism. God's Word and Attributes in Harmony, Being an Affectionate Attempt to Promote Union among Christians*. Dublin: 1830.

Ouseley, G. *Letters on Topics of Vast Importance to All Roman Catholics and the State, in Reply to Dr. Crolly's Letter to Lord Donegall*. Dublin: 1832.

Ouseley, G. *An Easy Mode of Securing Ireland's Peace. Letter to P. G. Crampton, Solicitor-General, 12 April 1833*. Dublin: 1833.

Ouseley, G. *A Dreadful Conspiracy against the Church of Christ Developed*. Dublin: 1837.

President of Queen's College, Belfast. *A Lecture on the Connexion Between Religion and Industry*. Belfast: 1852.

Printed Report of Case Submitted to the Rt. Hon. the Attorney General respecting the Legal Rights of the Methodists of Ireland and the Trustees of their Houses, Together with Saurin's replies, dated 7 July, 1816, and 14 July, 1816. Dublin: 1816.

Proceedings of the Great Presbyterian Demonstration. Belfast: 1868.

Protestant Defence Association of the Church of Ireland. Revision of the Prayer-Book. Dublin: 1875.

Purity of Worship Defence Association in connection with the Irish Presbyterian Church. An Address presented to the Ministers, Elders, and Members of the Church. Belfast: 1875.

Report of the Proceedings of the Synod of Aberdeen at its Meeting of October 13 1868 in reference to the Protestant Church of Ireland. Aberdeen: 1868.

Richey, Rev. W. Connor and Coleraine: or Scenes and Sketches of the Last Ulster Awakening. Belfast: 1870.

Ritualism in the Diocese of Dublin. A Correspondence between the Committee of the Protestant Defence Association of the Church of Ireland and his Grace the Archbishop of Dublin. Dublin: 1889.

Robinson, A. Facts for Irish Presbyterians. Broughshane: n.d.

Roden, Earl of. Progress of the Reformation in Ireland: Extracts from a Series of Letters written from the West of Ireland to a friend in England in September, 1851. 2nd edn. Dublin: 1852.

Seymour, W. D. Home Rule and State Supremacy, or Nationality Reconciled with Empire. London: 1888.

Smyth, Rev. E. An Account of the Trial of Edward Smyth, Late Curate of the Parish of Ballyculter in the County of Down. Dublin: n.d.

Speeches Delivered at the Great Meeting held in St. James' Hall on Wednesday afternoon, May 6, 1868, in support of the United Church of England and Ireland. London: 1868.

Staveley, W. War Proclaimed and Victory Ensured. Strabane: 1797.

Steele, S. Five Letters Addressed to the Rev. Adam Averell, Occasioned by his Coalition with the Clones Association. Dublin: 1818.

Stewart, W. A Plea for Original Methodism: a Letter Addressed to the Methodist Preachers in Ireland. Dublin: 1814.

Stopford, Rev. E. The Work and the Counter-Work: or the Religious Revival in Belfast, with an explanation of the Physical Phenomena, 4th edn. Dublin: 1859.

Stuart, Rev. D. A Sermon Preached by Appointment of the Irish Evangelical Society in the Scots Church, Mary's Abbey, Dublin, with Appendix and Description. Dublin: 1818.

Stuart, Rev. D. Sermon Preached in the New Meeting-House, Cookstown, at the Opening of the Presbyterian Synod of Ireland, distinguished by the name of Seceders, Tuesday, July 4th, 1820. Dublin: 1820.

Teignmouth, Lord. Letter to Rev. C. Wordsworth, D.D., in Reply to his Strictures on the British and Foreign Bible Society. Dublin: 1810.

The Home Rule 'Nutshell', examined by an Irish Unionist. Belfast and Dublin: 1912.

The Irish Protestant containing the Most Important Speeches Delivered at Conservative Meetings During the Parliamentary Recess, between August, 1834 and February, 1835. Vol. I (1). Belfast: 1835.

Trench, Rev. F. F. The Disestablishment and Disendowment of the Established Church in Ireland shown to be desirable under existing circumstances. London: 1868.

Venn, Rev. J. *The Revival in Wales: a paper read at the Conference of the Evangelical Alliance, held at Nottingham, October 1860, with subsequent additions*. 1860.

Walker, J. *Church in Danger*. Dublin: 1796.
Walker, J. *An Expostulatory Address to the Members of the Methodist Society in Ireland*, 3rd edn. Dublin: 1804.
Webb, A. *The Opinions of Some Protestants regarding their Catholic Fellow-Countrymen*. Dublin: 1886.
Webb, T. *Ipse Dixit or the Gladstonian Settlement of Ireland*. Dublin: 1886.
Weir, Rev. J. *The Ulster Awakening: Its Origin, Progress and Fruit with Notes of a Tour of Personal Observation and Inquiry*. London: 1860.
Whitehall Review. *'Rome's Recruits': a List of Protestants who have become Catholics since the Tractarian Movement*. Oxford: 1878.
Wilson, Rev. D. *A Defence of the Church Missionary Society*. Dublin: 1818.
Woodward, R. *The Present State of the Church of Ireland: Containing a Description of its Precarious Situation and Consequent Dangers to the Public*, 6th edn. Dublin: 1787.

(2) SECONDARY SOURCES

(a) Nineteenth-century books

Adams, J. *A Brief History of Belfast Methodism, 1805–1890*. Belfast: 1890.
Alley, G. *Our Class Meeting*. Dublin: 1868.
Anon. *Brief Memorials of the Reverend B. W. Mathias*. Dublin: 1842.
Arthur, W. *The Life of Gideon Ouseley*. London: 1876.

Ball, J. T. *The Reformed Church of Ireland, 1537–1886*. London: 1886.
Binns, J. *The Miseries and Beauties of Ireland*, 2 vols. London: 1837.

Campbell, W. G. *'The Apostle of Kerry', the Life of the Rev. Charles Graham*. Dublin: 1868.
Christophers, S. W. *Class-Meetings in Relation to the Design and Success of Methodism*. London: 1873.
Clarke, A. *An Account of the Religious and Literary Life of Adam Clarke: By a Member of his Family*, 3 vols. London: 1833.
Crook, [no initial given]. *Sketch of the Life and Character of the Late Rev. William Crook by his Son*. Dublin: 1863.
Crookshank, C. H. *A Methodist Pioneer: the Life and Labours of John Smith, including brief notices of the origin and early history of Methodism in different parts of the North of Ireland*. London: 1881.
Crookshank, C. H. *Memorable Women of Irish Methodism in the Last Century*. London: 1882.
Crookshank, C. H. *History of Methodism in Ireland*, 3 vols. London: 1885–8.

Dow, L. *Works: Providential Experience of Lorenzo Dow in Europe and America*, 3rd edn. Dublin: 1806.
Doyle, J. *Letters on the State of Ireland*. Dublin: 1825.
Drummond, A. L. *Edward Irving and his Circle*. London: n.d.

Drummond, W. H. *Autobiography of Archibald Hamilton Rowan*. Dublin: 1840.
Dwyer, Rev. J. *A Memorial of Thos. Averall Shillington, J.P.* Belfast: 1875.

Ferguson, Rev. S. *Brief Autobiographical Sketches of Some Irish Covenanting Ministers who Laboured during the latter half of the Eighteenth Century*. Londonderry: 1897.
Fitzpatrick, W. J. *The Life, Times and Correspondence of the Right Reverend Dr. Doyle, Bishop of Kildare and Leighlin*, 2 vols. Dublin: 1890.
Forster, C. *The Life of John Jebb, with a Selection from his Letters*. London: 1836.
Foster, T. C. *Letters on the Condition of the People of Ireland*. London: 1846.

Gamble, J. *View of Society and Manners in the North of Ireland in the Summer and Autumn of 1812*. London: 1813.
Gamble, J. *Sketches of History, Politics and Manners in Dublin and the North of Ireland in 1810*, 2nd edn. London: 1826.
Godkin, J. *Ireland and Her Churches*. London: 1867.

Haldane, A. *The Lives of Robert Haldane of Aithrey and of his Brother, James Alexander Haldane*, 7th edn. Edinburgh: 1860.
Hamilton, Rev. T. *History of the Irish Presbyterian Church*. Edinburgh: 1887.
Healey, Rev. J. *Maynooth College: Its Centenary History 1795–1895*. Dublin: 1895.

Inglis, H. D. *A Journey Throughout Ireland During the Spring, Summer and Autumn of 1834*, 2 vols. London: 1835.
Irish Intelligence: the Progress of Irish Society of London. London: 1848.
Irwin, Rev. C. H. *Famous Irish Preachers*. Dublin: 1889.

Jocelyn, R., Earl of Roden *Progress of the Reformation in Ireland*, 2nd edn. Dublin: 1852.

Killen, W. D. *Memoir of John Edgar, D.D., L.L.D.* Belfast: 1867.
Killen, W. D. *History of the Presbyterian Church*, 3 vols. Vol. 3. London: 1880.
Kohl, J. G. *Travels in Ireland*. London: 1844.

Lanktree, M. *Biographical Narrative*. Belfast: 1836.
Latimer, W. T. *History of the Irish Presbyterians*. Belfast: 1893.
Leadbeater Papers: a Selection from the Mss and Correspondence of Mary Leadbeater, 2 vols. London: 1862.
Lefroy, T. *Memoir of Chief Justice Lefroy*. Dublin: 1871.
Lynn, J. M. *A History of Wesleyan Methodism on the Armagh Circuit*, 3rd edn. Belfast: 1887.

McGregor, J. J. *Memoir of Miss Alice Cambridge*. Dublin: 1832.
MacWalter, J. G. *The Irish Reformation Movement in its Religious, Social and Political Aspects*. Dublin: 1852.
Madden, S. *Memoir of the Life of the Late Reverend Peter Roe, with copious extracts from his Correspondence, Diaries, and other Remains*. Dublin: 1842.
Mant, R. *History of the Church of Ireland, from the Revolution to the Union of the Churches of England and Ireland, January, 1801. With a Catalogue of the Archbishops and Bishops, continued to November, 1840*, 2 vols. London: 1840.
Mant, W. B. *Bishop Mant and his Diocese*. Dublin: 1857.

Moran, Cardinal. *The Catholics of Ireland under the Penal Laws in the Eighteenth Century*. London: 1899.
Morgan, J. *Recollections of My Life and Times*. Belfast: 1874.
Motherwell, Rev. M. C. *Memoir of Albert Blest, for Many Years Agent and Secretary for the London Hibernian Society*. Dublin: 1843.
Murray, J. W. *Sketches of the Life and Times of Eminent Irish Churchmen from the Reformation Downwards*. Dublin 1874.

Nelson, I. *The Year of Delusion: a Review of the Year of Grace*, 2nd edn. Belfast: 1860.
Noel, B. *Notes of a Short Tour through the Midland Counties of Ireland, in the Summer of 1836, with Observations on the Conditions of the Peasantry*. London: 1837.

O'Hanlon, Rev. W. *Walks among the Poor of Belfast and Suggestions for their Improvement*. Belfast: 1853.
O'Laverty, Rev. J. *Diocese of Down and Connor: Ancient and Modern*, 5 vols. Dublin: 1878.

Phillips, Rev. R. C. *Irish Methodism*. London: 1897.
Porter, J. L. *The Life and Times of Henry Cooke, D.D*. Belfast: 1875.
Prenter, Rev. S. *Life and Labours of the Reverend William Johnston, D.D*. London: 1895.

Reid, J. S. *History of the Presbyterian Church in Ireland*. 3 vols, 2nd edn. London: 1853.
Reid, W. *Authentic Records of Revival*. Belfast: 1980.

Savage, D. *The Life and Labours of the Rev. Wm. McClure*. Toronto: 1872.
Seymour, A. C. H. *The Life and Times of Selina, Countess of Huntingdon*, 2 vols. London: 1844.
Sirr, J. D. *A Memoir of Power Le Poer Trench, Last Archbishop of Tuam*. Dublin: 1845.
Smile, S. *The Huguenots, their Settlements, Churches and Industries in England and Ireland*. London: 1876.
Smiley, M. H. *The Life and Letters of the Reverend William Smiley of the Irish Methodist Conference*. London: 1888.
Smith, Mrs R. *The Life of the Rev. Mr. Henry Moore*. London: 1844.
Smyth, E. *The Extraordinary Life and Christian Experience of Margaret Davidson*. Dublin: 1872.
Stanford, C. S. *Memoir of the Late Reverend W. H. Krause, with Selections from his Correspondence*. Dublin: 1854.
Stevens, A. *The Women of Methodism: Memoirs of Its Three Founders*. London: n.d.
Stewart, A. and G. Revington. *Memoir of the Life and Labours of the Rev. Adam Averell*. Dublin: 1848.
Stock, E. *The History of the Church Missionary Society: Its Environment, Its Men and Its Work*, 4 vols. London: 1899–1916.

Thackeray, W. D. *The Irish Sketchbook, 1842*. London: 1865.
Thelwall, A. D. *Proceedings of the Anti-Maynooth Conference of 1845*. London: 1845.
Thomas, E. *Irish Methodist Reminiscences: Memorial of the Life and Labour of the Late Reverend S. Nicholson*. London: 1889.
Tonna, C. E. *Letters from Ireland*. London: 1837.

Urwick, W. *Biographical Sketches of the Late James Digges La Touche.* Dublin: n.d.

Vane, C. (ed.) *Memoirs and Correspondence of Viscount Castlereagh,* 12 vols. London: 1848–53.

Warneck, G. *History of Protestant Missions.* Edinburgh: 1884.
White, Rev. C. *Sixty Years Experience as an Irish Landlord: Memoirs of John Hamilton.* London: n.d.
Winskill, P. T. *The Temperance Movement and Its Workers: a Record of Social, Moral, Religious and Political Progress.* London: 1892.

(b) Twentieth-century books

Adams, J. R. R. *The Printed Word and the Common Man: Popular Culture in Ulster, 1700–1900.* Belfast: 1987.
Adams, W. F. *Ireland and Irish Emigration to the New World.* New Haven, Conn.: 1932.
Adamson, I. *The Identity of Ulster: the Land, the Language and the People.* Belfast: 1982.
Akenson, D. H. *The Irish Education Experiment.* London: 1970.
Akenson, D. H. *The Church of Ireland: Ecclesiastical Reform and Revolution 1800–1885.* London: 1971.
Allen, R. *The Presbyterian College in Belfast 1853–1953.* Belfast: 1954.
Allen, W. E. *The '59 Revival in Ireland, the United States of America, England, Scotland and Wales.* Belfast: 1955.
Anstey, R. *The Atlantic Slave Trade and British Abolition 1760–1810.* Atlantic Highlands, NJ: 1975.
Archibald, J. E. *A Century of Congregationalism: the Story of Donegall Street Church, Belfast.* Belfast: 1901.
Atkinson, E. D. *Dromore, an Ulster Diocese.* Dundalk: 1925.
Atkinson, N. *Irish Education. A History of Educational Institutions.* Dublin: 1969.

Bailey, W. D. *The Six Mile Water Revival of 1625.* Newcastle: 1976.
Baker, F. (ed.) *The Works of John Wesley,* Vol. 26, *Letters II 1740–1755.* Oxford: 1982.
Balleine, G. R. *A History of the Evangelical Party in the Church of England.* London: 1909.
Banks, O. *Faces of Feminism.* Oxford: 1981.
Bardon, J. *Belfast: an Illustrated History.* Belfast: 1982.
Barkley, J. M. *The Eldership in Irish Presbyterianism.* Belfast: 1963.
Beames, M. *Peasants and Power: the Whiteboy Movements and their Control in Pre-Famine Ireland.* London: 1983.
Bebbington, D. W. *The Nonconformist Conscience: Chapel and Politics, 1870–1914.* London: 1982.
Bebbington, D. W. *Evangelicalism in Modern Britain: a History from the 1730s to the 1980s.* London: 1989.
Beckett, J. C. *The Anglo-Irish Tradition.* Belfast: 1976.
Beckett, J. C. (ed.) *Belfast: the Making of a City 1800–1914.* Belfast: 1983.
Berger, P. *The Social Reality of Religion.* London: 1967.
Best, G. F. A. *Temporal Pillars: Queen Anne's Bounty, the Ecclesiastical Commissioners, and the Church of England.* Cambridge: 1964.
Biggar, F. J. *The Ulster Land War of 1770: the History of the Hearts of Steel.* Dublin: 1910.

Binfield, C. *George William and the YMCA. A Study in Victorian Social Attitudes*. London: 1973.

Bingham, H. *An Irish Saint: the Life Story of Ann Preston*. Toronto: 1909.

Bland, F. E. *How the Church Missionary Society Came to Ireland*. Dublin: 1935.

Bowen, D. *Souperism: Myth or Reality?* Cork: 1970.

Bowen, D. *The Protestant Crusade in Ireland 1800–1870*. Dublin: 1978.

Boyd, A. *Holy War in Belfast*, 2nd edn. Belfast: 1970.

Boyd, A. *The Rise of the Irish Trade Unions*. Dublin: 1985.

Boyd, R. H. *Couriers of the Dawn: the Story of the Missionary Pioneers of the Presbyterian Church in Ireland*. Belfast: 1938.

Bradley, I. *The Call to Seriousness: the Evangelical Impact on the Victorians*. London: 1976.

Broeker, G. *Rural Disorder and Police Reform in Ireland, 1812–1936*. London: 1970.

Brooke, P. *Ulster Presbyterianism: the Historical Perspective 1610–1970*. Dublin: 1987.

Brown, C. G. *The Social History of Religion in Scotland since 1730*. London: 1987.

Brown, F. K. *Fathers of the Victorians: the Age of Wilberforce*. Cambridge: 1961.

Bruce, S. *God Save Ulster! The Religion and Politics of Paisleyism*. Oxford: 1985.

Brynn, E. *Crown and Castle: British Rule in Ireland, 1800–1830*. Dublin: 1978.

Brynn, E. *The Church of Ireland in the Age of Catholic Emancipation*. London: 1982.

Buckland, P. *Ulster Unionism and the Origins of Northern Ireland 1886–1922*. Dublin: 1973.

Budge, I. and C. O'Leary. *Belfast: Approach to Crisis*. London: 1973.

Buick's Ahoghill. Antrim: 1987.

Burdy, S. *Life of the Late Reverend Philip Skelton*. First printed Dublin: 1792; reprinted Oxford: 1914.

Campbell, A. A. *Irish Presbyterian Magazines, Past and Present. A Bibliography*. Belfast: 1919.

Canton, W. *The Story of the Bible Society*. London: 1904.

Carson, J. T. *God's River in Spate*. Belfast: 1958.

Carwardine, R. *Trans-Atlantic Revivalism: Popular Evangelicalism in Britain and America, 1790–1865*. Westport, Conn.: 1978.

Clark, D. *Between Pulpit and Pew: Folk Religion in a North Yorkshire Fishing Village*. Cambridge: 1982.

Clark, S. and S. J. Donnelly. *Irish Peasants: Violence and Political Unrest 1780–1914*. Manchester: 1983.

Cnattigius, H. *Bishops and Societies: a Study of Anglican Colonial and Missionary Expansion 1698–1850*. London: 1952.

Coad, R. *A History of the Brethren Movement*, 2nd edn. Exeter: 1976.

Cole, F. J. *John Wesley and His Ulster Contacts*. Belfast: 1945.

Cole, F. J. *The Cavalry Preachers*. Belfast: 1945.

Cole, R. L. *Love-Feasts: a History of the Christian Agape*. London: 1916.

Cole, R. L. *A History of Methodism in Dublin*. Dublin: 1932.

Cole, R. L. *History of Methodism in Ireland 1860–1960*. Belfast: 1960.

Coles, M. *I Will Build my Church: the Story of the Congregational Union of Ireland 1829–1979*. Dublin: 1979.

Connolly, S. J. *Priests and People in Pre-Famine Ireland (1780–1845)*. London: 1982.

Connolly, S. *Religion and Society in Nineteenth-Century Ireland*. Dundalk: 1985.

Corish, P. *The Irish Catholic Experience: a Historical Survey*. Dublin: 1985.

Cott, N. F. *The Bonds of Womanhood: 'Woman's Sphere' in New England 1780–1835*. New Haven, Conn.: 1977.

Cox, J. *The English Churches in a Secular Society: Lambeth 1870–1930.* Oxford: 1982.
Crawford, W. H. *Domestic Industry in Ireland.* Dublin: 1972.
Crawford, W. H. and B. Trainor. *Aspects of Irish Social History 1750–1800.* Belfast: 1969.
Cross, W. R. *The Burned-Over District: the Social and Intellectual History of Enthusiastic Religion in Western New York, 1800–1850.* New York: 1950.
Cullen, L. M. *An Economic History of Ireland since 1660.* London: 1972.
Cullen, L. M. *The Emergence of Modern Ireland 1600–1900.* London: 1981.
Curnock, N. (ed.). *The Journal of John Wesley, Enlarged from Original Ms. with Notes from Unpublished Diaries, Annotations, Maps and Illustrations,* 8 vols. London: 1909.
Currie, R., A. Gilbert and L. Horsley. *Churches and Churchgoers: Patterns of Church Growth in the British Isles since 1700.* Oxford: 1977.

Davies, E. T. *Religion in the Industrial Revolution in South Wales.* Cardiff: 1965.
Davies, E. T. *A New History of Wales: Religion and Society in the Nineteenth Century.* Dyfed: 1981.
Davies, R. E. *Methodism.* London: 1963.
Davies, R. E. and E. G. Rupp (eds). *A History of the Methodist Church in Great Britain.* London: 1965.
Devlin, P. *Yes We Have No Bananas: Outdoor Relief in Belfast, 1920–39.* Belfast: 1981.
Donnelly, J. S. *Landlord and Tenant in Nineteenth-Century Ireland.* Dublin: 1973.
Dornan, W. E. *One Hundred Years: the Story of the City of Belfast Y.M.C.A.* Belfast: 1950.
Drummond, A. L. and J. Bulloch. *The Scottish Church 1688–1843: the Age of the Moderates.* Edinburgh: 1981.
Duffy, C. G. *My Life in Two Hemispheres,* 2 vols. Dublin: 1969.
Duffy, J. *Clogher Record Album: a Diocesan History.* Monaghan: 1975.

Eames, R. H. A. *The Quiet Revolution: the Disestablishment of the Church of Ireland.* Dublin: 1970.
Edwards, R. D. *Atlas of Irish History.* London: 1973.
Elliott, M. *Partners in Revolution: the United Irishmen and France.* London: 1982.
Elliott, M. *Watchmen in Sion: the Protestant Idea of Liberty.* Derry: 1985.
Emerson, N. D. *The Church of Ireland and the 1859 Revival.* Belfast: 1959.
Everitt, A. *The Pattern of Rural Dissent: the Nineteenth Century.* Leicester: 1972.

Fortescue Mss, Vol. IV. 1905.
Foster, J. *Class Struggle and the Industrial Revolution: Early Industrial Capitalism in Three English Towns.* London: 1974.
Foster, R. F. *Modern Ireland 1600–1972.* London: 1988.
Freeman, T. W. *Ireland: Its Physical, Historical, Social and Economic Geography.* London: 1950.
Freeman, T. W. *Pre-Famine Ireland: a Study in Historical Geography.* Manchester: 1957.
Fullerton, A. *Fifty Years an Itinerant Preacher.* Belfast: 1912.

Gallagher, R. H. *John Bredin.* Belfast: 1960.
Gallagher, R. H. *Methodism in the Charlemont Circuit.* Belfast: 1961.
Gallagher, R. H. *Pioneer Preachers of Irish Methodism.* Belfast: 1965.

Gibbon, P. *The Origins of Ulster Unionism: the Formation of Popular Protestant Politics and Ideology in Nineteenth-Century Ireland.* Manchester: 1975.

Gibson, W. *The Year of Grace: a History of the Ulster Revival of 1859,* 2nd edn. Belfast: 1903.

Gilbert, A. D. *Religion and Society in Industrial England: Church, Chapel and Social Change 1740–1914.* London: 1976.

Gill, C. *The Rise of the Irish Linen Industry.* Oxford, 1964; first published 1925.

Gillespie, R. *Wild as Colts Untamed: Methodism and Society in Lurgan, 1750–1975.* Lurgan: 1977.

Goodbody, O. *Guide to Irish Quaker Records 1654–1860.* Dublin: 1967.

Green, E. R. R. *The Lagan Valley: 1800–1850. A Local History of the Industrial Revolution.* London: 1949.

Green, W. J. *Methodism in Portadown.* Belfast: 1960.

Grubb, I. *Quakers in Ireland 1654–1900.* London: 1927.

Haire, R. *Wesley's One-and-Twenty Visits to Ireland.* London: 1947.

Halevy, E. *A History of the English People in the Nineteenth Century,* 4 vols. London: 1949–51.

Harbinson, J. F. *The Ulster Unionist Party 1882–1973.* Belfast: 1973.

Hardesty, N. A. *Women Called to Witness: Evangelical Feminism in the 19th Century.* Nashville, Tenn.: 1984.

Harrison, B. *Drink and the Victorians.* London: 1971.

Harrison, J. F. C. *The Second Coming: Popular Millenarianism 1780–1850.* London: 1979.

Hempton, D. *Methodism and Politics in British Society 1750–1850.* London: 1984.

Hill, C. *Puritanism and Revolution.* London: 1965.

Hobsbawm, E. J. *Primitive Revels.* Manchester: 1959.

Hobsbawm, E. J. *Labouring Men: Studies in the History of Labour.* London: 1964.

Hollis, P. *Class and Conflict in Nineteenth-Century England, 1815–1850.* London: 1973.

Holmes, R. F. *Henry Cooke.* Belfast: 1981.

Holmes, R. F. *Our Irish Presbyterian Heritage.* Belfast: 1985.

Hurley, M. S. J. (ed.). *John Wesley's Letter to a Roman Catholic.* Belfast: 1968.

Hurley, M. (ed.). *Irish Anglicanism 1869–1969.* Dublin: 1970.

Hutchinson, J. G. *Sowers, Reapers, Builders: a Record of over Ninety Irish Evangelists.* Glasgow: 1984.

Hutton, R. H. *A History of the Moravian Church.* London: 1909.

Jackson, A. *The Ulster Party: Irish Unionists in the House of Commons, 1884–1911.* Oxford: 1989.

Jacob, R. *The Rise of the United Irishmen 1791–4.* London: 1937.

Jay, E. *The Religion of the Heart: Anglican Evangelicalism and the Nineteenth-Century Novel.* Oxford: 1979.

Jeffrey, F. *Irish Methodism.* Belfast: 1964.

Jeffrey, F. *Methodism and the Irish Problem.* Belfast: 1973.

Johnston, E. M. *Great Britain and Ireland.* Edinburgh: 1963.

Johnston, E. M. *Ireland in the Eighteenth Century.* Dublin: 1974.

Johnston, R. *The Story of the Central Presbyterian Association, Belfast 1882–1932.* Belfast: 1932.

Jones, E. *A Social Geography of Belfast.* London: 1960.

Joyce, P. *Work, Society and Politics: the Culture of the Factory in Later Victorian England.* Brighton: 1980.

Keenan, D. *The Catholic Church in Nineteenth-Century Ireland: a Sociological Study.* Dublin: 1983.

Kent, J. *Holding the Fort: Studies in Victorian Revivalism.* London: 1978.

Killen, W. D. *Reminiscences of a Long Life.* London: 1901.

Kingdon, D. D. *Baptist Evangelism in Nineteenth-Century Ireland.* Belfast: 1965.

Koss, S. *Nonconformity in Modern British Politics.* London: 1975.

Krans, H. S. *Irish Life in Irish Fiction.* New York: 1966.

Laqueur, T. W. *Religion and Respectability: Sunday Schools and Working-Class Culture.* London: 1976.

Lecky, W. E. H. *A History of Ireland in the Eighteenth Century,* Vol. 3. London: 1913.

Lee, G. L. *The Huguenot Settlements in Ireland.* London: 1936.

Leslie, J. B. *Armagh Clergy and Parishes.* Dundalk: 1911.

Leslie, J. B. *Clogher Clergy and Parishes.* Enniskillen: 1929.

Leslie, J. B. *Derry Clergy and Parishes.* Enniskillen: 1937.

Leslie, J. B. *Raphoe Clergy and Parishes.* Enniskillen: 1940.

Leslie, J. B. and J. B. Swanzy. *Biographical Succession List of Down Diocese.* Enniskillen: 1936.

Lewis, D. *Lighten their Darkness: the Evangelical Mission to Working-Class London, 1828–1860.* London: 1986.

Livingstone, P. *The Monaghan Story: a Documented History of the County Monaghan from the Earliest Times to 1976.* Clogher: 1980.

Loughlin, J. *Gladstone, Home Rule and the Irish Question 1882–93.* Dublin: 1986.

Loughridge, A. *The Covenanters in Ireland: a History of the Reformed Presbyterian Church of Ireland.* Belfast: 1984.

Macauley, A. *Patrick Dorrian, Bishop of Down and Connor 1865–1885.* Dublin: 1987.

MacConnell, Rev. J. *Presbyterianism in Belfast.* Belfast: 1912.

McCutcheon, W. A. *The Industrial Archaeology of Northern Ireland.* Belfast: 1980.

McDowell, R. B. *Public Opinion and Government Policy in Ireland 1801–1846.* London: 1952.

McDowell, R. B. *The Church of Ireland 1869–1969.* London: 1975.

Machin, G. I. T. *Politics and the Churches in Great Britain.* Vol. 1, *1832 to 1868.* Oxford: 1977. Vol. 2, *1869 to 1921.* Oxford: 1987.

McLaren, A. A. *Religion and Social Class: the Disruption Years in Edinburgh.* London: 1974.

McLeod, H. *Class and Religion in the Late Victorian City.* London: 1974.

McLeod, H. *Religion and the People of Western Europe 1789–1970.* Oxford: 1981.

McLeod, H. *Religion and the Working Class in Nineteenth-Century Britain.* London: 1984.

McLoughlin, W. *Revivals, Awakenings and Reform: an Essay on Religion and Social Change in America, 1607–1977.* Chicago: 1978.

McMinn, J. R. B. *Against the Tide: J. B. Armour, Irish Presbyterian Minister and Home Ruler.* Belfast: 1985.

Maguire, Rev. E. *Fifty Eight Years of Clerical Life in the Church of Ireland.* Dublin: 1904.

Maguire, W. A. *Living Like a Lord: the second Marquis of Donegall 1769–1844.* Belfast: 1984.

Maguire, W. A. *The Huguenots in Ulster 1685–1985.* Lisburn: 1985.

Malcolm, E. *Ireland Sober, Ireland Free: Drink and Temperance in Nineteenth-Century Ireland.* Dublin: 1986.

Miller, D. W. *Queen's Rebels: Ulster Loyalism in Historical Perspective.* Dublin: 1978.

Moody, T. W. *The Social History of Modern Ulster: Ulster since 1800,* 2nd series. London: 1958.

Moody, T. W. and F. X. Martin. *The Course of Irish History.* Cork: 1984.

Moore, F. *The Truth about Ulster.* London: 1914.

Murray, S. W. *The City Mission Story.* Belfast: 1977.

Neill, S. *A History of Christian Missions.* London: 1973.

NIPRO. *Problems of a Growing City: Belfast 1780–1870.* Belfast: 1973.

Obelkevich, J. *Religion and Rural Society: South Lindsey 1825–1875.* Oxford: 1976.

O'Farrell, F. *Catholic Emancipation: Daniel O'Connell and the Birth of Irish Democracy.* Dublin: 1985.

Orr, G. E. *Lisburn Methodism.* Belfast: 1975.

Orr, J. E. *The Second Evangelical Awakening in Britain.* Edinburgh: 1949.

Orr, J. E. *The Light of Nations: Evangelical Renewal and Advance in the Nineteenth Century.* Devon: 1965.

O'Tuathaigh, G. *Ireland Before the Famine: 1798–1848.* Dublin: 1972.

Owen, D. J. *History of Belfast.* Belfast: 1921.

Paisley, I. R. K. *The 'Fifty-Nine' Revival.* Belfast: 1958.

Palmer, S. H. *Police and Protest in England and Ireland 1780–1850.* Cambridge: 1988.

Patterson, H. *Class Conflict and Sectarianism.* Belfast: 1980.

Phillips, W. A. (ed.). *History of the Church of Ireland,* 3 vols. Oxford: 1934.

Pickering, H. *Chief Men among the Brethren.* London: 1931.

Prochaska, F. *Women and Philanthropy in Nineteenth-Century England.* Oxford: 1980.

Rea, T. *The Life and Labours of David Rea, Evangelist.* Belfast: 1917.

Redmond, J. *Church, State, Industry 1827–1929 in East Belfast.* Belfast: 1960.

Rendall, J. *The Origins of Modern Feminism in Britain, France and the United States 1780–1860.* London: 1985.

Reynolds, J. A. *The Catholic Emancipation Crisis in Ireland 1823–9.* New Haven, Conn.: 1954.

Roebuck, P. *Plantation to Partition: Essays in Ulster History in Honour of J. L. McCracken.* Belfast: 1981.

Rogers, Rev. P. *Father Theobald Mathew: Apostle of Temperance.* Dublin: 1943.

Rouse, R. and S. C. Neill. *A History of the Ecumenical Movement 1517–1948,* 2nd edn. London: 1967.

Rowden, H. H. *The Origins of the Brethren.* London: 1967.

Rowell, G. (ed.). *Tradition Renewed: the Oxford Movement.* London: 1986.

Rule, J. *The Experience of Labour in Eighteenth-Century Industry.* London: 1981.

Schmidt, L. E. *Holy Fairs: Scottish Communions and American Revivals in the Early Modern Period.* Princeton, NJ: 1989.

Sellers, I. *Nineteenth-Century Nonconformity.* London: 1977.

Semnel, B. *The Methodist Revolution.* London: 1974.

Senior, H. *Orangeism in Ireland and Britain: 1795–1836.* London: 1966.

Shaw, T. *A History of Cornish Methodism.* Truro: 1967.

Sibbett, R. M. *For Christ and Crown: the Story of a Mission.* Belfast: 1926.

Sibbett, R. M. *Orangeism in Ireland and throughout the Empire*, 2 vols. Belfast: 1939.

Simms, J. G. *The Williamite Confiscation in Ireland, 1690–1703*. London: 1956.

Snyder, H. A. *The Radical Wesley and Patterns for Church Renewal*. Downer's Grove, Ill.: 1980.

Soloway, R. A. *Prelates and People: Ecclesiastical Social Thought in England 1783–1852*. London: 1969.

Stevens, A. *The Women of Methodism: Memoirs of its Three Foundresses*. Manchester: n.d.

Stevenson, J. *Two Centuries of Life in Down 1600–1800*. First published 1920; Belfast: 1990.

Stewart, A. T. Q. *The Narrow Ground: Aspects of Ulster 1609–1969*. London: 1977.

Stewart, D. *The Seceders in Ireland, with Annals of their Congregations*. Belfast: 1950.

Taggart, N. W. *The Irish in World Methodism 1760–1900*. London: 1986.

Thompson, D. M. *Nonconformity in the Nineteenth Century*. London: 1972.

Thompson, D. M. *Denominationalism and Dissent: 1795–1835*. London: 1985.

Thompson, E. P. *The Making of the English Working Class*. London: 1963.

Valenze, D. *Prophetic Sons and Daughters: Female Preaching and Popular Religion in Industrial England*. Princeton, NJ: 1985.

Vaughan, W. E. and A. J. Fitzpatrick (eds). *Irish Historical Statistics*. Dublin: 1978.

Vickers, J. *Thomas Coke: Apostle of Methodism*. London: 1969.

Walker, B. *Ulster Politics: the Formative Years, 1868–86*. Belfast: 1989.

Ward, W. R. *Religion and Society in England, 1790–1850*. London: 1972.

Ward, W. R. *Early Victorian Methodism, the Correspondence of Jabez Bunting 1830–1858*. Oxford: 1976.

Ward, W. R. and R. P. Heitzenrater (eds). *The Works of John Wesley*, Vol. 18, *Journals and Diaries I (1735–1738)*. Nashville, Tenn.: 1988.

Weber, M. *The Protestant Ethic and the Spirit of Capitalism*. London: 1930.

Weber, M. *Sociology of Religion*. London: 1966.

Westerkamp, M. J. *Triumph of the Laity: Scots-Irish Piety and the Great Awakening 1625–1760*. Oxford: 1988.

Whitley, W. T. *A History of British Baptists*. London: 1923.

Wickham, E. R. *Church and People in an Industrial City*. London: 1964.

Williams, R. D. (ed.). *Secret Societies in Ireland*. Dublin: 1973.

Wilson, B. *Religious Sects*. London: 1970.

Worsley, P. *The Trumpet Shall Sound*. London: 1970.

Yeo, S. *Religion and Voluntary Organisations in Crisis*. London: 1976.

Yeo, E. and S. Yeo (eds). *Popular Culture and Class Conflict, 1590–1914*. Brighton: 1982.

Young, A. *A Tour in Ireland, with general observations on the state of that kingdom made in the years 1776, 1777 and 1778*. Reprinted Belfast: 1983.

(c) Articles

(i) In books

Baker, S. E. Orange and green: Belfast, 1832–1912. In H. J. Dyos and M. Wolff (eds), *The Victorian City: Images and Realities*, Vol. 2, pp. 789–814. London: 1973.

Brown, E. K. Women of the word. In H. F. Thomas and R. Skinner (eds), *Women in New Worlds*, pp. 69–87. Nashville, Tenn.: 1981.

Chart, D. A. The broadening of the church. In W. A. Philips, *The History of the Church of Ireland from the Earliest Times to the Present Day*, 3 vols, Vol. 3, pp. 242–86. London: 1933.

Clark, G. R. K. The romantic element, 1830–1850. In J. H. Plumb (ed.), *Studies in Social History*, pp. 209–39. London: 1955.

Clarkson, L. A. Population change and urbanisation 1821–1911. In L. Kennedy and P. Ollerenshaw (eds), *An Economic History of Ulster, 1820–1939*, pp. 137–57. Manchester: 1985.

Connolly, S. J. Catholicism in Ulster 1800–1850. In P. Roebuck (ed.), *Plantation to Partition: Essays in Ulster History in Honour of J. L. McCracken*, pp. 157–72. Belfast: 1981.

Connolly, S. J. Religion, work-discipline and economic attitudes: the case of Ireland. In T. M. Devine and D. Dickson (eds), *Ireland and Scotland, 1600–1850*, pp. 235–60. Glasgow: 1983.

Crawford, W. H. The evolution of Ulster towns 1750–1850. In P. Roebuck (ed.), *Plantation to Partition: Essays in Ulster History in Honour of J. L. McCracken*, pp. 140–56. Belfast: 1981.

Drew, T. The rich and the poor. In *The Irish Pulpit: a Collection of Original Sermons by Clergymen of the Established Church*, pp. 251–69. Dublin: 1839.

Eversley, D. E. C. The demography of the Irish Quakers, 1650–1850. In J. M. Goldstrom and L. A. Clarkson (eds), *Irish Population, Economy and Society*, pp. 57–88. Oxford: 1981.

Fitzgerald, G. The decline of the Irish language 1771–1871. In M. Daly and D. Dickson (eds), *The Origins of Popular Literacy in Ireland: Language Change and Educational Development 1700–1920*, pp. 59–72. Dublin: 1990.

Ford, A. The Protestant Reformation in Ireland. In C. Brady and R. Gillespie (eds), *Natives and Newcomers: the Making of Irish Colonial Society 1534–1641*, pp. 50–74. Dublin: 1986.

Froggatt, P. Industrialisation and health in Belfast in the early nineteenth century. In D. Harkness and M. O'Dowd (eds), *The Town in Ireland*, pp. 187–202. Belfast: 1979.

Glassock, R. E. The growth of the port. In J. C. Beckett and R. E. Glassock (eds), *The Origin and Growth of a City*, pp. 98–108. London: 1967.

Gray, J. Popular entertainment. In J. C. Beckett (ed.), *Belfast: the Making of the City, 1800–1914*, pp. 98–111. Belfast: 1983.

Green, E. R. R. Early industrial Belfast. In J. C. Beckett and R. E. Glassock (eds), *The Origin and Growth of a City*, pp. 78–87. London: 1967.

Hempton, D. N. Religious minorities. In P. Loughrey (ed.), *The People of Ireland*, pp. 155–68. Belfast: 1988.

Hepburn, A. C. and B. Collin. Industrial society: the structure of Belfast, 1901. In P. Roebuck (ed.), *Plantation to Partition, Essays in Ulster History in Honour of J. L. McCracken*, pp. 210–28. Belfast: 1981.

Kelly, J. The genesis of 'Protestant ascendancy': the Rightboy disturbances of the 1780s and their impact upon Protestant opinion. In G. O'Brien (ed.), *Parliament, Politics and People*, pp. 93–127. Dublin: 1989.

Kennedy, L. The rural economy, 1820–1914. In L. Kennedy and P. Ollerenshaw (eds), *An Economic History of Ulster, 1820–1939*, pp. 1–61. Manchester: 1985.

Kent, J. Feelings and festivals. In H. J. Dyos and M. Wolff (eds), *The Victorian City: Images and Realities*, Vol. 2, pp. 855–71. London: 1973.

Liechty, J. The popular Reformation comes to Ireland: the case of John Walker and the foundation of the Church of God, 1804. In R. V. Comerford, M. Cullen, J. Hill and C. Lennon (eds), *Religion, Conflict and Coexistence in Ireland*, pp. 160–88. Dublin: 1990.

McCracken, J. L. The ecclesiastical structure 1714–1760. In T. W. Moody and W. E. Vaughan (eds), *A New History of Ireland*, Vol. 4, pp. 84–104. Oxford: 1986.

Malmgreen, G. Domestic discords: women and the family in East Cheshire Methodism, 1750–1830. In J. Obelkevich, L. Roper and R. Samuel (eds), *Disciplines of Faith: Studies in Religion, Politics and Patriarchy*, pp. 55–70. London: 1987.

Miller, D. The Armagh troubles. In S. Clarke and J. S. Donnelly (eds), *Irish Peasants: Violence and Political Unrest 1780–1914*, pp. 155–91. Manchester: 1983.

Moran, G. F. 'Sisters' in Christ: women and the church in seventeenth-century New England. In J. W. James (ed.), *Women in American Religion*, pp. 47–65. Philadelphia, Pa.: 1980.

O'Danachair, C. The penal laws and the Irish folk tradition. In *Proceedings of the Irish Catholic Historical Committee 1961*, pp. 10–16. Dublin: 1962.

Parsons, G. Irish disestablishment. In *Religion in Victorian Britain*, Vol. II, *Controversies*, pp. 124–46. Manchester: 1988.

Patterson, H. Industrial labour and the labour movement, 1820–1914. In L. Kennedy and P. Ollerenshaw (eds), *An Economic History of Ulster, 1820–1939*, pp. 158–83. Manchester: 1985.

Rule, J. Methodism, popular beliefs and village culture in Cornwall, 1800–50. In R. D. Storch (ed.), *Popular Culture and Custom in Nineteenth-Century England*, pp. 48–70. London: 1982.

Turner, C. B. Revivalism and Welsh society in the nineteenth century. In J. Obelkevich, L. Roper and R. Samuel (eds), *Disciplines of Faith: Studies in Religion, Politics and Patriarchy*, pp. 311–23. London: 1987.

Wall, M. The Whiteboys. In T. D. Williams (ed.), *Secret Societies in Ireland*, pp. 13–25. Dublin: 1973.

Wall, M. The age of the penal laws 1691–1778. In T. E. Moody and F. X. Martin (eds), *The Course of Irish History*, pp. 217–31. Cork: 1984.

(ii) In journals

Barkley, J. M. The Arian schism in Ireland, 1830. *Studies in Church History* 9 (1972), pp. 323–40.

Barkley, J. M. Tommy Toye – revivalist preacher. *Bulletin of the Presbyterian Historical Society of Ireland* 8 (November, 1978), pp. 2–15.

Bartlett, T. Select documents, xxxviii: defenders and defenderism in 1795. *Irish Historical Studies* 24, 95 (May, 1985), pp. 373–94.

Baxter, J. The great Yorkshire revival 1792–6: a study of mass revival among the Methodists. In M. Hill (ed.), *A Sociological Yearbook of Religion in Britain* 7 (1974), pp. 46–76.

Bebbington, D. W. Gladstone and the Baptists. *Baptist Quarterly* 26 (1975–6), pp. 224–39.

Bebbington, D. W. Nonconformity and electoral sociology, 1867–1918. *Historical Journal* 27, 3 (1984), pp. 633–56.

Belmore, Earl of. Some social notes of the Ulster plantation. *Ulster Journal of Archaeology* 1 (1894), pp. 51–61.

Brown, E. K. Women in church history: stereotypes, archetypes and operational modalities. *Methodist History* 18 (July, 1980), pp. 109–32.

Bumsted, J. Religion, finance, and democracy in Massachusetts: the town of Norton as a case study. *Journal of American History* 57 (1971), pp. 817–31.

Clarkson, L. An anatomy of an Irish town: the economy of Armagh, 1770. *Irish Economic and Social History* 5 (1978), pp. 27–45.

Conway, J. K. Politics, pedagogy and power. *Daedalus* (1987), pp. 137–52.

Cott, N. F. Young women in the Second Great Awakening. *Feminist Studies* 3 (1975), pp. 14–29.

Crawford, W. H. The origins of the linen industry in north Armagh and the Lagan Valley. *Ulster Folklife* 17 (1971), pp. 42–51.

Crawford, W. H. Economy and society in south Ulster in the eighteenth century. *Clogher Record* 7, 3 (1975), pp. 251–8.

Crawford, W. H. Landlord-tenant relations in Ulster 1609–1820. *Irish Economic and Social History* 2 (1975), pp. 5–21.

Cross, C. He-goats before the flocks. *Studies in Church History* 8 (1972), pp. 195–202.

Dunne, T. 'La trahison des clercs': British intellectuals and the first home-rule crisis. *Irish Historical Studies* 23, 90 (November, 1982), pp. 134–73.

Field, C. D. The social structure of English Methodism: eighteenth-twentieth centuries. *British Journal of Sociology* 28 (1977), pp. 199–225.

Gailey, A. The Scots element in North Irish popular culture: some problems in the interpretation of an historical acculturation. *Ethnologia Europa* 8 (1975), pp. 2–22.

Gailey, A. The Ballyhagan inventories 1716–1740. *Folklife* 15 (1977), pp. 37–64.

Garnett, J. Gold and the gospel. In W. J. Sheils and D. Wood (eds), *Studies in Church History* 24 (1987), pp. 158–83.

Geary, F. The rise and fall of the Belfast cotton industry: some problems. *Irish Economic and Social History* 3 (1981), pp. 30–49.

Geary, F. The Belfast cotton industry revisited. *Irish Historical Studies* 26, 103 (May, 1989), pp. 250–67.

Gibbon, P. 'The origins of the Orange Order and the United Irishmen', *Economy and Society* 1 (1972), pp. 134–63.

Gilbert, A. D. Methodism, dissent and political stability in early industrial England. *Journal of Religious History* 10 (1978–9), pp. 381–99.

Gribbon, H. D. Irish Baptists in the 19th century: economic and social background. *Irish Baptist Historical Society Journal* 16 (1983–4), pp. 4–18.

Haines, R. M. Wild wittes and wilfulness: John Swetsock's attack on those poyswunmongers, the Lollards. *Studies in Church History* 8 (1972), pp. 143–53.

Hall, B. The Welsh revival of 1904–5: a critique. *Studies in Church History* 8 (1984), pp. 291–330.

Harris, F. M. John Cennick in Ireland. *Irish Baptist Historical Society Journal* 15 (1882–3), pp. 21–9.

Harrison, B. Religion and recreation in nineteenth-century England. *Past and Present* 38 (1967), pp. 98–125.

Harrison, B. For church, queen and family: the Girls' Friendly Society 1874–1920. *Past and Present* 61 (1973), pp. 107–38.

Hempton, D. N. The Methodist crusade in Ireland 1795–1845. *Irish Historical Studies* 22, 85 (March, 1980), pp. 33–48.

Hempton, D. N. Evangelicalism and eschatology. *Journal of Ecclesiastical History* 31, 2 (April, 1980), pp. 179–94.

Hempton, D. N. 'Bickersteth, Bishop of Ripon: the episcopate of a mid-Victorian evangelical', *Northern History: a Review of the History of the North of England* 17 (1981), pp. 183–202.

Hempton, D. 'Evangelical revival and society: a historiographical review of Methodism and British society c. 1750–1850', *Themelios* 8, 3 (April, 1983), pp. 19–25.

Hempton, D. N. Methodism in Irish society, 1770–1830. *Transactions of the Royal Historical Society*, 5th series, 36 (1986), pp. 117–42.

Hempton, D. N. Methodism and the law, 1740–1820. *Bulletin of the John Rylands University Library of Manchester* 70, 3 (1988), pp. 93–107.

Hempton, D. N. Gideon Ouseley: rural revivalist, 1791–1839. *Studies in Church History* 25 (1989), pp. 203–14.

Hempton, D. and M. Hill. Godliness and good citizenship: evangelical Protestantism and social control in Ulster, 1790–1850. *Saothar* 13 (1988), pp. 68–80.

Hill, M. Popular Protestantism in Ulster in the post-rebellion period c.1790–1810. *Studies in Church History* 25 (1989), pp. 191–202.

Holmes, R. F. G. Eighteenth-century Presbyterian radicalism and its eclipse. *Bulletin of the Presbyterian Historical Society of Ireland* 3 (January, 1973), pp. 7–15.

Holmes, R. F. G. Ulster Presbyterianism and Irish nationalism. *Studies in Church History* 18 (1982), pp. 535–48.

Hume, A. Miscellaneous essays on topography, ethnology, language, etc. *Ulster Journal of Archaeology* 7 (Belfast, 1859).

Itzkin, E. S. The Halevy thesis – a working hypothesis? *Church History* 44, 1 (1975), pp. 47–56.

Ker, R. A. The origins of Primitive Wesleyan Methodism in Ireland. *Proceedings of the Wesley Historical Society* 43, part 4 (May, 1982), pp. 77–85.

Kerr, S. Voluntaryism within the established church in nineteenth-century Belfast. In W. J. Sheils and D. Wood (eds), *Studies in Church History* 23 (1986), pp. 347–62.

Kerrigan, C. The social impact of the temperance movement, 1839–1845. *Irish Economic and Social History* 14 (1987), pp. 20–38.

Kiernan, V. Evangelicalism and the French Revolution. *Past and Present* 1 (February, 1952), pp. 44–56.

Kincheloe, J. L., Jr. European roots of evangelical revivalism: Methodist transmission of the pietistic socio-religious tradition. *Methodist History* 18 (July, 1980), pp. 262–71.

Kingdon, D. P. Irish Baptists and the revival of 1859 with special reference to Tobermore. *Irish Baptist Historical Society Journal* 1 (1968–9), pp. 19–30.

Landsman, N. Evangelists and their hearers: popular interpretation of revivalist preaching in eighteenth-century Scotland. *Journal of British Studies* 28, 2 (1989), pp. 120–49.

Loughlin, J. The Irish Protestant Home Rule Association and nationalist politics. *Irish Historical Studies* 24, 95 (May, 1985), pp. 341–60.

Luker, D. Revivalism in theory and practice. *Journal of Ecclesiastical History* 37, 4 (October, 1986), pp. 603–19.

McLeod, H. Recent studies in Victorian religious history. *Victorian Studies* 21, 2 (1978), pp. 245–54.

McLeod, H. New perspectives on Victorian working-class religion: the oral evidence. *Oral History* 14, 1 (1986), pp. 31–49.

MaCourt, M. P. A. The religious inquiry in the Irish census of 1861. *Irish Historical Studies* 21, 82 (September, 1978), pp. 168–87.

Maguire, W. A. Lord Donegall and the Hearts of Steel. *Irish Historical Studies* 21, 84 (September, 1979), pp. 351–76.

Miller, D. Presbyterianism and 'modernization' in Ulster. *Past and Present* 80 (1978), pp. 66–90.

Munck, R. The formation of the working class in Belfast, 1788–1881. *Saothar* 11 (1986), pp. 75–89.

Murphy, J. A. The support of the Catholic clergy in Ireland, 1750–1850. *Historical Studies* 5 (1965), pp. 104–13.

Nuttall, G. F. Early Quakerism and early Primitive Methodism. *Friends' Quarterly* 7 (1953), pp. 179–87.

O'Brien, S. A transatlantic community of saints: the Great Awakening and the first evangelical network, 1735–1755. *American Historical Review* 91, 4 (October, 1986), pp. 811–32.

O'Farrell, P. Millennialism, messianism and utopianism in Irish history. *Anglo-Irish Studies* 2 (1976), pp. 45–67.

Prelinger, C. M. Religious dissent, women's rights and the Hamburger Hochschule fuer das weibliche Geschlecht in mid-nineteenth century Germany. *Church History* 45 (1976), pp. 42–55.

Savage, D. C. The origins of the Ulster Unionist Party, 1885–6. *Irish Historical Studies* 12, 47 (March, 1961), pp. 185–208.

Skevington-Wood, A. The eighteenth-century revival reconsidered. *Evangelical Quarterly* 53, 3 (1981), pp. 130–48.

Spence, J. L. Life in eighteenth-century rural Ulster as reflected in a parish record book. *Ulster Journal of Archaeology*, 3rd series, 6 (1943), pp. 35–8.

Stunt, T. C. F. Evangelical cross-currents in the Church of Ireland, 1820–1833. *Studies in Church History* 25 (1989), pp. 215–22.

Swift, W. F. The women itinerant preachers of early Methodism. *Proceedings of the Wesley Historical Society* 28 (1951–2), pp. 89–94; 29 (1953–4), pp. 76–83.

Thomas, K. Women and the Civil War sects. *Past and Present* 13 (April 1958), pp. 42–62.

Thompson, E. P. Anthropology and the discipline of historical context. *Midland History* 1 (1972), pp. 41–55.

Thompson, J. Irish Baptists and the 1859 revival. *Irish Baptist Historical Society Journal* 17 (1984–5), pp. 4–10.

Wall, M. The rise of a Catholic middle class in eighteenth-century Ireland. *Irish Historical Studies* 11 (1959), pp. 91–115.

Walsh, J. The Great Awakening in the First Congregational Church of Woodbury, Connecticut. *William and Mary Quarterly*, 3rd series, 28 (1971), pp. 543–62.

Walsh, J. Methodism and the mob in the eighteenth century. *Studies in Church History* 8 (1972), pp. 213–27.

Ward, W. R. The religion of the people and the problem of control, 1790–1830. *Studies in Church History* 8 (1972), pp. 237–57.

Ward, W. R. The relations of enlightenment and religious revival in Central Europe and in the English-speaking world. *Studies in Church History*, Subsidia 2 (1979), pp. 281–305.

Ward, W. R. Power and piety: the origins of religious revival in the early eighteenth century. *Bulletin of the John Rylands University Library of Manchester* 63, 1 (1980), pp. 231–52.

Ward, W. R. The renewed unity of the brethren: ancient church, new sect or interconfessional movement? *Bulletin of the John Rylands University Library of Manchester* 70, 3 (1988), pp. 77–92.

Ward, W. R. The way of the world: the rise and decline of Protestant social Christianity in Britain. *Kirchliche Zeitgeschichte* 1, 2 (1988), pp. 293–305.

Wright, F. Protestant ideology and politics in Ulster. *Archives Européennes de Sociologie* 14 (1973), pp. 213–80.

(d) Unpublished theses

Acheson, A. R. The evangelicals in the Church of Ireland, 1784–1859. PhD thesis, Queen's University, Belfast, 1967.

Binns, J. R. A history of Methodism in Ireland from Wesley's death in 1791 to the re-union of Primitives and Wesleyans in 1878. MA thesis, Queen's University, Belfast, 1960.

Brooke, P. Controversies in Ulster Presbyterianism 1790–1836. PhD thesis, University of Cambridge, 1981.

Brown, L. T. The Presbyterians of Cavan and Monaghan: an immigrant community in south Ulster over three generations. PhD thesis, Queen's University, Belfast, 1986.

Canavan, A. The Hearts of Steel: agrarian protest in Ulster, 1769–1773. MA thesis, Queen's University, Belfast, 1982.
Clayton, H. Societies formed to educate the poor in Ireland in the late eighteenth and early nineteenth century. MLitt thesis, Trinity College, Dublin, 1981.
Cooke, J. H. The development and distribution of Methodism in Ireland: a demographic study. MA thesis, Queen's University, Belfast, 1964.
Crawford, W. H. Economy and society in eighteenth-century Ulster. PhD thesis, Queen's University, Belfast, 1983.

Fahey, P. J. Ritualism, the revision movement and revision theology in the Church of Ireland 1842–1877. 2 vols. Doctorate of Sacred Theology thesis, Rome, 1976.

Hanna, S. G. The origin and nature of the Gracehill Moravian settlement 1764–1855, with special reference to the work of John Cennick in Ireland 1746–1755. MA thesis, Queen's University, Belfast, 1964.
Hehir, I. M. New lights and old enemies: the Second Reformation and the Catholics of Ireland, 1800–1835. MA thesis, University of Wisconsin, 1983.
Hempton, D. N. Methodism and anti-Catholic politics 1800–1846. PhD thesis, University of St Andrews, 1977.
Henry, J. M. An assessment of the social, religious and political aspects of Congregationalism in Ireland in the nineteenth century. PhD thesis, Queen's University, Belfast, 1965.
Hill, M. Evangelicalism and the churches in Ulster society, 1770–1850. PhD thesis, Queen's University, Belfast, 1987.

Jamieson, J. The influence of the Reverend Henry Cooke on the political life of Ulster. MA thesis, Queen's University, Belfast, 1950.
Jennings, R. S. The origins of Ulster Presbyterian revivalism in the mid-nineteenth century. MTheol thesis, Queen's University, Belfast, 1985.
Jordan, A. Voluntary societies in Victorian and Edwardian Belfast. PhD thesis, Queen's University, Belfast, 1989.

Kerr, S. P. The Church of Ireland in Belfast, 1800–1870. MPhil thesis, University of Edinburgh, 1978.

Liechty, J. Irish evangelicalism, Trinity College Dublin, and the mission of the Church of Ireland at the end of the eighteenth century. PhD thesis, St Patrick's College, Maynooth, 1987.
Loughlin, J. Gladstone, Irish nationalism and the home-rule question, 1882–93, with particular reference to the Ulster problem. PhD thesis, Trinity College, Dublin, 1983.
Lovegrove, D. W. The practice of itinerant evangelicalism in English Calvinistic dissent. PhD thesis, University of Cambridge, 1980.

McMullan, G. Change from within – change from without. The interaction of doctrine, politics and economics in the experience of the Church of Ireland, 1830–1880. PhD thesis, Geneva Theological College, 1987.
Martin, R. H. The pan-evangelical impulse in Britain 1795–1830: with special reference to four London societies. PhD thesis, University of Oxford, 1974.

Megahey, A. J. The Irish Protestant churches and social and political issues: 1870–1914. PhD thesis, Queen's University, Belfast, 1969.
Murray, N. The influence of the French Revolution on the Church of England and its rivals, 1789–1802. PhD thesis, University of Oxford, 1975.

Orchard, S. C. English evangelical eschatology 1790–1850. PhD thesis, University of Cambridge, 1969.

Rennie, I. S. Evangelicalism and English public life: 1823–1850. PhD thesis, University of Toronto, 1962.
Rodgers, R. J. Presbyterian missionary activity among Irish Roman Catholics in the nineteenth century. MA thesis, Queen's University, Belfast, 1969.
Rodgers, R. J. James Carlile, 1784–1854. PhD thesis, Queen's University, Belfast, 1973.

Sangster, P. E. The life of the Reverend Rowland Hill (1744–1833) and his position in the evangelical revival. PhD thesis, University of Oxford, 1964.
Scott, A. R. The Ulster revival of 1859. PhD thesis, Trinity College, Dublin, 1962.
Slater, G. J. Belfast politics 1798–1868. PhD thesis, New University of Ulster, 1982.
Stewart, A. T. Q. The transformation of Presbyterian radicalism in the north of Ireland, 1792–1825. MA thesis, Queen's University, Belfast, 1956.

Taggart, N. The Irish factor in world Methodism in the eighteenth and nineteenth centuries. PhD thesis, Queen's University, Belfast, 1981.
Thompson, J. The inter-relationship of the Secession Synod and the Synod of Ulster. PhD thesis, Queen's University, Belfast, 1980.
Thompson, J. Baptists in Ireland 1792–1922: a dimension of Protestant dissent. PhD thesis, University of Oxford, 1988.

Warner, T. E. The impact of Wesley on Ireland. PhD thesis, University of London, 1954.
Wright, F. A. Developments in Ulster politics, 1843–86. PhD thesis, Queen's University, Belfast, 1989.
Wright, J. R. R. An evangelical estate *c.*1800–1825: the influence on the Manchester estate, County Armagh, with particular reference to the moral agencies of W. Loftie and H. Porter. PhD thesis, Northern Ireland Polytechnic, 1982.

Index